WINNING CHOICE ON ABORTION

How British Columbian and Canadian Feminists Won the Battles of the 1970s and 1980s

By Ann Thomson

Note for Librarians: a cataloguing record for this book that includes Dewey Decimal Classification and US Library of Congress numbers is available from the Library and Archives of Canada. The complete cataloguing record can be obtained from their online database at:
www.collectionscanada.ca/amicus/index-e.html
ISBN 1-4120-4247-X
Printed in Victoria, BC, Canada

TRAFFORD

Offices in Canada, USA, Ireland, UK and Spain
This book was published *on-demand* in cooperation with Trafford Publishing. On-demand publishing is a unique process and service of making a book available for retail sale to the public taking advantage of on-demand manufacturing and Internet marketing. On-demand publishing includes promotions, retail sales, manufacturing, order fulfilment, accounting and collecting royalties on behalf of the author.
Book sales for North America and international:
Trafford Publishing, 6E–2333 Government St.,
Victoria, BC v8t 4p4 CANADA
phone 250 383 6864 (toll-free 1 888 232 4444)
fax 250 383 6804; email to orders@trafford.com
Book sales in Europe:
Trafford Publishing (uk) Ltd., Enterprise House, Wistaston Road Business Centre, Wistaston Road, Crewe, Cheshire cw2 7rp UNITED KINGDOM
phone 01270 251 396 (local rate 0845 230 9601)
facsimile 01270 254 983; orders.uk@trafford.com
Order online at:
www.trafford.com/robots/04-8298.html

10 9 8 7 6 5 4 3 2 1

Georgia Street, in front of Art Gallery, Vancouver International Women's Day Rally, 1989
[Photo by Karen Kilbride]

Dedication

To women throughout time, in every corner of the world,
who have braved fear, agony, and sometimes death
to exercise their fundamental right to control their bodies
and decide when and whether to bear children

To feminists and abortion-providers who have fought and
continue to fight for women's dignity and rights

CONTENTS

ACKNOWLEDGEMENTS

Many thanks to the following artists who gave permission to use their work in this text.

❧

'My Neighbour the Pro-Lifer' is used by permission of the author, Leona Gom, and Sono Nis Press, Victoria, B.C. It is from *The Collected Poems* by Leona Gom, 1991.

Thanks to Barbara Hicks for photos taken during the Abortion Caravan.

Thanks to Karen Kilbride for permission to use her photo, taken in front of the Art Gallery on Georgia Street, at a pro-choice rally, and other photos of pro-choice events.

Thanks to Katherine Kortikow for photos of the opening reception at Everywoman's Health Centre.

Thanks to Robert Krieger for permission to use his cartoon, showing an anti-choice protester threatening a pro-choice demonstrator with the words, '...Or I'll kill ya...' This first appeared in the *Province* newspaper, September, 1981.

Thanks to Donna Liberson for permission to use all and part of the Women's Caucus poster, 'Labouring Under A Mis-Conception.'

Thanks to Leon Rosselson for permission to use lyrics from his song, 'Don't Get Married, Girls!'

Thanks to Helene Wisotzki for encouragement and support.

Thanks to my wonderful cover artist, and also to text graphic designer Shirley Olson.

❧

Thanks to the nearly fifty participants and activists, who gave me their recollections in taped interviews.

INTRODUCTION

As I write this, it's hard to believe that only two or three decades ago, well within living memory, all of Canada, and even all of the western world, was fixated on the issue of abortion. So furious were the controversies that ranged daily through society that abortion was frequently the lead item in every newspaper, the first story on the evening's newscasts.

This book aims to capture a sense of the storm, and to tell at least part of the story of how feminists fought for their views and their rights. It is told from a base in British Columbia, because that's where I live and where I participated in the fight for nearly twenty years. But the story in western Canada is inextricable from the story in the rest of the country, and from parallel developments in Europe, the US, and around the world. It is tied up with other political movements and crises, and I've referred to these in the text.

I deeply regret that a chapter I prepared with love, about other wings of the women's movement which arose in BC along with the demand for choice on abortion, made the manuscript too long and, in the end, could not be included. The parallel struggles for holistic women's health and of midwive's fight for legality are two examples. This is the story of only one wing and one set of demands of a feminism that transformed everyone's life and all society.

For many Canadians, the towering figure of Dr. Henry Morgentaler is synonymous with abortion rights. And so it should be. A number of books and films have told his side of the story, while the story of the women who fought for the same victory is virtually untold. Here some of those women make their debut.

Library shelves are crowded with publications that tell the anti-abortion side. Students who elect to write essays on abortion for their history, law, or women's studies classes have trouble finding material that tells the winning side. The feminist side. I hope this book will help fill that gap.

This is also a contribution to writing women into history, and of writing the history of women. I want to honour those who helped us, as well. Their numbers are legion.

The impact of late twentieth-century feminism can only be compared to a collision of major tectonic plates. It re-shaped the landscape, and every sector of society was tumbled in its furious shock. Feminists, ordinary women who took on a big job, may sometimes seem less important players in the scenes you'll read about here than the governments at all levels, the courts and judges, the attorneys-general and the police, the hospital administrations and their medical staffs, the newspapers and their editors and commentators on TV, and round again to the colleges of physicians and surgeons, etc., etc. All those institutions were called into play. And that's without mentioning the opposition, those whose fervent declarations about 'life' virtually revise theology, so that the fetus seems to nudge Jesus Christ aside and take his place. I think readers will see that anti-abortionists are less concerned with the 'unborn' than with controlling women's lives as closely as the Taliban in Afghanistan. Beyond that, they want to impose an evangelical Christian dictatorship on our multi-cultural, multi-faith Canada.

Nonetheless the best part is, this is a story of victory. Here is one truly concrete triumph won by Canadian feminism. It deserves to be honoured and better known. It tells of a struggle that relied mainly on the strategies of educating on the issue, building broad-based coalitions, and demonstrating in the streets. But this is also a story that hasn't come to an end yet. Anti-abortionists still hope to turn back the clock. Feminist consciousness so alarms the rich and powerful that an avalanche of attacks has been unleashed in recent years. It has partially succeeded in re-casting middle class females as joyous 'ho's', who are obsessed with sex, clothes, and celebrities. Poor women are shoved deeper into poverty, and forgotten. Anti-abortion pledges rise again in every election campaign. So another reason I've written this book is to alert feminists of all sexes to the need to keep fighting.

See you on the barricades!

Ann Thomson 2004

CHAPTER ONE

FEMINISM ARRIVES AT SFU

Women's Liberation appeared in British Columbia at Simon Fraser University in the turbulent year of 1968. It was inspired by the new feminism sweeping across North America, and, in the beginning, it was also a branch on the burgeoning tree of radical campus politics. But it quickly developed its own character and became an important feature of the social landscape.

Most of the major issues of the women's rights movement popped up in the Women's Caucus, founded by students at SFU. Equal opportunities in education. Equal jobs, equal pay, and rights for women workers. Child care. And, of course, birth control and abortion. Some members of Women's Caucus were lesbians, although they did not begin to organize for lesbian rights until later. The major demand to end rape and violence against women took only another year or two to develop in Vancouver.

This book will trace the pursuit of women's right to control their reproductive lives from the time of BC's first feminist group, founded in 1968, through the opening of Everywoman's Health Centre, British Columbia's first free-standing abortion clinic, in 1988. When the struggle began, abortion was illegal, and everything to do with women's sexuality and reproductive capacities was treated as dirty and taboo. When this account ends, the law had been overturned, abortion was fully legal, and, in still-rare parts of Canada, women could end a pregnancy on demand.

Simon Fraser University in Burnaby, adjacent to Vancouver, opened in September 1965. Faculty members' political views ranged from left to right, and in a highly-politicized period, these had an impact on campus life. The university also attracted a student body for whom the major issues of the day vied with the curriculum for interest. In its short history, three radical student groups had already succeeded one another at SFU. It was a volatile time. There was intense interest on North American campuses in world-wide movements for peace and against nuclear weapons; in the US civil rights' struggle and development of the Black Liberation Movement; in the growth of the student left and its leadership in opposing the war in Vietnam; and in achieving respect and authority for youth. Leftist students and faculty felt the electric sense of a new era, not just a new university, opening up.

The 1968 summer term at SFU began amidst an avalanche of meetings, as both faculty and students of all political stripes discussed the university's future. The president had been forced to step down, when the Canadian Association of University Teachers had censured the administration and supported left-leaning faculty in a charge of discrimination in hiring. In the furore, few noticed the beginnings of a new constituency that would demand unthought-of rights. Feminism spoke up through a term paper for a course in the Political Science, Sociology, and Anthropology (PSA) Department.

Eighteen-year-old Marcy Toms had plunged into campus politics at the founding meeting of SFU's Students for a Democratic University (SDU) on January 22, 1968. She had attended her first anti-Vietnam war march the previous term. A Vancouver native, Toms recalls a defining experience from 1957, the year she was seven:

> ...one thing was watching the integration of the schools in Little Rock, Arkansas, on black and white TV...I can remember it like it was yesterday, seeing that little black kid with her pigtails and her white bobby socks walking up the stairs escorted by US marshalls ...this huge, huge, huge mob of people and one woman with her hair in curlers and a white kerchief...spitting at her...[1]

In secondary school, Toms was assigned to write an essay on "self-determination or not for Vietnam." That, too, helped form her political views.

During her first year at SFU, Toms took a Sociology course for which the one assignment was "to rewrite in modern terms...with a contemporary view, the Communist Manifesto." Into Toms's hands had recently fallen a pamphlet written by leftist women in Toronto. It was called, "Sisters, Brothers, Lovers...Listen."[2] In a tradition that grew out of the US civil rights movement — and some of the Toronto authors had been active in registering southern blacks to vote — it was a catalogue showing that women were not taken seriously by the 'new left'. Toms found in it the inspiration for her course assignment, which she wrote in partnership with some classmates. Looking back over the term and their own restricted role in SDU, these student activists noted, sardonically, that "what we were doing in SDU...wasn't exactly equal to what the guys were doing."[3] It seemed the "guys" were making the decisions and getting the glory. Toms and her writing partners called their term paper a "new manifesto for women" and titled it the "Feminine Action League."[4] It ended with the call: "Women of the world unite. You have nothing to lose but your apron strings."[5]

Soon afterward, a meeting was called to form a real Feminine Action League on campus. Toms and her friends eschewed the word 'feminist' at first. It had already been tinged by anxiety, aroused by the founding of the National Organization of Women (NOW) and other radical groups of the women's liberation movement in the US. The newly conscious women at SFU were determined to be taken seriously and wanted to avoid the derision heaped on NOW. Lest men dominate the meeting, they were barred from attending. That was enough to turn the founders' boy friends into clowns. Frantic to prevent the women in their lives from becoming independent, the male students tried to force their way into the meeting. Included were two prominent male activists and a photographer from the campus paper, *The Peak*. Toms described the scene to writer Frances Wasserlein: "...at least those three people were peering around the windows, they were knocking on the door, they were peering through the slit in the door to try to find out what was going on."[6]

The next issue of *The Peak* carried a front-page photo of some tense, but self-assured young women, seated around a table. Snapped just before the door was locked, the photo was captioned "Pussy Power Strikes at SFU." Those in the photo were identified as "the women of [male] [student] council members and sundry hangers-on," and readers were warned they were up to the same "diabolical plot" as Lysistrata, in the play by Aristophanes, in which the women of Greece withheld sex from their husbands until they stopped going to war.[7] The robust male chauvinism at SFU was threatened indeed.

A brisk retort appeared in the next issue of the paper. Using transparent pseudonyms, Marcy "Jones" [Toms] and Patty "Harding" [Hoffer; now Davitt] of the Feminine Action League, outlined the main points of their manifesto for change. It charged that society excluded women from economic production, confining them entirely to reproduction. Women were "appropriated as sex objects," and socialized into the narrow and obsolete channel of the nuclear family. *The Peak* headed the letter "Pussy power strikes back" and bracketed it between twin photos of a female breast.[8] The Feminine Action League was undeterred but met only two or three times.

Later that summer, fifteen women met in a Kitsilano apartment to continue the project. Not all were students, but all were supporters of activist politics, and they were not interested in introspection, or "consciousness-raising," which was then a major feature of budding feminist groups. The SFU women wanted to plan "what we should actually do, on the campus or even off the campus."[9] From the start, their gaze was fixed on changing the world, as well as changing the status of women. That did not mean their commitment to campus politics was diminished. The nucleus of women that met that summer continued to throw itself into SDU and to participate vigorously in ongoing political struggles. When classes resumed in the fall, the new group held a formal, founding meeting on September 11, 1968, and took the name of Women's Caucus. Beginning immediately, and for the next several years, Women's Caucus was intensely active, and it left an indelible mark on the Canadian scene.

The name Women's Caucus meant different things to its participants. Some considered it to be a caucus of women in Students for a Democratic

University (SDU). Others preferred to see themselves as a caucus of the human race, a group of those long disenfranchised.[10] Although women had belatedly been recognized in Canada as "persons" (1938) and had the vote, they could not get credit, enter most professions, or even get a library card without written permission from a man — father or husband. More importantly, they had no control over their own bodies and were required to carry every pregnancy to term and devote themselves to raising children.

From the start, Women's Caucus drew in activists with a variety of ages, occupations, and backgrounds. Many were students, but one of the founders was Margaret Benston, who was beginning a well-respected career on the Chemistry Department faculty.[11] Another was Andrea Lebowitz, a faculty member in the Department of English. Like Benston, she came to SFU from the United States. Other members had male partners who were students or faculty members at SFU. One was Liz Briemberg, who came to Canada from England, where she met her Edmonton-born husband while both were students. In 1968, she was at home with two children, feeling isolated from her husband's exciting work as one of the faculty members who had initiated the CAUT investigation.

Another Women's Caucus founder was Anne Roberts, a journalist from Michigan, whose partner was an assistant professor in the PSA Department. Marge Hollibaugh came to SFU from California. Though not a student, her husband was; he held such posts as Ombudsman and President of the Student Council. Marge, energetic and outgoing, was in her mid-forties at the inception of Women's Caucus, and was perhaps its senior member on the campus.

Jean Rands, originally from Regina, had accumulated an impressive record of political work before becoming a typesetter for the SFU student newspaper, *The Peak*, in September, 1968. Her commitment to leftist politics and women's issues made Women's Caucus a logical step for her.

The bulk of the members were students, of course. Among those who were influential in Women's Caucus was Marcy Cohen, who had done extensive progressive political work while an undergraduate in Calgary and at York University. She entered the graduate program in Education at SFU in January 1969 and was led to the Women's Caucus through SDU. Margo Dunn was doing graduate work in the Drama Department when she was drawn into Women's Caucus activities.

Cathy Walker, from a Burnaby working class family, was drawn into SDU and Women's Caucus because of her strong interest in politics. Like Jean Rands and several other women's liberation activists, Walker went on to become a leader in the labour movement. She served for several years as an executive officer of an independent Canadian union, CAIMAW, which has since disbanded. Pat Davitt, then Hoffer, from Saskatchewan, came to SFU for graduate study. Later, she served as president of the

Vancouver Municipal and Regional Employees Union (VMREU), and of the Canadian Union of Public Employees (CUPE) local that succeeded it.

Some members of Women's Caucus were studying not at SFU, but at the University of British Columbia. Candace Parker, from California, was a graduate student in sociology at UBC when she got involved in Women's Caucus. Ellen Woodsworth, great-niece of J.S. Woodsworth, founder of the CCF, and cousin of Grace MacInnis, was also studying at UBC. Women's Caucus was important to her as a women's organization, "but it was also a Marxist organization ...with a comprehensive social analysis, and...it was doing practical things...I wanted that kind of an organization. I needed it. I thought that that was where sanity was."[12] Donna Liberson, from Winnipeg, got an education degree from UBC, then opened a day care centre and, later, a Gastown boutique. She socialized with radicals from SFU, attended Women's Caucus meetings, and especially enjoyed guerrilla theatre.

Women's Caucus had wide-ranging activities, and it's not possible to name every participant. These women, mostly in their mid-twenties, were joined by others, some from the campus, and, later, by several vital women from the general community. When the moment came to apply their energies to women's needs, these products of the repressed 1950s became dynamos.

Marcy Toms announced the new group in the September 18, 1968 issue of *The Peak*. Women's Caucus, she wrote, was a "significant development within the student movement at SFU", and newcomers were invited to help draft priority issues for the group. In short order, a priority issue was addressed. The next edition of the weekly *Peak* featured a Women's Caucus comment "*on abortion*," written by Maggie Benston.[13]

This was, perhaps, the first time in the lower mainland that the horrific and taboo 'A' word was raised by politicized woman. Committed to feminism though she was, Benston approached the topic a bit gingerly. She made the basic points that women were illogically and unfairly denied control over their reproductive lives, and that poor women suffered most when access to birth control and abortion were not allowed. The piece was meant to be educational. It made no explicit call for a change in social policy or in the law, ending with the truism, "Until women are free, it should be clear that no one will be free."[14]

Three weeks later, Women's Caucus was ready to launch an ambitious plan, and it contacted the SFU administration and the Vancouver Family Planning Centre for help. It wanted to use the campus health centre two evenings a week "for an advisor on family planning and for medical examinations" — because of "concern about a pressing student (and societal) problem, the problem of unplanned and unwanted pregnancy."[15]

Access to birth control was then, and had long been, illegal in Canada, although to Women's Caucus activists it was vital. They needed it themselves. But unplanned pregnancies were genuine emergencies. While investigating possible ways of getting an abortion in Vancouver, Women's Caucus went ahead and placed a small ad in the October 9, 1968 edition of *The Peak*. It read:

> Girls — need help? in trouble? Contact the Women's Caucus Counsellor by letter c/o SFU Student Society or phone her at 299-**** evenings for information.

The response was immediate. Many phone calls came from students in the Vancouver area, as well as some from Alberta and Saskatchewan. The desperation of women seeking abortions was assuming volcanic force, irrevocably demanding to be addressed. Women's Caucus found it had bitten off more than it could chew, for it was nearly impossible to find practitioners of abortion to whom it could steer those who contacted it.

Those who now identify the 1960s as a time of hippies, free love, and psychedelic irresponsibility magnify the extent of such influences at the time. Even as the 'sexual revolution' gained steam, the overwhelming majority in Canada, and the world, remained strait-jacketed by suffocating sexual repression. Sex was a topic banned from thought, language, and discussion, associated with obscenity, and considered 'filthy.' But sexuality was not nearly so fearsome and despised as the question of abortion.

The American writer and crusader for birth control and abortion rights, Lawrence Lader, wrote "The abortion issue in 1965 was enveloped in a conspiracy of silence just as ruthless as the slavery issue in 1831."

> To be against slavery, dangerous as it was in Boston in 1831, gave the rebel a philosophic nobility. To be against abortion laws in 1965, however, involved one in a dirty business.[16]

Its practice was presumed to be, and often was, controlled by organized crime. Lader continued:

> "Abortion was a soiled and forbidden word. Many newspapers and broadcasting stations would not use it on their media. To advocate the right of abortion meant tearing down the key bulwark against immorality. Whether for the single girl or married woman, it meant destroying the ultimate punishment of sex, and allowing the pleasure of sex for its own sake without the concomitant obligation of childbirth. Abortion stood at the apex of all our nightmares and inhibitions about sex, and to tamper with it meant that the whole system could come tumbling down."[17]

Women's Caucus fumbled for contacts in the netherworld to which the illegal practice of abortion was consigned. It involved making whispered inquiries in veiled language to find someone who might know of a practitioner. It was a panicky search, for the dangers grew as pregnancy advanced. Often, it took weeks to find an abortionist — a person swathed in shadows to escape the law, who might or might not have any medical training, who invariably charged hundreds of dollars more than the desperate woman could afford, who might be a con artist, who might rape her instead of aborting her. To this person, who might operate in a back bedroom or on a kitchen table with little care taken against infection, whose methods one could not inquire about in advance and which ranged from simply packing the vagina with unsterile gauze, to the rare competent evacuation of the womb, the woman must deliver herself in trust. Whatever the abortionist did to her, no anaesthetic would be given. She would have to endure the pain without crying out, lest attention be drawn to the illegal operation. She would be expected to leave quietly, even if she were fainting or could barely walk, as soon as the 'doctor' was finished. Often, the woman was sent off to suffer alone, with no more than a promise that miscarriage would occur within a few days. If she hemorrhaged — as many women did — she was on her own. She would not know the abortionist's name, and there might be no clear link between him and the location to which she'd gone. If there was permanent damage that left her crippled or sterile, or if she died, there was no recourse. And even if it went well and her pregnancy was ended, the woman faced insurmountable taint and shame if she were found out by her family or the community at large.

Why should the female half of the human race be subjected to such sadism? Why should the law and all the institutions of society enforce it? Women go through hundreds of fertility cycles in a lifetime, each lasting up to a week. Why should a natural function for which our bodies were designed — getting pregnant — plunge so many into such agony? Why should society label sexuality disgraceful and make unwanted pregnancy a criminal offence? The only answer is because these are features of women's bodies, women's lives. And women have been a despised sex since prehistory, every aspect of whose lives has been ruthlessly dominated by men, and the economic and social institutions created by them.

The search for abortionists to help the women who wrote to Women's Caucus was seldom successful. The impasse the group met fuelled an important new stage for the fledgling feminists, one that developed in the coming year.

Yet the crust on the issue was buckling. Few in BC were aware of it, but change was afoot elsewhere as well. It happened that a revised law on abortion was under discussion in the House of Commons when Women's Caucus was founded. But the approaches of the feminists and parliament did not mesh well, and an explosive confrontation was in the works.

CHAPTER 2

BACKGROUND TO CHANGE IN THE ABORTION LAW

On June 25, 1968, the Liberals swept the federal election and installed Pierre Trudeau as Prime Minister. SFU radicals generally ignored both Trudeaumania and the election, which roughly coincided with the initial meeting of the Feminine Action League. Just a year before FAL developed into Women's Caucus, a House of Commons committee opened five months of hearings on abortion and its possible reform. Little about it was reported in BC.

Since 1892, discussing, procuring materials for, and performing abortions had been illegal under the federal Canadian Criminal Code. Nearly the same was true for contraception. A slight leniency allowed abortion when it would save the life of the pregnant woman, and the most severe penalty — life imprisonment — was reserved for practitioners of the procedure.[1] Abortionists were considered akin to rapists, creatures who preyed on hapless women. The devoutly-held belief was that motherhood was invariably desired by (middle-class) females, who wanted — and were virtually allowed — no other vocation in life. It was against the law to abort oneself, of course, but by mid 20th-century, women who were found out, usually because they were rushed to hospital bleeding or poisoned, were often not subjected to legal punishment.[2]

In fact, doctors did perform abortions in hospitals, in safe, antiseptic conditions, and had done so for decades. A well-known glossary of lies covered this patently illegal practice. In medical jargon, hospital abortions were called emergency appendectomies, or, more often, 'dilation and curettage' (D&Cs: dilation of the cervix and scraping out the uterus with an instrument called a curette) — euphemisms that do not mention pregnancy. D&Cs were said to be required for 'menstrual regulation.' Cautious about the legal risk being taken, but chiefly because of the deeply-entrenched view that females hadn't the mentality to exercise rights had such been granted to them, and because women and children had legal status only as trivial items of property belonging to men, physicians performed these safe, hospital abortions only rarely. Seldom at the woman's request. Usually to prevent scandal to families of men in the 'well-connected' classes.[3]

Of course, unwanted pregnancies occur at a consistently high level throughout society. The options for the vast majority of women were grim indeed. Abortion has been practised throughout history and pre-history, in every culture of the world. Women have an inextinguishable capacity, need and right to both give birth *or* to choose abortion, and they will find ways to terminate unwanted pregnancies, no matter what obstacles are put in the way.

Everything about the practice and effects of illegal abortion was and remains difficult to prove, but it was no doubt the leading cause of maiming and death for women in their child-bearing years, after 1892.[4] That continues to be the case in most underdeveloped countries.

By the 1960s, doctors were beginning to feel uneasy about this. Most family practitioners received requests for help in ending problem pregnancies. Many wanted to do abortions occasionally, or more often, without taking a legal risk. Like other Canadians, doctors had been jolted by the damaged children born to women who had taken the drug thalidomide, especially by the case of Mrs. Sherri Finkbine of Arizona, in 1962. Public approval for the abortion Finkbine obtained in Sweden encouraged a quest for change.

The Canadian Medical Association (CMA) began to think about protecting its members from the consequences of the increasing demand for safe procedures. After much deliberation, it voted in 1966 to call for legalizing the existing, but informal, hospital therapeutic abortion committees.[5] Abortions would remain strictly the medical profession's call. Doctors could perform them or not, as they wished. When they did perform abortions, a TAC would provide cover and confer medical respectability on what amounted to playing cat-and-mouse with women's bodies, needs, and lives.

Between October, 1967 and February 1968, the federal Standing Committee on Health and Welfare pondered numerous briefs and witnesses' calls for reform of the abortion laws.[6] Those carrying the greatest weight were from the Canadian Medical Association, supported by the Canadian Bar Association. These bodies had been deliberating the issue of abortion law reform for most of the decade.[7]

At the same time, public support for legalized abortion had grown throughout the sixties and was presented to the Standing Committee chiefly by mainline churches, including spokesmen of the United, Unitarian, Presbyterian, Anglican, and Jewish Reform congregations. The National Council of Women submitted its third appeal for abortion reform since 1964, and the Canadian Labour Congress put in its bid for change.[8] None of these, however, was as daring as a small, dapper, bearded doctor from Montréal who presented the views of the Humanist Association. Dr. Henry Morgentaler called for making abortion legal during the first three months of pregnancy, for any woman who requested one. Without her needing to give a reason.[9] The Committee was flabbergasted.

Proposals ranged from restrictive to compassionate, but consensus was for minor reform of the existing law, of the sort urged by the CMA. The Standing Committee's interim report, released December 19, 1967, recommended legalizing the role of hospital therapeutic abortion committees and broadening the grounds for abortion when "a pregnancy will seriously endanger the life or the *health* of the mother." This revision was slight but significant. Inserting 'health' as a ground for abortion sounded progressive, but it was so vague and undefined a term as to make the entire 'reform' unworkable, and, soon enough, it was odious even to the doctors who had lobbied for it.[10] Two days later, then-justice minister Trudeau stuck in the Committee's wording when he tabled his massive Omnibus Bill in the Commons.

The December 21, 1967 *Vancouver Sun* headlined its page-one story in the language of the day: "New Criminal Code Okays: Birth Control, Breath Tests, Abortion, Sweeps, Queers. Commons Gets Catch-All Bill."

It is surprising that in staid Canada, the first large body to broach the issue of abortion did so in 1960. The United Church, at its 19th General Council, adopted an internal study that bestowed respect on many non-traditional aspects of family life. It's section on abortion managed to both chastise and faintly approve it:

> Christian conscience cannot approve abortion, either as a means of limiting or spacing one's family, or as relief to an unmarried mother, because it involves the destruction of a human life. However, if, in the judgment of reputable medical authorities, the continuation of pregnancy seriously endangers the physical or mental health of the mother, therapeutic abortion may be necessary.[11]

Before that, only one mention of abortion had appeared in the mass-circulation media. In August 1959, *Chatelaine* magazine ran an article asking "Should Canada Change Its Abortion Law?" Writer Joan Finnigan reported, not on Canada, but on the reform movements underway in Great Britain and in the US. Most Canadians' eyes and ears remained closed, however, until the summer of 1961, when the *Vancouver Sun* shattered the silence in BC. In August that year, a 23-year-old North Vancouver woman, separated from her husband and the mother of two, collapsed and died while visiting a neighbour. The *Sun* relayed a public warning against self-induced abortion, the cause of the woman's death: "Pathologist Warns 1 in 3 Dies From Soap Injection" said the page 2 headline. "Its danger...lies in the entry of soap bubbles into the blood stream creating an embolism." Another doctor said "he had warned [Mrs. King] against any abortion attempt after she had indicated to him a strong desire to terminate her pregnancy."

Mrs. King's tragedy precipitated a spate of editorials, a 5-part investigative report, and several other stories on the impolite issue of abortion in the *Sun*. "Canadian abortion law is hypocritical, unjust and dangerous, as the public may again be reminded by the death of a North Vancouver woman," began the initial editorial.[12] Next day, the editor's charged:

> Illegal abortion in British Columbia is a flourishing minor industry with an annual income estimated to be somewhat above that of wheat farmers ($1.2 million) and below that of knitting mills ($2.4 million).
>
> One out of five BC women, at some time in her life, will trust her health, fortune, reputation and life to its practitioners...In doing so, she will be trusting them to an industry in which a hypocritical federal law encourages extortion, imposes unjust penalties, bestows privilege on wealth and peril on the poor...[13]

At the same time, a series by Tom Ardies was featured on page one. "Even Dogs Fare Better" was the headline on Friday, August 25:

> There is a prominent businessman in this city who has a pretty young daughter and a pretty scruffy dog. When his dog got sick he took it to a veterinarian and got it the best treatment money could buy. When his unmarried daughter got pregnant he took her to a quack abortionist and risked her health and life. This actually happened...[14]

An estimate by the BC Medical Association held that, in 1961, criminal abortions were equal to about 10 per cent of the province's 40,000 live births. Of these, "1000 [abortions] sent women to hospital for problems from infection to malformation to sterility."[15]

In 1967, the CMA *Journal* claimed that, in the eleven year period between 1954 and 1965, a total of 226 therapeutic abortions had been done in Canadian hospitals, which would average two per province per year. This extremely conservative figure was amplified by an estimated "50,000 to 100,000 illegal abortions" in the same period.[16] Popular Canadian medical writer W. Gifford Jones declared a figure of one million abortions per year in North America in 1969: "...illegal abortion...is believed to be the third biggest racket in the United States, ranking only behind gambling and narcotics."[17]

Still, arrests and convictions of illegal abortionists were few. These were publicly admitted only after 1954, when the *Vancouver Sun* began reporting about half a dozen per year. Those charged were chiefly amateurs, like Mrs. King's neighbour, whose motive was said to be money. No criminal syndicate was uncovered. The police told Ardies they felt sure local hospitals adhered closely to the law, but the hospitals were close-mouthed, saying no records were available on the number of post-abortion cases they handled.

Still, looking back to her days as a student nurse at Vancouver General Hospital, Barbara Hestrin, now Program Director at Women's Hospital in Vancouver, recalls her befuddlement about the patients in an off-limits room on the gynecology ward. Why was it that the women in that room were given only perfunctory treatment or even ignored? Sometimes they vanished, and it was clear that they'd died. When Hestrin asked, she was told "'you don't have to go in there...those people have had, you know, they've had operations, and don't worry about them.'"[18] The victims of botched abortions were looked on as carriers of moral contagion, from whom the student nurses should be protected. By having abortions, the patients' right to standard health care was put in question. Hestrin and her fellow students were stunned when, finally, a sympathetic nurse explained the mystery. They hadn't known that abortion existed.[19]

Nonetheless, a very few physicians dared to speak publicly about the need for abortion reform. Dr. Marion Rogers, who shared a practice with her husband, Dr. Roger Rogers, was one. Horrified when a young woman was admitted to hospital after shaking a carbonated soft drink bottle, then "pointing it up her vagina and letting loose," she began to speak out.[20] That self-abortion method "blew holes" in women, leaving them with life-threatening injuries and lifelong suffering. "We saw a lot of this when we were interns" recalls Dr. Roger Rogers. "And when we got out in practice, people were continually coming to us with unwanted pregnancies and asking if there was anything that could be done." Dr. Marion appeared occasionally on radio talk-shows, where she called for a change in the abortion law. This opened a limited public debate on the issue. A caller giving instructions for using slippery elm to self-abort was cut off in mid-sentence by the radio control room.[21]

Soon, the lack of options drove these doctors to take action. They made contacts in Japan and began sending women abroad. It was expensive. In addition to paying air fare and hospital fees, abortion patients were charged $100 for each month they were pregnant. But there were no legal hassles, and abortions were done no matter how advanced the pregnancy. Similar referrals to Japan were being made from cities across North America — surely, a comment on the absurdity of the situation here. Even for financially comfortable women, it was a "nightmare," recalls Dr. Roger Rogers. "It involved a tremendous amount of expense and anxiety."[22]

So great was the taboo against abortion, as well as fear that the College of Physicians and Surgeons would lift the licence of a doctor known to defy the law, that the Rogers's had only indirect knowledge of perhaps five to six other local physicians who shared their views. Even doctors had to rely on whispers coming through a grapevine. The Rogers's refused to send women to self-styled operatives of doubtful training, whose names sometimes surfaced. [23]

Ardies found, "There are some doctors who will admit off the record that they 'look the other way' if they know of a 'good abortionist' operating in Vancouver."[24] That led to front page charges of a cover-up by city prosecutor Stewart McMorran. He lashed out at the medical profession for refusing to help police shut down "a big abortion racket" in the city.[25]

The College of Physicians and Surgeons retorted that doctors were helpless as well. Dr. Lynn Gunn, the registrar, defended the patients' right to confidentiality, and said that many patients who had illegal abortions lied about it because they feared a police investigation.[26]

Interestingly, except for one reference to the Catholic Church's position, none of the editorials, articles, or the numerous officials interviewed by

Ardies, made mention of the fetus. The message of the *Sun's* series was that a unenforceable law spawned a shadowy trade in illegal abortions that flourished at great cost to women's health and wellbeing. Ardies' final report closed with the heading "Right to Choose." A businesswoman had sent him a note reading:

> I have had four abortions and will have as many as needed to remain childless. If I couldn't get a safe one, I would try everything and would willingly and knowingly risk my life to get rid of it. I would rather die than have a child...Women...should have the right to choose for themselves.[27]

Several doctors and MPs told Ardies it was time to study how the law might be modernized. This led Dr. E.C. McCoy, acting executive director of the BC Medical Association, to pledge that doctors were ready to co-operate with lawyers and legislators in expanding the grounds for performing legal abortions.[28]

Picked up over the wire services, the *Globe and Mail* quoted Dr. McCoy and ran the same story the next day, September 1, 1961. It followed that by an on-going editorial stance on the advisability of changing the abortion laws. The *Globe's* role in changing the climate of opinion is deplored by anti-abortion historians, who have called it a "crusade"[29] and as setting off "a chain reaction of lasting consequences."[30] The stimulus of the *Vancouver Sun* in August, 1961, and its editorial stance for change during the sixties, is virtually forgotten.

Spurred by the controversy, Vancouver city prosecutor Stewart McMorran himself spearheaded the rather sluggish progress toward the 1966 adoption, by the Canadian Bar Association, of a resolution to liberalize the Criminal Code on abortion.[31] Only months' earlier, the Canadian Medical Association had agreed on the type of reform that would be acceptable to doctors.

The machinery was in gear to send the issue to Ottawa. PM Lester Pearson appointed newcomer Pierre Trudeau to the justice ministry in April, 1967. The ambitious Trudeau urged the various parliamentary committees that were studying legal reform to rush him their deliberations. The CMA's proposal had been submitted as a private member's bill by Liberal MP Ian Wahn (St.Paul's, Toronto): it would transfer responsibility for abortions to the nation's hospitals and doctors. Grace MacInnis (NDP, Vancouver Kingsway), who was the lone woman in the House of Commons, submitted a similar bill, as did NDPer H.W. Herridge. Trudeau took the Standing Committee's report and the basic text of Wahn's bill and ran with them.

As the arrogant and debonair justice minister shrugged on his leather jacket, after tabling the Omnibus Bill to Amend the Criminal Code, with its 104 revisions, on December 21, 1967, TV reporters swarmed him on the steps of the Commons. Offhandedly, Trudeau dismissed opposition to his reforms by remarking, "The state has no business in the bedrooms of the nation."[32] Although it seems he lifted the quip from a column in the *Globe and Mail,* the man himself began to overshadow his astounding Omnibus Bill in the eyes of Canadians, and that phrase probably launched his climb toward becoming Liberal Party leader and then Prime Minister within the next six months.

So rapidly did this all happen that the Commons Committee on Health had not yet heard any opposition to the liberalization of abortion. Catholic historian Alphonse de Valk admits that, to that point, "articulate opposition to abortion law revision...had been almost non-existent.[33] The silence of the Catholic hierarchy, he explains, "was based on the assumption that the unacceptability of legalizing abortion was still as self-evident as it had always been."[34] He compared Catholicism's claim to immutable moral truth to the deplorable practice of the United Church "where principles of faith and morals are decided by majority vote."[35] The Catholic bishops addressed the Standing Committee a few months later.[36] However, de Valk admits the Canadian Catholic hierarchy had already "accepted revision of the Criminal Code in two other areas of marital morality: birth control and divorce."[37]

The Omnibus Bill had not yet been enacted when the Women's Caucus held its first meeting at SFU the following September. The Bill had had to be re-introduced to the parliament elected in June, 1968. When it reached second reading in January, 1969, debate — pro and con — was vigorous. The Ontario press gave it coverage, but news about parliament was apparently unable to surmount the Rockies, and British Columbians knew little about the Bill until the final vote came.

MPs from all four federal parties urged restrictions on the proposed abortion law. Nonetheless, with 111 MPs of all parties absent, the vote to eliminate the clause on abortion was defeated, with 36 in favour, 107 against.[38]

By this time, the addition of the pregnant woman's "health" as a ground for abortion was already perceived as troublesome. Only rarely is a woman's physical health threatened by pregnancy — although it can happen. In rare blood disorders, diabetes, or severe heart disease, pregnancy can be life-threatening to both mother and fetus. It was more likely, all agreed, that a woman's mental health would become the reason for terminating a pregnancy, and proof of such a threat would fall to psychiatric evaluation. Suddenly, psychiatrists found themselves being expected to take the weight so that their medical colleagues would be protected by the law. This became an issue during the Commons debate.

The burden of opposing the abortion and homosexuality amendments fell to the Raillement Creditistes. These fourteen Catholic MPs from rural Québec represented the traditional and religious points of view, and they mounted a filibuster to forestall the final vote. The abortion clauses were labeled "criminal, socialist and Communist."[39] Creditiste MP Gilbert Rondeau (Shelford, Québec) argued:

It [the proposed abortion law] is to give more freedom to the depraved people in this country, and to please the easygoing women of our society, who could not care less about their neighbors and our race. It is also to please credulous girls who fall easily into the gutter, and also to please flighty ones who go out night after night to conquer new lovers, and also to please dissipated women who lack foresight.[40]

Creditiste MP Leonel Beaudoin (Richmond, Québec) explained the dangers of permitting abortion on the recommendation of a psychiatrist:

Doctors will have to deal with women that will play on words, who will think up any reason to get a therapeutic abortion...They will trifle with the conscience and good faith of physicians and gynecologists. They will even threaten to commit suicide, but very few ever do it...[41]

Commenting on the remarks of Creditiste Leader Real Caouette, pro-choice activist Eleanor Pelrine wrote, "He too displayed a strong anti-woman bias, apparently feeling that, given half a chance, most women would choose to abort every pregnancy."[42] That was not the only spectre MP Caouette raised, however: "The Minister of Justice [John Turner] might not be here today, if such a legislation...had been passed fifty years ago. That is what I think. If such a bill had been passed fifty years ago, the Chinese would perhaps have taken over our country."[43]

If a woman's mental health became grounds for abortion, Caouette stated:

Before psychiatrists existed, there were women who gave birth to children...Psychiatry has seldom cured the insane. We realize it when we look at the other side of the house.[44]

Despite such edifying arguments, the majority of MPs were unconvinced by the Creditistes and other opponents to the bill. Note that no argument defended the fetus. It was freedom for women the MPs feared.

Rising to speak, tiny but fearless Grace MacInnis "lashed out at what she called the 'disgusting hypocrisy' of the debate. Some male MPs have talked of women as little more than 'baby machines' with no minds or rights or feelings of their own.'" Mrs. MacInnis said the failure of previous governments to open the law meant that "thousands of women were being butchered and tortured by quacks."[45] A feminist in her very marrow, Grace MacInnis kept on demanding the right to choose for all women throughout her parliamentary career.

The entire package of the Omnibus Bill was adopted by the Commons on Wednesday, May 14, 1969, by a vote of 149 to 55.[46] The sections on abortion were added onto the existing sections in the Criminal Code, those which made every imaginable aspect of abortion illegal. Thus the reforms co-existed with the old repressive law for the first several years — a recipe for disaster in itself. The new Criminal Code was sent on to the Senate, which endorsed it, and in due time the reformed abortion law took effect. By then, it was August 28, 1969.

Meantime, the Women's Caucus had gone about its business with a firm eye fixed on women's most pressing needs.

CHAPTER 3

THE ABORTION INFORMATION SERVICE

After a busy spring and summer, Women's Caucus members Marcy Cohen and Jean Rands reported on their work to a September, 1969 conference of the "Simon Fraser Left":

> Last February, Women's Caucus in Vancouver was a series of discussion groups which were discussing organizing but not organizing...Now Women's Caucus has regular monthly membership meetings, an office in the Labor Temple, a mailing list of over two hundred, most of whom are not students, and a newspaper.[1]

Women's Caucus had moved off campus. For $30 a month it was renting a small basement room in the Labor Temple, headquarters of the union movement, at 307 W. Broadway, near Cambie. It had produced the first issue of *The Pedestal*, a remarkable newspaper that continued publication until 1973. The *Women's Caucus Program*, drawn up in the spring, was printed as a four-page pamphlet, and as many as 20,000 copies were distributed between March and August 1969.[2] A public meeting, held with teachers studying at UBC, had discussed the channelling of female students into narrow vocational fields. Prime Minister Trudeau had been picketed when he visited the Seaforth Armories, shortly before the inadequate new abortion law took effect. The first Women's Caucus demonstration had taken place, to protest discrimination against women in hiring and promotion. And plans were nearly complete for a major event, the Western Regional Conference on Women's Liberation, to be held on the Thanksgiving Day weekend in 1969. Women came from all the western provinces and several US states to this conference, which then focussed the energies of Women's Caucus over the next eight months.

Cohen and Rands's "Report Back to the Simon Fraser Left" defined feminism as a "legitimate part of the movement against capitalism." Stung by the SDU male leadership's dismissal of them as lightweights in political theory, Women's Caucus members had prepared an impressive series of papers that explored the political ramifications of women's liberation. One was, in fact, published by the prestigious New York *Monthly Review* in September, 1969: "The Political Economy of Women's Liberation," by Dr. Margaret Benston.

Marxism had a big following among politicized youth in North America and Europe, which led student occupations and protests on every domestic and international issue. A politically eclectic alternative media mush-roomed, reporting on both politics and the counter-culture. The *Georgia Straight*, Vancouver's underground press, was full of protest against the established order, praise for cannabis, cartoons by R. Crumb — and end-less photos and drawings of naked women. It was cool to be misogynist.

Four issues were listed in the Women's Caucus's Program as top prior-ities: abortion and birth control, equal pay and equal work, child care, and channelling in the educational system.[3] The group set out to organize around these issues simultaneously. It also put out *The Pedestal*, which was published twice in the fall of 1969, and became a monthly in early 1970. Equal status for all was enshrined in the organizational structure, and there were no officers. One became a Women's Caucus member by declaring herself to be one. No oath of support was required, no membership dues or even duties. Every woman attending a meeting, including her first, and no matter how infrequently she came, had full voice and decision-making rights. As with the student left in general, Women's Caucus considered itself part of a movement, swimming in the sea of a like-minded populace — rather than a mere organization.

The move to Vancouver drew in several new women who were to play vital roles in Women's Caucus over the next year. The first was Betsy Wood, then known as Betsy Meadley. In her early forties, with prematurely white hair and the misleading appearance of a mild and conventional matron, Wood was recently divorced and was raising four children alone. She was a clerical worker in the BC Fire Marshal's office, and her bids for a better-paying job were routinely turned down. She sought out Women's Caucus after hearing about it on her car radio. "I went because I was interested in equal pay for men and women, and especially for myself."[4] She remembers being received with open arms.

Wood's job plight was perfectly suited to Women's Caucus concerns, and, indeed, it inspired the demonstration held on August 26 to protest discrimination against women in the workplace. For the initial issue of the *Pedestal*, Wood wrote an unsigned front page article, lambasting the sorry record of a BC government that supposedly pledged to uphold its employees' human rights.[5]

Equal pay and rights on the job were not the only issues of importance to Betsy Wood, however. Possessed of a shrewd sense of what the public was ready for, she believed abortion was the issue of the day. Women were just becoming aware of how much the heavily-touted abortion reform law, which took effect on August 28, 1969, cheated them. Wood's antennae picked up the rustle of incipient rage. She had already tried out a bold pro-posal on fellow members of the NDP, who chuckled admiringly but waved her idea aside. Wood wanted to revive the 'On to Ottawa' trek, which had set out from Vancouver to demand jobs and rights for the unemployed in

1935. This time the demand would be for repeal of the just-enacted abortion law. "But nobody took a serious interest in it," recalls Wood, until "I hit the Women's Caucus." She had a native understanding of what Cohen and Rands meant when they wrote "that all our demands [will] be raised in the context of building a mass, extra-parliamentary movement of women."

Also drawn to Women's Caucus that fall was Mary Stolk of Richmond. She was a nurse, staying at home to raise her family, active in the NDP and the anti-Vietnam war movement, and she saw feminism as "an organic part of these activities."[6] Mary Trew arrived from Toronto in September 1969, at age 19, and enrolled at Vancouver Community College. Her first experience with Women's Caucus came when she attended the Western Regional Conference. Like Wood and Stolk, Trew jumped into Women's Caucus immediately.

In the hippie era of the late sixties, Donna Liberson did not find it strange that, one day, a man she'd never met stopped her on a Gastown street. He introduced himself as Harvey Karman and told her he ran an abortion centre in Los Angeles. Karman invited her to refer women needing abortions to his clinic. He explained that he was not a doctor, but that he used the latest technique and charged women relatively little. Liberson was very interested in what Karman had to say.[7]

But, she thought, why should Vancouver women have to go to LA for an abortion? It was now legal in Canada. Liberson began to look into the possibilities for obtaining a local abortion. At the Planned Parenthood family planning clinic, she explained, "Look, it's legal for people to have abortions. But we need doctors...that will work with us [Women's Caucus] [from] within the system." The doctor misunderstood and assumed Liberson was pregnant. He told her the women he refused to abort later thanked him "as if he were a god."[8]

Next Liberson tried talking with her family doctor, but he wasn't interested in her plan. Both doctors, however, told Liberson: "'...if any women have abortions, (tsk, tsk), do send them to us afterwards and we'll clean them up.'"[9] It was clear that the medical profession had not caught up with the new law, and didn't regard an unwillingly pregnant woman as qualifying for medical attention, unless, after a botched backstreet operation, she suffered from hemorrhaging or septic infection, and was close to death.

Abortion was not specifically on the agenda for the Western Regional Conference, held at UBC and attended by about 130 women, but Liberson invited a spokesperson from Karman's clinic to speak. Mary Stolk, for one, was fascinated by what the young woman from Los Angeles told them. Betsy Wood circulated the room, getting a bounce on her idea for marching to Ottawa. As adjournment neared, Wood proposed this plan to the plenary session, and it was enthusiastically received.

Donna Liberson reported that the conference had focused on "specific ideas to deal with the economic oppression of women," in the *Georgia Straight*. Her final line mentioned that "an intensive campaign to legalize all abortions will be undertaken." The groovy crew at the *Straight* topped the article with a drawing of a bare-breasted dominatrix wielding a whip — their idea of what was meant by women's liberation.[10]

Betsy Wood remembers: "...I know that people in the Caucus were upset because abortion seemed to be taking the lead, and they didn't want that to happen. They wanted the four [issues] they were interested in to move ahead together. But the fact was, people weren't interested in equal pay for women at that time. But they were interested in birth control and abortion, so it was just a natural that it should move ahead."[11]

"Abortion Campaign" announced page one of the second issue of the *Pedestal* in December, 1969. Adjoining an article by Mary Stolk was a reproduction of the Women's Caucus poster, which showed a toga-draped, pregnant Justice, holding scales, described as "Labouring Under a Mis-Conception." "LEGALIZE ALL ABORTION NOW!" was the demand. In small print it said, "Ideology Surpasses Love" and gave the phone number for the Women's Caucus.

The article reported plans to educate women about the revised law. "Additionally, every Tuesday night at the Women's Caucus Office in the Labor Temple, legal abortion counselling will be available." This was the first public announcement of what some called The Abortion Information Service (AIS). Mary Stolk's article was reprinted in the *Georgia Straight*, and she was soon interviewed by both the *Province* and the *Sun*.[12] The tone of both daily papers was respectful. The *Sun* made much of Stolk's training as a "former nurse" and the fact that she was married and the mother of six children. A respectable, as opposed to a 'bra-burning', feminist.

Stolk is modest about her role in AIS and insists that "Donna [Liberson] was surely the catalyst and the leader" of the counselling service. Helen Potrebenko was another important player, and Melody Rudd, Janis Nairne, and possibly others were involved in the project. "We were very aware that we were opening a can of worms. In fact that was our firm intention. We wanted to blow the hypocrisy of the status quo sky-high," recalls Stolk. "The new legislation had gone through and women had less access to abortion and reproductive choice than before, because the medical profession was too timid to take the ball, run with it, and go as far as they could. Instead they'd held back, muttering about 'breaking the new law' and getting the advice of lawyers. It was a total bottleneck..."[13]

"Our position was that doctors could interpret the term 'health' in the new legislation according to the United Nation's definition, which, if memory serves me, included physical, mental, and social well-being. They argued they could not. What they meant was they would not. At least not until they, and not a bunch of upstart feminists, made the decision."[14]

Pulling no punches, Stolk wrote in *The Pedestal* the new service would inform women "about the options open to them under the present inadequate system." These were, almost entirely, illegal options, but "without them the whole system would collapse."[15] The Abortion Information Service intended to locate sympathetic doctors who would present pregnant women's cases to the required hospital Therapeutic Abortion Committees. "And Harvey [Karman] would be our backup," Stolk recalls.

They were a bit nervous and they were immediately swamped. Before AIS opened its doors, Donna Liberson began fielding calls made to her home by desperate women. "Where did you get my number from?" she asked, and discovered the doctor from the family planning clinic was sending abortion requests her way. "That was the man who gave me the lecture about being a god," she splutters.[16] "The doctors were very hypocritical."

From the outset, fifteen to twenty women showed up on Tuesday nights for AIS sessions at the Labor Temple. There were no divisions in the room to provide for privacy, and Stolk remembers "we just sat by the person we were talking with and dealt with their individual situation."

Liberson, Stolk, and Potrebenko had expected the women to be distraught, unsure whether they were truly pregnant, and needing a shoulder to cry on. Helen Potrebenko, then driving a taxi to pay her way through SFU while working on her first novel, was a trained laboratory technician. Although short of money, she bought pregnancy kits out of her own pocket and stood by to test urine samples.[17] "We felt that this service would be an inducement in itself, and it was," remembers Mary Stolk. Ordinarily, a woman could not confirm her pregnancy without going to a doctor, who then sent her specimen to a lab. That often took a week, and for a woman seeking an abortion, time is of the essence. At AIS, free pregnancy testing was done on the spot.

Potrebenko found that the women coming to AIS had "already made up their minds; they didn't want to talk about the abortion operation, they wanted to know what to do about [their pregnancies.] So counselling on making the decision wasn't needed."[18] To protect the women's identities as much as to protect themselves from possible criminal charges, the counsellors made no notes or records. Despite the law's revision, it was still illegal to counsel a woman about abortion, and AIS suspected its sessions and phone calls were tapped by the police. Cautious about being overheard giving out names and telephone numbers, AIS wrote that information on slips of paper and women then made their own contacts.[19] "However, we were very anxious for follow-up and I remember making some effort to keep track of at least a first name, so that when they phoned me with follow-up, I knew something about what their plans had been," recalls Stolk.

By the second session of AIS, a questionnaire was ready for women at the door.[20] No copy has survived, but in Donna Liberson's recollection it asked "'How did you hear about us?' and 'What's your term?' But there were no names, just ages and stuff.'" A surprising number were directed to the clinic by their doctors, and they wrote the doctors' names on the questionnaires. Later, that information proved useful.

What options could AIS suggest to the women? There weren't many, after all. The best outcome would be to get the medical establishment to open up the channels permitted by the new law. But local hospitals were reluctant to change their habits. After all, they saw the purpose of the new law to be, not a boon to women, but a cloak to keep the occasional legal abortionist out of jail.

Once a hospital bowed to the inevitable, it found creating an official Therapeutic Abortion Committee a cumbersome process, since the law required TACs to consist of at least three doctors, none of whom actually performed the operation. Many hospitals in small communities were lucky to have three doctors, altogether. In larger ones, many doctors were unwilling to condone legal abortions. Looking on from the outside, the women of AIS saw "a great deal of infighting, boycotting, backbiting and bitterness among doctors at VGH" as the hospital struggled to come to terms with the new law.[21] There was a shortage of operating room time, a lack of equipment, and widespread ignorance of how to perform an abortion — something medical schools didn't teach. Most hospitals' first response was to add tricky regulations, such as residency in the immediate area, on top of the byzantine requirements of the law, in order to stem the tide of demand. Little wonder that, for the next twenty years, only four or five hospitals in BC's major urban centres — Vancouver and Victoria — did abortions at all.

Those hospitals required women to locate at least two doctors willing to refer them to the requisite Therapeutic Abortion Committee. It came down to finding a psychiatrist who would claim the applicant's mental health was jeopardised by her continued pregnancy. Extraordinary anxiety, emotional trauma, shame, fear of scandal, and disruption of the woman's plans and/or economic situation frequently did accompany unwanted pregnancy — but true psychosis was rare. To enlist the help of a psychiatrist meant that women had to lie, to threaten suicide, and submit to being labelled unstable in their medical records. And that was only the beginning. Many times, TACs ruled against a woman's request, and the law allowed for no appeal. The TAC might or might not issue its ruling before a woman's pregnancy was too far advanced for an abortion. The arbitrary cut-off date used in BC was the end of the third month. It was a lengthy and uncertain ordeal. For some time, AIS was stymied in getting its clients into hospital settings.

So telling women about Harvey Karman in Los Angeles was the only option AIS could offer, at first. Of course, most hadn't the money or time to go there. Eventually, a doctor with a thick east European accent and "an extreme cloak and dagger approach" was located. "He made all his phone calls from pay phones and actually wore dark glasses and a trench coat," recalls Stolk. This man was fully trained as a doctor, but he wasn't licenced to practice in Canada. "His [medical] procedures were safe and professional", says Stolk. "He kept a small cabin in Point Roberts where he took his patients. Most of the women who used his services were satisfied, although awed by his secrecy and sometimes unhappy with his brusque manner."

Then the man was arrested and charged with performing illegal abortions. Illegal, because they weren't done in a hospital, and his patients had not been humiliated by a TAC. To be sure of a conviction, he was also charged with income tax evasion. Stolk's information was that he fled to his home country, thus escaping imprisonment.

Donna Liberson's search for sympathetic doctors got underway in earnest when a questionnaire for doctors was hastily typed on a stencil and run off on an ancient mimeograph machine. The result looked anything but professional. Never mind, it was mailed off to all the MDs in the local phone book. It was a frustrating search. Out of hundreds of inquiries, supportive replies were received from fewer than half-a-dozen doctors. They were invited to a meeting at the Labor Temple. Stolk recalls, "I think about three came."

They included Drs. Marion and Roger Rogers, who were pleased to learn about AIS. Their own efforts had turned up a new contact — Dr. Franz Koome, of Renton, Washington. A rebel, Dr. Koome had written to the governor in November, 1969, to inform him about his illegal clinic, where 140 abortions had already been performed, and to argue for a liberalized law. Abortion laws in the US were being reformed very gradually, state by state; there was no blanket federal law as there was in Canada. The Drs. Rogers had invited Koome to their home and were satisfied with the quality of his service. He then accepted their referrals from the lower mainland. At the next AIS session, several women were referred to Dr. Koome, and Stolk recalls, "they all phoned back and said they'd gotten appointments, no problem." Finding Dr. Koome was a great relief to both the Rogers's and AIS, because he was relatively inexpensive, close-by, and yet far enough away to assure privacy to the Canadian women who attended his clinic.

In the Drs. Rogers, AIS found what it had hoped for. Dr. David Claman and Dr. Gerald Korn were also supportive, and all worked to get Vancouver General Hospital to implement the new law. The Rogers's agreed to shepherd women sent them by Women's Caucus through the complex system for getting a legal hospital abortion. In Stolk's recollection, "we had to be very selective about which women we could, in fact, refer through legal channels. Married, white, middle class were best. I remember the first patient who we counselled to try the legal route and who was successful. She fit the above profile and was early enough in her pregnancy to have the time [for the time-consuming application process.] I remember how excited we were when the system went without a hitch. But it was clear that this was the exception, not the rule." [22]

However, there was a Vancouver physician who performed abortions in his office, and whose reputation for care and scrupulous cleanliness made him a godsend. His practice was an open secret. Dr. Robert Makaroff, located near UBC, was admired by the Drs. Rogers, who invited him, as well as Dr. Koome, to their home, and sent many women his way.

Dr. Makaroff was anonymously profiled in the *Georgia Straight* in January, 1970, under the by-line "Gratton Gray." In "Abortion, North American Style," Gray quoted extensively from a "Vancouver physician who had performed two illegal abortions last week, and was preparing to perform another while I spoke to him." This doctor was a reformer, arguing that "'The law is the murderer,'" and saying that, despite the threat to his liberty and medical licence, and to the living he provided for his wife and children, there were women in need whom he could not turn away. Introducing his prospective abortion patient to Gratton Gray, the doctor said:

> What would happen to this girl? She's perfectly healthy, mentally and physically. A hospital committee would likely not approve a therapeutic abortion. In desperation she might find someone who would penetrate her uterus with a rusty coat hanger. She might, or she might not, be admitted to a hospital in time to prevent a fatal hemorrhage or infection. [23]

Gray noticed an unmarked police car parked opposite the doctor's office when s/he left it at 11:14 pm. The writer declared, "I personally know of seven physicians operating [illegally] in Vancouver." AIS wished it knew of so many.

The women from AIS soon heard of Dr. Makaroff themselves and went to inspect his services. "It was a lovely, clean office, almost as large as a clinic. All these little rooms," recalls Potrebenko admiringly. Necessarily working alone, Makaroff provided his patients with a preview of what they could expect, by playing an audio tape that described the surgical procedure. Women received a D&C, or scraping of the uterus, under general anesthetic, and most said they had little pain afterwards. [24]

"He was a particularly fine human being who had allowed his inability to turn away desperate women to get him in too deeply to get out. I suppose a lot of other doctors, who found it useful to have such a service available, had helped push him to the point where he totally gave up his other practice, " says Mary Stolk. Liberson saw him as "kind of an innocent." She realized it would be unfair to flood him with referrals from AIS. First, because "we knew he was quite compassionate," and "would never refuse anybody." Although Makaroff's standard fee for abortion was $500 — which was more than it cost women to go to either Dr. Koome or Harvey Karman — Liberson knew he frequently charged less to poor women. (The doctor described by Gratton Gray was charging the nineteen-year-old student in the article $100.) Makaroff knew that he could lose his licence. He explained up-front that he charged a high price to enable him to hire a defence lawyer, when the time came. The second reason why Liberson wanted to use him sparingly was to help lessen the heat, in the hope that Dr. Makaroff might stay in practice longer.

Still, AIS was set on making doctors and hospitals live up to their responsibilities to provide *legal* abortions. The response to the new law was maddeningly slow. Reforming the law had not put legal abortions within reach. How to unblock the ice jam of the lordly medical establishment? "A lot changed because of the pressure of women," reflects Dr. Roger Rogers. "...if there hadn't been a groundswell, where women became really very outspoken and very aggressive," he believes doctors would have continued to ignore them.[25]

The AIS crew was invited to be guests on a radio talk show. Donna Liberson acted as spokesperson; she was informally regarded as the leader of the group. In Potrebenko's recollection, on air, Liberson threw caution to the wind and said, straight-forwardly, that the clinic was having little success directing women toward legal abortions, so it usually helped them get illegal ones. "God, I admired her guts," recalls the gutsy Potrebenko. However, she began preparing to be arrested, and she bought some jeans to wear in jail. Mary Stolk also bought a sweater to keep her warm in a prison cell.[26]

But there were no such repercussions. In retrospect, Potrebenko estimates "We could have set up a clinic at Granville and Georgia, and no-one would have cared — the time was right!"[27]

AIS was contacted by people with ties to the Unitarian Church who wanted to document whether or not the new law was working. This group wished to follow the case of a woman who would pursue the steps for obtaining a legal abortion. She would be directed by AIS to its short list of sympathetic doctors and make a bid to a hospital TAC. If she were found to qualify for an abortion on the only permitted grounds, as the doctors interpreted them — then hooray! If she were turned down, then the church group would pay her expenses to Harvey Karman's clinic. Mary Stolk remembers that "the young woman we chose had a low-key personality, a sense of humor, and a pretty street-wise manner." This woman's doctor referred her to a gynecologist, an essential first step in the process. But while she waited for an appointment with a psychiatrist, her pregnancy advanced too far for her to qualify for a hospital abortion in Canada.

So she flew to Los Angeles — her first time on a plane — and had her abortion without difficulty. "She had a good holiday, spending some time on the beach and she thanked the people who had paid the tab very nicely," recalls Stolk. Her own doctor said, nonchalantly, "'Oh, I see you've had a miscarriage.'"[28]

From this young woman Stolk, Potrebenko, and Liberson learned something about Harvey Karman they hadn't known before. It seems that after the abortion, Karman proposed having sex. She "...was quite good natured about the sex part. She declined," says Stolk. "However, I had to seriously re-think the feasibility of giving Harvey's number to very many people."

Donna Liberson decided to check Karman out. She had a woman friend who had just finished medical school, and the two of them drove to Los Angeles together. Liberson missed one Tuesday night session of AIS to do this, and, because of the crush of clients, she was missed. When the two reached Los Angeles, Harvey Karman remembered Donna and called her into the operating room while he was performing an abortion. "He said, 'Donna, hold the flashlight.' And he said, 'See? Look. This woman is three months pregnant, and this is all there is to it.'"[29] Liberson was surprised the procedure was so quick and uncomplicated. The patient was conscious, and she seemed to be in more anxiety than pain. Karman used a vacuum aspirator, which was indeed the latest technology; even Dr. Makaroff didn't have one of those. Consequently, women at Karman's clinic needed only a local anesthetic, which was much less dangerous and debilitating than the general anesthetic used in Canadian hospitals. Karman said, "'Now this is how you know it's a clean job.' I don't know if he was performing for me or what, but I was totally amazed...To me it was...like, what was all the fuss about?" Then Karman turned the patient over and gave her a massage.

Liberson's doctor friend did a tour of the clinic and decided it looked okay. It was certainly clean, and antiseptic procedures were being followed in the operating room. But like her peers, this BC doctor had never had any training regarding abortion. It was taboo in medical schools, so she really didn't know what to look for. Karman and his clientele were decidedly hippies. On their return, Liberson and her doctor friend concluded that "although he was weird and the place really wouldn't do for your average middle-class woman, it was safe and competent."

Liberson confronted Karman with the story about having sex with his patients, but in his view, he only did it as a means of comforting the women. And he never made having sex a condition for the abortion; he only suggested it afterward. "He wanted me to start up a clinic and he'd give me a percent up here. I said, 'I'm not interested; I don't do it for money.'...He was funny. So that was the story about Harvey. He was a character."[30]

Potrebenko and Stolk were less amused. Although this was 1970, and as Helen Potrebenko recalls, "women were still flattered to be sexually harassed," she objected to Karman's attempts to seduce his patients. "Nobody was indignant, because he'd gone to jail [for performing abortions] and was a martyr to the cause," she complains. In fact, scandal mounted over Harvey Karman, and *Ms. Magazine* later did an extensive exposé of him.

Meantime, Helen Potrebenko heard that Dr. Koome sometimes performed abortions without anesthetic. Stolk, on the other hand, had maintained contact with quite a few women she'd told about Dr. Koome, "and they were generally relieved that the whole situation could be dealt with so easily and competently."These AIS clients had not complained about a lack of anesthetic. Stolk concluded that Koome "used local anesthetic in varying amounts, perhaps not too lavishly."[31] Doubts about their main sources of help surfaced as the demand for abortions grew.

Liberson and Stolk were in telephone contact several times a day. It was impossible not to notice that their phones were tapped. The interference on the line was so obvious and heavy-handed that Stolk concluded that the object was to scare people. A friend who was involved in protesting nuclear experiments on Amchitka Island later described having the same experience. "It was vehemently denied, but I smiled. The things they described were very familiar to me...other phones ringing, clicks, several conversations going on in the background", etc. She also recalls that "Dr. Makaroff told me his phone calls used to be broadcast over taxi cab and ship-to-shore type phones. People used to phone and warn him."[32]

As spring 1970 advanced, the tactic of pressuring doctors to implement the new law and perform more legal abortions in local hospitals seemed to be having an effect. Very gradually, more of the women who came to AIS reported success through that route. Nonetheless, the process was so lengthy and complex that it was a rare for a woman to get through it before she was disqualified on the grounds that her pregnancy was too far advanced. In addition, many doctors were afraid to abort an obviously healthy woman. Liberson recalls being phoned by a doctor who sat on a hospital TAC. He was concerned about a fifteen-year-old patient who wanted an abortion, and he asked AIS to help her. "I said, 'You've got your own Therapeutic Abortion Committee!' He said, 'There's nothing wrong with her.' I said, 'She's *fifteen*, isn't that enough?'"[33] The law said her life or health must be endangered by the pregnancy, and the doctor felt that didn't cover his young patient, that she'd better find an illegal abortionist.

Then suddenly, the illegal resources dried up. On March 10, 1970, Dr. Robert Makaroff was arrested and his medical career came to an end. Vancouver feminists called for the charges against him to be dropped, but most medical colleagues, who had sent him more patients than he could handle, now shunned him. Dr. Makaroff's progress through the courts was front-page news for months.

Shortly afterward, an overloaded Dr. Koome began to require that women phoning him for appointments have a doctor's referral. He could not keep up with the demand. In late March, Harvey Karman, too, was put out of business. The *Georgia Straight* reprinted an article from Los Angeles that described cigar-smoking "homicide cops" invading the clinic, seizing the appointment book, interrogating patients, and arresting Karman and five volunteer staff members.[34]

However, Mary Stolk remembers that, in the spring of 1970, "a lot of American clinics opened, some in Bellingham, which were very anxious to cash in on the Canadian demand." From Dr. Claman, one of AIS's "sympathetic doctors," Helen Potrebenko learned that "pressure from women's groups" led VGH to gradually increase to forty abortions per week.[35] Nonetheless, the demand was skyrocketing. Recalls Helen Potrebenko, "The staff of the [VGH] Ob-Gyn Department went into a panic and decided to freeze the number at 40 per week, with no out-of-town people allowed except with extenuating circumstances (money). In October [1970], there was a backlog of three weeks" waiting time to get into the operating room, after all approvals had been obtained.[36]

With the arrests of the doctors, AIS lost its power and some of its significance. It was a great relief to Mary Stolk. "My phone had been ringing for months with calls from desperate women...It was more than I could handle, after awhile." The counsellors of AIS reported to a Women's Caucus general meeting, "We were exhausted...We couldn't go on" after the illegal clinics dried up.[37]

During the past few months, the tight group of women who operated AIS used the same office, but apparently seldom interacted with other members of Women's Caucus. No-one seems to remember how that isolation came about — possibly it was due to the anxiety of the AIS organizers who felt their service was clandestine. But toward April, as the departure date for the historic Abortion Caravan [see chapter five] neared, criticism of AIS developed within Women's Caucus. Potrebenko had quit AIS out of disgust for the methods of Karman and Koome. Other members of Women's Caucus felt the direction of AIS was wrong. They believed the first priority should be to politicize the women who came to the clinic and convince them that women were oppressed. A showdown developed. Feeling burned out, Donna Liberson agreed to hand over AIS to those in Women's Caucus who demanded it.

Under this new management, AIS began another phase that lasted through the summer months of 1970. Women coming for help were persuaded to join sit-ins in the VGH Outpatient Department, and AIS threatened to sit-in at meetings of the TAC, unless many more abortions were approved.[38] Potrebenko believes that "due to this outside pressure, and the pressure inside from Dr. Claman and others, the hospital policy was changed and the number of abortions rose to 70 a week." Still, reporting on their experience in the *Pedestal*, the original members of AIS said "the same problems are frustrating the counsellors now, as before. Many of the new doctors who say they are sympathetic use the situation to moralize, keep the women waiting for weeks and then refuse to help." Even worse,

> The hospitals are still doing barbaric and unnecessary hysterotomies (cutting through the stomach and uterine walls) on women over three months pregnant.39

There was only one solution: 'this present system for obtaining abortions must be removed" altogether.[40] The new abortion law must be repealed.

CHAPTER 4

GOING THROUGH THE PROPER CHANNELS

The exuberance and sass of the Abortion Information Service characterized other Women's Caucus projects, as well, although those focussing on women workers may have had the most down-to-business manner. Pleased by the reception given to her proposal for a Caravan to Ottawa, Betsy Wood first thought the appropriate moment would be on Valentine's Day.[1] She saw an obvious irony in the celebration of romantic love — and its frequent outcome for women: unwanted pregnancy and the danger of a bloody illegal abortion. But February proved to be too early; more time was needed for organizing the march.

Despite its members' readiness for daring projects, the scope of what became known as The Abortion Campaign was a matter of debate in Women's Caucus. There was much to do on the local scene, and some outside the tight group in AIS were eager to focus on British Columbia. Ottawa and its dealings were remote from BC; was it really necessary to go so far? "It was actually hard to convince them," recalls Wood, the newcomer among politically sophisticated student radicals,"that it was a federal law. And you had to work at the municipal level, the provincial level, *and* the federal level."

Wood envisaged holding public meetings at every stop between Vancouver and Ottawa, with new people joining the Caravan along the way. They would be so colourful and garner so much notice that the inadequate 1969 law would be dispatched by parliament upon their arrival. Repeal it altogether! No law was needed on abortion. Existing federal and provincial health acts could guarantee its safe performance. However, with no network of contacts and the barest beginnings of feminism in Canada, a search was required to locate people willing to set up meetings in their areas, do advance publicity, and, not least, find places for caravaners to sleep. Marge Hollibaugh is credited with doing much of that spade work, just as Anne Roberts sent press releases to media across the country.

As the glamorous Abortion Campaign drew more internal interest and womanpower, some resentment surfaced. Wood, whose job situation was the focus of the first Women's Caucus demonstration, and who had presented a paper on the problems of women workers at the Western Regional Conference[2], felt she had to explain her apparent switch in loyalties.

"We knew abortion affected one in four," was her argument, although the source for this figure is unknown. "It crossed all political lines. It affected both men and women. And it didn't matter whether you were Social Credit, or Liberal, or NDP. When you had a problem with an unwanted pregnancy, it was a big problem. So its time had come." Wood saw the essential need to draw new people to the women's liberation movement. Equal pay was certainly needed, but it was not a hot issue with the public just then. What *did* excite the public, in part because of news about the revised law, was the need for birth control and abortion, "so it was just a natural that it should move ahead. And if you could move ahead on one thing that people could identify with, then you would begin to build momentum. And then you could work on the other three areas [of the Caucus program]."

Valentine's Day had irresistible symbolism for Betsy Wood, and if the Women's Caucus couldn't get to Ottawa then, she wouldn't let the occasion pass unmarked. She helped organize a march through downtown Vancouver on Saturday, February 14, 1970, which is remembered as the first public demonstration on abortion in Canada. It got off to a shaky start: at the appointed hour, only twelve people were assembled in front of the courthouse (now the Art Gallery) on Georgia Street. An embarrassed Wood spotted another embarrassed group out of the corner of her eye. The Women's Caucus guerrilla street theatre troupe, formed days before, had planned to rehearse its skit outside the public washrooms at the courthouse. But the rehearsal site had disappeared down a forty-foot hole, the excavation for the new Eaton's (now Sears) store. High-spirited performer Diana Moore wrote of mock nervousness in the March, 1970 *Pedestal*: "So the troupe that had quailed before an audience of four in its first rehearsal, had its second in front of the courthouse and the whole city."[3]

Rising to the occasion, the troupe stepped forward and gave the first of four performances that day. To everyone's relief, the expected demonstrators were just late in arriving and by the time the procession set out, the marchers numbered 250.[4]

Fiery feminist writer Jeannine Mitchell had demanded *The Georgia Straight* print her material, and she gave the demonstration high marks. She called it a "good start for the national campaign to legalize abortions in Canada...While there was some confusion in the front ranks as to where we were heading and whether or not we should stop for red lights or just charge ahead, things pulled together within a few blocks," she wrote. She reported on the skit with enthusiasm.[5]

This skit, or variations of it, came to be performed again and again in Vancouver, and at every stop on the way to Ottawa later on. The mimed performance illustrated the unequal and cruel treatment meted out to women who applied for legal abortions under the new law. Three 'doctors', representing a hospital Therapeutic Abortion Committee, stood with their hands thrust through a large piece of cardboard that was hung by cord around their necks. Another 'sympathetic doctor' presented this 'board' with anxious women, wearing identifying signs. The shabbily dressed 'Mother of Six' was summarily turned down for an abortion, as the TAC doctors wound her in red tape and thrust forth signs saying 'NO.' An applicant with 'German Measles' and one who had been raped met the same fate. A user of the Catholic method of birth control wore a sign saying 'I Got Rhythm;' she was also turned down. But when a woman appeared in a fur coat, with a 'Silver Spoon' in her mouth and handfuls of money, the TAC doctors signaled 'Yes.' "Particularly effective," wrote Mitchell, "was the evil, hooded butcher abortionist who whooshed up deathily [sic] to the girl with rhythm...The butcher snatched a variety of things out of her totebag, including a leather punch, which got a big laugh. Anyway, Rhythm decided on a drink — meant to be compounds of ergot or quinine sulphate — and died."[6]

Years later, Wood is still elated by the march's success. "It is true that [bystanders] joined in on that march...I've met people since who joined in on that abortion march! Really straight, straight types joined in." "The TV coverage was fantastic," in Wood's view. Jeanine Mitchell noticed, too, the reactions of observers. "A lot of people laughed at first glance, and many men in particular gave us the kind of tolerantly-amused smile parents give children. But as they got to reading such signs as 12,000 DIE FROM ILLEGAL ABORTIONS A YEAR IN NORTH AMERICA, smiles faded. It wasn't a joke after all, these nutty women and longhaired men parading down the streets and holding up traffic, beating old pots with metal spoons."

Half-a-dozen anti-abortionists tried to blot out the banners saying "Abortion is Our Right" with smaller placards claiming "Abortion is Murder."[7] Mitchell reported that, while some bystanders were confused by the conflicting signs, "relations between the opposing factions were quite peaceful." She gave an example: "When a guy with an anti-abortion sign crowded into prominence at a sidewalk skit performance, the girl playing the butcher put her arm around him, holding a sign beside his. It read OLD WIVES' TALES."

The march wound up at the Cenotaph in Victory Square. At the site of Remembrance Day ceremonies to honour men who died in men's wars, the women butchered in women's wars were recalled in a short set of speeches. A final performance of the skit, and the demonstration was over.

That evening, a public meeting on abortion was hosted by Women's Caucus at the Hotel Georgia. The featured speaker was Dr. Richard Foulkes, then Medical Director of Royal Columbian Hospital in suburban New Westminster. Foulkes endorsed the view that, after consulting with her doctor, it must be the woman faced with unwanted pregnancy who makes the final decision on whether or not to abort.[8]

A new, even more symbolic target date for the caravan had emerged: Mother's Day. On the weekend of May 9, 1970, Canadian women would demand that abortion be completely legalized. An unsigned article in the March, 1970 issue of the *Pedestal*, headed "Women Declare War," began by boldly pointing out that "Laws can be changed very quickly in war time, a state of national emergency." The death toll from illegal abortion and the suffering inflicted by unwanted pregnancy were just such an emergency. "On Mother's Day, thousands of women across Canada will declare war on Ottawa...Women are no longer prepared to sit quietly while our lives are determined by others; while our sisters die. Now is the time to act! Join the campaign. Call Women's Caucus..." The extremity of the situation and the analogy with war were made even clearer at the Caucus general meeting on February 26:

> If 2000 Canadian women were lined up and shot by any other country Pariament [sic] would allow only a matter of hours for the offending country to stop killing these women — before declaring war on that country.[9]

Then came the blow of Dr. Robert Makaroff's arrest on March 10. Some within Women's Caucus and AIS were conscious-stricken, worried that their public profile had helped force the hand of the police. At once, a press release and a public information leaflet were printed, demanding that charges against Makaroff be dropped. At the doctor's first court appearance, Women's Caucus staged a protest in front of the Main Street police station.

Undercover policewoman Mary Lynn Hinston had entrapped Makaroff by pretending to need an abortion. He agreed, but because he did not actually abort her, the original charge against him was of 'conspiring to procure...' Therefore, the police took the doctor's files and systematically interrogated his patients until they got admissions that abortions had been performed. Two counts of actually 'procuring' abortions were then laid against Makaroff, for which the Criminal Code demanded life imprisonment.[10]

Hinston's name had figured in news accounts of raids on unsavoury abortion mills in the late 1960s and 1970s, but Dr. Makaroff's highly competent and compassionate practice was clearly of a different order than those. An "Open Letter to Mary Lynn Hinston, Policewoman" was written by Jean Rands for Women's Caucus and printed in the *Georgia Straight* of March 25-April 1, 1970 :

> We are aware that workers, and particularly women workers, are asked to do many degrading tasks in the course of earning a living. We are aware that in order to survive in this society, women workers are doing inhuman jobs, such as the one you were asked to do to make possible the charges against Dr. Makaroff. Please accept our sympathy. We hope that one day you will have the strength to resist; risk losing your job; to work with other women as sisters to

ease our common oppression. If you feel that any assistance is required in regaining your humanity, and if you wish to help free other women from disgusting jobs such as yours, please call Women's Caucus...[11]

Throughout his trial, which stretched through the summer and fall of 1970, Women's Caucus rallied in support of Dr. Makaroff and demanded that the charges against him be dropped.

Later on April 19, the day of Makaroff's arraignment, Betsy Wood went to the Labor Temple and typed out letters to the prime minister and to the federal ministers of health and justice. They rang with indictments of the government, which she held responsible for the deaths and mutilation of thousands of illegal abortion victims, and they spelled out the minimum steps towards remedy: that the government fund research on safe methods of birth control for both women and men; that it fund research into improved methods of abortion; and that techniques of abortion be mandatory courses in medical schools. The immediate task was for the government to remove Section 237[12] — the combined old and new abortion laws — from the Criminal Code. Pardons should be issued to anyone convicted under that section, and all pending prosecutions should be halted. The letter concluded in Betsy Wood's inimitable style:

> We consider the government of Canada is in a state of war with the women of Canada. If steps are not taken to implement our demands by Monday, May 9, 1970 at 3:00 p.m., we will be forced to respond by declaring war on the Canadian government. We are angry, furious women and we demand our right to human dignity.[13]

Thus were federal government officials notified of the plans for the Abortion Caravan. The theme of war was very familiar to feminists who were also active protesters against the war in Vietnam. There was strong identification with the people of that small nation. Women's Caucus was determined to make it clear that death was routine for women in Canada, too, and that the federal law and the legislators were to blame.

Meantime, steps were underway to take the issue to the provincial government, as well. The first shot was a neatly typed letter to Leslie Peterson, attorney-general, and to Ralph Loffmark, minister of health services, with copies to the BC Medical Association and to the College of Physicians and Surgeons. It made six clear demands.[14] The only reply was a form letter.

On March 23, Betsy Wood, with grandmotherly white hair, and a youthful Dodie Weppler took the ferry to Victoria. Wood approved of Weppler's neat pant-suit. She was firmly of the opinion that you could speak more forcefully to politicians if you were well-groomed and appeared to be middle-class. What elected official would want to offend a potential voter, donor, or campaign worker? They stopped at Loffmark's office, but he brushed them off. So Wood contacted the *Victoria Daily Colonist,* which carried an interview with her the next morning.[15]

A second group of Women's Caucus members left for Victoria, to be met at the ferry by an excited, good-natured woman named Alet McLeod. A life-long campaigner for social justice of every sort, McLeod, who worked in the credit office at Hudson's Bay and had spent years trying to form a union there, was so well-known for protesting the Vietnam war on Vancouver's many talk-radio shows that she had the sobriquet of "Hanoi Hannah." She had heard of the Women's Caucus expedition to Victoria, and she set out to join it. With her she carried a thick sheaf of news-clippings and letters demanding legal abortion, which she had been circulating for years. McLeod was a crusader ahead of her time. Waving cheerily, she rushed up to the Women's Caucus delegation and was puzzled to be met with blank stares. She was not welcomed. With the snobbery of those who have a different dress code, the jeans-clad feminists brushed past the fiftyish McLeod in her skirt and cardigan, leaving her behind.[16]

Joining Wood and Weppler, the thirteen-strong group of women pulled out their placards and bed-sheet banners and marched up and down before the legislative building. Then they presented themselves at health minister Loffmark's office. Joining them were women from the University of Victoria and a few reporters. Despite the minister's rude remarks to them, they asked him to provide funds for and approve the use of special hospitals, or clinics, specifically to meet the increasing demand for abortions. Loffmark said he hadn't the power to do so, whereupon the women produced a copy of the Criminal Code, in which provinces were charged with 'designating' any facility as a hospital, and proved him wrong.[17]

Discussion moved to the medical profession. "Loffmark refused to recommend that BC doctors employ the World Health Organization definition of 'health' — 'complete physical, economic, social and mental well-being' — as grounds for abortion."[18] He spoke of the "morality" of the issue and said, "I have a responsibility to protect the unborn children of BC." Perhaps the abortion law was not "humane enough", but he refused to demand that the federal government repeal it. "He told us that we should approach the medical profession rather than the government." The stonewalled women left the room.

After lunch, the women's delegation filed into the public gallery of the legislature building and spaced itself across the front row of seats. Moments later, a spectacular action began. Women in the gallery above the Socred side hurled long streamers of red tape onto the heads of the MLAs below. Other women unfurled banners reading, "Abortion is Our Right," and "Just Society, Good Life — KILLS 12,000 Women in North America Each Year." Down pelted bumper stickers with the genetic symbol for woman, encircling a fist, and saying 'Abortion Now.'[19] The startled but uninjured legislators leaped up, and Loffmark shouted out, "There are strangers in the House!" Someone cried, "Those woman don't understand the democratic process!"[20]

As the gavel pounded for order, women were already hurrying down the stairs, while the obviously frightened commissionaires rushed to eject them. This inspired bit of mischief was the brainchild of Marcy Cohen and friends. They sprinted out of the gallery, while Betsy Wood looked at the officials' faces and thought, "Boy, they're going to really get us now." But the commissionaires ran right past Wood and Weppler, who were not recognized as rebels. In fact, the action had been a surprise to Wood; she had not been told about the plan to throw down red tape.[21]

TV cameramen arrived and filmed the scene. On the whole, the women felt they got positive media attention in Victoria, and they felt the whole experience helped prepare them to stand up to the federal government in Ottawa.

Two weeks later, a long and decidedly friendly article appeared in the Vancouver *Express*, a paper put out by striking staffers of the *Sun* and *Province*. Headed "They want simple change in law: get rid of damned thing," the story gave the itinerary for the caravan to Ottawa and described its purpose.[22]

Caucus members learned that Trudeau would change planes in Vancouver on his way to Whistler for a ski trip. Some feminists jumped in a van and drove to the airport late on Friday, March 27. By chance, they and the prime minister arrived at the same place at the same time. Trudeau ambled over. "He noticed us when I bellowed ABORTION NOW!" wrote Bonnie Beckwoman (née Beckman) in the April issue of the *Pedestal*.[23] "He said, 'Gee — did you come out specially to see me?'" Glancing at their picket signs, Trudeau said the abortion question was already taken care of and seemed surprised the women weren't satisfied. "He also suggested we organize our medical people if we want the law changed," and commented that "obviously" the doctors didn't want to do abortions. After a few more quips, the two parties went their separate ways, but a telegram was sent to the PM on March 30: "We are coming to Ottawa to demand removal of abortion from the Criminal Code...Since we met Friday night, 16 Canadian women have died of illegal abortion."[24]

The Caucus asked for meetings with the BC Medical Association and the BC College of Physicians and Surgeons. Both requests were spurned. However, the women learned that the college council would meet at the Vancouver Lawn and Tennis Club on Friday, April 10. The role of the college, which governs the curriculum in medical schools and physicians' conduct within the profession, was well understood by Women's Caucus. They had told Loffmark that it "elicits more fear from doctors than the law does, for it has the power to take away [medical] licences."[25] A brief was drawn up, containing five demands on the college.[26] While it pulled no punches, a brief or letter from Women's Caucus was always well-researched, thorough, and very pertinent.

Arriving early at the tennis club, the women planted their banners on the lawn. Ordered to leave, they retreated as far as the sidewalk on 10th Avenue, near Burrard. The college registrar, Dr. McClure, came out and told them, "'We don't want you here!'" He threatened to call the police.[27] Whereupon two women found an unlocked door, and slipped inside to admit their sisters. An argument broke out with the building manager, Mr. Pauls, but when they explained they'd been referred to the doctors by both Trudeau and Loffmark, Mr. Pauls went to report that to the council. The doctors offered to admit two women for ten minutes. The Caucus countered by suggesting eleven women — there were eleven doctors — for half an hour. No! The doctors retreated behind locked doors, and the women sat down in the waiting area. When the police arrived, they found mini-skirted women demurely leafing through magazines, just what one does while waiting for a doctor.[28] True, eight-foot political banners are unusual at a doctor's appointment. Inspector Ken Evans admitted the scene was peaceful, just as the picketing on behalf of Dr. Makaroff was always peaceful. Peaceful, but trespassing. Reluctantly, the women went back to the sidewalk, spread their sleeping bags and brought out a guitar, while the police consulted with the "injured party" inside. Somehow TV reporters showed up. As the Caucus explained its position and sang for the cameras, passersby waved the peace sign, and the tennis club janitor gave a quarter to the cause. Thus, the members of the college council probably watched what the rest of Vancouver saw on TV, and the objective of the day was accomplished. The caper may seem tame to present-day readers, but it was decidedly unconventional by standards for female behaviour, at the time.

The BCMA also refused to meet with the women and issued a statement saying "'The association takes the stand that our doctors carry out laws and do not make them. Some changes in abortion laws have been required, and some changes have been made.'"[29]

Learning that a conference of obstetricians and gynecologists was planned for April 23-24, Women's Caucus assembled its ranks. Unable to get inside, the skit was staged on the lawn, and the women noticed a lot of doctors' noses pressed against the window glass. This was a variation of the skit performed on Valentine's Day, to which an angel, played by Helen Potrebenko, had been added. With a halo above her blond hair, the angel comforted women who'd died from botched abortions.

Toward late afternoon, the patience of the women on the lawn expired and they marched on the entrance. Again, guards struggled with them, but before the door was locked, at least three women got inside. There is confusion now about who they were; some accounts mention 'Jean' (Rands?). However, Helen Potrebenko, whose angel's wings got bent in the process, was the last to squeeze in. She hurried after Donna Liberson and Pat Davitt or Jean Rands, who were sauntering into the midst of the doctor's Happy Hour. Catching sight of a friend, the women called out "Hi, Roger," and Dr. Roger Rogers admits that, in the company of his medical colleagues, he winced.[30]

Climbing upon a table set for dinner, Liberson, clad in a doctor's white coat for her role in the skit, delivered an indictment of the physicians. She recounted the flood of needy women who came to the Abortion Information Service for help, and the pitiful number who got through the legal hurdles in time. "Abortions are legal, and it is your job to provide safe health care for women," she reminded the hushed and open-mouthed assembly. Her tone was conversational, her manner relaxed, but her anger was apparent. "There is no reason why the majority of women seeking abortions must still put themselves at the mercy of backroom hacks." Then she mentioned that many women coming to AIS were sent there by their doctors — the very doctors in that room, who were too cowardly to help the women get hospital abortions. If the situation didn't change, announced Liberson, Women's Caucus would take out a full-page news-paper ad and publish the names of doctors who used AIS as a conduit to illegal abortionists. "Never think we haven't written down how women find out about the Abortion Information Service," she said. With an elo-quent shrug, Liberson climbed down from the table and the women casu-ally walked out. Later, she heard from her doctor friend, "'Donna, we may not agree with your tactics, but abortion was all we talked about after you left.'"[31]

Thus, all the 'proper channels' had been appealed to. The politicians had referred the women to the medical profession, and the doctors had said they must obey the law and sent them to the politicians, and most of British Columbia knew about it. It was time to march on Ottawa.

CHAPTER 5

THE ABORTION CARAVAN

At last, on a sunny spring morning, a hundred well-wishers gathered at the courthouse on Georgia Street (the present Art Gallery) to send off the Abortion Caravan.[1] They climbed the steps between the stone lions and unfurled banners to inform rush hour drivers that "Abortion is Our Right," "Women Demand Safe Birth Control," and "Illegal Abortions Kill 12,000 Women a Year." The familiar "We Are Furious Women" banner was there, with the women's symbol surrounding a militant fist.[2]

Pulled up before the steps were the vehicles that would take the Vancouver delegation to Ottawa. "They were all decorated," recalls Cynthia Flood, who had joined Women's Caucus a month earlier and regretted she could not leave her job to go on the trip. Some observers might presume that seventeen, rather disheveled-looking women in a parade of old beater cars would have little impact on parliament. But Flood and the rest believed otherwise. "There was a sense of importance to it," she recalls of the occasion, "a great feeling of pride and, sort of, ownership of the event." The unexpected sunlight, the tang to the air, and the high-spirited determination of Women's Caucus members heightened the certainty of success among the crowd of "scruffy students, welfare mums, and leftists" whom Flood recalls on that early Monday morning, April 27, 1970. She saw "banners and placards and boxes of food, and somebody's dog running around and barking excitedly," and she felt "quite envious of the women who were going" off to make history.[3] Despite its portent, the event was not written up in Vancouver newspapers, for the unions at the *Vancouver Sun* and *The Province* were on strike, and there had been no daily papers since mid-February.

At a preparatory meeting, the caravaners had discussed what the main slogan should be. Marcy Cohen and Ellen Woodsworth favoured "Free Abortion on Demand." Mary Trew felt that was addressed too broadly to hit the target. Could parliament supply women with free abortion on demand? No. Parliament passed laws. Since they were heading to Ottawa, she preferred to put the onus on the state and to demand what it could actually do for women: "Repeal the Abortion Laws." Each viewpoint reflected a wing of the left. Cohen voiced the take-no-prisoners anti-capitalism of many activists at SFU. Trew, who had joined the Trotskyist student group, the Young Socialists, shortly after joining Women's Caucus, wanted a no-less-uncompromising slogan that the public could identify with and support. She was of the school that aimed to involve the masses in action against capitalism. After much debate it was decided to use both slogans. When the crowd gathered at the courthouse on April 27, however, one side of Cathy Walker's van was painted with "On to Ottawa", and the other side read "Smash Capitalism." Nostrils began to flare.[4]

There was no time for debate just then. Mary Trew stepped before the banner that read "Vancouver Women's Caucus" to give the send-off address. The caravan could cite letters of support from the BC New Democrats, The BC Federation of Labor, the Victoria Labour Council, the Stewardess Emeritus Association, and a few more. Sisterly blessings were bestowed by 84-year-old Mary Norton, a suffragist, who was thrilled by the revival of feminism and who continued to attend women's liberation events in Vancouver until her death. Finally, the caravaners climbed into their vehicles and drove away amid cheers.

Betsy Wood drove her large, yellow, Pontiac convertible, with a full complement of passengers. She had quit her job with the fire marshal, and the *Pedestal* printed her angry resignation letter, detailing wage discrimination against women in her office.[5] Setting off on the caravan, Wood was pleased with the long paper streamers reading "Abortion is Our Right" that stretched down each side of her car, attached with masking tape. Masking tape would not damage the car's paint if used for less than thirty days, she believed, but she wasn't confident the streamers would last past Hope, 160 kilometres east of Vancouver. "It was just amazing. We never had any trouble with the signs coming off until just outside Ottawa!" The hood of Wood's car read "On To Ottawa," the slogan of the unemployed in 1935. Women's Caucus believed its cause was no less desperate or just. Flying from her aerial was a pennant that also read "Abortion Is Our Right."[6]

Cathy Walker's Volkswagen van had a homemade black coffin on top, in which the caravaners put their suitcases for the time being. A sign in front commemorated the women who'd died from illegal abortions, and anti-capitalist slogans were painted along the sides. Another vehicle bore a loudspeaker and sound system atop its cab.[7]

The itinerary was ambitious, tight, and well-publicized. The caravan would travel 300-400 miles a day and stop in ten cities, arriving in Ottawa, the eleventh stop, on Friday, May 8. Strangely, despite the voluminous records kept by the Women's Caucus, no-one thought to write down exactly who went on the caravan. From research and interviews, writer Frances Wasserlein reconstructed this list of the Vancouver delegation, given here in alphabetical order:

Bonita Beckman, Charlotte Bedard, Marcy Cohen, Margo Dunn, Hannah Gay, Vicki Goodman, Gwen Hauser, Barbara Hicks, Colette Malo,

Mary Mathieson, Melody Rudd, Maxine Schnee, Mary Trew, Cathy Walker, Betsy Meadley Wood, Ellen Woodsworth, and Dodie Weppler.[8] Dawn Carrell flew ahead to do publicity, and Marge Hollibaugh, who had a back problem, flew to Ottawa together with Sharman Kanee in time to meet the caravan there. In the end, there were nineteen or twenty women from Vancouver.

As they drove across the prairies, a few more cars joined the parade, and by the time the women reached Ottawa, busloads had joined them from southern Ontario, Toronto, and Montréal. Margo Dunn recalls that Colette Malo, who traveled from Vancouver, was actually visiting BC from Halifax. Therefore, the caravan could truthfully claim there were participants from coast to coast.[9]

At the haphazardly-attended planning meetings before departure, some rules had been agreed on. There were to be no "stars", no personalities that outshone others. To ensure equality, the role of spokeswomen rotated daily: two women, one experienced with the media and one less so, would speak to the press at each stop.[10] Further, they might choose to call themselves by the names of political forebears, such as Emma Goldman, Margaret Sanger, Emily Murphy, Nellie McClung, Helena Gutteridge...[11] Through the *Pedestal*, Women's Caucus had been educating itself about women's history and was secretly amused when reporters failed to recognize the anachronism and proceeded to interview "Emma Goldman," the World War I-era anarchist, in all seriousness. Looking back, caravaner Margo Dunn believes the use of pseudonyms was partly to bring "these forgotten womens' names to the public," and partly through a desire to don anonymity and become Everywoman.[12]

The first stop was Kamloops, where they were offered a meal of chili and salad — "We had chili con carne at absolutely every stop across the country!"[13] and where they unrolled their sleeping bags on the floor of a church basement. Local United and Unitarian churches billeted the caravaners all the way across the country, and often they were sites of the public meetings held at each stop.

Too excited to sleep, the women talked late into the night. The major topic was the surprise slogan of "Smash Capitalism" gracing the van. Betsy Wood and Mary Trew led the objections to it. What had that slogan to do with abortion? Everyone on the caravan opposed capitalism, but dislodging it was a major, longterm struggle. Right now, they had a serious mission, and it had to do with abortion. People along the way would be puzzled rather than enlightened. "So the focus was to be taken off abortion and put on 'Smash Capitalism'?" asked Wood, astonished. "That would alienate a lot of people across the country." She mentioned "the church groups [who] had been putting in petitions [for legal abortion] for a long time," and who were billeting the caravan most of the way to

Ottawa.[14] It was time to educate Canadians in small towns, insisted those who liked the slogan. The source of women's oppression was capitalism. These caravaners, led by Marcy Cohen and Ellen Woodsworth, with the support of Dawn Carrell, objected to tailoring their pitch to the opinions of the "lowest common denominator" in society. That would be to go backward, not forward.

Tired already on the second day out, Betsy Wood realized that she had never met some of the other caravaners before they'd left Vancouver. The passengers in each vehicle changed, for the women believed that rotating their seats would be sisterly and democratic. Indeed, it helped cut across the strangeness felt by these essentially self-selected travelers. Those who went were those who could find the money and take the time off to go.

Margo Dunn, for example, thought it sounded like a fun idea. A graduate student in drama, she had thoroughly enjoyed the Women's Caucus campaign to disrupt a student beauty pageant in early 1970, and was active in the WITCH group that staged feminist guerrilla theatre. When she received a President's Grant to work on her thesis that spring — at $400 a month, it substantially boosted her resources — she decided to postpone her research and go on the caravan. Despite the censure, the sit-ins, and the strikes at SFU, Dunn felt herself to be a "political *naif.*" The intense debates on the caravan were "my political education...All of a sudden I could see all the connections between the pharmaceutical industries and...[why] there was no safe birth control. [And] the economic reasons that women were kept separated in [our individual] homes, and not allowed control over our bodies. [Why], in fact, women weren't supposed to have sexuality at all, outside of marriage. And that whole thing made sense to me, around the arguments over 'Smash Capitalism' on Cathy Walker's van."[15] Dunn came to agree with Cohen and Woodsworth about the value of the slogan.

Leaving Kamloops, the women drove to Calgary, where they were met just outside the city by the media and an excited gathering from the Women's Union. The two women's liberation groups drove slowly through the city, their loudspeakers blaring music, while they handed leaflets to downtown shoppers. They circled Foothills Hospital and then headed to the Unitarian Church, where a public meeting was scheduled that evening.[16]

The Women's Caucus skit, which opened the meeting, was a novelty, and it was described in detail the next day in the *Calgary Herald*. The discussion afterward was lively, due in part to the "surprise presence of a local gynecologist," said the *Herald*: "The gynecologist admitted that the 'liberalized' abortion law merely brought it up to the 1900 era," but, he argued, many doctors favoured making abortion even more available than the recent reform allowed. However, he said of the medical profession, "'Our hands are locked, let's face it. Any change is going to have to come through political action.'"[17] The women from Vancouver agreed; they had heard it before.

On the third day, the caravan went to Edmonton. Again, intrigued reporters, alerted by Anne Roberts's press release from Vancouver, gave detailed coverage to the visit. Accompanied by a vivid photo of the crowd, the banners, and the skit, the *Edmonton Journal* told its readers:

> The group assembled in Sir Winston Churchill Square and staged a grisly mime play showing the horror of a back-street abortion before 200 curious onlookers. ...The mime play told about a woman who was denied a legal abortion. She went to a back-street abortionist who put on a blood stained gown and then showed the crowd his instruments — a knitting needle, a bent coat hanger and an egg beater.
>
> After a moment of deliberation, the abortionist covered the victim with a black cape. The crowd applauded.[18]

That night, the public meeting in Garneau United Church featured guest speaker Dr. Michael Ball, director of student health services at the University of Alberta. His insistence that something be done to end the epidemic of illegitimate births hinged on "volunteer agencies across Canada to advise women where they can go for a legal abortion, in Canada or another country."[19] Again, the Women's Caucus Abortion Information Service had already tried that and found little chance for legal abortion, in Canada or another country. "'People don't need laws to govern their human relations,' said an unnamed woman, to loud applause."[20]

After Edmonton came Saskatoon, and after that Regina. At each stop, the caravaners tried to do a series of things, all aimed at stirring up debate and winning support. They would link up with local feminists, speak to the media, and take the campaign to the heart of town. Their sound system blasted out music by Judy Collins, or by Elaine Brown and the Black Panthers. They'd stop, do their skit, and sometimes augment it with poetry or readings from Sylvia Plath. Caravaners Gwen Hauser, Melody Rudd, and Maxine Schnee might read their own poems, as well. The group tried for TV coverage, a press conference, or a spot on a radio talk show wherever they stopped. They constantly urged local women to join the caravan, and a few did. Then they'd eat and get ready for the evening's public meeting.[21]

"At the open meetings we tried very carefully to show why the caravan came out of an understanding of women's liberation in all forms — from the right to have free abortion on demand...[to] tearing down capitalism and building a movement and a society in which women and men can participate in the decisions which control their own lives...[and] can make the laws which govern...matters such as birth control," reported the caravaners in the June issue of the *Pedestal*.[22]

"Every public meeting went way longer than it was supposed to go. It always seemed like there were hundreds there. And women would get up and tell horror story after horror story, about abortions, or not being allowed abortions — just appalling things. [It] was so emotionally draining," recalls Margo Dunn.[23]

Afterward, debate continued among the women spread out on the church floor. 'Struggle sessions' until two or three in the morning became a nightly routine. Debate around the "Smash Capitalism" slogan continued. Further, "instead of getting on with what we should say to the press tomorrow, we'd have these big long meetings about whether or not pot should be smoked on the trip. Because, obviously, some people were smoking it," recalls Betsy Wood. "I had a hard time with that."[24]

In Saskatoon, the format was followed as usual and was covered favourably in the *Saskatoon Star-Phoenix*.[25] Pacific Press strikers ran a negative headline in the Vancouver *Express* story about Saskatoon: "Abortion group meets hostility."[26] However, the *Express* went on to describe a public meeting that drew 175 people, and it quoted Saskatoon law student Norma Sim, who argued that the 1969 liberalized abortion law might even be more stringent than the old one because it required the approval of three doctors, instead of one. "'Too much injustice is perpetrated on behalf of the unborn fetus," said Mary Trew..."'Having the right to choose is a prerequisite of liberation and denial of that right is an important way to keep us down.'"[27]

As sleepy caravaners prepared to leave town on Friday morning, May 1, 1970, they picked up the local paper to see what coverage they'd got and were jolted by the front page story: *"Nixon surprises: orders troops into Cambodia."*[28] The women were horrified. Deeply opposed to the war in Vietnam, many of them had marched on April 18, nine days before they started for Ottawa, in an anti-war demonstration that had meshed with others drawing hundreds of thousands across North America.[29] Now the US President had widened the war, snubbing Congress as he snubbed his youthful opponents. Shaken, the caravan drove on to Regina.

Mary Trew remembers riding in the van beside Marcy Cohen as the Vancouver women drove through downtown Regina. The crowd was curious about the caravan.

> And people had come out of offices and stores downtown and lined the streets on both sides as we drove through...People on one side could see the panel truck that said, 'Free Abortion on Demand.' And they were kind of shyly waving and friendly; smiling at least. And on the other side, the side with 'Smash Capitalism,' people just gazed with their mouths open, as we passed. Not knowing what to make of it.[30]

Their contact in Regina was a well-established psychiatrist, Dr. Margaret Mahood. Her daughter Sally joined the Abortion Caravan, and Dr. Mahood later flew to Ottawa for the Mother's Day weekend events. Talking with these prairie socialists, the Vancouver women were at last persuaded to wash "Smash Capitalism" off the side of the van. Margo Dunn agreed to scrub it, partly so that everyone could quit arguing about it and get some sleep.[31]

As it traveled, the caravan grew. In its sweep through the prairies, 23 new women joined the journey.[32]

Winnipeg gave the caravan particular notice. *The Free Press* offered background on Women's Caucus, included an interview with Betsy Wood, and reprinted the full text of the letter sent to Trudeau, containing the caravan's demands. An accompanying photo showed women with fists raised in the air.[33]

On Sunday, May 3, the caravan reached Thunder Bay. A dynamo of energy there named Joan Baril had corresponded with Women's Caucus for months. The public meeting, called "A Conference on Abortion," included two speakers and a 30-minute multi-media presentation, to which the Women's Caucus repertoire was added.[34] It was a hit. But describing the scene in a subsequent Thunder Bay *Women's Liberation News Letter,* Baril saw trouble seated in the front rows. A delegation announced it came from St. Agnes Catholic Church, and it heckled the speakers during the discussion period. Finally, the Catholics made an angry departure, which was followed by an angrier confrontation in the church parking lot. One of the Catholics turned on a local, pregnant teen-age feminist — not a member of the Thunder Bay Women's Liberation group, or the caravan — and called her a "gutter slut, filthy hippy", and the insulted young woman responded by striking out and hitting the Catholic woman in the face. She was immediately sorry and apologized in tears. Finally, the pastor of Knox United Church came out and ordered an end to the fracas.[35]

As the caravan was leaving the next day, its vehicles were pelted with stones.[36] Undaunted by the mêlée, the Thunder Bay group announced it would soon open a service to refer pregnant women to clinics in New York state, where legal curbs on abortion expired in April, 1970, only weeks before the caravan's trip.[37]

Good will returned as the caravan moved on to Sault Ste. Marie. Nan Rajnovich, women's news editor of *The Sault Daily Star,* had sent this enthusiastic letter to Betsy Wood on April 20:

> We have run a story on the material you sent and would be delighted to hear full details of your Abortion Cavalcade...We have put your poster up in the news room and have startled all the men in the place. Several have approved however. We have just completed a study of local hospitals and learned that chances of getting a legal abortion here are worse than ever![38]

Eight days after leaving Vancouver, the caravan rolled into Sudbury. For many of these spirited anti-capitalists, it was their first experience in an industrialized, working-class town. "It was just the most desert-like place on the planet," recalls anti-capitalist Margo Dunn.[39] In Sudbury, social and political life centred on the union hall, and that is where local members of the Young Socialists, the group to which Mary Trew belonged, arranged the caravan's public meeting. Loyal to a different political stripe than the Trotskyist YS, some "women on the caravan...wanted to boycott this meeting," wrote Trew in the June, 1970 issue of the *Pedestal*. "The meeting itself was one of the most successful ones held across Canada — drawing over 100 people in a mining town, and being the first impetus for the creation of a women's liberation group there. All this would have been lost had the sectarian attitudes led to the proposed boycott."[40]

Sudbury was memorable for another reason, too. Dunn recalls "going to this corner store...and seeing the headlines: 'FOUR KILLED AT KENT STATE.'"[41] The US National Guard had opened fire on a student strike at the small Ohio college, which was protesting the extension of the war into Cambodia. Guardsmen had also fired on students at Jackson State, a Black college in Mississippi. "I remember taking the paper back, and we were just — devastated! Devastated...that they were shooting us! I mean, we certainly identified with those students. So that changed everything...We were just in shock."[42]

Behind them, in unmarked cars, the RCMP had followed the caravaners across the country.[43] Cathy Walker told writer Frances Wasserlein:

> We were closely watched by the police all the way across. In fact, when we got to Ontario every ten miles there was an OPP [Ontario Provincial Police] following us, and every day in Toronto we got stopped.[44]

Paranoia racheted upward. These were women, primarily students, who had declared war on the federal government. What had the powers-that-be in store for them?

While the cavalcade was in Winnipeg, Marcy Cohen and Dawn Carrell flew ahead to Toronto. On Tuesday, May 5, with most of the group in Sudbury, Cohen and Carrell were the major speakers at a Town Hall meeting at St. Lawrence Arts Centre, televized by the CBC. Their fiery defence of their mission was supplemented by Toronto feminists Alma Marks and Judy Darcy (then D'Arcy) and was widely reported in the Toronto media. They demanded an immediate, emergency session of parliament, in which abortion laws would be dropped altogether from the Criminal Code.

Citing the efforts of the Women's Caucus Abortion Information Service, Dawn Carrell "said that in four months...265 women have asked for abortions (most of them married) and only eight were able to get them legally."[45] Darcy had learned from hospital officials that "three to four women are admitted every night to Toronto General Hospital following 'botched up' abortion attempts."[46] Marcy Cohen called for pardons for doctors prosecuted for performing illegal abortions, and for their reinstatement in medical practice.[47] She outlined the need for community-controlled clinics, "staffed by women and supported financially on a 50-50 basis by the provincial and federal governments," which would provide information, birth control and abortions. "'We don't expect to get it all right now,' she said, 'but we do expect the government at least to take us seriously.'"[48]

The next day, Wednesday, May 6, 1970, the Abortion Caravan pulled into Toronto, fifty women strong.[49] The parade through town was followed by a rally outside Trinity United Church, joined by a throng of Toronto feminists. Speaking at the rally and at the televized press conference afterward, Mary Trew wondered what her mother's response would be to her unannounced arrival and to this exposure of her non-traditional views. "As soon as I got a chance, I called my mom to say I was in town." She had told her mother — Catholic, born in Ireland, and in her sixties — nothing of the caravan and had no idea of her mother's views on abortion. "And she said, 'Oh, I know. I just saw you on TV!' And she said, 'I'm proud of you, Mary.'" For Trew, that was a wonderful moment.[50]

A meeting was held to inform Toronto women about the plans for the big weekend. Afterward, the caravaners had a night off for the first time since leaving Vancouver. Buoyed by youth's indefatigable energy, most, like Margo Dunn, took the opportunity to join a large demonstration against the invasion of Cambodia and the killings at Kent State and Jackson State colleges. The candlelight protest at the American Embassy on that Thursday was tame, compared to the near-riot between protesters and police the night before. That anti-war event had resulted in numerous injuries and arrests. The caravaners were, like others, in mourning for the dead, but they were also in "fighting mode," and they broke into the songs they had sung as they crossed the country.[51] Some tried to 'shush' them, but the women's voices rose in "Bread and Roses," and other familiar tunes with modified lyrics:

Women in chains for a long, long time,
Use our bodies, ignore our minds
Keep your eyes on the prize, Hold On!
The only thing we ever did right,
Was when we decided to go and fight
Keep your eyes on the prize, Hold on!
Going to Ottawa with our cause,
Sisters murdered by abortion laws
Keep your eyes on the prize, Hold on!
Hold on, hold on, keep your eyes on the prize,
Hold on![52]

And so, in strength, the cross-country Abortion Caravan arrived in Ottawa on Friday, May 8 and proceeded to inform Canadians it was there.

CHAPTER SIX

INVADING PARLIAMENT

Just as planned, hundreds of women descended on Ottawa for the Mother's Day weekend in 1970. On Friday night, women's sleeping bags were rolled out on the floor of the vacant Percy Street public school. At the time, it was being used by the Trudeau-era make-work project, Company of Young Canadians.[1] As usual, animated discussion lasted late into the night.

Details of women's situation had become better known as the troupe moved from town to town. In addition to Vancouver, two cities stood out for offering birth control and related services to women. In Edmonton, Dr. C.A. Ringrose began giving out birth control information through a group he founded in 1964. This was illegal until Trudeau's Omnibus Bill became law, but Alberta premier Ernest Manning assured Dr. Ringrose he did not intend to prosecute. In May, 1969, the city of Edmonton began offering another family planning clinic one night a week.[2]

In Winnipeg, where the legacy of the 1919 workers' General Strike was not forgotten, Mrs. Anne Ross, wife of the president of the Communist Party of Canada, was executive director of the Mount Carmel clinic. Publically funded, the clinic had a busy birth control service and was making arrangements to send Winnipeg women to Buffalo for abortions, as soon as the reformed New York law went into effect.[3] Apart from these significant exceptions, however, Canadian women were customarily treated as breeding stock in the year of the Abortion Caravan.

Crammed into the Percy Street School, three to four hundred excited human beings were bound to chafe one another somewhat, and gaffes soon occurred. For example, feminists in Toronto were divided into rival groups. Marcy Cohen and Dawn Carrell allied themselves with Toronto Women's Liberation, and there was an expectation that other Vancouver women would do the same. The New Feminists, led in part by journalist and filmmaker, Bonnie Kreps, had broken away from TWL, to base their fight against sexism, "rather than capitalism."[4] The New (or "Radical") Feminists were not welcome at meetings in Toronto to plan for the cross-Canada caravan. Many New Feminists went on to Ottawa anyway.

Betsy Wood, known for saying exactly what she meant, found the rift distressing. The caravan had set out to unite all possible support for fully-legal abortion, and Wood was bothered by the coolness shown the New

Feminists.[5] She had been billeted in Toronto at a communal house where Peggy Morton, one of the most influential members of Toronto Women's Liberation lived, but, in Ottawa, Wood found a chance to slip out and meet some of the New Feminists for breakfast. The political differences between them and TWL did not interest her; she simply wanted to make contact with a contingent she felt the caravan could not afford to drive away.

By then, Wood herself was a frequent target of her sisters. As if in retribution for getting "Smash Capitalism" scrubbed from the van, Wood remembers, "I actually had people follow me around...there were two people who, sort of, always kept an eye on me." These women had joined the caravan at a stop on the prairies. "[One] came up to me and she said, as if, you know, I was an absolute stupid pumpkin from the Great Farm, did I know that there were people assigned to the press? And I wasn't to be speaking to the press...Don't ask me why there was such a close guard — it was like I was the enemy." Wood had taken care not to overstep after that. She decided not to mention her meeting with the New Feminists, because "I would have been severely chastised" for it. But word got out.

On Saturday morning, May 9, the caravaners were jubilant and raw nerves were forgotten in the rush of events. The city was already plastered with posters, silk-screened by hand in a blue, psychedelic script that said, "THE WOMEN ARE COMING!" There was to be a march through the streets, followed by a meeting with MPs in a committee room within the House of Commons. Despite all the caravaners' efforts, the three government officials they wanted most to meet — PM Pierre Trudeau, justice minister John Turner, and health minister John Munro — had cancelled out. The women were offended but undeterred.

Media estimates of 300 to 650 women, plus crowds of well-wishers, gathered in front of the Supreme Court. Banners flapped and placards were waved; chants and songs stirred the air. Two further busloads of demonstrators pulled in from Toronto. And to the astonishment of those who thought Québec was uniformly Catholic, two busloads arrived from Montréal. The impact on women of Québec's politicization had been underestimated on the west coast. Still, the women bringing their fervent belief in abortion rights from Montréal to Ottawa were Anglophones. The larger 'Front de Libération des Femmes Québecoises' refused to go before the parliament in Ottawa, whose powers it did not recognize. However, le Front proclaimed its solidarity with the women of Canada because its members suffered from the same oppression. On Mother's Day, May 10, the Québecoises would demonstrate in Montréal to obtain abortion free and on demand for all women. In rough translation, they announced they would trade the land of fatality for liberty. "P.S. pas de Québec libre sans femmes liberées."[6]

Betsy Wood turned as the wife of a prominent Ontario NDP MP approached with the gleeful news that Trudeau's office had misplaced the Women's Caucus' Declaration of War and was phoning around parliament hill to find out what was going on. She pressed a donation of cash on Wood. Other high-profile demonstrators were NDP MP Lorne Nystrom and his wife Gayle, who wore a hand-lettered sign around her waist that read: "This uterus is not government property."[7]

Chanting and singing, the procession wound through the streets to parliament hill. Still singing, caravaners filed into the prestigious Railway Committee Room, which had been booked for them by Grace MacInnis, NDP (Vancouver Kingsway). No-one from the Liberal government came to meet them. The Prime Minister's excuse was that he was preparing for a tour of the far east, which would begin the next day. Health minister John Munro, who had assured feminists in Saskatoon that he would meet with the caravan in Ottawa, went to a conference in Geneva instead. John Turner, minister of justice, opted to play tennis that morning, after lobbing this reply to the Women's Caucus:

> Minister of Justice will not be available to meet your group May 9th in spite of ultimatums, demands, and threats as set out in your letter of Mar 19th.[8]

Instead, the Abortion Caravan was greeted by three NDP MPs and one opposition member. Joining Grace MacInnis were David Lewis (York South) and Lorne Nystrom (Yorkton-Melville), as well as Gerald W. Baldwin, the PC Whip from Peace River, BC. Judy Darcy of Toronto read a brief demanding that, "in this session of parliament" the government sponsor a bill removing all mention of abortion from the Criminal Code. "We are here to tell you what our needs are, and to find out whether you are prepared to act," proclaimed these unsettling females.[9]

Grace MacInnis rose to tell them "I'm solidly behind you," and to remind the women that she had twice submitted a private member's bill for repeal, to no avail. Urging the caravaners to inundate Trudeau and Turner with petitions, she said dryly, "If you can break up the solid ranks of the government, then you've done something."[10] In response, the demonstrators groaned; they wanted immediate action and they found letter-writing boring.

Toronto welfare rights activist Doris Power, mother of three and eight months pregnant, protested, "To send me around with a [expletive] petition is just not the answer."[11] Power then gave what is remembered as a "blockbuster", the most compelling speech of the afternoon. She spoke as a poor woman, a representative of the 'Just Society Movement,' who viewed abortion in the context of a soulless, bureaucracy-ridden society. "Developers and slum landlords...make decisions about *where* I'm going to live and *how* I'm going to eat." When Power requested a legal abortion at a Toronto hospital, the social and economic prospects for the child were not considered. The only question was the state of her own health, as judged by others. It was put to her bluntly that if she would agree to be sterilized, then she might be offered an abortion. She refused and was refused an abortion. Whereupon the doctor asked whether she would obtain one illegally. "I replied that many women did. He then said, 'Well, take your rosary and get to Hell out of here.'"

> We, the poor of Canada, are the dirt shoved under the rug of a vicious economy. In obtaining abortions, we pay a price second to none, *our lives*. We can't afford to fly off to England for a safe, legal abortion. We have to seek out back street butchers.

"The Just Society Movement of Toronto recognizes that the liberation of women means the liberation of men — *the liberation of society*," cried Power, to a crescendo of applause.[12]

A lone man stepped toward the microphone. He was an invited speaker, but few knew him, and he was booed. It was Dr. Henry Morgentaler. Unaware that the speaker, who was introduced as the president of the Humanist Association of Canada, was in reality a crusader for women's rights and was performing abortions in his small Montréal clinic, the feminists objected to his remarks because of his sex. He was not "radical enough," recalls Margo Dunn, with regret. The behaviour of her sisters made Betsy Wood "so embarrassed I could have gone through the floor."

Ignoring the audience's hostility, Dr. Morgentaler labelled Canadian abortion laws as "archaic" and "ineffective", and said that "only one out of 1,000 women who want legal abortions is granted it under the present laws." "It is unfair to turn doctors into judges," said the doctor, referring to legalized hospital Therapeutic Abortion Committees. He was optimistic that public opinion would force a change in the law: "For every woman here today, there are 100,000 others who feel the same way."[13]

Less than three weeks later, on June 1, 1970, Dr. Morgentaler was arrested and charged with performing abortions that were illegal because they were done in his clinic. His patients had not been forced to beg a hospital TAC for consent.[14] Thus began Morgentaler's long, expensive court battle which culminated in the 1988 decision by the Canadian Supreme Court that the 1969 abortion law was unconstitutional.

When the two-hour rally ended that Saturday in Ottawa, the women were restless. Angry that government members had given them the brush-off, they were in no mood to simply go home.

Margo Dunn had foreseen this and recalls raising the matter with Marcy Cohen and Ellen Woodsworth the night before. "I felt we should have something scheduled for after the Committee Room meeting, because we'd be so high, and there'd be nowhere to go."[15] Someone cried: "'Let's bring the coffin to Sussex Drive!'" and 150 to 300 women, and perhaps fifteen men, set out to walk the kilometre and a half to the prime minister's residence. Meantime, Cathy Walker ran off to get her van with the coffin on top of it.

Dunn remembers being "high, high, high on this incredible energy" as they walked, and being astonished to find that the gates were open at 24 Sussex Drive. "They took us so non-seriously! There were just two RCMP-uniformed guards." The guards began to scuffle with the male protesters at the head of the march, while the women linked arms and simply swept through the gates, pushing the guards backwards ahead of them. Someone yelled, "Sit down! Sit down!" and the group dropped onto the lush lawn bordered with spring tulips. "Probably it was a very good thing that we sat down," considers Margo Dunn, with hindsight. "If we had not sat down, we would have somehow gotten into 24 Sussex Drive. I deeply believe that. People would have smashed in windows and whatever." More armed police were arriving, and while their guns were dismissed by the crowd at the time, looking back, and remembering the events at Kent and Jackson State, Dunn realizes the situation could have got out of control.

The sit-down continued for an hour and a half. Between chants of "Trudeau coward," and "Trudeau assassin," the group sang its songs. The prime minister did not appear, but eventually a man slipped casually out the door. He did not identify himself but said, "'Just thought I'd come out and see what I can do.'"[16] The easterners didn't know him and objected to this "lackey," but the women from BC recognized Gordon Gibson, Trudeau's top aide in the PMO. "Look, you idiots," said one, "this is as high-up as we're going to get." Gibson's intervention was not very effective.

...any hope of dialogue collapsed when Gibson addressed one of the women as 'Miss,' a title which, like 'Mrs.', Women's Liberation militants reject. He was shouted down in spite of his explanation that he was only saying "what my mother always taught me."[17]

The head man at the PMO backpedaled into chiding the women for calling the RCMP "pigs." That's "not very nice," he told them.[18] Courtesy was not a topic to raise carelessly in the presence of Betsy Wood, who has high standards in that regard. "I remember he was chewing gum. And it was so annoying, because here it was, something that was very serious...And I can remember telling him that this was a serious occasion and he should stop chewing his gum." Gibson retreated inside.

Margo Dunn laughingly recalls, "We were in a difficult position, because some people...started saying, 'We're not getting off this lawn until abortion's removed from the Criminal Code.' Which, of course, as it was starting to rain and we hadn't had lunch, was not exactly a workable strategy." But how to get away gracefully? Although police attempts to locate and speak with 'your leaders,' had met with stony faces and non-co-operation, negotiations eventually began. If it would get the women off the lawn afterward, the RCMP agreed they might make a few speeches and deposit the coffin at the PM's door.

The coffin was carried forward. Then, in a gesture that hushed them all, Margo Dunn stepped forward and opened the paper bag she'd begun putting together in Saskatoon and had carried unchallenged by the guards into the Railway Committee Room earlier. It contained household items used by women to abort themselves. In the July 1970 issue of *Saturday*

Night Magazine, Toronto WLM member and caravan participant Kathryn Keate, gave this description of Dunn's dramatic exposition:

> ...There are garbage bags on top of that coffin. These are used to pack the uterus to induce labor. Since they are not sterile, they often cause massive infection, resulting in sterilization, permanent disability, or death...There are knitting needles on top of that coffin. These are used to put in the vagina in order to pierce the uterus. Severe bleeding results...There is a bottle which is a container for lysol on top of that coffin. When used for cleaning, it is in solution. Women seeking to abort themselves inject it full strength into their vaginas. This results in severe burning of tissues, haemorrhage, and shock. Death comes within a matter of minutes. Intense, agonizing pain is suffered until the time of death...There is a part of a vacuum cleaner on top of that coffin. The hose is placed in the vagina in order to extract the fetus, but results in the whole uterus being sucked out from the pelvic cavity...[19]

"I remember those cops just turned green at the gills," recalls Dunn. So did many demonstrators. Some began sobbing. The crowd shuffled somberly from 24 Sussez Drive as a heavy rain began to fall.

Taking stock, the women of the Abortion Caravan felt they'd accomplished something, but not enough. They weren't ready to quit until they'd met with the government. So, while those who had to, returned home, a core of about one hundred women stayed on in Ottawa until Monday, when parliament would re-convene.

Buoyed by television footage of the Saturday march in the capital, the scheduled Mother's Day demonstrations across the country were highly successful. In four cities, feminists marched for abortion rights on Sunday, May 10, 1970. Anglophone and Francophone women marched together in Montréal, some carrying signs in French that said, "Mother's Day is one day — Father's Day is 364 days a year."[20] A half page of photos in *The Montréal Star* showed young women with picket signs in English and French, handing out leaflets to mothers pushing strollers in Lafontaine Park.[21]

The Winnipeg Tribune gave serious coverage to a march by 100 women and friends, describing the guerrilla theatre action. "Doreen Plowman, a representative from the Congress of Canadian women, addressed the crowd and said in part: 'As women won the right to vote — they'll win the right to abort.'"[22] Another demonstration was held in Edmonton.[23]

In Vancouver, marchers held a spirited rally at the courthouse, after performing a skit near Catholic-run St. Paul's Hospital. Coverage was scant. The *Vancouver Express,* still replacing the usual dailies, ignored the demonstration; nor did it report on the Abortion Caravan's action in Ottawa. The *Georgia Straight* published only a small, dark photo, with a brief caption, showing the Mother's Day skit in progress.[24]

The women who remained in Ottawa took a rest on Sunday. But that night, Percy Street School reverberated with discussion into the wee blue hours. The caravan had thrown down a gauntlet with its much-publicized

"Declaration of War," and the women now had to plan how that war against the government would be launched.

Enthusiasm rose for copying an action of the English suffragists, whereby members of the caravan would chain themselves to seats in the House of Commons. They would fling their demands upon the MPs' heads, not with red tape this time, but with words. Each woman would stand, in turn, and proclaim as much as possible of a single speech until she was silenced. After that, a woman in the next gallery would stand up and continue the same speech, and after her, another woman would rise...

The idea had delicious appeal, but some were hesitant. What risks would they be taking by such a show of disrespect? Would they at last be arrested? Jailed? Few expected to be shot, but the shades of the dead students at Jackson and Kent State seemed to hover among them. Margo Dunn recalls being persuaded by Myrna Wood of Toronto, one of the authors of the document, "Sisters, Lovers, Brothers, Listen..." who argued that the suffragists had acted with great dignity, and that the caravaners would likewise command the MPs' respect. They would not present themselves as hysterics.

Although any number could enter the public visitors' gallery, tickets were required to enter the government and opposition galleries in the Commons. More than one hundred women were waiting for Monday in the Percy Street School, and there weren't enough tickets to go around. Who should go inside?

Women's Caucus members clustered in a corner. The person regarded as the dominant personality, in this anti-leadership group, rose to set out guidelines. She and friends had consulted a lawyer before leaving Vancouver, and he'd advised that arrest and trial were very likely for any disruption in the Commons. What had happened at SFU in November, 1968, when 114 students had been arrested for setting up a picket line, had lessons for the caravan now, ran the argument. Bail for the 114 had been high. But in the present case, expenses for those arrested would be much higher, because Ottawa was so far away. So, in choosing those to go inside the Commons, women with independent means should be considered first. Secondly, certain categories of women ought not to be put at risk of arrest: single mothers, for example, and anyone without Canadian citizenship.

Most important of all was that a bond of trust and a common viewpoint should exist among the women who entered the Commons from BC. SFU's arrested 114, for example, had argued bitterly among themselves, and their disagreements fragmented the defence and made it easy for them to be manipulated. It was vital that those who might be arrested from the Abortion Caravan maintain a united front.[25] Given all that, there were only three women from the Vancouver Women's Caucus who fit all the criteria, in the speaker's view: Marcy Cohen, Ellen Woodsworth, and Dawn Carrell.

In the excitement and the exhaustion of the moment, not everyone recognized the implications of this argument. Betsy Wood, who had proposed the Abortion Caravan and had been a driving force in making it a reality, heard the argument through an emotional fog. "From Vancouver, there were only to be three to go in. Now, if you came from Toronto, any number could go in. But from Vancouver, only three could go in. And that excluded me."

> ...I really didn't know what was happening, at that point...I mean, I was feeling pretty badly by that time...I was in tears. But I didn't really figure it out until Mary Trew got up from the circle, and she said, 'Are you doing this to keep Betsy from going into the parliament buildings?' And it hadn't dawned on me that that was exclusively what was happening.

In Trew's recollection, "by the time we got to Ottawa, there was a lot of heavy baiting going on." She herself had been red-baited as a "'sort of 'Leninist-Trotskyist from Hell.'" At the same time, she was accused of being the polar opposite, an "agent" — the most scurrilous of turncoat roles. Both charges were meant to discredit her contributions to the caravan. Trew also remembers, "There was a serious attempt to marginalize Betsy by saying she was crazy. Betsy, of course, was not crazy; she just disagreed with them. So, that kind of ruthless behaviour is sometimes difficult to deal with. Betsy and I concentrated on trying to convince the other women on the politics [of our position.] Bless her, Betsy's political instincts are very, very good. She's a real fighter and she doesn't give up easily."

That evening in Ottawa, Dunn remembers, "there were about ten of us who really, really wanted to be inside" for the caravan's Declaration of War. However, the proposal that only Carrell, Cohen, and Woodsworth should enter the Commons from BC was accepted. Musing on it decades later, Dunn says:

> It's kind of funny because, at the time, it so clearly seemed the right decision. And I don't know now. ...Certainly, on a rational level, I think it was the right decision. But in terms of fairness and personal pain, and personal deserving, it was the wrong decision. ...I think if we had known no-one would get arrested — well, first of all, we would have all gone in! ...I think it would have been very clear Betsy had a real righteous cause, there, in going in.

When the selection was over, Betsy Wood's devastation was "obvious — and awful" recalls Dunn.

However, there was work to be done. Wood joined Dodie Weppler in making preparations for a demonstration to be staged, simultaneously, outside the Commons. A typically colourful plan was worked out, and Weppler and Wood went shopping for fabric early on Monday morning. Hurriedly, they cut this up and handed out a kerchief of red cloth, and a somewhat larger square of black cloth, to each woman planning to march around the Centennial Flame. This action would reinforce the caravan's demands and also deflect suspicion from those going inside.

Meantime, those chosen to go into the House of Commons were scurrying about to the left-wing and feminist co-ops of Ottawa, borrowing "dresses, make-up, shoes with heels, jewellery, hats, gloves — all those lovely unnecessities."[26] Male friends were sent out to buy bicycle chains. The speech each woman would read a part of was written, although who its authors were is uncertain and no copy seems to have survived in Vancouver. Carbon copies were typed and these were tucked into purses, together with the chains. At the appointed hour, thirty-some innocuous-looking women, some with male escorts, presented their tickets at the entrance to the parliamentary galleries. Once again, the women showed how quickly they could devise and carry out a complex plan of action.

As the first phalanx was taking seats inside, the outside demonstrators took up their places. Among them were spotters, like Marge Hollibaugh and Sharman Kanee, who sat on opposite park benches watching the entrances and exits. In her bag, Hollibaugh held donations to use for bail money. In her recollection, male supporters on idling motorcycles sat ready to follow any police van carrying off arrested feminists. The women were prepared for the worst. Approximately eighty women began a slow, silent, funereal procession around the Centennial Flame, beneath the Peace Tower. They carried a coffin and banners proclaiming '12,000 women die.' On their heads were black babushkas, and, secretly, their tension was high as 3 pm., the hour for declaring War on Canada, approached.

In the aftermath, nearly every major newspaper in the country carried the story of the caravan's climax on page one. A delighted Marge Hollibaugh made a point of collecting these articles and making a scrapbook of them.

In the midst of a plodding question period in the House of Commons, shortly before 3 pm, "a woman in the top row of the visitors gallery suddenly stood up and began a speech demanding the repeal of the present abortion law...As security guards made a beeline for her, another feminist popped up on the other side of the gallery with a similar speech. From there it snowballed, with feminists bolting to their feet in all sections of the galleries faster than security officers could quiet them."[27] *The Globe and Mail* devoted reams of space to the outburst. "One guard said, 'They were popping up all over the place.'"[28]

The caravaners had slipped into their seats in time to hear the issue of abortion rise on the floor. Andrew Brewin (NDP — Toronto-Greenwood) stood to quote from the Dominion Bureau of Statistics report, issued the previous Friday. It said that a total of only 235 abortions had been performed in six of Canada's provinces in the first three months of 1970 — well after the liberalization of the law. Did the government intend to "find remedies for what must remain a large number of 'back-alley abortions,'" asked Mr. Brewin. Justice minister John Turner mumbled that it would take time to review the figures. "'I doubt whether this law would be reviewed in this parliament,'" he said.[29]

When she was later ejected from the Commons, Marcy Cohen told a writer for *The Globe and Mail* that Turner's dithering was not acceptable. He "apparently expected [us] to 'wait two years for the statistics,'" she objected. "'We will not stand for women to die or be mutilated.'"[30]

Another MP demanded to know what the government was going to do about "a large group of hoodlums, queers and just plain fools" from Canada, who had stormed through the border at Blaine, Washington, south of Vancouver, in a mock invasion of the United States to protest its action against Cambodia.[31] Moments later, notes Hansard, "...there was an interruption from the public gallery..."[32] This was, of course, the women's "Declaration of War."

"The demonstration was a masterpiece of timing and organization," admitted the *Montréal Gazette* the next day.[33] Speaker Lucien Lamoureux rapped his gavel and called for order in vain. "It took security guards more than 15 minutes to clear the chamber of the demonstrating women...One apparently had connected a microphone to the simultaneous translation system connected to every gallery seat, adding an electronic assist to the din her companions were creating with pure lung power."[34] In the galleries, the women gave up trying to speak above the racket. "Then from all corners, they chanted in unison: 'Free abortion on demand.'"[35]

"Removal of chains from about 10 [other reporters said 20 wore chains] of the women was a slow process for the nonplussed guards. The women had used choker chains, wire or bicycle padlocks, and chains around their ankles, and guards had to obtain cutters to snip them loose."[36] They weren't gentle. "Several of the women are nursing lacerated wrists after security officers tried to yank them free...At least one officer, who tried to clap his hand over the mouth of a protester, was bitten in return."[37] "One woman screamed as guards worked to free her; another said...'they took the chains off after nearly breaking our arms.'"[38] "One Vancouver girl who refused to give her name told reporters: 'They gagged us. They lifted my sister beside me and pushed her throat against the wall so she was coughing and couldn't breathe. The other guy...[was] trying to stick his hand in my mouth. He forced me backward over the chair so I was almost fainting and wouldn't let me sit down.'"[39]

MPs were alarmed or outraged — or impressed. "After the initial surprise some MPs reacted with loud laughter, others with desk thumping."[40] Some smiled and congratulated the "young ladies" on the effectiveness of their organization: "'They had guts and they got their point across,' said Andrew Brewin."[41]

Speaker Lamoureaux finally adjourned the House until the uproar could be quelled. "It was the first time in the 103-year history of the Canadian Parliament that such an adjournment was provoked by a disturbance in the galleries," reported the *Vancouver Sun*, which had resumed publication after a long strike. The *Sun* joined other papers in warning of "fears that any kook group or individual could do the same thing."[42]

Released by adjournment, the MPs wandered outside, followed by the press. Safely in the open air, some MPs expostulated angrily. PC member for Oxford, Wallace Nesbit, declared, "'It was something like the tactics the Nazis used in the thirties to break the German parliamentary system.'"[43] Solicitor-general George McIlraith, who had responsibility for the RCMP, asked, "How do you keep parliament an open forum free of violent minority pressure groups?'"[44]

Justice minister Turner, however, kept his stuffed shirt on. Echoing BC's Ralph Loffmark, he told the media, "'I think these ladies don't understand the democratic process...I would not think this would be the way to convince the Canadian public of the legitimacy of their cause."[45] He didn't add that he'd stood them up when they came to meet him on the Saturday.

From the vantage point of more than thirty years, one looks back at a clear over-reaction. Members of Parliament were obviously scared to death of women. Treating them with contempt, in the manner of Samuel Johnson, who once compared a talking woman to a dog that believes it can walk upright, was no longer working to keep Canadian females down. Barking excitedly, the upright parliamentarians — ironically, Grace MacInnis was not in the House that day[46] — seized on any topic but abortion law repeal. In the days to come, they rushed into committee to discuss installing a plexi-glass shield "to protect the Commons from thrown objects and disruptive noise."[47]

As they were ejected from the building, caravaners joined their sisters marching around the Centennial Flame. Cheers broke out when it was clear they had not been arrested. At the stroke of three, the black scarves had been pulled off to reveal that the women marching outdoors were wearing red ones underneath, "in the style of the French revolution."[48] The red color, which signified blood, also meant, said one demonstrator, "'that we have declared war. We have given up black for mourning.'"[49] A few speeches were made, and then a large sheet of heavy paper, hand-lettered with the text of the abortion law, was set aflame. A Vancouver woman who refused to identify herself but was probably Margo Dunn, explained this to the press: "We no longer recognize laws that destroy rather than protect lives...Women of Canada answer with fire the blood of their sisters."[50]

In the daily papers there were many photos of the caravan's activities over its three days in Ottawa. A dozen of the women were quoted in the print media, and more appeared on TV. One was Betsy Meadley Wood, who had signed the letters declaring war. Although she had been denied a speaking role, even in the demonstration outside the Commons, the *Globe and Mail* sought her out and devoted four inches of its story to her remarks.[51]

And so, the Abortion Caravan came to an end and its participants drifted back to their home cities, confident they had inaugurated a new consciousness among Canadians. No-one had been arrested. But the abortion law was still in place.

CHAPTER 7

WRAP-UPS and THE EARLY 1970s

The confrontations in Ottawa were watershed events for Canadian feminism. Women's organizations were sprouting across the country. Entrenched taboos against mention of pregnancy, birth control, abortion, the real-life agonies of childbirth — indeed, anything about female sexuality and women's reproductive role — began to lift somewhat, as the media caught the tail of an irreversible social trend. Days after the caravan disrupted the House of Commons, a *Globe and Mail* headline admitted, "Amateur [illegal] abortions a large part of Toronto's everyday life: doctors; Figure may be hundreds a week."[1] A Canadian Press survey in March substantiated the charge that the amended abortion law hadn't changed much for pregnant women. In most of the country, hospitals had either refused to set up therapeutic abortion committees or had staffed them with anti-abortionists to insure that the operation remained unavailable.[2]

In Vancouver, the momentum of the abortion campaign continued to fuel events during the next few weeks. However, change was coming, and it arrived in full force during the summer, transforming Women's Caucus and the course of the fight for abortion rights.

Returning from the Pacific, Pierre Trudeau stopped in Vancouver for a press conference on Friday, May 29, 1970. He had scarcely begun a languid discourse on Asia when eight feminists seized the microphone and demanded repeal of the abortion law. The June issue of the *Pedestal* reported that "Trudeau's arrogance was exposed." The only argument the PM gave for not changing the law was that "the law was changed once already." The fact that the change had had no effect in practice was ignored.

> WOMEN: If someone close to you needed an abortion, she'd get one. Rich women can get safe abortions. It's poor women who suffer.
> TRUDEAU: So?[3]

The *Vancouver Sun* regarded the prime minister as a man with élan, and the women as screaming harridans:

> Trudeau remained calm throughout the onslaught, sipping water and waiting for the women to quiet down so he could answer. The women complained that they had gone to Ottawa to see him...but had seen nobody. ...Trudeau said he was 'sorry' and that the incident was 'rather unfortunate.'
> A woman: 'Sorry is not enough.'
> Trudeau: 'Well then I'm not sorry.'[4]

Shortly afterward, the prime minister arranged another get-together with Women's Caucus. During a *Pedestal* editorial meeting, on Sunday, June 14, 1970, the telephone rang. It was an aide to Trudeau, with an invitation to send, "say, six or eight" women to meet with the PM, either that night or the next day. Monday was an inconvenient time for working women, so the meeting was set for 10:30 that night, at the Bayshore Inn.

At 7 pm, forty activists sat down to plan how to avoid being manipulated or having their demands trivialized once again. From the start, they rejected the notion of sending a few representatives or, as had been requested, identifying a single speaker whom the PM could address by name. No media depictions of a cosy tête-à-tête between the nation's first lady-killer and a comely feminist.

Arriving early at the hotel, the women re-arranged the chairs from rows into a circle. They sang protest songs as Trudeau entered, wearing an apaché scarf around his neck. Some of the women were remarkably dressed, also. They arrived in bathrobes and slippers, with their hair in unaccustomed rollers. The point wasn't entirely clear, but perhaps it was to indicate that preparing for the real-life world of Monday morning was more pressing for women than listening to the prime minister spin tales.

Costumed women were in a minority, however. As planned, the feminists kept the discussion to the point, demanding repeal of the law, women's clinics, and pardon for doctors. Reported *The Pedestal,* when asked to remove abortion from the Criminal Code, Trudeau "tried a whole series of dodges." He said that, by repealing the abortion law, he would damage his chances of re-election. The women laughed. "He said, 'You are saying that the law doesn't fall equally on the poor and on the rich. But this is true — it doesn't apply only to abortion laws.'" "So much," scoffed *The Pedestal,* "for Mr. Trudeau's 'Just Society'!"[5]

Responding to the official report that, in the first six months of 1970, only 235 therapeutic abortions had been done in the only six provinces to perform any at all, an incensed *Chatelaine* magazine made these comparisons:

> In England, with a more humane and liberal law, there were 6,162 abortions in *only one month* (March)...New York City's municipal hospitals reported a total of 1190 abortions performed in the first three weeks following the state's liberalized law, effective July 1.[6]

By the end of 1970, according to the Dominion Bureau of Statistics, a total of 11,200 abortions — triple the number for 1969 — had been performed in all of Canada. In December, 1970, 2,252 abortions were done, or thirteen times the number in January of that year. Ontario had the highest total, 5,657, followed by 2,981 in BC. Commented the *Province,* this made Canada's legal abortion rate about three per 100 live births, "compared to 46 for England and Wales, eight in Denmark, and 38 in Japan."[7]

It seems paradoxical that the triumph of the Abortion Caravan led to a buckling of the organization, but, in truth, the tensions boiling just beneath the surface made an eruption predictable. As the glow from the Ottawa events faded, Women's Caucus was rushing toward a new phase. A Strategy Conference in June, 1970, began the group's unravelling. *The Pedestal* announced it as a conference to "decide how best to co-ordinate the various campaigns — such as abortion, day care and job issues..."[8] With characteristic energy, position papers were written and exchanged. Some of the old-guard, such as Anne Roberts who had moved to Edmonton, returned for the conference. Other attendees were newcomers, seldom or never drawn into Women's Caucus events before, such as Claire Culhane, known then as an anti-Vietnam War activist and later as an advocate for prison reform.

The meeting opened an hour late on Saturday, June 20, in Women's Caucus's new headquarters at 511 Carrall Street. As reports began on the year's numerous activities, Cynthia Flood took meticulous notes. She jotted down the name of each speaker and the gist of her remarks. About noon, two dozen more members trailed in, and DJ O'Donnell rose to announce that the latecomers were leaving Women's Caucus. It had become, in Flood's notes on O'Donnell's speech, no more than a "multi-issue reform group" that had failed to confront the "total oppression" of women. A position paper was passed around to the stunned meeting.

That afternoon, the planned workshops were cancelled. Discussion focused on the charges of the 24 women who were leaving, including Marcy Cohen, Dawn Carrell, Ellen Woodsworth, Margo Dunn, Maxine Schnee, and Judy Darcy (visiting from Toronto). Consistent with the slogan, "Smash Capitalism", these women believed that ending the oppression of women required immediate revolution. They were joining forces with a mostly male group, the Vancouver Liberation Front, and would call themselves Vancouver Women's Liberation. Arguing that feminism was already established, undergoing "'spontaneous growth,'" and no longer needing nurturance by groups like Women's Caucus,[9] the VWL intended to leap to the forefront and raise the red banner for full-scale revolt.

Many Women's Caucus veterans opposed the splitters arguments. Cynthia Flood shook her head to hear the VWL claim "'that the women of Vancouver are ready to rise!'" Her eyes met those of Sheila Dunnachie, who, like Flood, then worked as a secretary in a large downtown office. Both were thinking, "We could confirm one hundred percent that this was inaccurate!"[10]

Another woman, attending her first Women's Caucus meeting, also disputed the split. Flood's notes identify her as Kim Campbell. Early in the afternoon, the previously unknown Ms. Campbell spoke like a seasoned political scientist and historian. Addressing the VWL document, she referred to the "stages" of development in a revolution — a keystone of

Marxism as developed under Stalin — at one of which, revolutionaries join with other groups in order to reach certain unified goals. She gathered that the split people thought this level had been reached and surpassed, and that the revolutionaries could now break away. Campbell disagreed with this notion — "thinks not", jotted Flood. Later, Campbell, clearly acquainted with the writings of Lenin, spoke again, saying that the split "'reeks of infantile communism.'" Arguing that we "'must keep women's liberation as *prime* goal,'" she reminded the meeting that no political system had yet liberated women. Not even Ms. Campbell herself guessed, at that moment, that the first female prime minister of Canada was in attendance that afternoon.[11]

Nothing, however, could deter the group of 24 from walking out of the Women's Caucus. Its departure was a blow, involving more than one third of those at the Saturday session. On the Sunday, June 21, just over forty women addressed the remaining agenda. Newcomers had not returned after the previous day's debacle.

Those remaining fell into two groups, one tight and one looser, but larger. The tightly-co-ordinated group were the women from the Trotskyist Young Socialists and League for Socialist Action (YS/LSA). They argued that "[m]ost women are not yet convinced that they are oppressed, but in growing numbers they are supporting our fight for free abortion on demand."[12] The majority accused them of paring the complex number of women's needs down to a single issue. In reply, the YS/LSA wrote in the July *Pedestal*, "Far from being a restricted 'single issue', the abortion question reaches out to women and draws them to an ever-widening awareness of their over-all position in society and teaches them to question the basis of that society which has oppressed them for so long." And, the group insisted, "it's a battle we can win."[13]

The larger group at the Sunday meeting consisted of many founding members: Jean Rands. Maggie Benston, Pat Davitt, and others. These women intended to focus on working women and on the educational system, and the conference ended by adopting their proposals. "The goal," reported *The Pedestal*, "is not to mobilise large numbers of women who can be called out to demonstration[s]," but to politicize individuals so they might "confront the institutions and people who oppress them." Action around "specific issues like abortion should take place within this context."[14]

Thus, after the momentous June conference, Women's Caucus showed little interest in abortion, the issue it had thrown into extraordinary prominence. With tragic irony, the issue was spotlighted in the news when, days later, Gwytha Pearse, a 34-year-old Vancouver mother of two, died of a self-induced abortion. An immediate protest was called by about thirty Young Socialist members of Women's Caucus, who assembled at the Federal

Building at Hastings and Granville on Wednesday, June 24. They chanted "Every child a wanted child, every mother a willing mother."[15] Mary Trew told the *Vancouver Sun*, "'We feel that the federal government is responsible — more than the hospitals, more than the reactionary medical profession — for what is happening to women who want abortions.'"[16] The focus on the federal government was consistent with the Trotskyst purpose of exposing the capitalist state's refusal to govern in the interests of the people.

The Pedestal ran a story on Mrs. Pearse and the protest, although no-one from the majority at the previous weekend's conference attended it.[17] Within ten days of the intense confrontation with Trudeau at the Bayshore Inn, the issue of abortion was virtually dropped by the majority of Women's Caucus. Very soon, the tension between the majority and the Trotskyist YS/LSA members mounted to a showdown. At the August 27, 1970 meeting — one year less a day after the amended abortion law came into effect — the Women's Caucus voted to exclude members of the YS/LSA. They withdrew, but others believed the YS/LSA women were treated unfairly and went with them. Of the twenty-four signers of a final leaflet, titled "For Unity — Against Expulsion," at least one third were not members of the YS/LSA. Within three weeks, these women had founded a new group called The Women's Liberation Alliance.

So ended the initial, vital, and vibrant period, in which Vancouver Women's Caucus carried the banner for women's right to birth control and abortion. The Caucus did not fold at that time, but its transformation into other organizations was underway. *The Pedestal* continued publishing until late 1973. The struggle to win control over our reproductive lives was continued by other women in new organizations: in 1971, the Women's Liberation Alliance morphed into the B.C. Coalition to Repeal the Abortion Laws, which later became a wing of the cross-Canada Morgentaler Defence Campaign.

Some observations may be in order. The incredible activity level of Women's Caucus has already been noted. At a mid-1980s reunion, and others later on, most Women's Caucus members were still actively working for social justice and social change. Many were in the labour movement, as activists or elected leaders. Women's Caucus efforts resembled a charge of dynamite, forcing local doctors to put the new abortion law into effect, seeding the growth of women's liberation groups elsewhere, and bursting into public consciousness on a national scale. If they were cheeky, so were the times, which witnessed tie-dyed be-ins in Stanley Park and the marijuana smoke-in in Gastown. The feminists' behaviour was often regarded as refreshing by the very society it set out to affront. "We were very good at being very dramatic," recalls Pat Davitt with satisfaction, "and we did generate a fair amount of press."[18] Its legacy of fighting for women's rights as workers, and to control their bodies by choosing abortion if they wished, made Women's Caucus an effort of first magnitude, in whose debt Canadian women will forever be.

Close on the heels of the Abortion Caravan by supposedly disreputable feminists came a tide of opposition to the 1969 abortion law from the most reputable of quarters. Less than a month after the caravan closed the House of Commons, a Liberal Party meeting in Edmonton voted two-to-one for legalizing all abortions. Forwarded to the federal Liberal Party convention in November, 1970, the resolution was adopted by more than four to one. It called for removing abortion from the Criminal Code, and it agreed that the decision to abort should concern only a woman and her doctor. "In other words, free abortion on demand, the great cry of the Women's Lib group," commented the *Vancouver Sun*.[19] The prime minister ignored the vote.

In June, 1970, both the Canadian Medical Association and the Canadian Psychiatric Association took stands that repudiated their former support for the 1969 abortion law. The CMA removed all mention of abortion from its code of ethics,[20] while the CPA voted for removal of abortion from the Criminal Code. A strongly-worded editorial in the CMA *Journal* in August 1970, said, "Doctors should not be obliged to assume the function of gatekeepers to decide which unwanted children should be allowed into this over-populated world and which ones should not."

Meantime, Dr. Henry Morgentaler's modest clinic in Montréal was raided, and he and his nursing staff were arrested on Monday, June 1, 1970.[21] The doctor, a survivor of Auschwitz, asked why it was necessary "'in a civilized society such as ours" that women should "needlessly suffer at the hands of the law."[22] Debate raged on across Canada for decades.

This change in public opinion was of no help to Vancouver's Dr. Robert Makaroff. The three counts against him were based on the technicality that his patients had not gone before hospital therapeutic abortion committees. On August 26 — as a reported 80,000 protesters from across the US paraded in a gigantic Women's Strike for Equality led by Betty Friedan in New York City[23] — the soft-spoken Dr. Makaroff pled guilty in provincial court, and submitted a lengthy statement. "The new law is simply not working," he said. It was "outrageous," inequitable, and humiliating to women.[24]

Makaroff gave the court his story, describing the many requests he'd received from desperate women, who, when turned down, had been forced to take the "physically and psychologically traumatic" route of searching for a back street practitioner. Finally, a heartbreaking case had led him to break the law and do the procedure in his office. "Like most physicians, I had little idea then how vast the underground demand for abortion was," he said. Within a year, he was so swamped by requests for abortions that he could not keep up with his general practice. He cut it back, unable to turn away from the urgency of the women's plight. Working eighteen-hour days for three "harrowing," "nightmarish" years, before and after the 1969 legal change, he had provided medically safe abortions and compassionate care for up to twenty-four women per day. Only once had a patient suffered ill effects. Makaroff inserted an intravenous tube into the women's arm and admitted her to hospital under his own name.[25]

His standard fee of $500 was partly meant as a deterrent, he said, but he also said he had never turned away a woman who could not pay. Indeed, two of the women named in the three counts against him had paid the doctor nothing. They were fully eligible for a legal abortion, except that they needed one before the law was changed.[26] Therefore, he pointed out, "my crime consists solely of having bypassed bureaucratic protocol...This single consideration makes the questions about the morality of abortions *per se*, my motivations, volume of practice, fees, irrelevant."[27]

The in-house *Newsletter* of Vancouver General Hospital reported in the September 10, 1970 issue:

> To the end of June, 1969, 25 sterilizations and 36 therapeutic abortions had been done here. This year in the corresponding period, 365 sterilizations and 241 therapeutic abortions have been undertaken.[28]

Clearly, if VGH had performed about 1.5 legal abortions per week in early 1970, that illustrates the great pressure put on doctors like Makaroff by the overflow demand. He had been performing 24 careful abortions per day, while, at the same time, an unknown number of other women were forced to use equally expensive, often non-medical, clandestine services.

At the sentencing hearing on September 17, five physicians did testify on behalf of Dr. Makaroff, each of them arguing that abortion was a medical, not a legal, matter.[29] The Rev. Jack Kent, of the North Shore Unitarian Church, told the court he had referred three, greatly anguished, women to Dr. Makaroff. The *Vancouver Sun* omitted mention of the supportive doctors and headlined its story, "Pastor admits abortion aid; Doctor made $300,000 in year."[30]

Justice Harvey Sedgwick insisted on examining Dr. Makaroff's assets, to his lawyer's distress.[31] He acknowledged that "the abortion laws of the country could be considered inadequate, as they stand today,"[32] However, the courts' function was to uphold the law, not to suggest change, or to disagree with it. "I believe," he said, "that a therapeutic abortion committee should be consulted before an abortion is undertaken by any doctor." He sentenced Dr. Makaroff to three months in jail on each of three counts against him, to be served concurrently. Sedgwick levied a fine of $15,000 and took note of his own leniency, since conviction for illegal abortion could incur a sentence of life imprisonment.[33]

The claim of leniency was exposed as untrue by *The Georgia Straight*, which reported briefly on the cases of two other local doctors caught performing abortions. Both went to trial in 1968, before the law was changed, but after Dr. Makaroff began helping women at his clinic. Both received suspended sentences and were allowed to keep their medical licences.[34] Presumably, neither took a political stand against the law, as Makaroff did so publicly.

The passionate doctor was humble in defeat. He was escorted to Oakalla Prison in Burnaby to begin his sentence, while his wife Shawna was left to support their daughters. His personal humiliation was made as complete as possible: when he was released from jail in December 1970, Makaroff was allowed to keep his medical licence but was denied hospital privileges. It was impossible for him to resume a practice.

At the sentencing, about ten members of the newly-formed Women's Liberation Alliance protested outside the courtroom at Main and Hastings. A smaller number of Women's Caucus members marched alongside.

On December 7, 1970, the long-awaited report from the Royal Commission on the Status of Women was released. Its 167 specific recommendations included abortion on demand for women who were pregnant twelve weeks or under, and abortion after that time when the woman's physical or mental health was endangered, or when the fetus was deformed.[35]

The Women's Liberation Alliance (WLA), successor to the Women's Caucus, took up the campaign for legal abortion after its formation in the summer of 1970. It was not a single-issue group, for its program had six points for women's rights. It was at once as busy as the Women's Caucus had been. Part of its plan was to follow the broad outline of the work done by its predecessor. In 1971, the WLA went to Victoria seeking greater access to abortion; a demonstration was held on Valentine's Day; there were debates, educational events, and events to reach out to high school women.

Dr. Makaroff accompanied the WLA delegation to Victoria on February 10, to meet with health minister Loffmark. Alas, Mr. Loffmark did not see matters as the women did. He scorned to recommend reinstatement of Dr. Makaroff's licence and rejected all of the Alliance's requests.[36]

The demonstration on Saturday, February 13, 1971 was held in conjunction with actions in other Canadian cities and with a March on Ottawa organized from Toronto. This author joined the WLA just in time to take part in the march. I was assigned the role of 'Mrs. Menopause' in the latest version of the skit. The very high expectations for the Vancouver action made organizer Cynthia Flood break out in a rash and have to go on tetracycline. "The word 'abortion,' and publicity of that word was still so novel and extraordinary — and so dreadful,"[37] Flood recalls, that it was hard even for sympathizers to associate themselves publicly with it. The day itself was very wet, and the turnout of 150 disappointed Alliance members. Flood recalls that the notion of mass action, which the Trotskyist women supported, "was perceived as wrong-headed, and, indeed, kind of pathetic." Where were the masses? Why didn't women who had had abortions come out? Why had no bystanders stepped into the street to march along with them, as they'd heard so often happened the year before? Standing at the threshold of a decades-long effort for legal abortion, the group learned the hard way that building a movement is not done overnight.

In extant copies of the monthly *Women's Liberation News,* names of about thirty-five WLA activists appear. Ten of them were also involved in the YS/LSA. Among the independent members were Reva Dexter, Carolyn Jerome, Muggs Sigurgeirson, and Betsy Wood. Mary Norton, the suffragist, often attended WLA meetings.

Just as I joined it with idealistic fervour, a sour note was creeping into the WLA. Again, the membership began to divide between the Trotskyists and the other members. Looking back, Gail Riddell, Carol La Bar, and Heather Johnson believed the YS/LSA minority "controlled everything": the agenda, most of the proposals for activities, even the colour of paper for leaflets.[38] Margaret Birrell was among the knot of women that began caucusing separately, just as they knew the Trotskyist women were doing. "We met for ages and planned a variety of things," recalls Carol La Bar. "But it came to naught." In retrospect, Heather Johnson believes the group got together "just because [we] were not the Young Socialists." Others, like Perry Millar (formerly Becker), did not feel personally threatened by the Trotskyists. "I felt that, as much as I understood anything, I did understand what their point of view was. And if I disagreed with it, I would argue about it. But if I didn't disagree with it, what was the problem?"[39]

May was coming and with it the anniversary of the Abortion Caravan. Canada's 'Royal Family' — former SFU student Margaret Sinclair and the PM, still honeymooning after their surprise March wedding — were expected in BC on May 1, and a broadly-based anti-Trudeau protest and Mayday festival began to take shape. The Trudeaus were coming to open the whale pool at the Vancouver Aquarium.

That inspired the unique imagination of Betsy Wood, who devised a plan to make a feminist point to the prime minister. It was not easy to stand out among the crowd of protesters, well-wishers, and police at the Aquarium, but the Women's Liberation Alliance made the national news. As the prime minister began his speech, over the hill across from the whale pool came the WLA, chanting, singing, and carrying the usual banners about abortion, plus another one that read 'Women Before Whales!' "He couldn't speak because we were chanting," recalls Wood. "And, of course, it carried right across the water." Later, discovering how cramped the whales' quarters were, Wood says, "Afterward, I felt very sorry for the whales that we'd even said this."[40]

Euphoria over the May Day success was short-lived, however, for at the following Tuesday's meeting of WLA, a terse, angry announcement was made and six members of the Independent Caucus walked out.[41] They amounted to less than a quarter of the membership, but the rift affected everyone, and it could not be healed. The Alliance did not dissolve, but it faded over the summer of 1971. In the fall, a new organization, a coalition of many groups, was formed. The Vancouver movement took another turn.

About then, Joseph Borowski, then NDP highways minister in Manitoba, weighed in with an anti-abortion rant. On an open-line radio show, Borowski told a caller that teen-age girls wouldn't need abortions "if they'd start keeping their hot pants on...or maybe we'll do to them what we do to dogs, and have them spayed.'"[42]

On July 10, 1971, the *Journal* of the Canadian Medical Association published a computer analysis of the first 500 abortions done at VGH in 1970. Written by a team headed by Dr. David Claman, it showed that the 1969 partial legalization wasn't satisfactory by medical standards. The red tape required under the new law, "led to an increasing backlog of patients with a waiting time of over three weeks." Eighty percent waited that long by mid-September, 1970. As a result, many women didn't get into the operating room until they were past the first trimester, the safest period for an abortion. The complication rate was an incredible 17%.

Abortion was well-known to be vastly safer for women's health than pregnancy ending in birth: this was shown by the record in eastern Europe and Japan[43] Even for those Canadians indifferent to the suffering of women, a 17% complications rate was an embarrassment in a country that prided itself on its health care system.

A cross-country body was needed to fight the abortion law, one that would draw organizations with established clout into a coalition. The Women's Liberation Alliance and similar groups in other cities were not large enough and hadn't the resources needed to mount an effort that would succeed. Thus went the thinking of the League for Socialist Action and Young Socialists, whose ranks I had joined that summer. Accordingly, the BC Women's Abortion Law Repeal Coalition (the BC Coalition) was founded at a conference at UBC in October, 1971. More than forty prominent women publicly supported the group, and endorsements soon included student societies at UBC and Vancouver City College, as well as the BC Family Planning Association, the NDP Women's Rights Committee, the Vancouver and District Labour Council, and the BC Federation of Labor. Nonetheless, more than a quarter of the 100 people at the founding conference were from the YS/LSA. The Trotskyists understood that the first job would be to get active participation from the groups that supported the Coalition, and that, in the beginning, they would have to do most of the work.

Indeed, during its two-three years of existence, most of its activists were from the Trotskyist movement, and organizations that joined the Coalition seldom sent delegates to participate. Still, valuable and committed work was done by a number of women not part of the YS/LSA, including Donna Aubert, Marjorie Clark, Holly Devor, and Elizabeth Godley. The indomitable Mary Bishop, whose prodigious writings and efforts on behalf of women were capped by her long presidency of the BC Family Planning Association, was often involved in the Coalition. Pia Shandel, whose views have since changed, was one of five women who devised and performed a skit at the Coalition's founding conference.

The BC Coalition was notable for organizing demonstrations, conducting a petition drive, deepening support for abortion rights among students, presenting a breathtaking Tribunal, in which women publicly told their abortion stories, and for carrying a defence campaign in support of Dr. Henry Morgentaler. In concert with other provincial coalitions established by the YS/LSA, the group organized demonstrations across Canada on November 20, 1971. Afterward, its members dove into collecting signatures on a petition that called for repeal of the abortion law.

The next great event was a conference in Winnipeg in March, 1972, called to found the Canadian Women's Coalition to Repeal the Abortion Laws. Six of us from Vancouver went by train, including Jan Bulman of the United Church, who played an active role in the BC Coalition. Among the 230 at the conference were women from various YWCAs, the Unitarian Church, the NDP, student societies, and many small feminist groups — 65 organizations in all. Rita MacNeil was there, and I bought my first MacNeil album, one she self-produced.

Eleanor Wright Pelrine was there; her first book was *Abortion in Canada: The Reform that Hardly Was,* and she was at work on a moving biography of Dr. Morgentaler. But the Canadian Women's Coalition was too far-left for her. In November, 1974, Pelrine founded the Canadian Association for Repeal of the Abortion Law (CARAL), which became a powerful lobbying and fund-raising organization, with chapters across the country.

The CWC set up an office in Toronto, put out a handsome monthly paper called *Spokeswoman* that we sold on streetcorners, and focused its provincial chapters on the petition campaign. Thousands of signatures had already been collected, and on May 15, 1972 — Mother's Day — 77,500 signatures were accepted by Liberal MP Ray Perrault in Ottawa. The 12-person delegation included Dr. Harriet Christie of the United Church and Mary-Lou Church of the Unitarian Church. The coalition was augmented by a chapter in Nova Scotia, making seven provincial bodies, and there were nine chapters in Ontario.[44]

May 1-6, 1972 was declared an international week of actions on abortion by the Trotskyist movement, which had organizations in a sufficient number of countries to bring it off. As reported in *Spokeswoman*, there were demonstrations on May 6 in England, France, three cities in Scotland, six cities in New Zealand, a dozen cities in the US and seven cities in Canada.[45] A rally in Vancouver heard speeches by NDP MLA Rosemary Brown, lawyer Nancy Morrison, and Dr. Robert Makaroff. In a mock trial, Pierre Trudeau was found guilty of injustice to women and sentenced to repeal the abortion laws.

By December, a new project developed. The Women's Action Group at UBC announced plans for a Women's Week on campus. Through student members of the BC Coalition, we proposed holding a Tribunal in that week, on abortion, contraception, and forced sterilization. Skeptical at first, the Women's Action Group accepted the plan, and the Tribunal was held on February 15, 1973.

I remember it as a luminous and profoundly moving evening. A capacity crowd sat in the Student Union Building ballroom, which was dark except for a spotlight at the front. The atmosphere was hushed. Fourteen women had responded to our call for volunteers. Some delivered their testimonies in person; others asked that their stories be read for them. Later, ten of the stories were typed on Gestetner stencils and put together in a booklet by the BC Coalition.

One woman told of being forced to travel from Ontario to New York for an abortion; another's story was of being granted a therapeutic abortion but kept on the maternity ward for two nights and scolded by hospital staff for her decision. In two cases, women were forced to pay $100 or more in cash to the doctors who performed their legal abortions, a fairly frequent but entirely illegal practice. A particularly fertile woman told of having given birth six times, as well as undergoing seven or eight abortions. All but the last, which was done in a hospital on condition that the woman be sterilized, were illegal, terribly dangerous, and excruciatingly painful. An incest survivor told of being forced to agree to sterilization as a condition for getting a hospital abortion in 1971, when she was barely twenty; her grief was unending. Another young woman went to an MD in Merritt to request an abortion. He harshly refused her, saying he had seven children and she should have the same. Then he agreed to perform the operation and tie her tubes at the same time. She objected. Finally, he slyly demanded a cash payment which she could not afford. At last he sent her to a gynecologist, who operated on her in hospital. She lost a lot of blood — entirely unnecessary with a competent doctor — and felt too ill to go home right away. Seven weeks later, she began to bleed again, and the next day, she discharged "placenta and fetus all intact. At last, the gruesome ordeal was over." But the final story was unforgettable. It was read by Bonnie Geddes, a Y/S and Coalition member who was just out of high school herself.

> This is not my own testimony but the testimony of a woman named Karen, a high school student of the age of 17. Karen can't be here herself because Karen is dead.

Karen had lived in Abbotsford and went to her family doctor, who refused to help her. Besides, she would have needed parental consent to get a hospital abortion. She ran away to Vancouver, where she somehow located a backstreet practitioner. He aborted and left her to bleed to death.

The audience was shaken. When asked to return a verdict on the culpability of the law, there was a long moment before stunned and croaking voices could call out "Guilty."

Such tribunals were being held everywhere. Across Canada, the provincial coalitions organized them on the same theme as in Vancouver: "Repeal Abortion Laws! Free and Effective Contraception! No Forced Sterilization!" In New York City, an International Tribunal was being planned for March. Simone de Beauvoir, the great French feminist, had agreed to sit on the presiding panel.

Then a reverberating thunderclap: the US Supreme Court decided on the case of *Roe versus Wade*. On January 22, 1973, it ruled that abortion was a constitutional right, protected by the right to privacy. It could not be restricted or refused to a woman, up to twenty weeks of pregnancy. The outcome of *Roe v. Wade* was, for many years, the greatest victory won anywhere in the world by what were beginning to be called the Pro-Choice forces.

But in Canada, the miserable law was sealed in place. Nearly three years after the arrest of Dr. Henry Morgentaler, he had yet to go to trial. He continued to operate his abortion clinic in Montréal, where women got competent and compassionate service without being made to answer to a TAC. The government was not eager to try him in Québec, where separatist sympathies were very strong, the wounds of the War Measures Act imposed in October 1970 were still fresh, and the labour federations had combined in a *front commun* with spectacularly successful strike actions. So accepted was the pro-choice view that the governments of Québec and Ottawa suspected Henry Morgentaler was right, when he claimed that no jury would convict him. The doctor was determined to bring the law to its knees through the courts.

At a Canadian Women's Coalition conference in Toronto in March, 1973, Dr. Morgentaler was the featured speaker at a session open to the public. I had the good fortune to be there. He used the occasion to announce he had performed more than 5000 technically illegal abortions at his clinic. All were done to the highest medical standards. Not one of his patients had died in four years. He called on other physicians to join him in defying the law, for it was the law that was criminal.

It was a calculated move: Morgentaler was demanding to be put on trial. There was no government response. He then performed an abortion, live, on CTV's popular public affairs show, *W5*. The pregnant patient consented to the cameras, and also insisted on being identified to help dispel the shame unfairly attached to the procedure. Her name was Petra Hartt. The film went to air on Sunday, May 13, 1973 — Mother's Day.

It caused an uproar. Still, Québec justice minister Jerome Choquette stalled. Three months went by, and police raided Morgentaler's clinic on rue Honore Beaugrand again. The doctor, his staff, the patients and those who had accompanied them were all arrested and taken away. Only Dr. Morgentaler was charged, and within two weeks, the number of charges against him rose from three to thirteen. At last he went to trial, in late October, 1973, and as he'd predicted, Henry Morgentaler was acquitted.[46]

He was jailed anyway, while the Crown appealed the acquittal and scheduled another trial on the second charge against him. It was a low point for everyone who valued women's right to choose. Dr. Morgentaler was acquitted by a second and a third jury, but those verdicts were overturned by the Canadian Supreme Court in 1975, which pronounced him guilty. The crusading doctor was kept in jail until 1976, when the newly-elected Parti Québecois released him and declared that Québec would no longer honour the Criminal Code on abortion. Morgentaler resumed operating his clinic in Montréal.

Across Canada, the fight went on.

CHAPTER 8

HOSPITAL BOARD ELECTIONS: I

What about opponents of abortion? They were abundant and made their presence felt in most BC communities. For more than a dozen years, their money and connections put them in the lead, forcing the pro-choice movement to scramble after them.

Vancouver's first Birthright Centre opened on Marine Drive in 1971 to dispense moral coercion and fear — not medical advice — to women who consulted it. According to the *Vancouver Sun*, the centre relied on the views of a psychiatrist from Washington, D.C:

> [Dr.] Fogel does not claim that mental illness automatically follows an abortion..."Often,"he said, "the trauma may sink into the unconscious and never surface in the woman's lifetime. But a psychological price is paid. I can't say exactly what."[1]

Birthright aimed to prevent pregnant women from having abortions; the Pro-Life Society aimed to organize the general population, and a third group aimed to corral government members. All these groups still exist today. Betty Green and Bernice Gerard formed the Pro-Life society of BC in 1973, as an educational and lobby group,[2] and the triad was completed by the political arm, called variously Alliance for Life, Coalition for Life, and Campaign Life. It was/is devoted to electing candidates who pledge(d) to outlaw abortion completely, and to unseat politicians who did/do not subscribe to that goal.[3]

These three strands of the anti-abortion movement were joined by a fourth in the 1980s that engaged in direct action — invading, blockading, and fire-bombing abortion facilities; harassing and intimidating abortion providers and patients. And, as James Kopp, the chief suspect in the shooting of three Canadian physicians proved, by his proud confession to killing Dr. Barnett Slepian of Buffalo, N.Y. in 1998, in assassinations.

In Ontario, Catholics are the backbone of the anti-abortion movement. But, in BC, the organizing centre is just east of the urban lower mainland, in the Fraser Valley — often called the 'Bible Belt,' or the heart of evangelical Protantism. Most anti-abortionists are church-goers, but, as we have already seen, not all Protestant churches are against abortion.

Even among Roman Catholics, opposition to abortion is a relatively recent phenomenon. It was only in 1869 that Pope Pius IX proclaimed against abortion in *A Syllabus of Errors.* Before that, there had been no particular Catholic concern about it since the middle ages. Abortion before 'quickening' (when the woman feels the fetus moving about) had usually been regarded as natural and unremarkable, and was exceedingly common.[4]

Catholicism had little influence in 19th century US, but a secular opposition to abortion arose in the medical profession. Among histories of the procedure, one of the most insightful is by James C. Mohr, whose *Abortion in America* (1978) traces its general toleration up to the mid-1800s. Then, in a concerted drive to gain a monopoly on medical practice, physicians in North America began to campaign against their many competitors. Midwives, pharmacists, surgeons, homeopaths, and other practitioners who had different training than members of the fledgling American Medical Association, founded in 1847, were targeted as dangerous. Of course, medical treatment of the female sex, one-half of the human race, was highly lucrative. A major part of the physicians' efforts was to brand the services of midwives, who traditionally ministered to women, as sleazy and unethical. It was more difficult to pin that label on midwives' assistance at births than on the widespread practice of controlling reproduction through early birth control methods and abortion. Patent medicines, 'ladies remedies,' and the equivalent of abortion clinics were very common in nineteenth-century North America. Against them, doctors began a steady effort to make abortion illegal. Mohr details their success in getting anti-abortion laws passed state by state in the US, until by 1900, the practice was almost uniformly banned. In asserting their sole right to practice medicine, and practice as their patriarchal beliefs inclined, physicians raised a great 'moral' clamour against abortion — toward their own professional ends.[5]

Regarding Mohr's book, the *New York Review* noted: "It is helpful to know that what is presented as an eternal verity — the criminality of abortion — has been with us for less than a hundred years." In Canada, abortion was made illegal in 1892, in language very similar to an 1861 law in Britain.[6]

This, of course, only forced abortion underground and guaranteed that enormous numbers of women would have to face the stark terror of visiting backstreet providers. But why was it that ordinary people tolerated this suffering for so long? Feminism's answer is hard to ignore. It describes the origin of 'family values' this way:

Throughout history, societies have been controlled by men. In every patriarchy, males have been so dominant that females were rendered not only powerless, without legal rights, but identity-less, existing only in the shadow of their fathers, husbands, or sons. Male-directed Church and State dictated 'family values,' which can be translated as keeping a woman in her place: married to a man and the bearer of 'his' children. If children were the legal property of their father, then his other property — the wife — had no right to control her own sexuality or reproduction. To prevent women from bearing heirs to the wrong man, they were permitted sex only in marriage, and evidence of extra-marital sex was harshly punished. Keeping women powerless and, whenever possible, invisible, and placing emphasis on the progeny of the male, is still the norm in many cultures in the world, and is elevated as the inalterable natural order by those who rule by force and who fear change. Thus, all concern is shifted to the 'unborn', the better to delete the female from the equation of pregnancy, and to protect the patriarchal right to rule through 'male' progeny and to dominate women.

Conveniently classed as property already, women in the private-wealth-and-property system of capitalism have faced exclusion from every index of power: legal status, education, jobs and decent wages, positions of authority, etc. Security is exposed as an illusion. Every feminist advance has been a struggle.

In late 20th century Canada, patriarchy's hold was loosened by determined effort, but domination of women underlies the 'perfect world' which fundamentalists of every stripe revere. The advent of the pill in the 1950s turned fairly reliable birth control into a mass-market item, undercutting enforcement of the patriarchal ideal in North America. The 'sexual revolution' irrevocably changed Western social attitudes, although stalwart believers fight on to crush the female, invoking the authority of whatever god they prefer.

Patriarchal premises are the basis of the anti-abortion movement. If its efforts have not succeeded in stemming change, that is due less to the work of the small, de-centralized pro-choice movement than to a genuine and generalized sea-change in societal outlook. For a majority of Canadians, extreme disapproval of sexuality, an entirely submissive role for women, and strict control of reproduction, including a total ban on abortion, are no longer accepted without question. Still, if feminism had not emerged to battle for women's rights, the opportunities that opened for them in the late 20th century might have shrunk instead of expanding. And if feminism can be silenced yet, all its gains will surely be overturned.

Anti-abortionists put great energy into getting their cause before the courts. Since the 1970s, no complaint has been too small, for, once before a judge, it might be argued and appealed all the way to the Supreme Court of Canada, which anti-abortionists believed would surely rule that all abortions should be banned.

So, for example, in October, 1977, 25 Vancouver Island doctors calling themselves Physicians for Life, placed an ad in *The Victorian*, a weekly paper. It offered to pay cash for unwanted babies. "If a pregnant woman has the right to abort the unborn child in her womb, why can't she sell the fetus instead," Nanaimo child psychiatrist Phillip Ney argued to the *Vancouver Sun*.[7] Reportedly, the doctors hoped to be charged with an offence so they could go to court and get the fetus declared to be a human being. The Canadian Criminal Code defined human beings, then and now, as those who had proceeded through the birth canal and begun to breathe independently, and the fetus was consistently ruled to have no legal status. In order to equate abortion with murder, it is necessary that the victim be legally human. However, the ad was dismissed with a chuckle by the attorney-general, with concurrence of the BC Medical Association.[8] Still beating this drum, Dr. Ney got a standing ovation at an anti-abortion conference at UBC in June 1979, when his passion for 'life' led him to advise:

> Snatch an aborted baby out of the operating room. If it dies, report the doctor to the College of Physicians and Surgeons, suggesting a charge of negligence.[9]

But the tactic used most often in BC, from the mid-1970s to the late 1980s, was to seize hold of the publicly-funded, community-controlled hospital system. In no other province was this scheme used so extensively.

During the 1970s and 1980s, there were just over 100 publicly-funded hospitals in British Columbia. The vast majority did few or no abortions, and the new law of 1969 did not rectify that. Investigations during these years showed that between 49 and 67 of the province's public hospitals simply refused to set up the necessary therapeutic abortion committees.[10] The law gave hospitals that leverage. Vancouver General, Royal Columbian, Lions Gate, Victoria General, and Victoria's Royal Jubilee Hospital, in the urban centres, did the majority of abortions in BC. They soon adopted residency requirements, which shut out women from elsewhere in the province.[11] Most BC women who were unwillingly pregnant had only the age-old choice between giving birth, aborting themselves, or having the luck to find a backstreet practitioner — whose ministrations they might not survive. That is still the case today.

Publicly-funded hospitals had publicly-elected trustees, and it was generally cheap and simple to become a voting member of a hospital society. At Vancouver General, it required only filling out a form and paying two dollars. The Pro-Life Society turned the usually sleepy VGH Annual General Meeting into a challenge in 1975 by signing up hundreds into the hospital society. Its candidates lost, but the following year, voters at the AGM rose to 500. Again, the anti-abortion candidates lost, and the hospital continued its fairly liberal abortion policy. By 1977, the race started early, and by the cut-off date a month before the AGM, the meeting was expected to draw more than 2000 people. Although only one-third, or six seats, on the board were vacant, there was nervous apprehension about Pro-Life's intentions.[12] Facing that threat, a coalition of women's groups, including the Vancouver Status of Women, the Vancouver Women's Health Collective, and the Women's Book Store, conducted its own sign-up campaign. Earlier pro-choice groups in BC had folded after Dr. Morgentaler was freed from prison by the Parti Québecois, in late 1976.

On the evening of April 20, 1977, the atmosphere was electric at the Hyatt Regency Hotel, as bus after bus from Surrey, Chilliwack, Abbotsford, and other parts of the Fraser Valley discharged 'pro-life' supporters into the lobby. Quick thinking by a hospital administrator saved the day. It was moved and carried that only residents of Vancouver be accepted as voting members in the society.[13]

But warning had been given: careful planning would be needed to protect the hospital board from an anti-abortion takeover. The hospital itself was concerned, and so were feminists. By January, 1978, a new group was begun, involving women in the small early wave of professionals — those who had recently broken through the quota system and obtained degrees in medicine and law. Dr. Liz Whynot and lawyer Barb Findlay (before she abandoned using upper-case letters in her name) were among them. Another was Hilda Thomas, an instructor in English at UBC, and, at the time, an NDP-appointed member of the VGH board.

At an early meeting, another person appeared and sat quietly at the back. She gave her name as Betty Green, but she was not recognized, at first, as the president of the Pro-Life Society. The feminists, who called their group Concerned Citizens for Choice on Abortion (CCCA), were horrified to find it had been infiltrated, and they closed it to new members. After passing a security check, I was one of the last to win admittance, and I attended my first CCCA meeting on April 30, 1978.

CCCA was active for more than a decade and did stellar work for women's rights and for repeal of the abortion law. Without an office, officers, or a reliable income, the group's frequent public events gave it a high profile, and it was looked to for inspiration and guidance by pro-choice groups around the province.

In an extraordinary effort, CCCA signed-up more than 4000 pro-choice members of VGH in 1978. By July, however, the hospital reported that 40,000 application forms were in circulation.[14] No-one knew how many 'pro-lifers' there were, although Betty Green later confessed her campaign had "not been as successful as hoped."[15] "It just staggers the mind," was the hospital's comment, as it worried about finding a venue large enough for the September meeting.[16]

However, another development involving women upstaged the titanic battle. During the summer of 1978, senior nurses at VGH began resigning, first in a trickle, then in a flood, to demand their inclusion in decision-making bodies and protest demeaning treatment by superiors. Half-hearted gestures by the hospital failed to conciliate them. Suddenly, a truly ham-fisted solution was imposed. Socred health minister Bob McClelland placed the hospital under provincial trusteeship. A retired RCMP officer was appointed its president, and he assumed all the powers of the board of directors. McClelland also cancelled the VGH AGM "because of an expected battle over abortions."[17]

Taking-over hospital boards became the preferred method for exercising anti-abortion power. In June, 1978, two anti-abortionists were elected in Powell River, joining two other Pro-Lifers on the thirteen member body.[18] At Lions Gate Hospital, anti-abortion candidates lost.[19] By 1979, the battle for control of hospital boards had spread to Victoria, Williams Lake, Fort St. John, Richmond, Langley, Abbotsford, and, most dramatically, to Surrey, with mixed results. There were both pro-choice and anti-abortion victories. Anti-abortion candidates were successful at Lions Gate in 1979. Vancouver General Hospital did not return to publicly electing its board of directors, but in many parts of the province, feminists rushed to sign up members before each local hospital AGM — and this had to be repeated again the next year. It was exhausting.

Eight years after Canada approved the practice of very-circumscribed therapeutic abortions, a report card was issued. February 1977 saw the release of the Badgley Report, the result of a two-year investigation into the "Operation of the Abortion Law," commissioned by the federal Liberals. Every complaint made by feminists was underscored in it: widespread unevenness in interpreting the law, an average delay of two months between the time a woman first contacted a (sympathetic) doctor and when she got an abortion; a pronounced complications rate directly attributable to those delays. Getting an abortion was "illusory for many Canadian women," and "often a matter of chance," said the report. The complications rate could be cut if there were "specially equipped regional centres" for the procedure — in other words, abortion clinics.[20] The government quickly shelved the report.

Meanwhile, the Health Sub-Committee of the BC Federation of Women — founded in 1974 — conducted a minimally-funded but ambitious study on the availability of abortion in the province. Their *1977 Abortion Handbook for British Columbia* reported that of 103 public general hospitals in BC, only 53 had therapeutic abortion committees; 40 did not. The remainder were in communities too small to meet the federal guidelines, which required at least four pro-choice doctors on staff (three for the TAC and the fourth to perform the operation). The researchers found it took an average of eight weeks to get an abortion after a woman found a sympathetic doctor, and it was frequently impossible to get one within the 12-week limit imposed by many hospitals. After fourteen weeks of pregnancy, the procedures used were much more traumatic to the woman and had much greater risk of complications. These 'late abortions' involved injecting either a saline solution or the hormone prostaglandin into the uterus, which resulted in the woman undergoing labour for from five to 24 hours and then expelling a dead fetus and placenta. The other method, hysterotomy, was like a

Caesarean section, entailing major surgery and leaving a woman permanently sterile. The *Handbook*, a highly-valuable resource, identified seven parts of BC where anti-abortionists dominated hospital policy.[21]

After September 1978, CCCA effectively dissolved. It was still needed but how to generate interest, now that VGH no longer had an elected board? Events in Europe helped revive it. At a June 1978 meeting in London, feminists from thirteen nations founded the International Campaign for Abortion Rights (ICAR) and notified feminists around the world. In Vancouver, a new group of thirty pro-choice activists crowded into a meeting to re-form CCCA on November 22, 1978. We agreed to add "Repeal Abortion from the Criminal Code," to the CCCA slogan of "Defend a Woman's Right to Choose," and to organize a demonstration on March 31, 1979, ICAR's date for co-ordinated actions worldwide. The ICAR Manifesto ended with:

You do not beg for a just right. You fight for it. And we are fighting.[22]

A 100,000-strong demonstration in Rome had, not only won Italy's first legal abortions, but actually toppled the Christian Democrat government in 1976.[23] But victories for women usually generated a backlash, and *Roe v. Wade* in the US was trimmed by the Hyde Amendment in 1976. It cut off federal Medicaid to poor women seeking abortions. The result was inevitable. *Ms. Magazine* reported the death of Rosaura Jimenez, of Texas, who died of massive infection due to an illegal abortion in Mexico. She was forced to cross the border because she could not get an abortion in the US. Jimenez was a single parent raising a five-year-old daughter on welfare, working part-time at an electronics plant. She was six months away from getting a bachelor's degree in education. Jimenez was described as "the Hyde Amendment's first reported victim."[24]

Similarly, in the UK, the liberalized law of 1967 was subject to a series of parliamentary attacks. But in November, 1978, another ambitious feminist effort was extraordinarily successful. The British National Abortion Campaign (NAC — not to be confused with the Canadian National Action Committee on the Status of Women, also known as NAC) joined with the Labour Party Abortion Rights Committee (LARC). Together they held a conference for union members on how to defend abortion rights, which was attended by nearly 500 women and men. Delegates then went to the annual meeting of the Trades Union Congress (TUC), equivalent to the Canadian Labour Congress, and won a vote pledging the TUC to fight against any further legislative moves to restrict abortion. A sixth effort to curb abortion had recently been put before parliament by Conservative MP John Corrie.

British NAC's careful plans reached a crescendo on October 28, 1979, when, true to its pledge, the TUC organized a mammoth demonstration in London against the Corrie Bill. The turnout was greater than 50,000, a dramatic expression of links between feminists and the labour movement. With such a crowd in the streets, debate on the Corrie Bill crumpled, and MPs voted it down.[25] Jubilation!

The link with labour was paying off in Québec, too. "Abortion-performing clinic exists uneasily in Québec" said the *Vancouver Sun* on December 17, 1979: "Something important is happening down a clean, airy corridor...of the Confederation of National Trade Unions building in Québec City. [It is] the Centre de Santé pour les Femmes, a woman-organized health centre that gives advice on family planning, contraception, birth, and the menopause. And that performs abortions."[26]

A woman-founded, women-run abortion clinic? It happened in Québec nearly a decade before it happened in British Columbia. And only because the labour movement gave space in its offices and helped to fund it. Feminists in Québec pushed on after Dr. Morgentaler was released from jail and demanded that the PQ government authorize more abortion clinics. This defied the Canadian Criminal Code, but the strength of the separatist movement kept Ottawa off Québec's back. Even in Québec, however, the feminist-controlled Centre de Santé pour les Femmes was unique.

Because VGH no longer had elected trustees, CCCA was not bound to fight on that terrain and was able to focus on the larger issue of repealing the law. Anti-abortionists were only our secondary foe, we argued: they were pressuring the federal government for a change in the law, too — a ban on all abortions. It was the Criminal Code that must be defeated to win legal and accessible abortion. CCCA's March 31, 1979 demonstration for abortion law repeal was endorsed by nearly fifty organizations and drew out 300 people. There was some disappointment that the turnout had dropped from the 700 who came out to the CCCA demo organized on July 28, 1978 by Jackie Simpson and me. It always took effort to pull the pro-choice majority of the population into active participation in the movement, and that effort had its ups and downs.

During 1979 and early 1980, CCCA activists included Vicki Camp, Anne Dwyer, Cynthia Flood (who left the Trotskyist movement in 1974), Jeanette Frost, Sharon Hager, Jan Lancaster — a staffer at the YWCA — Dr. Lynne Potter of the Pine Free Clinic, Debra Rooney, Tessa Stewart, Nancy Wiggs, and Ann Thomson. Only Sharon Hager and I were Trotskyists. Other non-Trotskyists, such as Dita Gill, Julie Healey, Evelyn Leaf, Danielle Sclaratta, Jenifer Svendsen and Jean Young also contributed.

The hospital board election season was full of angry battles in 1979, but the race at Surrey Memorial on June 20 was the cliffhanger. There were already two anti-abortion trustees; if they won all three vacancies, they would be close to controlling the eleven-member board. Doctors Silvia Glen and Pat Blackshaw helped spark a pro-choice organizing drive, which signed up 2500 people. But more than 5000 streamed into the AGM, and on first count, two of the three board positions went to anti-abortion candidates. It took two recounts to confirm that the pro-choice candidates had actually won, by 58 votes.[27] Whew! But in fact that was only the beginning of a lengthy and dramatic contest in Surrey.

Throughout these decades, the Social Credit (Socred) BC government was decidedly against abortion.In November, 1979, a new health minister, Rafe Mair, began his term by announcing he would lower the number of abortions.[28] Almost at once, some hospitals stiffened up. "It is becoming tougher, not easier, for women in some parts of BC to get abortions in their local hospitals,"reported the *Vancouver Sun*. The story named ten communities, including all the suburbs of Vancouver as well as most of the Okanagan, Prince Rupert, and Nanaimo, where restrictions were multiplying and abortion approvals dropping. Many out-of-town women were showing up at VGH, which had finally dropped its local residency requirement, and thousands more went to Washington state for abortions.[29] Nonetheless, Mair fired off a letter to all hospitals, in which he said abortion was "morally offensive"to his "personal feelings."[30]

Immediate condemnation came from hospital administrators[31] and feminists.[32] Dr. Lynne Potter of CCCA said, "Mair would be better off to put his energy into distributing birth control literature, especially to young people."[33] At the Pine Free Clinic on West Fourth Avenue, where Dr. Potter worked, there was a constant stream of confused and frequently desperate teen-agers, who had no reliable source of information about sex, sexual diseases, birth control, pregnancy, abortion, childbirth, childcare, etc.

A January 15 editorial in the *Vancouver Sun* questioned "Mair's Law." "Where was provincial Health Minister Rafe Mair when lessons in political sophistication were taught?" It argued that no government could legislate an end to abortions, for women would seek them anyway, wherever they could. The next day, Mair announced he preferred sex education to abortions. He clearly meant to teach the quite-unenforceable method of chastity. Then he hopped on a plane for a two-week holiday.[34]

At Victoria General, the TAC was quick to pick up on Mair's cue. In the first two weeks of 1980, it approved only four out of 31 abortion applications, although, previously, it had approved 99 per cent of them. A single TAC served both hospitals in Victoria, but when approvals at Vic General dwindled to zero, Royal Jubilee Hospital set up its own TAC, which approved the applications Vic General turned down.[35]

The short-lived Joe Clark government fell and a federal election on February 18, 1980 returned Pierre Trudeau and the Liberals to government in Ottawa. Anti-abortionists did their utmost to unseat NDPers, especially MPs Svend Robinson and Margaret Mitchell, who had filibustered an anti-abortion debate in the Commons to death. Robinson and Mitchell were re-elected.

Soon afterward, an uproar developed on Vancouver City Council. The March 4 meeting considered a proposal for a grant to the Vancouver Status of Women. Councillor Bernice Gerard objected, accusing VSW of "pro-abortion" work. She waved copies of the VSW paper, *Kinesis*, and the Newsletter of the BC Teachers' Federation Status of Women Committee, called herself a feminist, and said she opposed giving taxpayers' money to a group of "activist gays teaching in little Catholic schools." Councillor Marguerite Ford explained the sexual orientation story had not run in *Kinesis*, and Councillor Darlene Marzari asked how Gerard could call herself a feminist while opposing a group that did advocacy work for women. Gerard maintained she was a feminist: "I don't have to accept their definition...They can't just classify me out." The *Vancouver Sun* quoted Marzari accusing Gerard of "outright lies, outright slander," and of misleading "the gullible and vulnerable males that don't know their ass from their elbow." Not all the males considered themselves gullible, and Councillor Harry Rankin warned against returning to the days when women aborted themselves with coathangers. Mayor Jack Volrich called a five-minute recess in the midst of general clamour, as four Councillors tried to outshout one another. The *Sun* described it this way:

> The adjournment came as Rankin, who had the floor, called [Councillor George] Puil a "sawed-off little runt" and said Gerard produced documents critical of the Vancouver Status of Women with the same discrimination as a monkey "producing peanuts at a zoo."[36]

The shouting continued at the April 29 Council meeting, but VSW did not get its grant.[37] The verdict of voters came the following November, when Mike Harcourt was elected mayor, and Bernice Gerard and her anti-VSW co-thinker Doug Little were defeated. The far-left Harry Rankin, as usual in his long career, topped the polls.

CCCA's response to Rafe Mair was to organize a day-long conference for pro-choicers on March 22, 1980. It was a veritable war-council, with groups from the lower mainland and Fraser Valley, Vancouver Island, and the Kootenays. "An exciting, energizing day,"[38] said *Kinesis*.

For CCCA, the most important workshop was on repealing the abortion laws. Jointly facilitating it were Joan Newbigging of the Trotskyist Revolutionary Workers League (RWL),[39] and Margaret Birrell, Woman's Organizer of the BC NDP. Their proposal to a plenary session was adopted enthusiastically: to hold a major action in late November, coinciding with the convention of the BC Federation of Labor. Dr. Henry Morgentaler would be invited, and speakers would be sought from the US and from the Labor Party Abortion Rights Campaign in Britain. An international focus.

Soon after, Rafe Mair was in action again. At the Vancouver Centre Socred constituency office, he shared a platform with Betty Green at a public meeting in late May. Green announced plans for a counselling service in eight to ten BC communities. Mair announced a pilot project, which would "reduce the number of abortions" in the province.

Commented the *Vancouver Sun*, "Mair said he does not know if the Birthright group, which counsels pregnant women against having abortions, will be a participant in the project.[40] An editorial titled "Starting at the middle" advised "The province does not need a program oriented toward the Birthright method of counselling women *after* they become pregnant with an unwanted child."[41]

CCCA responded to Mair with a public meeting. A standing-room only crowd pushed into Robson Square media centre on July 11, 1980.[42]

Over the summer, both Vancouver dailies ran in-depth series on birth control and abortion. A very *a propos* piece by Dr. Marlene Hunter of the north shore addressed the stakes for hospitals. Describing a competent hospital board nominee, Dr. Hunter asked: "Has a candidate had years of experience in building hospitals, in extended-care units, in the needs of engineering, construction, architecture, union negotiation, litigation, community service, in women's opinion?" In her view, doctors have the right to perform abortions or not, according to their consciences, but "To deny any woman the option of abortion...can be adequately described by only one word: punitive."[43]

With summer, the season of hospital board elections began. The outcomes seesawed from right to left and back. On June 18, 1980, all the vacant seats at Langley Memorial Hospital were taken by anti-abortionists. In Richmond on June 26, the election went the other way, and two of the three candidates elected were pro-choice. Lions Gate Hospital remained pro-choice, in a meeting with 4000 voters that was as raucous as a political convention. Then came a series of pro-choice defeats. The first, and most dramatic, was in Surrey, followed the next evening at Victoria General — with a turnout of 1500 — and after that, at Royal Jubilee Hospital, in which 500 people voted, more than six times the number in 1979.

In Surrey, on September 24, anti-abortionists obtained a majority on the hospital board and pledged a rapid end to the hospital's TAC. From that moment until the end of the year, the battle at Surrey Memorial was news across Canada. The whole hierarchy of power in BC was dragged into it, as well as the numberless women whose futures were at stake. The medical staff saw it coming, and two weeks before the election meeting, they had voted unanimously to support abortions at the hospital. But what could they do? The only recourse was to appeal to Rafe Mair to "intervene and prevent this single issue from dominating...[the] running of a most complex and extremely important community facility."[44] It was like asking the fox to guard the hen house.

Nearly a week later, the health minister deigned to notice the situation, commenting to the *Vancouver Sun* that he was very concerned by the turn of events in Surrey. He said that abortion was Ottawa's responsibility. "My obligation is to see that the hospital is well run," he cogitated, adding that he did not plan to "interfere" in Surrey unless the quality of health care was "threatened."[45]

A squabble developed between the group around Margaret Birrell in the NDP Women's Rights Committee and some members of the RWL then participating in CCCA. Even though Birrell had put the motion for a Day of Declaration before the CCCA-sponsored conference on March 22, in the July-August issue of *Priorities*, published by the NDP WRC, she wrote that CCCA didn't really believe in repealing the law, after all.[46] Then on September 29, 1980, the NDP women founded their own pro-choice group, dubbed the Repeal 251 Committee. (Section 251 of the Criminal Code was the 1969 abortion law; it had previously been numbered 237.) It was to be a lobby group, and therein lay part of the rub: for CCCA, lobbying the federal government was considered wasted effort, and the only way to win repeal was to mobilize actions on the ground. The disagreement was partly over tactics, and largely a personality dispute and a power play. The NDP women scheduled something else for November 29, forcing CCCA to move its Day of Declaration to November 30 and rename it a Day of Action.

The NDP women dropped out of CCCA, and the BC Federation of Labor permitted only the Repeal 251 Committee to put up an information table at its convention — thereby blocking any address to the delegates by Ann Kingsbury of the British Labour Party Abortion Rights Committee (LARC), who was in Vancouver at the invitation of CCCA.

As expected, the new board at Surrey Memorial Hospital voted to dissolve the therapeutic abortion committee at its first meeting, on October 2.[47] On October 6, the hospital's physicians voted non-confidence in the board and called on Mair to overturn the decision on the TAC. If the dispute was not resolved by November 15, doctors would withdraw from all 20 administrative committees — thus bringing most of the hospital to a halt.[48] The health minister had just set out on a month-long jaunt to Britain, which is why the doctors' deadline was set so far into the future.

Meantime, the academic journal *Canadian Women's Studies* ran an article by Dr. May Cohen of McMaster University. Summarizing the impact of the 1969 abortion law, Cohen quoted the renowned Population Council in New York:

> ...India and Canada share the dubious honour of having the highest rate of second trimester abortions (after the 13th week of pregnancy) in the world. In India, this is due to poor access to medical care, but in Canada, it is due to the fact that...of all the western countries, Canada has the most restrictive law and the most cumbersome authorisation procedures.[49]

Rafe Mair returned to BC on November 3 and began to consider the situation at Surrey Memorial. He held a meeting or two, then seemed to forget about the crisis. When November 15 came with no resolution, the 150 members of the medical staff resigned from hospital committees as they'd said they would.[50]

It was an unprecedented revolt, and it generated headlines and debate across the country. For three weeks the doctors' strike held. Reluctantly, slowly, the board came around, agreed to re-instate the TAC and to accept the doctors' nominees for its composition.[51] By December 4, the doctors had won a clear victory for medical autonomy and a liberal pro-choice policy. Almost unnoticed was the fate of *women*, who were seldom mentioned by any side.

CCCA's November 30 rally was a great success. As the speakers took their seats onstage at Kitsilano High, and chairperson Joyce Meissenheimer, a Trotskyist and also member of the NDP provincial executive committee, was about to open the meeting, a tall latecomer hurried down the aisle. 'Joyce told me I'd better be here, or I'd never live it down,' called out Mike Harcourt, NDP mayor-elect of Vancouver. Two weeks after his victory, he hadn't taken office yet, but he'd come, to CCCA's surprise, to introduce Dr. Henry Morgentaler and welcome him to the city. The mayor's appearance signaled the enormous respect for the doctor, held, then and still, by supporters of social justice.

Seated beside Dr. Morgentaler were Anne Kingsbury of British LARC, Dr. Silvia Glen of Surrey Memorial, and Dorothy Young Sale of the US NOW. Everyone loves a success story, and when Ann Kingsbury stood up to tell how feminists had got the labour movement to call the enormous demonstration that defeated an anti-abortion bill, there was enthusiastic applause. Then a duo consisting of singers Sharon Hazelwood and Celia O'Neill, performed the Leon Rosselson song, *'Don't Get Married, Girls.'* Despite its anti-male lyrics at a rally welcoming the movement's most honoured male doctor, the song broke the tension, brought laughter, and was prominent in media coverage of the event:

> *Don't get married, girls, it's very badly paid.*
> *You may start off as the mistress*
> *but you end up as the maid.*
> *Change your lover every Friday,*
> *take up tennis, be a nurse,*
> *But don't get married because marriage is a curse.*

At last came the moment everyone was waiting for. Even before Dr. Henry Morgentaler rose to speak "The crowd had risen in one movement to greet the bearded Montréal doctor when he stepped to the microphone..."[52]

'What sustained me during my persecution [in jail, where he suffered a heart attack after being tossed naked into solitary confinement] was the support of women across Canada,' said the doctor. He said he had accepted CCCA's invitation to speak because 'I was outraged at what happened in Surrey.' With a shrug toward the protesters milling outside, Dr. Morgentaler called them "fanatical busybodies, who want to impose their views on everybody." "They're not 'pro-life," he said. We are pro-life! It is we who care about the quality of women's lives, who fight for good medical care and for children who are wanted and loved."[53]

The Canadian Supreme Court reserved its decision on hearing the government's appeal against Joe Borowski. The Manitoban had won his suit holding the federal Liberals responsible for allowing therapeutic abortions, which he claimed were illegal and which tax money should not support.[54]

Like tar-baby, the 1969 amended abortion law was sticky. It had no friends, yet neither the women's movement, the anti-abortionists, nor anyone in-between could shake free of it. Only in Canada, you say? Yes, unambivalently Canadian.

CHAPTER 9

HOSPITAL ELECTION BATTLES: II

Pierre Trudeau returned to the prime minister's office in 1980 with a mission: he would repatriate the constitution. The work progressed rapidly, and in only two years it was done. On April 17, 1982, the Queen proclaimed the new Canadian Constitution. The voting public was not consulted, and self-determination, or separatism, for Québec was presumably contained and had no future.

Nonetheless, it didn't happen without protest. The Liberals were apparently startled to find that objections came from such negligible Canadians as the First Nations, human rights groups, and women. Sparked by Doris Anderson, a prominent Liberal, more than 1300 women flew to Ottawa in February, 1981, for a non-partisan protest conference on women and the constitution.[1] Their work led to adding a new section to the Charter, Section 28, in which men and women are equal under the law,[2] as well as strengthening the principle of non-discrimination in Section 15.[3] These were important additions to the final text. The crucial Section 7 recognizes that "everyone has the right to life, liberty and security of the person."

Feminists worried that Section 7 might be used to confer personhood on the fetus and argued strongly for guarantees for abortion in the Constitution and Charter.[4] Anti-abortionists wanted unalterable rights for the "unborn."

The anti-choice view was gaining steam elsewhere. With high-profile anti-abortionist Ronald Reagan elected to the White House in 1980, expectations rose that the US Constitution would be amended to ban abortions. On the 8th anniversary of the *Roe v. Wade* decision, January, 1981, a resolution was introduced into the Senate for a 'Human Life Amendment,' which would designate the embryo as a person from the moment of conception. Women who had abortions or used some types of birth control would then face life in prison, or even the death penalty for premeditated murder.[5] The process for amending the US Constitution is lengthy and difficult, and the proposal, later called the Hatch Amendment, failed in the end. The Irish Republic, however, installed a constitutional ban on abortion in 1983. In most parts of the world, the procedure was still illegal.

Anti-abortionists in Canada took up the cause with enthusiasm — only to run into a snarl with the Catholic Church in Toronto. In his book, *Catholics Against the Church,* Michael W. Cuneo details the campaign of lay Catholic "militants" on the issue in the early 1980s: "...anti-abortionism for many... had become a definitive badge of Catholic authenticity...and any Catholic who did not wear this badge proudly was branded a traitor to the faith."[6]

It was a shock, then, to find some of the highest-ranking churchmen insufficiently devout on the issue. Emmett Cardinal Carter, archbishop of Toronto, met privately with Trudeau in early 1981 and afterward announced his satisfaction that the proposed Charter did not provide for abortion on demand. Because it had "many positive values," despite no clause on fetal rights, the Cardinal would not oppose it on moral or religious grounds.[7]

Anti-abortionists responded with denunciations in the public dailies and with appeals over the Cardinal's head to Rome. Gwen Landolt, Campaign Life's chief legal advisor, fumed in the *Toronto Star*: "...in ten years of fighting abortion it never entered my mind a Catholic cardinal could take the stand Carter has taken."[8] The Cardinal's response was carried in all three Toronto papers at the end of April. That triggered the first volley to Rome, fired by the hot-headed Family Life Survival Fund in Prince George, BC. Its letter to Pope John Paul II labeled Carter a "traitor" and "a Judas" and urged the pontiff to change the Cardinal's mind "before it was too late."[9] Two weeks later, the national group Campaign Life sent a similar missive to the pope, describing Carter's position as, in Cuneo's terms, "an act of sabotage against the pro-life movement."[10] The pope's response is not known. However, he was leading a massive, but losing battle against an Italian referendum on abortion at exactly that time. The pro-choice victory in Italy, 70% in favour of retaining partial legalization of abortion, was even more pronounced since the vote began only four days after an assassination attempt on the pope, which might have drawn sympathy to his cause.

In what Cuneo says was "fast becoming a cold war" within Canadian Catholicism,[11] anti-abortionists found one church leader worthy of admiration: Archbishop of Winnipeg Adam Exner — who moved to Vancouver in 1991. *The Interim,* launched by Campaign Life in May 1983, wrote: "Bishop Exner is the only Bishop in Canada who has spoken up loud and clear on the subject of abortion."[12] The Charter of Rights and Freedoms, nonetheless, makes no mention of either abortion or "the unborn."

While this debate was going on in central Canada, the west, as usual, had little news of it and was mostly removed from the ruckus. Pro-Choice groups in BC continued to focus on repealing the law and on endless hospital board contests.

Although the 1981 International Women's Day rally in Vancouver heard nothing about abortion, it was the main theme of the Montréal IWD rally. 6000 marchers demanded the Parti Québecois government open more abortion clinics, in a demonstration called jointly by the four major labour federations. After vociferous feminist insistence, the issue of abortion had become part of Québec's agenda against federalism.

Support from labour was building in British Columbia, too, though on a smaller scale. On April 15, 1981, delegates to my union, the BC Teachers' Federation, voted overwhelmingly at its AGM for a three-part policy supporting women's right to choose. This policy withstood annual attacks from anti-choice teachers for nearly a decade.

In 1981, battles to control BC hospitals intensified. Small, local pro-choice groups did valiant work, but anti-abortion candidates captured or maintained the majority on six hospital boards: Victoria General, Richmond, Surrey, Powell River, Prince George and Langley. Unexpectedly, these boards did not move to ban abortion immediately. Part of the reason why had to do with another blow-up in Surrey.

Six months to the day after the medical staff brought the anti-abortion board to its knees, abortions were again banned at Surrey Memorial Hospital. The issue was not even on the agenda for the trustees' meeting on June 4, 1981; a committee report triggered the board's knee-jerk response. This caused more than half of the 150 doctors on staff to launch a furious repudiation of the board and call for the health minister to replace it with a public trustee. They also wanted to remove hospital boards' authority over therapeutic abortion committees, and attempted to get Surrey Memorial's accreditation lifted.[13]

Jim Nielsen had replaced Rafe Mair as health minister, and he made soothing sounds but took no action.[14] Dr. Pat Blackshaw, deputy head of the medical staff objected. "The doctors at Surrey Memorial have been waiting too long for a solution which is always supposed to be coming next week," she said. The doctors gave Nielsen a month to place the hospital under trusteeship. Hostility between zealous board members and the medical staff had reached such a pitch, Blackshaw told *The Province,* that board members called the doctors "neo-Nazis" and suggested they did abortions only for the money.[15] Chairman Lyle MacMillan took exception to the doctors' charge that the board was interested solely in the issue of abortion.[16]

Meanwhile, at Burnaby General Hospital, the TAC pushed its colleagues to submit two letters, rather than one, to support referrals for abortions. When general practitioners voted that down, TAC members resigned in protest. Here, the strikers — physicians on the TAC — were opposed to abortions, in contrast to the situation in Surrey.[17] The demand for an additional letter won out in Burnaby.

Near the end of June 1981, four anti-abortion candidates were elected at Chilliwack General Hospital, giving the group a footing but not control there.[18] Anti-abortionists had a strong majority already at the June 29 AGM in Richmond — the vote was reportedly 378 to 124[19] — when twenty-five late-comers stormed the doors after the meeting began. A grim-faced man in a white cowboy hat scuffled with guards. He was stopped but broke into a defiant shout with upraised fist, as five or six others pushed their way in behind him.[20] But at its first meeting, the new board in Richmond referred the membership's call for a ban on abortions for further study. Clearly, they thought it wiser to avoid a head-on clash with the medical staff, which had already threatened an administrative strike if the TAC were dissolved. Health minister Nielsen, who represented Richmond, distanced himself from the fray while insisting he wouldn't tolerate "politics" on the hospital board.[21]

After dithering for two months, Nielsen acted on the Surrey crisis. He appointed Victoria physician Dr. Ray LeHuquet to investigate and report to him directly. That did not quell the uproar. Three weeks later, on August 12, 1981, LeHuquet was made public trustee of the hospital, with the proviso that the elected board would remain in place. Nielsen then cancelled the AGM scheduled for September 9, making it clear that he wanted no challenge to the existing anti-abortion board. LeHuquet was given broad powers, but he delegated most of them back to the board.[22] The ban on abortions continued until February, 1982, eight months after it was imposed.[23]

However, anti-abortionists failed to topple the incumbent, pro-choice majority at Lions Gate Hospital in North Vancouver on September 2. Women of the North Shore Association for the Right to Choose (NOR-SACA) phoned 4000 hospital members over the summer, urging them to attend the AGM and vote.[24]

When the evening came for the now-cancelled AGM in Surrey, anti-abortion activists were in an ugly mood. This was despite the continuing ban on the procedure. About 700 of them rallied on the hospital grounds and heard speakers attack the government for meddling. The board was doing just fine, and the government's intervention was unwarranted, shouted board member Tony Upton. After two hours of this, the crowd began a candlelight procession around the hospital grounds. They were greatly out-numbered, but half a dozen members of Surrey-Delta Association for the Right to Choose (ARC) felt compelled to represent the pro-choice side. Reported the *Vancouver Sun*, "Within minutes a man, who had earlier addressed the meeting from the floor, grabbed the placard of pro-choicer Vicky O'Connor and shoved her to the ground." A photo showed a terrified woman, looking over her shoulder at a man following close behind her. His picket sign was ready to descend on her head; in his other hand, he crumpled the sign she had been carrying. When he was pulled off O'Connor, the unidentified man grabbed the sign of another pro-choice woman and broke its handle. The broken handle struck her in the face.[25]

Immediately, the all-male anti-abortion faction began denying responsibility for the fracas, while mounting a ferocious campaign for the media to report the events its way. Pro-Life Society spokesman Allan Garneau, a school principal from Delta, said, "I will swear that those men did not lay a hand on or touch that woman." Surrey Pro-Life president Ben Schroeder reluctantly admitted that a pro-choice sign had been seized but said "He [the assailant] never hit the lady in the face or anything." Schroeder knew who to blame: "And then that lady just threw herself in among the group just as if she'd been hit. They were just trying to provoke something." But Vicky O'Connor showed her bruises to reporters and said that her friend, also attacked by anti-abortionists, was pregnant. "[He] told her to go have an abortion," she recalled.[26]

In an unusual twist, the writer and photographer assigned to the story publicly declared they had truthfully reported what they'd seen. The *Sun's* reporter Ted Townsend and photographer Mark Van Manen wrote another story to defend what they had already reported: that one woman had been pushed to the ground and another struck in the face with a broken picket by anti-abortionists.[27] *Province* cartoonist Robert Krieger also departed from tradition by submitting a letter to the editor defending his cartoon. It showed a trembling woman with a sign saying 'Free choice on abortion' being threatened by a burly man with a raised fist and a 'Pro-Life' placard. The man is snarling, "...or I'll kill ya!!!" Krieger said he meant to highlight the "hypocrisy" in the "deplorable behavior demonstrated by anti-abortionists Sept. 9 at Surrey Memorial Hospital," and he was surprised that was not understood by readers.[28]

There was no donnybrook at the election meeting the following evening, September 10, 1981 — just an anti-abortion victory that gave them control of Victoria General Hospital. More than 7000 people had signed membership forms, requiring rental of Memorial Arena for the meeting. Although half that number showed up, the incumbent pro-choice candidates were thoroughly defeated. Victorious Michael Hall-Patch, describing himself as a moderate, said he opposed abortion in any circumstance, even rape or incest. To avoid a collision with the medical staff, however, the new board would not abolish the TAC but apply "continual pressure to get doctors to see the law in a slightly different way." Defeated pro-choice candidate Cathy Mountain told of being phoned at home by anti-abortionists, who screamed "baby killer' at her.[29]

Two days later, on Saturday, September 12, 1981, both CCCA in Vancouver and CARAL in Victoria held demonstrations. Former Liberal cabinet minister, Iona Campagnolo, spoke to the rally in Victoria, holding a sign showing a coat-hanger with the caption "No! No!" In her view the Criminal Code was satisfactory: "Women have a right to abortion when the operation is necessary. The spirit of the law is being subverted [by anti-abortion hospital trustees]..." Glancing at the crowd, she challenged the government: "Social Credit has danced round this issue through three successive health ministers. They have to come out and support the law."[30]

In Vancouver, where September 12 was a sparkling late-summer day, CCCA made sure the NDP and labour sent speakers. Contingents from Nanaimo, Nelson, Powell River, and Terrace brought their banners, with the help of travel grants from CCCA. We had a rare and short-lived surplus from the collection at the Morgentaler meeting in 1980, and we used it to support groups fighting hospital elections. Pro-choice feminists came from the north shore, Richmond, Surrey, and Victoria, and the march from QE Theatre Plaza to Robson Square included groups from several unions. Addressing the rally, Dr. Silvia Glen of Surrey Memorial linked the fight at her hospital with Vic General, saying "What we are seeing is mob rule by narrow-minded bigots."[31] Then the microphone went dead just as CCCA spokesperson Wendy Francis-Oakley approached it. Apparently, an opponent on the Robson Square maintenance staff had cut the electricity. When chairperson Jan Lancaster announced this, the crowd took up a joking chant: "What do we want? Power! When we do want it? Now!" A battery-operated bullhorn saved the day. A few members of a minor ultra-left group stood in the crowd, incongruously chanting, "Hail the Red Army in Afghanistan." They were drowned out by women shouting "Not the church! Not the state! Women must control their fate!"

We were accustomed to being ignored by the media, but, to our astonishment, the CBC national TV news gave six minutes to the Vancouver march and reported a turnout of 1200 people. I had carefully noted every marcher: by my count, there were about 500. The cameras gave prominent coverage to a very-pregnant Astrid Davidson of the BC Federation of Labor, who led the march wearing a scarlet dress and holding her four-year-old daughter's hand. It was wonderful! Was the media's turn-around due to the scandalous behaviour of anti-abortionists in Richmond and in Surrey just days before?

Langley anti-abortionists won control of their hospital board on September 15. Again, incoming trustees said they would achieve their ends by non-confrontational means. It was the second anti-abortion victory in a week.

To general surprise, anti-abortion candidates went down to defeat in Prince George, on September 22. It was another mammoth meeting for the size of the community: 1,000 people, four times the number in 1980. The hospital board had no-one left on it of the anti-abortion stripe.[32] The opposite happened in Fort. St. John, which already claimed to be an anti-abortion stronghold. On October 15, three candidates who opposed abortion were elected to the hospital board. Once more, citing Surrey Memorial, the Pro-Life Society said it didn't expect dramatic moves against the TAC.[33]

That followed an anti-abortion victory at Royal Jubilee Hospital in Victoria on October 8. They did not manage to control the board, because nine of the 13 members were political appointees. However, the situation was precarious for women in the capital region, since Royal Jubilee had been providing abortions to some of those turned down at Victoria General.[34] Within weeks, Campaign Life mailed out a letter urging a vote for the Socred slate, names enclosed, in the municipal elections. The reason was that Victoria city council appointed some members of the Royal Jubilee Hospital board.[35]

Now that they controlled the majority of hospital boards in the lower mainland and Victoria — the exceptions were Vancouver General, Lions Gate, and Royal Columbian — the anti-abortionists set about their new "persuasive" approach. Rather than ban abortions outright, they would issue new guidelines for approving them. In short, they aimed to drastically shrink the number of abortions performed, while paying lip-service to the public demand and support for the procedure.

For example, Richmond trustees voted to allow abortions to continue. However, an applicant would be subject to "thorough counselling" on "alternatives." If such counselling didn't change her mind, the woman had to co-sign her doctor's application to the TAC, indicating, in effect, that she knew what horrible thing she wanted to do. No abortions would be performed after the twelfth week of pregnancy, whereas the previous cut-off date had been twenty weeks at most hospitals. In this case, Richmond went further than Surrey did, where the cut-off date was set at eighteen weeks. The woman's doctor had to submit an additional letter to the TAC spelling out just how a continued pregnancy threatened her life or health. No longer would its members be selected by the medical staff; now the TAC would report directly to the hospital board.[36]

Similar highly-restrictive guidelines were adopted by other hospital boards. Only the spunky *Richmond Review,* published twice-weekly, found out what the trustees had decided in their in-camera session, and it printed a summary of the guidelines on its front page. The 'guidelines' approach did little to soothe relations between anti-abortion trustees and doctors, but it did reduce the number of abortions in BC. Friction continued at hospitals in Langley, Richmond, Surrey, and, especially, in Victoria.[37]

The offended medical staff at Victoria General rejected the guidelines and polled its members, showing that doctors preferred the guidelines in the Criminal Code. In retaliation, the trustees suspended the TAC in February, 1982, and no abortions were performed at the hospital in the ensuing months.[38] After it erupted into the news too many times, health minister Nielsen finally took notice and assigned Dr. Ray LeHuquet to look into the matter. LeHuquet was still public administrator of Surrey Memorial Hospital when, in October 1982, he added Victoria General to his responsibilities.

For awhile at Surrey Memorial, the dual authority of elected trustees and government appointed super-trustee LeHuquet continued, albeit shakily. The anti-abortionists succeeded in imposing their guidelines on the doctors and the rate of abortions dropped, but the board wasn't happy about co-existing with LeHuquet. They wanted the government out of their business. Trustees Tony Upton and Allan Garneau, both members of the Surrey-Delta Pro-Life Society, went to court demanding that the appointment of LeHuquet be quashed. The court did not agree.[39]

Then at Lions Gate, where anti-abortion trustees were in a minority, another lawsuit was filed. Trustees George Carruthers and Michael Whelton argued that the hospital approved abortions on frivolous and unnecessary grounds and asked the Federal Court of Canada to rule that 2000 abortions, done between September 1979 and December 1980, had been illegal. The community didn't like that. Three months afterward, on September 2, 1982, Carruthers and Whelton were defeated at the Lions Gate AGM. The new board was entirely pro-choice. The case went before a judge a week later and lurched along until May 1983, when the court upheld the hospital's generally pro-choice policy.[40]

During all this, the tiny, poor, loosely-organized and de-centralized pro-choice movement had done its utmost to get its message out and draw its supporters together. Only the North Shore group, NORSACA, had succeeded in organizing enough hospital society members to defeat the anti-abortion candidates at Lion's Gate, in 1982. Surrey-Delta ARC had no election meeting to work toward, and the group that had beat off anti-abortion candidates in Richmond in 1980 dissolved, leaving the entire burden to Emi Yoshida. She was a tireless worker but she could not do the job alone. In Victoria, the pro-choice CARAL chapter was an energetic and powerful group, headed by Maxine Boag, Jennifer Lowen, and Freya Korning, but they were unable to prevail against the anti-abortion and Socred alliance.

Between 8 and 15 activists formed the core of CCCA then, with others attending from time to time. Women who had been involved during part of 1980 continued on, including Rita Chudnovsky, a working mother and left activist; Krys Constabaris, a student; Joan Frost, a musician; Helen Glavina, a member of AUCE at UBC; Jan Lancaster, a staffer for the YWCA; Angela Schiwy, a working woman, and Michele Valiquette of the SFU Women's Centre. They were augmented by an enthusiastic new group drawn in by the Morgentaler, Kingsbury, and Sale rally the previous November. Among these were Marie Abdemalik, a high school student;

Marva Blackmore, temporarily a stay-at-home mom; Kathleen Eddy; Wendy Francis-Oakley, and Deb Patrick, who were recent university graduates; Judith Snider and Janet Vesterback, Vancouver teachers; and Melinda Suto, a professional woman. Shelley Rivkin from the NDP Women's Committee was angry that so few of her sisters had turned out for the Morgentaler meeting, and she made a point of attending CCCA meetings. Maureen Dymond of NORSACA often came, and Emi Yoshida from Richmond and Sandra Letts from Surrey were regulars. After the September, 1981 demo, we drew in arts-co-ordinator Gwen Kallio, and our first male activist, Jeff Finger. Two of the new women were from the neo-Maoist group In Struggle! The half-dozen women from the Trotskyist Revolutionary Workers League, who had worked in CCCA during 1980, had dropped to two: Barb Horst and me.

Jeff Finger volunteered to prepare a newsletter for CCCA. How proud we were of the first issue, dated December, 1981. The typed pages were photocopied, producing clear and readable text — in contrast to the Gestetnered efforts of years past. Eagerly, we printed 3000 copies of our first edition for less than $100; mailed 700 to the CCCA mailing list, and persuaded the feminist papers, *Kinesis* and *Priorities*, to stuff copies into their issues. The masthead featured CCCA's two demands: 'Repeal all anti-abortion laws,' and 'Defend a woman's right to choose.' The centerfold listed B.C. hospitals that had therapeutic abortion committees. There were 56, out of a hospital total of 105. The back cover listed organizations that endorsed CCCA's demands. In December, 1981, these included 4 pro-choice groups, 24 women's rights groups, 21 unions and labour organizations, 9 bodies of the BC NDP, 8 student groups, 6 political groups (including Liberal Party women) and 5 community organizations, 77 in all. The *Newsletter* came out for several years and was a major step forward for CCCA.

Another breakthrough came when the BC Federation of Women voted to sponsor a province-wide demonstration on abortion rights on Mother's Day 1982.

However, an ominous development came in December, 1981: the Canadian Supreme Court agreed to hear Joe Borowski's challenge to the constitutionality of the 1969 abortion law. Borowski had undertaken a dramatic 80-day hunger strike in Winnipeg the previous spring.[41] Now his suit, aimed at getting abortion banned in the new constitution, was no longer a joke.

Lawyer Gayle Raphanel met with CCCA to review the court's rationale. It had agreed to hear the case, brought by Borowski on behalf of the "unborn," since fetuses could not represent themselves. Feminists were alarmed that the court had given legal standing as an "interested" party to a man — who could never get pregnant — while presuming that pregnant women seeking abortions were beneficiaries of the law and had no interest in challenging it. The status of a fetus was already defined in the Criminal Code, in Section 206, which predated the 1969 amendments on abortion. Section 206 held that a "child becomes a human being" only when it has been born alive, breathing, with its own circulation independent of the mother.[42]

Already, organizations like the National Action Committee on the Status of Women (NAC) and the National Association of Women and the Law (NAWL) were making plans to intervene in the Borowski hearing. CCCA was too poor and too far away to take part in the court proceedings. Its role would be to inform and rally the troops at home. The date of the hearing was then unknown and might be more than a year away. Women's struggle for reproductive choice was far from over.

In 1982, CCCA organized two major actions, put out six copies of its *Newsletter* and a 52-page booklet, and followed pro-choice developments outside BC.

The often fractious process of jointly organizing a demonstration with the BC Federation of Women got underway in February, with a planning meeting at Trout Lake Community Centre. Then nearly eight years old, BCFW was a large, very-loosely knit body, somewhat unsure what it was about. When launched in 1974, the idea had been to join up all feminists in the province, and many small new groups formed under its banner. With funding from the Secretary of State, BCFW officers met regularly in locales around BC, but its members were so anxious not to tread on one another and so fearful of hierarchy, that little was agreed on beyond a broad feminism. Overworked member groups of BCFW had trouble sparing women to organize the Mother's Day 1982 abortion actions, but Nicole Kennedy from Rape Relief and Lorna Zaback from the Vancouver Women's Health Collective did meet regularly with CCCA. It scarcely needs saying that no money from government agencies, such as the Secretary of State, ever came the way of pro-choice groups, who were pitted against the government and a cherished law.

We felt the initial planning meeting on February 13 was well-attended. People came from 18 different organizations, including the Unitarian Church, the Canadian Union of Postal Workers, and many women's groups. One woman apiece came from BCFW groups in Port Hardy, Sardis, Victoria, and Vernon. The NDP Women's Rights Committee, still stand-offish toward CCCA, sent an "observer." No-one recognized Sissy von Dehn, an active anti-abortionist, who registered as "S.Dane" and claimed to be from the Vancouver Status of Women. She sat silently through the meeting, which adopted a plan for province-wide actions on Mother's Day, May 8.

A 52-page booklet that Marva Blackmore and I wrote was ready for the

Trout Lake planning meeting, and it sold out immediately. Lack of time and money prevented its being properly published, as we had intended when CCCA members voted to approve its contents. Titled *A Woman's Choice: A Strategy for the Abortion Rights Movement*, it was a handbook on how to organize. The chapter, "How to Fight and Win," written by me, explained that the pro-choice campaign was aimed toward all levels of government — just as the misnamed 'pro-life' movement was: "While anti-abortionists are a serious threat to our cause, they do not have the power to directly achieve their goal of outlawing abortion." They relied on lawmakers for that. As for tactics, "We in CCCA are convinced that lobbying has its place, but it is not the most effective way to campaign. Numbers are more persuasive than logic when dealing with politicians. Since numbers are more persuasive, there's more power in our numbers when all our supporters march with us down the street than when a few of them lobby."

For the first time, pro-choice actions were held simultaneously in several parts of the province. Powell River leafletted at a mall; Nanaimo showed a pro-choice videotape; Vernon women informed themselves about the Borowski challenge and drove to nearby towns to distribute leaflets and speak, and Victoria held a march and rally with a turnout of about 125. Prince George and Port Hardy women held events. The event in Terrace succeeded in getting a debate going in the local media. It was risky and daunting for women in smaller communities to go public about choice on abortion. Another first at this rally was that the BC Federation of Labor sent a letter to its affiliated unions urging endorsement and donations to CCCA. There was good media coverage both before and following the event, and the Borowski threat became better known.

In Vancouver, on May 8, a lively crowd of 600 marched to the Hotel Vancouver for a rally. Such extravagance brought criticism from within, but we'd rented the ballroom when we were still hoping to get an international speaker. That didn't work out, and the hotel was nervous when it found out CCCA dealt with abortion, but there were no disruptions.

In the April 1982 CCCA *Newsletter*, Melinda Suto's article "BC Hospital Scoreboard" tallied replies from 36 hospitals to a questionnaire on their abortion practices. Five turned down all applications. Only two — Lions Gate and the hospital on Saltspring Island — approved every request. Vancouver General and Surrey Memorial refused to divulge information, but Suto was able to document that 17 hospitals did 4,271 abortions in 1981, while turning 115 women down. This specific information fleshed out the annual report by Statistics Canada.

Our focus on organizing actions in the street set CCCA apart from the largest pro-choice group, the Canadian Abortion Rights Action League (CARAL), which conducted letter-writing campaigns and raised funds. It was headquartered in Toronto and had chapters across the country. Some, like the chapter in Victoria, were as radical in their tactics as CCCA was. The CARAL national AGM, at the end of April every year, was a highlight of the pro-choice movement. In 1982, CCCA managed to send Wendy Francis-Oakley to Toronto for that meeting, and she returned with electrifying news.

Always a keynote speaker for CARAL, Dr. Henry Morgentaler chose that venue to announce that he was "ready to jump in" the fight again, and he would establish (still illegal) abortion clinics across the country: "The best way to test the law is to set up clinics nation-wide," summarized the *Globe and Mail*.[43] Nothing about this blockbuster news appeared in the BC media. Morgentaler believed that if he could win three acquittals in Québec, then no jury in the country would convict him. He wanted to help the women of Toronto, who found it increasingly difficult to get hospital abortions, and in Alberta, "where 50 per cent of the women who want abortions must go to the United States." Already his clinic in Montréal drew women from seven provinces, because of the red tape and delays they met at home. The doctor dismissed the chances of Borowski's bid to ban abortions: "It's not going to have any consequence at all...It's preposterous for a man to want to delegate himself guardian of a fetus."

Wow! Should we believe it? If we'd known Henry Morgentaler better, we would never have doubted he would keep his word.

Meantime, a different turn of events was underway in Toronto, where a group of feminists decided to open their own clinic. They believed it should be planned and controlled by women, and anyway, they had found a doctor to work with them. In September, 1982, six to eight Toronto feminists formed what they called the Committee to Establish an Abortion Clinic (CEAC). CEAC formed an alliance with Dr. Leslie Smoling, who had performed thousands of abortions in his native Hungary before coming to Canada.

Soon afterward, fifty to sixty groups joined in founding a political arm for the partially-secret plans for a clinic. It called itself the Ontario Coalition for Abortion Clinics (OCAC). Within a week, OCAC had obtained enough in donations to buy space for a full-page ad in the November 12 *Globe and Mail*, bearing nearly six thousand signatures: "Women need access to safe medically-insured abortions."[44] Women columnists in the Toronto dailies hailed the news, explaining how tedious and often impossible it was for women to get through the bureaucratic barriers to hospital abortions.[45] Less than 30% of Canadian hospitals approved abortions at all, and one third of the women of Ontario lived in communities too small for hospitals to meet the requirements of the Criminal Code: a minimum of four pro-choice doctors.

Henry Morgentaler's re-emergence on the national scene coincided with the 1982 publication of his book, *Abortion and Contraception*,[46] written for the general public and aimed at answering "almost all the questions a woman could have about controlling her own fertility." Penny Kome's emphatically pro-choice review of it in *Homemaker's Magazine*[47] led anti-abortionists to boycott the digest-sized magazine's advertisers and force it to abandon its feminist editorial line. Morgentaler began a book tour that swept Canada from west to east, beginning in British Columbia, which enabled him to publicize his promise for more clinics.

Morgentaler's high profile drew a crowd to CCCA's public meeting at Charles Tupper School where he spoke on October 23. He did many radio and TV interviews and went on to Victoria the next day. In his speech, Morgentaler disputed the claim that a fertilized ovum is the same as a fully-developed human being: "What can one say of people who seriously believe that one or even a hundred cells constitute a baby, a human being?"[48]

Furthermore, Morgentaler argued that nature is the greatest abortionist: "It is safe to estimate that eighty percent of the products of conception do not go to term and are rejected" in spontaneous abortion. That must be seen as a "self-regulating mechanism to protect the health of the species" by eliminating defective organisms. Since not even the Catholic Church baptized or buried the products of spontaneous abortion, was it only therapeutically-aborted fetuses that were fully human from conception?[49]

In fact, the vexing question of "When Does Life Begin" had been taken up in the CCCA *Newsletter* in February. Kathleen Eddy quoted Harvard professor John D. Biggers, who addressed the issue in *The Sciences*, December, 1981. "Life began. It is as simple, or as complicated, as that. Something happened over three billion years ago to turn inanimate matter into animate cells, and started a continuous process commonly known as life." Human beings are temporary participants in this continuum. "There is no beginning to a human life. In fact, there can be no new beginning to any life on earth."[50]

Despite organizing the Morgentaler meeting, followed a week later by a fund-raising event, CCCA stayed in touch with the hospital board elections scene. In June, it put together a kit on organizing and sent it out to groups preparing for these confrontations. Soon, Chilliwack Citizens for Choice was formed and drew sixty people to its first public meeting; membership rose to 150 and extended to neighbouring communities of Sardis, Agassiz, Rosedale, Yarrow, and Cultus Lake. Four pro-choice candidates stood for the September 21 election at Chilliwack General Hospital — none of them won that year, but the group was encouraged. Anti-abortion victories occurred in Langley and at Royal Jubilee, but at Lions Gate Hospital, the pro-choice candidates were successful for the third year in a row.

The clinic planned by CEAC, to be operated by Dr. Leslie Smoling with the support of Dr. Morgentaler, was supposed to open in Toronto on November 2, 1982. A building had been rented, staff hired, and equipment ordered, when the landlord backed out and cancelled the lease. The organizers viewed it as a temporary setback. Afterward, Henry Morgentaler assumed a principal role in the project, and the clinic that eventually opened was the Morgentaler Clinic of Toronto.

So the year came roaring to a close. At the BC Federation of Labor convention, a resolution submitted by postal workers was approved, calling for free-standing abortion clinics. About the same time the Canadian Labor Congress adopted similar policy. In September, 1982, the US Senate defeated a proposal by Jesse Helms to permanently ban the use of federal funds for abortions — even though President Reagan had thrown his weight behind the bill.[51] Further, the national Coalition of American Nuns announced its opposition to overturning the 1973 US Supreme Court decision, *Roe v. Wade*. Although that was a priority goal of Catholic bishops, Sister Donna Quinn of Chicago said that, while nuns opposed the practice of abortion, they believed it should remain "within the realm of women's morals to make the choice."[52] Despite the rash of anti-abortion hospital takeovers in BC, 1982 was ending on a high note.

In British Columbia, we did not yet know of the racist and other attacks that greeted Dr. Morgentaler's announcement that he would open an abortion clinic in Winnipeg.

CHAPTER 10

DR. MORGENTALER FIGHTS BACK

Abortion burst onto the national scene again in 1983, when free-standing clinics opened outside of Québec, first in Winnipeg and then in Toronto. The resulting furore was the beginning of the long last stretch, which brought victory to Canadian women and to Henry Morgentaler. In 1988 the abortion law was at last struck down by a decision of the Canadian Supreme Court. Of course, no-one could foresee or count on that, in 1983.

Still, beginning in 1983, the tide began to turn for the pro-choice movement. Let it be clearly said that, without the stubborn dedication of Henry Morgentaler and the skill of his legal teams, the whole enterprise could have foundered. Without the agony he suffered in Québec prisons — where he had a heart attack after being thrown naked into solitary confinement in 1975 — without his willingness to risk life imprisonment yet again, beginning in 1983; without the personal fortune he committed to lawyers and to opening clinics, and the stubborn years it took for his case to wind through the courts, women would probably still be unable to get legal abortions on demand. And, *quid pro quo,* without the public education work, the fund-raising, and the alliances made with the larger community by the pro-choice movement, the doctor couldn't have succeeded. The role played by the many women organized into the pro-choice movement was, and remains, over-looked. But he, *and we,* did it! We did it *together* with the doctor — and the few doctors who joined him — each of us playing indispensable roles.

In reality, it was necessary to set up real abortion clinics to open the route to making them legal. Parliament remained stony to the last and would not alter the 1969 abortion law. It was only in the process of fighting against criminal charges in court that it could be indisputably proved that the law was iniquitous, inequitable, unenforceable — and unconstitutional. That was how women's needs and the social failure to serve them caught the country's attention. Although cabinets and parliamentarians, both Liberal and Tory, proved they knew this but didn't care, other sectors of the Canadian power structure were eventually brought to listen.

At the time, however, the anti-abortion movement was on a roll and could not imagine failure. Events in the US directly affected us; for example, in 1981, at least 4000 abortions, or six per cent of the Canadian total, were done on Canadian women who went to the States.[1] It mattered here whether a US ban would succeed. In 1983, a 90-page essay purportedly by President Ronald Reagan was published as a book with his photo on the cover. The only book written by a president while in office, the tract was titled "Abortion and the Conscience of the Nation." It was full of the platitudes of the anti-abortion movement, comparing *Roe v. Wade* to the 1857 Dred Scott decision, whereby the Supreme Court re-enslaved a free man; dubbing abortion a 'holocaust;' quoting the Declaration of Independence and Mother Theresa, and so on.[2] In June, 1983, however, the US Supreme Court — stacked with Reagan appointees — delivered a powerful re-affirmation of *Roe v. Wade*, when it struck down a myriad of local restrictions on access to abortion. The odious regulations adopted in Akron, Ohio, that required doctors to harass a woman seeking an abortion with the heavy suggestion that she was contemplating murder (very similar to the anti-abortion 'guidelines' imposed on BC hospitals) were declared unconstitutional. The 6-3 decision was seen as a "decisive pro-choice victory" by the *New York Times*,[3] and it had the effect of scuttling chances for passage of the Hatch Amendment, which would have added an anti-abortion plank to the US Constitution.

Early in the year, CCCA set out to locate pro-choice doctors. We got a break when the Federation of Medical Women and its president, Dr. Lorena Kanke, helped us select the most likely names from its provincial directory. Armed with a list of 115 doctors, we invited them to meet with us on February 23, 1983 at the Unitarian Church. We assured the doctors of strict privacy and no publicity, for we wanted neither anti-abortionists nor the media to come. Lawyer Jack Woodward and two doctors — Nelson Savein of Burnaby and Mary Conley of Victoria — agreed to speak and answer questions about free-standing abortion clinics. Our hope was to see a group emerge that might be called "Doctors for Choice," and we were ready to propose running a newspaper ad as OCAC in Toronto had done. But, as luck would have it, a heavy snow fell on the meeting night. The turnout from our earnest invitations and phone calls was exactly eight doctors, two of whom were speakers. They listened quietly for an hour, and then they vanished before the snowstorm got worse. We were to contact that list again and again over the following years, without much success.

When Henry Morgentaler selected Toronto, it seemed an obvious choice for an abortion clinic. Then he announced he would simultaneously open a clinic in Manitoba. What followed was an incredible polarization in the only province with an NDP government. Why Winnipeg? Why within the NDP, when the federal convention of 1971 had adopted the first of many, frequently re-affirmed, policies calling for removal of abortion from the Criminal Code?

It is hard to untangle that question, especially from the distance of years and kilometres. Morgentaler hoped that newly-elected Manitoba NDP premier Howard Pawley, and especially his openly pro-choice attorney-general, Roland Penner, would stand on long-established party principle and support him. Little chance. The ensuing, gloves-off set-to in Winnipeg rocked the party across Canada, and increased the iciness of the BC NDP toward the BC pro-choice movement.

For some time, though, we in CCCA had little information about the problems of the Winnipeg clinic. Recent as the 1980s seem, it was an era before fax machines, the internet, or cell phones, and as the Vancouver media reported little that happened outside BC, we were often in the dark. We were also unfamiliar with the intricacies of Manitoba's political climate. From the beginning, there was open and vicious anti-Semitism toward the doctor. Beyond that, as Ellen Kruger, long-time NDPer, and Morgentaler's choice to lead his political defence in Winnipeg, explained to author Anne Collins:

> We have the dichotomy on the Prairies of groupings of people who are very progressive on economic issues, but because of religious socialization, and so on, are less progressive on social issues.[4]

Nor was CCCA aware of the personal animosity that flared up between Roland Penner and Dr. Morgentaler. Had we known more of the story, which kept NDPers' tongues wagging across the country, we might have understood the sudden distrust for Morgentaler shown by NDPers in British Columbia.

After Dr. Morgentaler publicly announced his choice of Winnipeg, he met with Penner, whom he asked to "stand on principle" and refuse to prosecute.[5] Instead the new attorney general sent Morgentaler a letter, saying that he would not personally order that charges be laid against clinic operators, but the law was the law. If the crown prosecutor chose to move against the clinic, it would be a matter for the courts to decide.[6] Stung, Dr. Morgentaler lambasted Penner and the NDP for their "lack of courage" and for "caving in to a fanatical minority."[7] Further exchanges led to an ongoing state of personal animosity and personality conflict.

The outcome was that the Winnipeg clinic, in a renovated house on Corydon Avenue, was subjected to police attacks even more savage than at the Toronto clinic. It opened on Friday, May 5, 1983, a month before the clinic in Toronto — after every effort to prevent it had been exhausted.

Joe Borowski was serving lunch to the faithful from a trailer on the front lawn of an adjoining house. His long-awaited constitutional challenge was to begin in Regina the following Monday, and when the clinic didn't open after all on the Thursday — due entirely to a bureaucratic muddle his side had orchestrated — Borowski told reporters, "Dr. Morgentaler is deliber-ately delaying the opening of his clinic until I have to leave town."[8] Then Borowski was served with a 48-hour notice to remove his trailer from residential property, or face a $5000 fine. Nearly beside himself, he tossed reporters what a historian calls "one of his typical screwball metaphors." Borowski said: "'If we can't stop an illegal clinic, how are we going to stop abortions in hospitals? It's like Custer's last stand. Either I'm Custer or he [Morgentaler] is Custer.'"[9]

Anticlimactically, the clinic opened the next morning with only a dozen protesters out front. Manitoba doctors were not keen on the project, so Morgentaler was seconded by an Ontario doctor whom he had selected and trained, Dr. Robert Scott. Neither had illusions about the intentions of officials. They not only expected action from the crown, but their Winnipeg lawyer, Greg Brodsky, had already offered to furnish proof of illegal activity. As recounted by legal scholar F.L. Morton: "In what is presumably the first time in the history of Canadian criminal law, a lawyer had actually gone to the police and explained that his client wanted to be arrested and charged with violating the Criminal Code."[10]

The clinic was allowed to operate for a month. Scott took charge while Morgentaler returned to Toronto to purchase the building at 85 Harbord Street for his Ontario clinic. When the raid came in Winnipeg on June 3, Dr. Scott and head nurse Lynn Crocker locked the operating room and finished the abortion they were doing. Then they were taken out by the front door through a crowd of jeering anti-abortionists. Nine others at the clinic — staff and patients — were also removed to the police station through the back door, away from the cameras. No charges were laid for the moment, and all were released within hours. On the steps of the jail, Lynn Crocker announced to cheering supporters and TV crews, "The clinic is open. We're on our way back to work."[11] But the clinic had been stripped of equipment and could not resume performing abortions until another vacuum aspirator was obtained.

Almost a week later, the charges laid against Morgentaler, Scott, the four RNs and two social workers at the clinic were not for performing illegal abortions, but for conspiracy to violate section 251. As Morton puts it, "The conspiracy charges caught Morgentaler and Brodsky offguard and posed serious problems for their defence. It would be much more difficult to persuade a jury that the defence of necessity applied to a plot to perform illegal abortions."[12] The doctor had won his three Québec acquittals by pleading he performed abortions at his Montréal clinic out of medical necessity, to prevent the women patients from greater harm elsewhere.

Undeterred, the opening of the Toronto clinic went ahead on June 15. Anti-abortionists did not picket, so the sunny day was one of celebration. Except, that is, for the passerby who suddenly lunged at Dr. Morgentaler, wielding a wicked pair of garden shears. Judy Rebick, his assistant at the time, stepped in front of the doctor and pushed the man away. He lowered the blades and rushed off, while Morgentaler entered the clinic safely. It all happened so fast that it was only when they saw the TV news that Morgentaler and Rebick realized how dangerous the moment had been. The attacker was easily located and arrested, and he chose to inflate the story and claim he'd said to Morgentaler, "'You want to butcher children? Butcher kids? I'll butcher *you*.'" Then he added for benefit of the media, without the slightest credibility, "'I didn't mean nothing bad to him.'"[13]

When the Winnipeg clinic got new equipment and resumed operating, a second raid was staged in true commando style. The police broke down the front door, injuring the clinic worker who was about to open it for them. They also swarmed in through the back door and herded everyone upstairs. The abortion in progress was interrupted — a horrible experience for the woman on the table, although she later managed to get treatment in hospital. Clinic volunteer Suzanne Newman, a mother of four, remembered how frightening everything was: "Many of the women there [as patients] spoke little English and were terrified. There were TV cameras...That was the hard part for the women who were there for the service, not for political reasons. They wanted their faces covered. This is the most personal of decisions, and to have their faces broadcast over the evening news..."[14]

Each staff member was interrogated separately in the clinic kitchen, while the patients were already on their way to jail. They were let go, but Dr. Scott and five women staffers were put in cells. They were denied bail unless they promised not to go near the clinic, which they refused to do. Scott was put in his own cell, but the women were treated harshly: strip-searched, denied combs, toothbrushes, belts, shoes, or their own clothing.[15] After two nights in jail, the six still-defiant staffers were released, but new charges of performing illegal abortions were levied against Morgentaler, Scott, and Lynn Crocker.

On Canada Day, July 1, the NDP met in Regina. This was the city of its roots, where the On to Ottawa trek had been halted halfway to its destination in 1935. Out of its genuine grievances had come the Cooperative Commonwealth Federation (CCF), which morphed into the New Democratic Party in 1961.

Columnist Jamie Lamb commented in the *Vancouver Sun*: "An outsider never knows whether to laugh, cry, or cheer at an NDP convention." Lamb was astonished that, "On Thursday it rebuffed...its only provincial government."[16] An emergency resolution from the party's Federal Council condemned the Manitoba NDP for its criminal charges against the Winnipeg clinic and for "police harassment against employees and patients." It was passed by 95% of the delegates, who also pledged that a federal NDP government would remove abortion from the Criminal Code, pardon doctors convicted under it, and establish facilities in both hospitals and clinics for abortions.[17]

Regrettably, none of the pressure against its treatment of the clinic corrected the Pawley government's ferocious attitude toward Dr. Morgentaler. Pawley came up with a clever, but dishonest way to rationalize this. *Priorities*, the BC NDP Women's Rights Committee publication, ran a letter from the Manitoba premier in its August 1983 edition:

> With respect to Dr. Morgentaler's clinic, we have said from the beginning that such facilities must operate within the law and that we will not give support to the *privatization of health care.* [emphasis added]

This excuse was used at a later time by the NDP in British Columbia, when an abortion clinic was being planned for Vancouver. The truth was that Dr. Morgentaler did everything he could to place all three of his clinics within the health care system. It was the provincial governments that would not accept his repeated and unequivocal offers to *give* the clinics to Québec, Manitoba and Ontario, so that they might be public, not private facilities.

Back in Toronto, the clinic on Harbord Street was allowed to operate for just three weeks. On July 5, the police moved in like gangbusters. Anne Collins witnessed the raid on that hot afternoon, and she described the scene vividly in *The Big Evasion: Abortion, The Issue that Won't Go Away.* The plight of patients being led down the back fire-escape by police shocked her out of her desire to tell pro-choice and anti-abortion sides with equal emphasis. Collins wrote: "The police had raided the clinic as if it were a brothel or an illegal drug factory...the police behaved exactly as if [Drs. Henry Morgentaler, Robert Scott, and Les Smoling] were garden-variety crimi-nals."[18] The absurdity of the situation did not lessen the brutality of the assault on the clinics and all involved in them. Two weeks later, an arsonist set fire to the building on Harbord St. that housed the Toronto clinic.

Just before the clinics opened, the CARAL AGM took place in Toronto. Two BC women were there: Marva Blackmore from CCCA, and Maxine Boag of the CARAL chapter in Victoria. Following Henry Morgentaler's annual speech, constitutional lawyer Morris Manning sketched the pos-sible approaches to the courts. Manning was Morgentaler's lawyer, but CARAL officers had hired him to launch their own constitutional challenge to the abortion law. It would be filed in the name of CARAL's president, Norma Scarborough. Boag and Blackmore were skeptical — how many court challenges could the pro-choice movement afford — but the pro-posal had Morgentaler's blessing. It was only later that the virtue of this plan became apparent.

Manning argued that the government was in a tough spot. The defen-dant in the Borowski case was the federal law. If government lawyers vig-orously defended the law against Borowski, they couldn't very easily oppose the law in the Scarborough suit. Manning's chief argument would be that a woman's security of the person — Section 7 of the Charter — was violated by her exclusion from the deliberations of the TAC, against which she had no appeal. He anticipated the case would go before a judge in Ontario within the year.[19]

OCAC held a lunch-hour rally, attended by the eighty CARAL delegates along with 400 Torontonians, to hear Dr. Morgentaler speak. Afterward, Judy Rebick took women from the strongest chapters of CARAL aside and proposed a National Day of Action for the fall. It sounded good to Blackmore and Boag, and they returned to the AGM to move that CARAL sponsor and support this plan. Somewhat to the executive committee's dismay -its time was filled with support for and fund-raising for the trials — the motion was enthusiastically adopted, after the BC women volunteered to co-ordinate the organizing.

Back in BC, work toward the October 1 National Day of Action on Abortion was slow. Everyone's energy and attention was focused on defeating the Socred 'Restraint' Budget. With its own heavy agenda in the year of the Winnipeg and Toronto crises, CCCA joined none of the protest groups, although we went as individuals to the numerous meetings and rallies. Jeff Finger and Melinda Suto made a lightweight sandwich board publicizing the fate of the clinics, and I wore it over my shoulders when 50,000 budget protesters filled Empire Stadium on August 10. Some seemed startled that an issue not related to the BC budget should appear there, but people pulled out their wallets and $400 was donated to the clinic doctors' defence fund.

The turnout for the Day of Action in Vancouver was average — 500-600 people. The Solidarity groups against the budget did not spill over to swell CCCA's continuing struggle. Lynn Crocker, head nurse at the Winnipeg clinic, was the rally's featured speaker. Facing charges for "conspiracy to procure miscarriage," Crocker described how she went from being a conscientious public health nurse to being charmed by Dr. Morgentaler into joining the clinic staff, and within weeks, to being arrested and charged. Joining her on the podium at the much-loved Commodore Ballroom was Carmen Wernli, wife of Dr. Henry Morgentaler. In addition to songs by the endlessly delightful Euphonious Feminists and Non-Performing group, the mood was lightened by a poet. Leona Gom read three of her poems, including one called "My Neighbour the Pro-Lifer":

> says it's not that he
> doesn't believe in woman's rights,
> nothing like that,
> it's that he's afraid of communism,
> how there's more of them than us,
> and it's getting worse.
> he'll see me
> at the hospital meeting, he says,
> but he has to vote what's right,
> he has to vote for democracy."[20]

On the following Monday, an anti-abortion petition with 50,000 names on it was presented to the BC attorney-general.[21] However, a Gallup Poll had found a jump in support for our side. Across Canada, 83.2% replied "Yes" to the question, "Do you think it should be a woman's right to decide whether or not to have an abortion?" This was an 11% increase over the previous poll of July 1982. In Vancouver, only the CCCA *Newsletter* reported the new results, reaching a few hundred subscribers but not the general public.

At last, the verdict came in the Borowski case. Conducted in grand style for more than two weeks in May, nine expert witnesses had been summoned from as far as Paris, New York, and New Zealand. Dr. Bernard Nathanson of New York went to lengths to convince the court that the science of 'fetology' had grown exponentially since the 1970s, and it was now proved that the fetus was human from conception. But the pro-choice side was jolted by the government's refusal to call any witnesses to defend the abortion law. On October 13, 1983, Justice W.R. Matheson released his judgment against Borowski: "There is no existing basis in law which justifies a conclusion that fetuses are legal persons."[22] He acknowledged that the law could be changed, but only by parliament, not by the courts. He found no conflict between the abortion law and the Charter and dismissed the case.

A week after the budding general strike against the Socred budget ended, scuttled by IWA leader Jack Munro and NDP official Jerry Stoney, the Revolutionary Workers League expelled me. Ironically, I was the only member in BC who had actually been on strike. But the RWL's brand of Marxism was changing, and it had developed doubts about the women's movement. So ended my membership in the far left.

On November 21 the case against Drs. Morgentaler, Scott, and Smoling began in Toronto. The charges in Manitoba were put on hold, pending the outcome in Ontario. Immediately, Morris Manning made a pre-trial motion to quash the charges on grounds they were unconstitutional. Judge William Parker of the Ontario Supreme Court allowed the motion, and Manning then launched the challenge that would otherwise have been the Scarborough case. Until the constitutional question had been heard and decided, there would be no jury trial of the doctors. Instead of the expected two weeks, the pre-trial arguments took more than four months, until April 5, 1984. In July, Justice Parker ruled as expected — that only parliament, not a judge, could strike down the abortion law.

That meant the three doctors would go to trial on charges of conspiracy. But Manning, by setting out the basics of his constitutional challenge ahead of time, laid the groundwork for an anticipated future hearing before the Supreme Court of Canada. Since that is an appeals court, which reviews cases that have already gone through the system, new cases and arguments not heard before cannot be made for the first time to the country's highest judiciary.

An era ended in early 1984 when Pierre Trudeau took a walk in the snow and announced he would step down. John Turner became prime minister. Since he had no seat, he called an election for September 4 — won by the Tories — and the campaign brought surprises for both the leaders and for Canadian women.

It was also an election year in the United States. For the first time in history, a woman from a major party won nomination for executive office, when the Democrats named Geraldine Ferraro its vice-presidential candidate. Although Walter Mondale and Ferraro were defeated by Republicans Ronald Reagan and George Bush, the profile of women and the issue of abortion erupted with force during the campaign.

And, late in the year, Dr. Henry Morgentaler and his associates, Drs. Robert Scott and Les Smoling, were acquitted by a Toronto jury of conspiracy charges for opening an abortion clinic. The smug assumption that only the crazy, separatist Québecois were susceptible to the doctor's message was struck down. It was a splendid, if not a final, victory.

Across British Columbia, social activists were deflated by the sell-out of the 'Solidarity' movement. CCCA was no exception. We continued to meet rent-free on alternate Tuesdays, in the board room of the NDP provincial office, whose staff was indifferent to the animosity borne us by some in the Women's Rights Committee. But we were pretty low-energy in 1984.

Elsewhere in the province, abortion continued to spark conflict. Anti-abortionists won the hospital board elections in Vernon, Langley, and the Bulkley Valley, while Lions Gate remained pro-choice. The now-merged hospitals in Victoria resumed performing abortions with a TAC that followed fairly liberal guidelines. Feminists in Terrace, Nelson, and Trail stayed in touch with us, as did Chilliwack Citizens for Choice, represented by Margaret Brady, who often drove to Vancouver for CCCA meetings.

Alicen Keamarden of Smithers visited CCCA while in Vancouver, and she described the formation of the Bulkley Valley Pro-Choice Alliance in the April CCCA *Newsletter*. As in other mostly-rural centres in BC, Smithers' many churches ensured a strong anti-abortion climate. All denominations combined to demand the district hospital disband its TAC. The medical staff made the by-now familiar withdrawal from hospital committees, and the Pro-Choice Alliance, with some courage, conducted a petition campaign, held a public meeting, and appeared on talk shows. When the TAC was re-installed, it was with guidelines so strict they made abortion unavailable. Meantime, anti-abortion ads in the local paper presented fetuses as fully-developed babies, warned that abortion was unsafe, and accused women of wanting the procedure so they could "afford designer jeans."[23]

Nearby, in Quesnel, anti-abortionists snuck onto the board of the Amata Transition House and altered its constitution. Admittance to the shelter was thereafter refused to battered "women and teenagers considering abortion." It took obtaining a court order for feminists to have that bylaw set aside.[24]

Passionately committed to the need for a cross-country movement, CCCA found a way to retain our independent character and mass-action focus and still participate in CARAL. Marva Blackmore was elected an at-large member of the CARAL national executive in April, 1984.

She returned to Vancouver with a report on anti-abortion violence, as presented by Dr. Uta Landry, outgoing director of the US National Abortion Federation. This was a network of 240 abortion clinics that shared news, medical protocol, and security measures. While Canadians fought to be free of hospital restrictions, few abortions were done in US hospitals, where private clinics were the norm. There had always been anti-abortion pickets at US clinics, reported Landry, but with the death of the Hatch Amendment and the 1983 Supreme Court reinforcement of *Roe v. Wade*, more than three dozen abortion facilities had suffered attacks. In the first ten months of 1984, the scale of such attacks rose to triple the total in all of 1983.[25]

Even then, before abortion-providers began being murdered by 'pro-lifers' — the first death was that of Dr. David Gunn of Pensacola, Florida, who was shot in the back on March 10, 1993 — the degree of violence was shocking. *Ms. Magazine,* in October 1984, described "firebombings, vandalized clinics, slashed tires, crosses on an abortion staffer's front lawn, midnight phone calls that threaten injury and death" as all too common. One of the hardest-hit was the Hope Clinic for Women in Granite City, Illinois, across the Mississippi River from St. Louis. Firebombed in 1981, the clinic's medical director, Dr. Hector Zevallos and his wife Jean, were abducted in 1982, held for eight days, and threatened with murder if they didn't stop doing abortions. The couple survived and was released. Their kidnappers, who dubbed themselves the Army of God, were caught and convicted. The supposedly moderate chair of Catholics United for Life accused the pro-choice movement itself of staging the abduction. Mark Drogin told the St. Louis *Post-Dispatch* that a "real anti-abortion group" would not have returned Dr. Zevallos unharmed. "He might have been released without a hand or something," said Drogin.[26]

Openly violent groups were gaining respectability. Chicago's Joseph Scheidler, a one-time Benedictine monk who went on to found the Pro-Life Action League and to write a book called *Ninety-nine Ways to Close the Abortion Clinics,* zealously championed direct action methods. He publicly linked himself with convicted anti-abortion arsonists and the leaders of Army of God. But he was also welcomed as a speaker at the 'respectable' national Right-to-Life convention. And in January, 1984, Scheidler was among the anti-abortion leaders invited into the White House by Ronald Reagan.[27] Scheidler soon linked up with Canadian anti-abortionists and made an appearance in Vancouver in the early 1990s.

Close to home, the Feminist Women's Health Center in Everett, Washington, just north of Seattle, opened in August, 1983. Crowds of protesters repeatedly assembled outside. Staffers began receiving death threats. On December 3, an arsonist destroyed the clinic, and staffer Diane Hale was threatened with a possible firebomb in her car.[28] The brave women of Everett rebuilt and re-opened their clinic on the eleventh anniversary of *Roe v. Wade*, January 22, 1984. An overflow crowd attended a rally to celebrate, including three from BC: Carol Rosset, a former staffperson for the Morgentaler clinic in Winnipeg who had moved to Vancouver; Margaret Brady of Chilliwack Citizens for Choice; and me. Two more arson attacks followed, costing the clinic its lease and fire-insurance and forcing it to close. Curtis Beseda, who had led a 'respectable' effort for a ballot-initiative to ban abortions in Washington state, was arrested and charged with three arson attacks in Everett, and one on a clinic in Bellingham, Washington.[29]

In Canada, a right-wing group calling itself R.E.A.L. women (Realistic, Equal, Active for Life) popped up in February 1984 and commandeered enormous media attention. Claiming to represent bedrock Canadian values, the group demanded an end to government grants to feminist groups, opposed any universally-available, subsidized day-care plan as a threat to the traditional family, objected to affirmative action and equal pay — and, of course, was severely opposed to abortion. It bid for, and eventually won, government funding — whereas pro-choice groups were denied funding because we were 'political.' The BC R.E.A.L. leader, Peggy Steacy, also put out a 'Pro-Life' newsletter.[30]

On July 20, Justice Parker rejected Dr. Morgentaler's case, as put in the 'pre-trial motion.' A key argument of Parker's was that, since abortion had been outlawed in Canada for one hundred years, then, despite the limited 1969 reform, "no unfettered legal right to abortion is deeply rooted in the traditions or conscience of this country."[31] Really!! responded Toronto writer June Callwood in the *Globe and Mail*. What about the long Canadian tradition of women deciding to limit their families or to not bear children at all? "Fertile women would give birth to twenty children in their lifetimes," she wrote, unless they practiced birth control. "Modern families rarely have more than two babies...even women who march in anti-abortion demonstrations are not leading twenty children by the hand."[32]

So both Borowski and Morgentaler failed to get rid of the abortion law through the courts in that go-round. Parker's ruling meant the criminal charges against Drs. Morgentaler, Scott, and Smoling would proceed. A trial date was set for late October, 1984, and the jury would decide whether or not opening a clinic in Toronto warranted a guilty verdict.

In the meantime, Canada's media was obsessed with federal power politics. A riding was found for the new PM, Ontarian John Turner, in Quadra, a tony area of Vancouver, and an election was set for September. As elections go, that one had its moments.

Borowski himself came to BC to blast three incumbent MPs who sought re-election: NDP MPs Svend Robinson and Margaret Mitchell, and Iona Campagnolo, who had bid for the Liberal leadership. Holy Joe exposed them as honorary directors of CARAL. His followers nearly broke down the door at Robinson's campaign office and menaced Campagnolo at her nominating meeting.[33] Startling four-page leaflets appeared on doorsteps, bearing the Campaign Life imprint and a Delta, BC address. Above a photo of a fetus sucking its thumb were captions like: "Protect All of Our Children — Born and Unborn!" — a slur on Robinson's sexual orientation, and "Svend is a personal friend of Morgentaler" — which Robinson was proud to acknowledge.[34] Mitchell and Robinson were re-elected; Campagnolo went down in the general Liberal defeat.

This election had a twist: "News flash — The parties have discovered women voters" announced the *Montréal Gazette*.[35] The political beast stirred and cast its boiled eye at this unsuspected crop. It was uncertain how to harvest it. Then the National Action Committee on the Status of Women arranged for a CBC 'Women's Debate,' featuring a panel of feminists and the leaders of the three major parties. It was the last of three televized debates and took place on Sunday, August 15.

Before that, TV cameras caught the new PM in the act of "slapping Mrs. Campagnolo's bottom after giving her a friendly kiss." This took place in Edmonton, and a week later in Montréal, Turner did the same to the "attractive" vice-president of the party's Québec wing. The prime minister, who struck even pundits as about as warm and sincere as The Man From Glad, laughed the whole thing off. "I'm a hugger. I'm a tactile politician. I'm slapping people all over the place...That's my style."[36]

It may or may not have inspired the question that brought the house down and closed the 'Women's Debate.' Many pressing issues were raised, including abortion. Would the new government be prepared to finance family-planning and free-standing abortion clinics? John Turner, although eager to take credit for having introduced the 1969 law, said it was impossible to make changes because the pro-choice and anti-choice sides were at odds. "The best we can do...is the present state of the law," he said.[37] Mulroney promised nothing. He was ahead in the polls and presented his "usual glycerine...self."[38] The last question was put by Toronto teacher and co-founder of NAC, Kay Sigurjonsson. Pointing to the long history of unkept promises on women's needs, going back to the Status of Women

Report in 1970, she asked, *"SO WHY SHOULD WE TRUST YOU NOW?"* Indeed! Cheers from the live audience went on so long that the debate ended without answers to that question being risked.

Pope John Paul II visited Canada at summer's end. To contain the crowds at the open-air mass in Abbotsford, BC, security holding pens were constructed to divide the devout from one another. In fact, the faith itself was divided, and this secret was getting out. *Chatelaine* magazine ran a major report by Heather Robertson in September 1984, titled "Women vs. The Pope." She interviewed highly-placed Catholic women — theologians, lay activists, and nuns — who were especially concerned by the Vatican's archaic views on sexuality and the ordination of women. Sister Diane Bridges summed it up: "'When the Pope gets off his airplane, I wish he'd kiss the women and step on the ground.'"[39]

It was in the 1984 US presidential election that Catholics rose up on the issue of abortion. By then the Washington, DC-based group called Catholics for a Free Choice was ten years old and had at least 5000 members. The group published a number of readable booklets arguing that abortion is not wrong if it is the best decision in a given woman's circumstances, and that God means each woman to make responsible decisions when she becomes pregnant. Geraldine Ferraro, a Catholic, refused to pledge to abolish abortion if she were elected vice-president, and Catholics for a Free Choice wanted to support her against the flak this was causing. It pulled together a group of professionals, which drew up a statement on the issue. This ran as a full-page ad in the *Sunday New York Times* on October 7, 1984, beneath a headline reading: "A Diversity of Opinions Regarding Abortion Exists Among Committed Catholics." It pointed out that "only 11% of Catholics surveyed disapprove of abortion in all circumstances," and it challenged the Pope and the church hierarchy's claims that abortion is always morally wrong. The ad called for "candid and respectful discussion on this diversity of opinion within the church," and was signed by nearly 100 prominent Catholics, including four priests and 24 nuns.[40]

It caused an uproar and was followed by theological bloodshed. The 24 nuns who had signed it were ordered to publicly retract by their superiors in the church. Instead, most knuckled down to renewed study and renewed struggle for their beliefs. Calling themselves the Vatican 24, the nuns published a second ad in the *New York Times* on March 2, 1986. This one was signed by one thousand Catholics from seventeen countries, including at least five priests and forty nuns, and was headlined "We Affirm our Solidarity with all Catholics whose right to free speech is under attack."[41]

Back in Vancouver, CCCA was excited about a new film released by Studio D, the women's division of the National Film Board. Called *Abortion Stories from North and South*, it looked at six countries and the obstacles to abortions they placed in women's way. The film gave graphic meaning to its estimate that 30-45 million abortions were performed in the world each year, half of them illegal, and that an estimated 84,000 women died as a result. CBC refused to broadcast a film dealing with abortion, but the NFB in Vancouver readily agreed to CCCA's request for a benefit showing to aid the doctors' legal fund. We scheduled it at the community-minded Ridge Theatre on Sunday November 18. It was a miserably wet day and — something we had overlooked — the day of the Grey Cup game. Barely a third of the seats were filled. Still, we put the proceeds together with other funds we'd raised and sent off another $1000 to CARAL for the doctors' defence.

That defence was underway in the Ontario Supreme Court before the same judge, William Parker, who'd heard and denied the long pre-trial motion. The charge of conspiring to perform abortions was put to a jury, beginning October 25. The crown's case was told mainly by police who had raided the Toronto clinic, and they painted it as just another sleazy operation, where desperate women were taken advantage of by men who would do anything for a price.

Once again, Henry Morgentaler relied on the defence of necessity, which had won his three acquittals in Québec. He'd performed abortions in Ontario to prevent greater harm to his patients; he'd opened the clinic in Toronto because women there were routinely blocked from obtaining legal abortions. Among the numerous witnesses were Dr. Diane Sacks, director of a birth control clinic at the Hospital for Sick Children, who described the many teen-age patients who were forced to undergo dangerous late abortions or even go to New York, because of the difficulty of getting into Toronto hospitals. "I'm ashamed, as a physician, that we're not doing better," she said on the stand.[42] Psychiatrist Wendell Watters, long a Morgentaler associate and a faculty member at McMaster University, had a succinct answer when crown counsel told him, "many people view abortion as a crime against humanity akin to genocide or slavery." "'If you want to talk about slavery, I think it is women who have been the slaves,' Watters said. 'They have been enslaved by laws made by men.'"[43]

There were many others, but perhaps the most powerful testimony was given by feminist social workers Janis Tripp and Carolyn Egan. Tripp was an original member of CEAC; Egan was a leader of OCAC. Both worked at the Toronto Birth Control and VD Clinic, and Janis Tripp took the jury step by step through the impossible frustration of trying to get a hospital abortion in Toronto. Unlike in Vancouver, where TACs scheduled abortions, once a Toronto woman got past a TAC, she had the responsibility of arranging an appointment for the surgery herself. On the one morning a week when Toronto General Hospital scheduled abortions, only those women who managed to get through to the telephone switchboard before 10am had a chance. So women — regardless of whether they had jobs to go to, or children to be fed and sent to school — would have to cancel everything else for a marathon telephone effort. "'You keep dialing and dialing and dialing. There is no other way. You can't stop and have coffee and dial again. And by the time you get through, all the appointments are taken. So you start again'" at another hospital, the next scheduling day, recounted Tripp.[44] Her testimony made the defence of necessity compelling.

Far from quailing at the prosecution's depiction of him as a greedy crime-syndicate boss, operating a dangerous, back-street establishment, Dr. Morgentaler took the stand and gave the jury his history. He described childhood poverty in Poland, how most of his family perished under the Nazis, and how he himself had been a teen when he was sent to Auschwitz. He called himself a "coward" when, after opening his medical practice in Montréal, he had turned away women who came to him for abortions. One incident that changed his mind involved a woman who tried to abort herself with a bicycle pump. The woman died. He began performing abortions at his Montréal clinic, but never in a clandestine or furtive way. "Everything has been done above board," he said, describing his Toronto facility as a luxury clinic. His only concern was the best care for his patients. About 60 per cent of the women coming to his Montréal clinic were from outside Québec, which made him see the need for clinics elsewhere. He described his many efforts to get the federal government to legalize clinics, but it was like "going against a brick wall. The politicians seemed to be scared of the anti-abortion lobby."[45]

In his closing address to the jury, Morris Manning cut directly across Justice Parker's ruling in July, when the judge insisted only parliamentarians could make or change the law. "Send a message to Mr. [Ontario attorney-general Roy] McMurtry saying 'stop prosecuting doctors for trying to help people.' You are the only independent body that can do this. Politicians can't. They are dependent on votes," he argued.[46] Justice Parker retaliated by instructing the jury for four hours and, according to Manning, breaching his duty to appear impartial. He forced the judge to re-charge the jury without the implicit instruction to convict. When they retired for a second time, the jurors took only six hours to reach a verdict, and, on November 8, 1984, they acquitted the three doctors of all charges.

A jubilant Morgentaler announced his Toronto clinic would re-open within days, and it did. But the response from anti-abortionists was unrelenting, and it didn't take them long to pressure attorney-general McMurtry to launch an appeal of the acquittal. While Morgentaler listened from the Ontario legislative gallery, McMurtry made his announcement on December 4. For good measure, he ordered another police raid of the clinic and laid further charges on Drs. Morgentaler and Scott. Still, in the spring of 1985, during the crown's appeal of the acquittals, the Morgentaler clinic in Toronto remained open. And McMurtry was soon defeated at the polls.

Elsewhere, though, bombs were shutting clinics down. Three abortion facilities in Pensacola, Florida exploded on Christmas Day, 1984, followed by a bombing that destroyed a Washington, DC clinic on January 1, 1985. The Florida bombers were quickly rounded up. Matthew Goldsby, 21, James Simmons, 21, and Simmons' wife Kathy, 18, admitted to having blown up another clinic before that, on June 25, 1984. They believed it was a "sign from God" when they got away with destroying The Ladies Center in June. Goldsby's fiance, Kay Wiggins, 18, explained they had planted bombs on Christmas Day "as a gift to Jesus on his birthday."[47] Intoned New York Archbishop John J. O'Connor, the fetus always comes first.[48]

CHAPTER 11

A BIG YEAR IN VANCOUVER

1985 was one of CCCA's most exciting years. We planned a full calendar and gladly expanded it when Dr. Morgentaler came to BC in mid-April. What a tour! There were four main events during his brief stay in Vancouver, and few soon forgot the stormy protest that greeted his public address at John Oliver Secondary School. We felt we had done the best organizing job ever. But we were also shown to have been naïve and blind in some respects.

Marjorie Maguire, Catholic theologian and a co-founder of Catholics for a Free Choice in the US, came to Vancouver at our invitation in early July. There was a tug-of-war for her allegiance between the pro-choice movement and evangelical, or 'charismatic' Catholics. Maguire remained poised, articulate, charming, and resolutely pro-choice, even when an enraged band of her co-religionists pursued her through the downtown streets.

Afterwards, CCCA devoted itself to planning a full-scale Tribunal, in which the Criminal Code was to be put on trial and found guilty of violating the rights of women. The 1985 CARAL AGM agreed to hold a staggered series of Tribunals across the country. We first planned to hold the Vancouver version in November, but it got re-scheduled to January, 1986.

A major feature on abortion appeared in the *Vancouver Sun* in January, that proved BC had the same crisis of access that had been highlighted in Ontario by the Morgentaler trial. The *Sun* found that half the province's 105 public hospitals had no therapeutic abortion committees and performed no abortions at all. Only 34 of the 52 hospitals with TACs would tell how many abortions they performed in 1983, and four reported doing none. Vancouver General, at 4,300, did half the total of 8,650 abortions that year; Lions Gate did "about 700" and Burnaby General "just under" 400. Hospitals in the Vancouver area were clearly serving the majority of women in BC who managed to get through the complex system.[1] Clinics in northern Washington state reported that Canadian women "often" sought their services, even though it meant making three visits across the border and paying between $240 and $650 US. Marva Blackmore of CCCA and Lorna Zaback of the Vancouver Women's Health Collective were interviewed about their groups for the story.[2]

Pro-choice forces were augmented when a Fraser Valley chapter of

CARAL was begun in mid-January, 1985. It was initiated by Eileen Suffrin of White Rock, already well-known for years of trying to unionize the staff at Eaton's. Coalescing older groups, it was well-situated to fight against anti-abortion take-overs at Valley hospitals, and it served as a counter-point to the Delta base of Campaign Life. In the battles to come, this CARAL group and pro-choice women in Vancouver co-operated closely.

An addition to the anti-abortion arsenal was a 27-minute-long video, *The Silent Scream*. It purported to be an ultrasound record of an abortion on a 12-week-old fetus. Narrated by Dr. Bernard Nathanson of New York, its audience had a brief view of dizzyingly-indistinct lines on a TV screen. One had to take Nathanson's word for it that the video showed a) an ultra-sound of b) a fetus which c) recoiled from d) an abortionist's probe. With evangelical fervor, Nathanson proclaimed that it showed the terrified 'scream' of the fetus. The video got a lot of play after its release in late 1984. CCCA's Marva Blackmore, together with Dr. Nelson Savein, debated the video with Betty Green of the BC Pro-Life Society on TV. Mass-produced copies of it arrived, gratis, at churches, community organizations, and on the desks of every MP in Ottawa, where it was played many times over the in-house parliamentery TV system. In response, a video was developed by Planned Parenthood of Seattle, and CCCA ordered a copy.

Almost unnoticed in Vancouver at the time, a sometime cabinet-maker in Nelson walked unseen into the operating room at Kootenay Lake District Hospital and stole the machine used for abortions. Before the January 27 theft was discovered, Jim Demers took the vacuum aspirator to his shop, drilled a hole through its motor, and added a shelf to transform it into a 'book cart.' He then returned it to the hospital, claiming to have done a community service[3] He was arrested, charged with public mischief and possession of stolen goods, and was convicted in October that year. As usual when anti-abortionists got into a courtroom, Demers and his lawyer tried to escalate the case into a trial of the hospital and its abortion prac-tices. The judge in Nelson ruled that line of argument out of order and fined Demers $2000 toward replacing the aspirator. Demers refused to pay and filed an appeal, and in early November, Joe Borowski himself was in Nelson to applaud him. Jim Demers played a role in attacking the Vancouver pro-choice movement later on.

Meantime, having finally switched to a paid membership system, CCCA felt it was time to call its first Annual General Meeting. Seventy people came on the evening of February 20, and we were able to report having forwarded donations of $8500 towards the doctors' legal defence in the previous eight months. At that point, a core of about seven worked in CCCA, including Marva Blackmore, Jeff Finger, Sharon Hager, Theresa Kiefer, Ron Peterson, Ann Thomson, and Penny Tilby. We were gradually joined as the year progressed by Val Cain, Carol Chapman, Rebecca Frame,

Lynn Gary, Cameron Hay, Norah Hutchinson, Lynda Raynard, Cherie Scott, Janet Shaw, Cindy Shore, Maureen Sugrue, and others.

The morning after CCCA's AGM, a ruckus erupted at the Surrey elementary school where I taught. Although activists in the Surrey Teachers' Association knew of my work in the pro-choice movement, the topic had never arisen at school itself. I was assigned elsewhere that morning, and, knowing this, the teacher in the classroom next to mine tried to corral the principal and my colleagues into an *ad hoc* staff meeting. He was demanding that they condemn me in my absence for an article I'd written about the doctors' acquittals in Ontario. It had appeared in the BCTF Status of Women *Newsletter*. This low-budget publication had a total printing of fewer than 300 copies, which went out to teacher locals across the province. Somehow it had fallen into the hands of anti-abortionists like my colleague, and *Voila!* they saw the opportunity to make trouble.

Typically presuming that everyone else shared his mindset, this colleague was confident I would be tarred and feathered at once. In fact, the rest of the staff was non-plussed. The guy next door used the school's photocopier to make dozens of copies of my article, plus three pages of a hysterical rebuttal, which he distributed widely. Parents came in to get copies, and the next morning a writer and photographer from the *Province* roamed the halls. Outrage focused on the effrontery of the BCTF's pro-choice policy — which had been in place for nearly four years — as well as on one of the closing lines of my article: "What can pro-choice teachers do?" I suggested "Bring the issue into your classrooms, staffrooms, local associations..." Well organized anti-abortionist speakers' bureaus frequently went into secondary school classrooms, taking with them gory photographs, videos, and plastic fetuses. A 'pro-life' statement, attached to my article, expressed "vehement" resentment that the BCTF should address "such a divisive and politically volatile topic."

"Abortion article causes uproar" was the headline in the Saturday, February 26, 1985 *Province*. "A Surrey teacher faces an investigation, and family life curriculum in the district will be screened in an uproar over abortion politics..." Next to the article was a half-page photo of a parent and her two children, standing in front of the school from whose evil teacher she vowed to protect them. I was given a line to explain that I meant the issue could be raised in secondary schools, and the head of the parent-teacher association at my school commented "[Thomson] is entitled to her own beliefs and right now it's not affecting us."[4]

But that was not the end of it. On the Tuesday following, my clock radio woke me with the same story headlining the 6:30am news on the CBC. It gave my name and said I was being investigated. This was repeated at 7:30 and at 8:30. At school, I contacted the president of the Surrey Teachers' Association, who assured me the story was false. He had already heard from the chairman of the Surrey trustees, and despite what the *Province* and the CBC said, the trustees were not concerned and did not intend to investigate. Patrick Clarke, then president of the BCTF, appeared on CBC radio's *Afternoon Show,* where he defended teachers' right to make policy on whatever we chose, and fielded calls from both sympathetic and hostile listeners.

That ordeal paled when two weeks later, CCCA received news from Alicen Keamarden of the Bulkley Valley Pro-Choice Alliance in Smithers. An arsonist had burned her out of her house, which also served as the Alliance's meeting place, and all their files and material were lost.[5]

As CCCA members marched in the International Women's Day parade, we distributed a leaflet announcing that Dr. Morgentaler would come to BC in April. Accompanying him would be Carolyn Egan of OCAC and Selma Edelstone, the beautifully-groomed Torontonian who had succeeded Judy Rebick as Morgentaler's publicist.

We were anxious to insure the doctor's safety. Death threats to him were frequent. In mid-January 1985, as Morgentaler stepped off a plane in Calgary, the head of Christians Concerned for Life sprayed him in the face with catsup. Photos showed the terror of the moment, as a hostile crowd surged around the diminutive doctor, nearly lifting him off his feet. The attacker was wrestled to the ground by police but was released without charge.[6] Carried away by her reverence for life, one woman screamed at Morgentaler, 'Kill him, kill him!' and a Baptist minister proposed that women who had abortions should be executed.[7]

Such incidents drove CCCA to request police protection for Morgentaler while he was in Vancouver. Janet Shaw and I secured a meeting with an inspector at police headquarters in mid-March. I remember refusing to visibly squirm under his leering gaze; the issue of abortion clearly inspired lewd thoughts in the man. He delighted in baiting us and testily insisted that the city had no responsibility to protect Henry Morgentaler. Absolutely not. However, the police would protect the *public* (from what?) by assigning two plainclothesmen to trail the doctor around. If 'Doctor' Morgentaler needed protection, that was entirely up to, heh heh, 'you girlies.' Toward this end, he considered it mandatory that CCCA hire off-duty cops as bodyguards and at least two cars, which should be ready at every moment to whisk Morgentaler away from danger. One should be parked with motor running by the door whenever he went inside a building, and one should be near the rear exit. The inspector seemed to think Morgentaler and CCCA were gangsters (whom off-duty cops would guard for money?) We left stunned by his attitude and by the expenses ahead.

Janet Shaw followed up by meeting with the RCMP assigned to the airport and to UBC. They were more polite. However, CCCA minutes for March 19 noted concern that the police "were either not offering enough security or were unwilling to reveal" what they would provide. "We cannot afford to buy adequate security," so Shaw continued to negotiate for it, without success.

We all felt we did a super job of organizing the tour, publicizing it, and scheduling maximum media coverage. On the night of the big rally, the program listed 112 organizational endorsers, plus 14 individual endorsers, of CCCA's demands. As usual, the money we needed came mainly from the 35 unions and labour groups on our list. Our budgets were always modest.

We also worked to draw the uncommitted into supporting women's right to choose. Despite lengthy and delicate discussions with the Liberal Party's Women's Commission, its president decided against holding a fund-raising luncheon with Morgentaler. John Turner, a Catholic, 'hit the ceiling' at the idea, I was told; Iona Campagnolo had been frightened by anti-abortionists during the 1984 election campaign, and Liberals had turned 'very negative' toward Morgentaler after he denounced Robert Bourassa, who was aiming to defeat René Lévesque and had promised to overturn the PQ's permissive policy on abortion clinics.

Similarly, the NDP brass was sour on Dr. Morgentaler in the wake of the debacle around the Winnipeg clinic. Surely the party should have been embarrassed by the Pawley government, instead. But Mike Harcourt, mayor of Vancouver, who had been eager to introduce the doctor from the stage of Kitsilano Secondary School in 1980, now refused all calls from CCCA or its supporters. Libby Davies, who represented the civic party COPE on city council, agreed to chair the 1985 public meeting to take place at John Oliver School, but even she queried whether Morgentaler's clinics, which were excluded from every medical plan and had to charge women a fee, weren't a threat to the publicly-funded health care system.

Even the BC branch of NAC declined to be associated with Henry Morgentaler. (That organization's squeamishness on some feminist issues later led to a show-down convention, from which Judy Rebick emerged as its leader, and after that NAC didn't look back.) A crack developed in CCCA's previously strong support in the labour movement. When a motion to endorse the Morgentaler tour was placed before the Vancouver and District Labour Council, it was shouted down by Doug Evans, an official of the International Woodworkers Association (IWA).

However, the media was eager to receive the doctor. By the time Henry Morgentaler arrived on the afternoon of Wednesday, April 10, 1985, CCCA had arranged fifteen media interviews — electronic and print — and once he was in town, the clamor from other sources was intense. Jeff Finger of CCCA made a lot of those arrangements. I remember predicting to a fellow delegate at the BCTF AGM that Vancouver would be wall-to-wall Henry Morgentaler in another week.

The doctor's energy never flagged. He cheerfully rushed from venue to venue, speaking at two public rallies and appearing at two catered fund-raisers in Vancouver. Then he went to Victoria for further appearances. We in CCCA and the Victoria CARAL group worked hard, but had we been fully aware of the schedule Dr. Morgentaler was following in the weeks before he arrived here, we might have been chagrined that his energy and dedication so far outpaced our own. Morgentaler had just turned 62 years old.

His four days in Vancouver included a lovely wine-and-hors-d'oeuvres event hosted by CCCA at the UBC Faculty Club. Spring was in full bloom. It was a spiritual experience to glimpse the sunset on the water against the backdrop of the north shore mountains. The doctor seemed refreshed, despite the non-stop media appearances he had made during the previous twenty-four hours. He climbed on a chair to address the 200 professionals we had invited to the fund-raiser. *Province* columnist Jeanie Read found Morgentaler to be genial but the atmosphere "bizarre." Reflecting on the gratitude, respect, and hatred that swirled about the doctor, she realized that "people can still be at risk for their beliefs... Still, it seems safe enough. I look at Dr. Morgentaler standing on his chair, surrounded by good, right-thinking pro-choice liberals, his face intelligent, his handshake when we shook hands a masterpiece of mixed warmth and reserve."[8]

After mingling for an hour, Morgentaler retired to an adjoining room with a small group of doctors that CCCA and Dr. Nelson Savein had laboriously persuaded to come. We partied on politely, knowing he was making his case to them: 'Come to my clinic in Montréal, and I'll provide the training in doing abortions that medical schools refuse to offer'— then, as he put it to a *Vancouver Sun* reporter, "Take the risk of helping women."[9] The BC doctors smiled, some of them sheepishly I thought, as they departed. None of them took up the challenge.

The next afternoon, speaking to 1,000 students at UBC, Dr. Morgentaler made his case once again:

> Hospital abortions are not as good as clinic abortions in many ways...you have the red tape of a hospital abortion committee, hospitals are impersonal, cumbersome, often cold institutions, where women are not treated the way they should be.[10]

Inspired by the enthusiasm he was meeting, the ever-optimistic doctor updated his prediction. On arriving in BC, he told reporters he had come to raise funds for his legal defence and had no plans to open a clinic in Vancouver. The next day he was speaking of a possible clinic in BC by the end of the year 1985. At UBC, he ebulliently declared; 'I would like to open one as soon as possible...maybe two months, three months, four months..."[11] He was met with prolonged applause.

When he finished speaking, Morgentaler left by a back door and was driven away by the CCCA members who piloted the two rental cars we had dutifully obtained. We declined to pay for bodyguards to do the driving. The next stop was a wine-and-cheese fund-raiser hosted by the NDP Women's Rights Committee. Marilyn Parliament headed the organizing committee.

Equipped with walkie-talkies, the CCCA drivers phoned ahead to Trout Lake Community Center and were assured there were no signs of danger. The doctor was very amiable toward the admiring NDPers at the party, and, for the moment, the friction in Manitoba seemed to be forgotten.

On his final day in Vancouver, Saturday, April 13, Dr. Morgentaler had time in the afternoon for some relaxation. Laurier Lapierre of CKVU TV planned to drive him up Howe Sound. Meantime, CCCA finished preparations for a public meeting at John Oliver School, in working-class southeast Vancouver. The auditorium held 930 people and was the largest venue we could find. In a break with our tradition of admitting everyone free, we had decided to sell tickets for this event — $5.00 ($2.00 for low-income people.) Sixty to 100 volunteers were lined up to keep order, many of them from Rape Relief. We felt good; everything had gone smoothly, and we anticipated that good-will would continue. In retrospect, the signs of trouble were there; we hadn't been paying attention.

Ten days before Dr. Morgentaler arrived, the *Vancouver Sun* reported a call to the faithful from Catholic Archbishop James Carney. Send Morgentaler a powerful message, he instructed, but "avoid hysterical responses...[and] reject outright any temptation to resort to violence in [your] protests to abortion clinics."[12] CCCA failed to read between the lines.

What we noticed, instead, was the sympathetic profile of Morgentaler in the *Province* on Easter Sunday, April 7.[13] In its editorial the same day, the *Province* said, "It is to be hoped that...Carney's warning to Catholics to 'avoid hysterical responses'...will be heeded." This caution was prompted by events in Toronto in February, when four days of escalating protest at the Morgentaler Clinic had been orchestrated by Emmett Cardinal Carter. On the final day, buses of Catholic school students arrived from all over southern Ontario. OCAC's demonstration the following day drew out 5000 pro-choice supporters, compared to the 3000 Catholic opponents. But only one item about those events had appeared in the Vancouver press, and CCCA had not realized the scope of them.[14] However, the *Province's* editors' main point was to warn politicians to stop imagining they could make the abortion law effective by continuing to "persecute" Morgentaler. 'Granted, if they stopped charging him, abortion clinics would become 'legal' in a *de facto* way,"ran the editorial. The *Province* seemed to think that would be the lesser of two evils, given the damage to the jury system and to respect for the law that the state's obstinacy was furthering.

Arriving early at John Oliver on the evening of April 13, CCCA activists were surprised to find two dozen youthful members of the volunteer 'militia'called The Guardian Angels there, looking tense in their red berets. They knew what we didn't. Their usual role was to defuse threats of student violence, but the Guardian Angels showed up that night to help us.

Soon afterward, the anti-abortionists began coming, by busload, car-load, and motorcycle. An hour before the meeting began, the entire city block on which the school stands, as well as both sides of 41st Avenue, was swamped by 3000 anti-abortionists. They carried pickets and candles, sang hymns and shouted, "Let the babies live!" The noise was deafening. A school wall was spray-painted "Dial M for Murder." A pile of dismembered dolls was heaped beside a cup of red liquid and a misspelled sign that read, "As often as you drink of this cup remember Morgenthaler."[15] Leather-clad bikers menaced the arriving pro-choice crowd near the school entrance.

Our "safety women," as the Rape Relief team called themselves, were out-numbered and, in the end, overwhelmed. They linked arms to create a cor-ridor from the street to the school door. But it was narrowed by shoving, screaming protesters, so that people with tickets had to struggle through it inch by inch. The pro-choice banner Rape Relief had strung up to direct people to the entrance was ripped down and destroyed. A pregnant, 20-year-old told The *Province* she was "manhandled" as she tried to get into the school. "I was pushed and shoved by the anti-choice people," she said. "They talk about respect for life but they told me, 'No, we're not going to let you in.'"[16]

Reporter Rick Ouston spoke to a pregnant fifteen-year-old who insisted, "'I won't kill my baby.'" When a doctor told her that what she'd thought was stomach flu was pregnancy, "she didn't really know what that meant — the doctor had to explain it to her, what would happen to her body, how long it would take, what it would feel like." 'Eunice's' parents urged an abortion, but she didn't know what that was, either. However, a friend of her foster family told her it meant killing a human being and took Eunice along to the protest at John Oliver. Her decision to continue her pregnancy, she told Ouston, was based "entirely" on that friend's advice. "Asked what decision Eunice would have made if her advisor had been pro-choice instead of an anti-abortionist, she looked puzzled and smiled and shrugged her shoulders."[17]

Undoubtedly, the police had intelligence about this protest which they withheld from CCCA. There were twenty uniformed officers present, but they simply watched the melée. Keith Baldrey of the *Sun* reported seeing "at least 12 minor scuffles that resulted when demonstrators tried to break through the human barricades on the school steps," but the police told him the crowd was "orderly." Betty Green denied there was violence. "I didn't see the scuffles," she told Baldrey. "To me it was very peaceful."[18]

CCCA had stationed two people in a tiny ticket booth, where they could not see the desperate scene at the door. There I stood, the lone person assigned to take tickets as people entered, and I struggled to help the pro-choicers get in and keep the screaming, pushing protesters out. Finally, the defences collapsed and anti-abortionists rushed the entrance.

It took all the strength that I and by-standers had to pull the glass doors closed before we were stampeded. In the scrimmage, an elderly NDPer I knew was wrenched from her daughter's side and both the daughter and I were horrified to find her marooned outside in the snarling crowd. At the last minute, uniformed police pushed into the school, but they made no effort to help us prevent it from being overrun. Instead, they headed at once to the basement cafeteria, where they huddled by the vending machines until the meeting ended.

Fortunately, Dr. Morgentaler and the other speakers were already safely inside. After a thirty-minute delay while the shaken audience struggled to find seats, they erupted in the first of many ovations when Dr. Morgentaler walked on stage. He further electrified the evening with his prediction of victory. He would continue to be acquitted, the law would be defeated, clinics would become legal in Canada. "Even the country of the Pope has a better abortion law than Canada has," he said. He shrugged off the hostility outside. "They call themselves pro-life, yet they threaten to kill me." Anti-abortionists are "the same kind of people who burned women as witches."[19] When the meeting ended, most of the protesters were gone. Donations in Vancouver came to nearly $13,000.

When we met to evaluate the tour, CCCA members were relieved to have got through the Saturday night near-riot, and otherwise pleased. Except with the police. Janet Shaw sent a blistering letter to Police Chief R.J. Stewart, to which we got no reply. It made the point that "We do not feel that the police should have stood by while protesters physically assaulted the citizens entering John Oliver."[20]

For weeks afterward, so many letters — mainly from pro-choice supporters — flooded the *Vancouver Sun* about that riotous crowd on April 13 that the paper ran pagefuls of them on three separate dates.

So then what. Many in CCCA, especially the newcomers, wanted to work toward a clinic in BC. They were blind to the fact that clinics were still against the law and that the law would certainly descend on any clinic we might open. CCCA, of course, lacked everything — money, doctor, venue, even information about how to start. Despite his enthusiasm, Dr. Morgentaler did not want to commute to BC to run a clinic. There was Dr. Nelson Savein. His wife, Norah Hutchinson, became active in CCCA following the Morgentaler tour of 1985. But while Morgentaler was in town, Dr. Savein told CCCA members flatly that he was not interested in opening a clinic himself. The doctors who had met with Morgentaler at the Faculty Club weren't interested either. After some discussion, CCCA postponed striking a clinic feasibility committee until we had more information. The place to get that was in Toronto, and, because OCAC had called for a strategy conference to coincide with the CARAL AGM, CCCA authorized three members to go: Marva Blackmore, Theresa Kiefer, and me.

Just before the CARAL meeting convened, on April 29, the Ontario government's appeal of the doctors' acquittals opened in court. When Henry Morgentaler addressed the CARAL AGM, he didn't mention it. But after him, Morris Manning gave a succinct summary of how he would counter the crown's case. The appeal ended on May 7, but it was October before Chief Justice William Howland released his decision.

CARAL's keynote speaker was Marjorie Maguire, Ph.D. in Catholic theology and co-founder of Catholics for a Free Choice. Maguire spoke simply, as if in conversation, but one sensed her fierce commitment to her ideals and to children. In Catholicism, she said, the spirit of ecumenism, heralded by Pope John Paul XXIII and Vatican II in the 1960s, was at odds with a one-sided condemnation of abortion. Historically, the Church had been unperturbed by it until well into the 19th century. As a theologian, she called for a new ethic: "a feminist ethic, the empowering of women and all other people who are dominated in any way." Feminism was the needed antidote to the present condition of the Church because "feminism is non-hierarchical and egalitarian."[21]

She illustrated her understanding of the morality of women's reproductive choice this way: In God's covenant with his people, argued Maguire, He made women responsible for reproducing humanity. Thus the decision about when to bring children into the world was clearly assigned to them. Therefore, the moral response was to support a woman's choice. For example, a sincere Catholic would rejoice with a woman who was delighted on becoming pregnant. And with those women whose pregnancies were unwelcome — and Maguire reminded us that many women have little power in their sexual relationships with their husbands or boyfriends, many are raped, many are poor, and most are ignorant about sexuality — a sincere Catholic would support their choices, too. If, on reviewing her situation, a woman chose not to carry through with a given pregnancy, that was her moral prerogative, according to the responsibilities God had equipped her for and entrusted to her. "We can never establish when personhood begins," said Maguire; personhood is "not a biological concept; it is an ontological, a theological concept." A "person" begins when a pregnant woman personally consents to carry her pregnancy to term, as part of the human community in covenant with God.[22] Though I am not religious, I found her argument persuasive and moving.

The next day, OCAC convened a strategy session attended by the CARAL delegates. Linda Gardner identified five political points for defending "community-based, woman defined, and medically-insured clinics." All of them presumed the conditions that existed in Toronto from 1983 on, and her first and fourth points, in particular, did not apply in Vancouver. They were 1) active involvement in the clinic from the women's movement; 2) "significant ties with labour and the NDP;" 3) co-ordinating the work with CARAL's fund-raising and its focus on the court cases; 4) "doctors who are prepared to come forward to work at clinics as the need arises;" and 5) when the documented need and the problem of access is known to the local community. Henry Morgentaler supported these points and succinctly pointed to four forces that must be dealt with: "state, police, anti-choice group, and the college of physicians and surgeons." Judy Rebick then proposed the pro-choice movement hold a series of tribunals, to take place one after the other until the momentum culminated in an action in Ottawa. It was an idea CCCA had already discussed. It seemed an excellent response to *The Silent Scream,* and the meeting took up the idea.[23]

When we three returned to Vancouver, we found CCCA prepared to hold a tribunal and to invite Maguire to visit Vancouver. But above all, members wanted to know how to open a clinic. The best information we'd obtained didn't offer much on what interested CCCA most: the 'nuts and bolts' of finding financing, a venue, a doctor. So we were little further ahead.

However, Marjorie Maguire responded promptly to our inquiries and said she could come to Vancouver in July. CCCA already had a supply of the educational pamphlets put out by Catholics for a Free Choice. One was the clearly written "Abortion: a Guide to Making Ethical Choices," by wife and husband team Marjorie and Daniel Maguire. Both were trained in theology at the most prestigious school of their faith in the US, Catholic University in Washington, DC. They pointed to the hypocrisy of making opposition to abortion the very touchstone of the Catholic faith. They offered a theologically-based challenge to the church hierarchy's unilateral pronouncements about doctrine, stressing that polls showed many Catholics did not agree with its clergy. Indeed, in June 1985, the *Globe and Mail* found that 54% of Canadian Protestants were pro-choice, while Catholics were evenly divided: 48% were opposed, 47% were pro-choice.[24]

In the build-up to the Morgentaler tour in April, efforts were made to involve local churches. But the doctor's forthright actions, going so far beyond debate on policy, scared off even those who were otherwise pro-choice.

However, persistent, polite efforts to locate open-minded Catholics had begun to lead somewhere. In March, 1985, I made contact with an active member of a six-month-old, small, devout, and deliberately informal group calling itself Concerned Catholic Women. It had ties to St. Mark's College at UBC. The articulate woman I spoke with on the phone was as angry as any of the Catholics interviewed in *Chatelaine* in 1984. She characterized the Vancouver diocese as "like a totalitarian country." I asked whether a Catholic might sit on the platform with Dr. Morgentaler. She replied that the "celibate male clergy has declared that the only sin that calls down immediate excommunication is to be 'an agent of abortion.'" I contacted this woman again in June, sure that Marjorie Maguire's visit would interest

Concerned Catholic Women. I was invited to visit a different woman at her home. This woman radiated graciousness, and she served me tea as we had a spirited talk about the role of women in the church. Abortion was not the major interest of her group, despite the hierarchy's obsession with it. Concerned Catholic Women was focused on winning the right for women to say the Mass. My hostess declined a luncheon meeting between her group and Marjorie Maguire.

Shortly before that, a Catholic priest was convicted of "terrorist violence" in Birmingham, Alabama, for entering an abortion clinic and smashing its equipment with a sledge hammer. The Rev. Edward Markley had previously been convicted of splashing paint on another abortion clinic.[25]

Locally, hospital election battles stormed on. Anti-abortion candidates were finally returned to the board of Lions Gate Hospital in June, 1985, although pro-choice board members remained in the majority.[26] But at Vernon Jubilee Hospital, the result of the September vote was to place 7 anti-abortionists on the nine member board. The familiar conflict with the medical staff then ensued.[27]

In the end, two local church speakers joined Marjorie Maguire at the public meeting at Robson Square Media Centre on July 6, 1985. Dr. Shelagh Thompson, a vivacious feminist and public speaker, represented the Unitarian Church. New CCCA member Carol Chapman was instrumental in obtaining a United Church speaker, Ms. Leslie Black.

Maguire arrived and began the round of media appearances and interviews. Relaxed and fresh-faced, she looked like a competent young-mother-next-door, rather than a feared and despised heretic. Yet, after appearing on a CBC radio show, ashen-faced men in suits chased her down Richards Street, waving copies of the Douay Bible and shouting in fury. Callers to the talk-shows on which she appeared were far angrier that Maguire should challenge the authority of the Pope, than about her "absurd" support for choice on abortion. She met their questions head on. It was her Ph.D. and scholarly study of church doctrine that led her to her views:

> Many people think that Catholics believe the Pope is infallible every time he opens his mouth to speak, that he cannot make a mistake and therefore Catholics have to follow him...but that is mistaken. The Pope can't just decide out of the blue that something's going to be an infallible teaching. It has to be something that has always been believed in the Church.[28]

All in all, Marjorie Maguire's visit to Vancouver was a triumph for her and for CCCA.

Afterward, CCCA returned to its preoccupation with how to organize itself. Attendance had trebled after the Morgentaler tour, and twenty or so people were now actively involved. We had never changed our totally informal, everyone-has-equal-standing structure, and although some of the newcomers found that ridiculous (and were clearly itching to become the 'president' or something like it), we settled for a three-person 'agenda committee,' which had limited responsibilities and rotated every two months.

Next up was the tribunal we had agreed to hold, in conjunction with pro-choice groups in other provinces. We invited women to come forward and tell their stories, about legal or illegal abortions. Testimony could be presented in person, or anonymously, either through being read aloud by someone else, or printed in the program. A panel of prominent people was invited to sit at the front of the room and serve as judges, and those in the audience would constitute the jury. We were confident the testimony would produce a verdict that found the abortion law guilty of crimes against women. In the end, testimony from twenty women was presented.

The tip of what we knew to be an iceberg — that some women were forcibly sterilized, that eugenics continued to be practiced in BC — got a bit of public notice in the summer of 1985. Most of the forcibly sterilized were aboriginal or ethnic minority women, and their stories were hidden by officialdom. However, the *Province* reported that a 25-year-old homemaker with one child went into Vancouver General Hospital in May for an abortion "but ended up sterilized without her consent." She and her partner were devastated. The hospital said it was just a mistake.[29]

Planned Parenthood published data from a recent World Fertility Survey showing that more than 150,000 women, who were denied access to contraception, died annually from abortions.[30] As the Coalition for Reproductive Choice in Winnipeg put it, "Saying that women will use abortion as a means of birth control is like saying that people will stop brushing their teeth because of easy access to root canal."[31]

On October 1, the Ontario Court of Appeal ruled that Morgentaler's use of the defence of necessity did not apply to opening abortion clinics, and that the doctors' 1984 acquittals must be set aside. It further held that the Charter did not support an implied right to abortion, so that Manning's request for the courts to rule against the abortion law was inadmissible.[32] The Harbord Street clinic in Toronto continued to perform abortions, and, in fact, a second clinic had been opened by Dr. Robert Scott. Henry Morgentaler immediately announced he would appeal his case to the Canadian Supreme Court. It took a further year before that case was heard, and it was 1988 before the verdict came down.

Joe Borowski also went to court in late 1985, when the Saskatchewan Appeal Court heard his protest of the decision against him in 1983. The upshot was to open the way for Borowski, too, to carry on to the Canadian Supreme Court.

We knew none of this in the fall of 1985, as we made our way toward a Vancouver tribunal that was held in January, 1986 and was dubbed "Crimes Against Women — The Abortion Law on Trial."

CHAPTER 12

A TAKE-OVER OF CCCA

It was an extraordinary afternoon. The fifteen women who took turns at the microphone to tell their abortion stories to a capacity crowd on Saturday, January 25, were not ashamed to reveal their personal histories. Controlled anger was the prevailing mood. Many described a relentless fertility that required years of vigilance to outwit, and to which they refused to yield their wills or their independence. It was the 1986 Vancouver tribunal, "Speak Out for Choice."

Ranging from nineteen to 80 years, the women told of having legal abortions in hospitals, as well as having horrifically painful, frightening, and life-threatening illegal abortions. One surprise was that their experiences in hospitals, with sterile conditions unlike the frequent grime of the illegal trade, were almost as distressing to the women as the prospect of submitting to a nameless practitioner of uncertain qualifications and skills. In hospitals, shame and humiliation continued to be heaped on abortion patients.

One testifier compared her abortion at the Morgentaler clinic in Montréal with a later one in a hospital. In the clinic, she received excellent and considerate care. In the hospital, "I felt I was being subjected to indignities and generally treated as a non-person...treated as a naughty girl. I was 31 years old."

A student from another province became pregnant in Vancouver before she was eligible for BC health insurance. She told the hospital that she could not afford the usual overnight stay. But patients who received a general anesthetic were not allowed to leave the same day as their surgery, unless someone picked them up. On her back on the operating table, heels in stirrups, with observers in attendance, the student was upbraided by the doctor when her muscles contracted against the insertion of a cold speculum. "He asked angrily why I didn't have anyone picking me up. By this point, I was in tears, explaining to six masked strangers what I was doing in this predicament...Though I was sure of my decision, I had continual nightmares for months afterwards, and only now can I begin to tell the horror story."

Another testifier managed to get a legal abortion, but, as she was leaving the hospital, her doctor stopped her and began a lecture. He told her the operation was "horrible" for *him*. She felt she made the right choice, but said, "My regrets are about the inhumane experience around abortion."

Routinely, women were forced to persuade doctors that they were mentally unfit to bear a child, in order to get through the bureaucratic red-tape and into a hospital. That was the fiction required to show that their health was endangered, and it was degrading. Worse, it put the women at some risk of having their existing children taken away by authorities, because they were self-described as incapable, highly-neurotic women, with crying spells and suicidal tendencies.

A number of the testifiers had had several abortions — as well as having several children — due to their exceptional fertility. Ann K., who had five living children, became pregnant repeatedly and endured agonies to limit her family. She married at nineteen, in post WWII Scotland. "For me, one of the fears around pregnancy was that housing was very scarce. We lived in rooms, which wasn't easy with small children. My husband was a displaced person, a refugee from the war, and could not get permanent work until he became a citizen." It was up to Ann to support the family, which was difficult when she became pregnant so easily and often. Contraception was illegal at the time. When at last she obtained a diaphragm, it failed and she became pregnant anyway. Unable to find competent help, Ann was forced to abort herself. Pills ordered through a newspaper ad worked for her twice, but, another time, she had to resort to knitting needles. "It was scary," she told an audience that was frightened along with her. "I induced abortions with a very dangerous method and I didn't die. I was lucky." Years later, she was fitted with an IUD. It caused unceasing cramps and bleeding. In a final struggle with her doctor, her last pregnancy ended with a caesarian, followed by a tubal ligation. Since he was "already in there," the doctor decided to remove her appendix. That unnecessary surgery was available to her, but Ann was refused help in dealing with the more frequent, more urgent need to control reproduction.

Suzanne, a mother of two, had six abortions, "two illegal, three self-induced and one legal." Her story was printed in *The North Shore News*: "I don't consider myself to have been careless or irresponsible — just very fertile. I have become pregnant despite the calendar, despite condoms, despite diaphragm and spermicidal cream, and despite the pill."[1]

Janet experienced a seesaw of fear and need, as she stared at the rundown tenement in Montréal, whose stairs she forced herself to mount alone. She became pregnant in her student days. To her surprise, she was treated with apparent kindness by the abortionist, who packed her uterus with gauze and, without explaining anything, sent her away, thinking it was all over. "So when my friends came back, we went out and celebrated a bit, got back on the train to Toronto. On the way back I went into labour. By the time I got home and was in my own bed, I was in absolute agony. This lasted a week. I just lay there hemorrhaging heavily, wishing I was dead or unconscious."

A former nurse described seeing many women with septicemia — often-fatal blood poisoning — resulting from illegal abortions. Women would be brought to hospital having used knitting needles, clothes hangers, or shaken-up bottles of soda. What seemed like the dark ages, for women living in or near major cities where they could get hospital abortions, was still the reality for vast numbers of Canadian women in 1986. It is still their reality as this is written, because abortions are hard to get.

Marguerite, indomitable at 80 years, stood tall in her stylish hat and told of having seven abortions. She was fortunate to have found a compassionate and able physician, who provided illegal abortions with follow-up care. Her description sounded close to the experiences of women at the Makaroff or Morgentaler clinics: she was treated with respect and did not suffer undue pain. "It is not terrible if it is done properly," she re-assured younger women. Unfortunately, her Calgary doctor was eventually arrested and lost his licence.

The moral outrage heaped on women who have more than one abortion flies in the face of women's reality. On average, a healthy woman has nearly 500 fertile cycles over the course of sometimes forty child-bearing years. For many, birth control information or devices are not available. And no contraceptive method is foolproof — several women testifying at the Vancouver tribunal told of becoming pregnant while using birth control. The 1969 reforms that legalized birth control and made a few safe abortions available in hospital, did not dispel the sexual double standard. Canadian doctors and public opinion might overlook the 'indiscretion' that led to one unwanted pregnancy in a lifetime. But after that, women were expected to keep their knees together, seemingly even if they were married.

At the end, tiny Grace MacInnis, who never let the pain of severe arthritis keep her from public events she supported, rose to charge the jury. "We have no reason to allow the minority to force their will on the majority," she told the audience. Sitting at the front of the room were five other 'judges.' They were Lorna Zaback, of the Vancouver Women's Health Collective; Rev. Ken Wotherspoon, a United Church minister, writer, and broadcaster; Dr. Ingrid Pacey, a feminist psychiatrist; Lauris Talmey, president of the National Women's Liberal [Party] Commission as well as the "mother of twelve, grandmother of 10;" and Art Kube, president of the BC Federation of Labor.

To report its verdict, the audience rose to convict the law. Four anti-abortionists, including Betty Green, spoiled the unanimity. They had sat hushed through the proceedings. Marva Blackmore, acting as chair, declared "the Canadian abortion law has been found guilty of crimes against women" and announced that telegrams would report the verdict to the prime minister and minister of health in Ottawa.

I felt the warm satisfaction of a job well done, as the work of four months of organizing came to an end. Nearly all of it had been done by the two or three of us on the Program Committee, and those on the Publicity Committee.

A tribunal evaluation was arranged for Sunday, January 26 — scarcely 24 hours after the event. We gathered at a member's house, and, to my surprise, more than half a dozen people who had dropped out of CCCA in the past were also there. The few chairs were soon filled, and, with most of the others, I took a seat on the floor. It was agreed that the tribunal had gone exceedingly well, and that we'd got good coverage in the media.

Ten minutes into the meeting, the tone changed. The chair announced that the remaining time would be spent airing grievances, and she set the rule that no-one could speak until every other person had spoken. It was a trashing, very like one that CCCA had indulged in against me in 1984. Nearly two hours were spent attacking me — not that any genuine complaints were made. Only dramatic and vague assertions, such as 'I just can't stand this any more!' Stand what? I was not allowed to ask or speak until the end, and after I had, as calmly as I could, tried to get the meeting back on the track of discussing ways to win legal abortion, I was not allowed to speak again until everyone in the room had had another turn. It was an ugly evening. Newer members, especially those who had worked closely with me to arrange testimony for the tribunal and had had no problems with it, were astonished at first, but the hostility in the room quenched their impulse to support me. It was an especially crude take-over of CCCA, arranged by a clique that had no commitment to the tradition of public education and mass action.

I took a leave from the organization I'd worked so hard in. That was what the trashing had aimed for. For five months, I was sidelined.

In Victoria, BC's new health minister, Stephen Rogers of the wealthy sugar family, charged that women were using abortion as a form of birth control. He saw no need to restore financing for preventive measures because, in his view, women knew perfectly well how to avoid getting pregnant. To paraphrase, they should 'just say no.' Rogers told the *Vancouver Sun* that females are "either blasé (about birth control) or whatever. They don't think about it." He implied that nothing could dissuade the promiscuous female sex from fornicating. That included teen-agers. The problem "was one of attitude not ignorance," as the reporter explained Rogers's views. She had the sense to seek out responses from Dr. Mary Conley of Victoria and Margaret Prevost, co-ordinator of the South Vancouver Island Family Planning Society. Said Prevost, "Of course, there should be more preventive programs...not just in BC, but all through North America. I think Rogers is one of the least intelligent of all those people in government, who aren't very intelligent, anyways, for sure, but I just wouldn't pay any attention at all to what he says."[2]

Alas, Rogers had little chance to expound his views further. Less than a week later, he resigned in tears, minutes after attorney-general Brian Smith announced charges against him for breach of the Financial Disclosures Act. Rogers had neglected to declare a measly $100,000 investment in government-promoted stock.[3] Premier Bennett re-instated Jim Nielsen as health minister. Nielsen was in a spot of trouble, himself, for someone from a party proud of its Bible-thumping roots. The husband of a woman he was romancing caught him with her and blackened his eye, requiring stitches to close the wounds. Nielsen's wife told the press, "He's going through a tough time, okay? Maybe he should be left alone, too, okay, because this is between him and me and not the public." Bennett said, "Quite frankly, I would have no comment on domestic disputes that have not affected the minister's ability of doing his job."[4]

What did it matter, anyway, as the province stampeded toward the opening of EXPO '86 in May. "Invite the world," was the Socred's theme, while elderly and sometimes infirm residents of cockroach hotels on the Downtown Eastside were evicted to make room for visitors to the fair. Some of them died.

The Reagan administration's last hope of defeating *Roe v. Wade* died when the US Supreme Court upheld it, again, on June 10. In a 5-4 decision, the court struck down a Pennsylvania law that put restrictions on abortion and limited state financial support for it.[5] Credit was clearly due, in part, to the National Organization for Women (NOW), which held pro-choice demonstrations in Washington, DC, and in Los Angeles on March 8. Celebrities such as Jane Fonda, Ed Asner, Morgan Fairchild, and Cybill Shepherd joined the 20,000 who turned out in pouring rain on the west coast, and more than 100,000 marched in Washington — a three mile parade.[6]

Meanwhile, CCCA had changed. A constitution was adopted, which was brief and to the point. It set out the group's aims of defending women's right to choose and repealing the law, which were appropriate — but CCCA's long-standing mass action approach disappeared. For the first time, leadership was vested in a designated body, a Steering Committee, to be elected every six months. That seemed innocuous at first, too. The first Steering Committee consisted of Norah Hutchinson, Rebecca Frame, Lynda Raynard, and, a last-minute addition, Lynn Gary. All four had become active in 1985.

To my surprise, I was phoned and asked to appear for CCCA on a panel to debate abortion on Vancouver Co-operative Radio. I did. Then I attended the CCCA meeting on June 17.

That night, the new Steering Committee introduced a six-month plan for the majority of CCCA members — routine tasks like putting out the newsletter, updating the membership list, networking with endorsers.

Then Norah Hutchinson proposed establishing a "Free Standing Abortion Clinic Planning Committee...with the view of opening a...clinic sometime within the next 12-month period." The committee would consist of "one, two, or a number to be decided" from CCCA and would invite "specific people in the community" to join in with it. This group would be "parallel" to CCCA, authorized to make decisions on its own and to "keep certain matters secret from the general membership" for security reasons. The vagueness of this "two-tier structure" for the pro-choice movement rang alarm bells and many questions were raised. The upshot was that another CCCA meeting was set to discuss the idea.[7]

That meeting, on July 3, divided between those who argued against reducing most CCCA members to second-class status, and those who favoured transferring control to a small 'autonomous' group that would open a clinic. Hutchinson, who said she was prepared to be very flexible, made a proposal. 'We should put out a call to the community, see who responds and allow them to decide their own course.' Who was this "community" and why should it supersede CCCA? The truth was, Hutchinson's plan had already been launched. Sometime between April and June, approximately 35 people came to a meeting called by Hutchinson and Marva Blackmore to discuss opening a Reproductive Health Clinic. Attending were unnamed health care professionals, the Vancouver Women's Health Collective, and the Midwives' Association, according to Blackmore. Theresa Kiefer told the July 3 meeting, 'We do have a proposal, though it's not written down.' It was that an abortion clinic be located in the Reproductive Health Clinic, whose advocates would meet for a second time at the end of July. Hutchinson and her associates were not willing to trust a clinic, which they saw as a medical project, to CCCA, but they saw a role for CCCA in running political interference. CCCA members saw things differently and demanded a "semi-public meeting" of the broad feminist and pro-choice community to discuss the matter of a clinic.[8] Talk of a Reproductive Health Clinic dried up when the second meeting failed to draw a turnout.

If there was division on who should participate in opening it, there was agreement that Vancouver needed a clinic. A leaflet to announce the exciting news was needed. Theresa Kiefer and I were struck off, and we met at Joe's Café on Commercial Drive to draft the text. It was easy to write, for the arguments were long familiar to us. Within days, thousands had been printed on buff coloured paper, with a photo on the front page showing a modest two-story house — the Morgentaler clinic on Corydon Avenue in Winnipeg.

In Toronto, 2000 anti-abortion teachers attended a conference called by Catholic priest Alphonse de Valk in July 1986. He told a reporter that, in grades "7 and 8, we have to start defending human life." The *Globe and Mail* described a slide presentation on the growth of the fetus "aimed at students up to the Grade 8 level."[9] I thought back to February 1985, when my short article on the Morgentaler trial, read by about 300 teachers — not students — had caused hysterical protest against discussing abortion in BC schools.

We began to prepare the August issue of the CCCA *Newsletter*. It would be on newsprint, so that we could afford to circulate more copies than usual. Marva Blackmore reported on the CARAL AGM in early May and wrote about abortion clinics in the US and the US National Abortion Federation. We were pleased that Hilary Clark, identifying herself as a member of CCCA, wrote about the "Narrow Victory at Lions Gate," whose hospital board she chaired. On June 25, that year's anti-abortion candidates had been defeated. For laughs, there was a feature on a zany theatre group from California that dubbed itself "Ladies Against Women." Its members boasted "'I'd rather be ironing,'" and called for women to "get into the kitchens and out of the streets." CCCA's Jeff Finger had buttons made for sale with one of Ladies Against Women's choicest slogans: "Protect the Unconceived — Citizenship for Sperm."

The editorial for the issue was assigned to me. I wrote of the prospects for a clinic in BC, emphasizing the need to "build enough public support to defend a clinic from harassment by the government, courts and police." Following that was an article by Dr. Nelson Savein, who identified himself as "a practicing gynecologist [who had] provided abortion services in three provinces over the past ten years." The title was "A doctor's Perspective on Abortion Clinics," and beside it was a photo of Savein. His article concluded: "For those of us physicians who cannot wait for an archaic Criminal Code to change, we may be forced to follow in Dr. Morgentaler's footsteps and defy the law."[10]

British Columbia's attention was turned elsewhere, however. Shortly after presiding at the opening of EXPO, Premier Bill Bennett stunned the province by resigning from politics. In the free-for-all leadership race that followed, an even dozen candidates vied to succeed him. Some were newcomers, several were cabinet ministers, and others weren't even in government, such as William Vander Zalm.

Vander Zalm had held several cabinet posts in the past, but he'd "quit in a snit," as the *Vancouver Sun* put it,[11] after calling his cabinet colleagues "gutless," when they defeated his land use plan in 1983. He'd spent the interim building a biblical theme park in Richmond called Fantasy Gardens and running, unsuccessfully, for mayor of Vancouver against Mike Harcourt of the NDP. He was remembered for uttering threats against welfare recipients who "refuse to pick up a shovel," when he'd been minister of human resources; for calling Parti Québecois premier René Lévesque a "frog;" and for vowing, as education minister, to resume the use of the Lord's Prayer in schools and to ensure that students learned to "write good." In their 1989 book about him, journalists Keith Baldery and Gary Mason gave this summation: "Anyone who had ever worked with Vander Zalm in cabinet considered him to be inept at administering anything."[12] He was popular with the public, however.

The leadership convention in Whistler at the end of July was raucous. Delegates were wooed with parades, barbecues, and beer fests, and rumours persisted afterward that Bank of BC head Edgar Kaiser had offered to pay the campaign debts of those who would deliver their supporters' votes to his personal favourite, Bill Vander Zalm.[13] All twelve candidates addressed the floor, and Kim Campbell, a recent Socred MLA and late entrant for the leadership, who got only fourteen votes, made an impression when she warned, "Charisma without substance is a dangerous thing."[14] Her allusion to Vander Zalm was unmistakable.

Bill Vander Zalm triumphed on the fourth ballot and assumed the premiership late on July 30, 1986. As he hugged his wife Lillian (whose mother voted NDP), groans issued from various quarters. From the *Toronto Star*: "Bill Vander Zalm's victory in Socred race may bring wackiness back to BC politics." Columnist Allan Fotheringham in the *Calgary Herald*: "Vander Zalm win underlines BC's goofiness." And, presciently, in the *Montréal Gazette*: "Vander Zalm can make or break BC Socreds' future."[15] Editorialized the *Vancouver Sun*: "...It is safe to say [his] are the politics of the unexpected...He was not our choice for premier."[16]

Two days after being elected, an expansive Vander Zalm outlined his priorities to the Canadian Press in an interview that was printed in the *Toronto Star* but did not appear in BC. "Premier-designate Bill Vander Zalm, a staunch Roman Catholic, has vowed to scrutinize abortion procedures in British Columbia hospitals."[17] Almost a month went by before the premier formally gave health minister Nielsen the task of determining the availability of abortion in BC hospitals. He said he believed hospital TACs sometimes approved abortions as a means of birth control.[18] There was such an outcry that, by the end of the week, Vander Zalm withdrew his request to Nielsen, who had also expressed the belief that TACs followed the law. Instead, the premier hinted he would undertake a personal investigation of the matter, while, in future, an "in-depth" look was "something I intend to pursue." He called an election for October 22, a week after EXPO closed but before the glitter-dust had time to settle.

In Toronto, the situation seemed more positive. Dr. Robert Scott, long-time associate and co-defendant with Dr. Morgentaler, opened a second abortion clinic in May. Ontario was in the throes of a province-wide doctors' strike, and because women needing abortions could not wait for the strike to end, many Toronto doctors unhesitatingly sent their patients to the Morgentaler and Scott clinics.[19] The two clinics worked expanded hours to handle the demand. This boosted their standing in the medical community, and led CARAL president Norma Scarborough to call for an end to the continuing police investigation of the clinics. When the strike ended, however, doctors began charging abortion patients $200-$400 for referring them to hospital TACs.[20] This was followed by the unexpected arrest of Drs. Morgentaler, Robert Scott, and Nikki Colodny — who performed abortions at the Morgentaler clinic and was also a leader of OCAC. They were released the same day and charges were stayed, but the arrests came less than three weeks before Drs. Morgentaler, Scott, and Smoling returned to the precincts of the Canadian Supreme Court. The case was nominally an objection to the Appeal Court's capsizing of the doctors' 1984 jury acquittal for opening the Harbord St. clinic. In fact, Morgentaler and Morris Manning's careful groundwork would now open a challenge to the constitutionality of the abortion law before the highest court in the land.

As the case opened on October 7, 1986, the Supreme Court was somewhat changed. Only two judges remained of those who had replaced Dr. Morgentaler's initial Québec acquittal with a conviction, in 1975. For the first time, a woman — Justice Bertha Wilson — sat on the bench. But the most important change was the adoption of the Charter of Rights. Chief counsel Morris Manning would rely on it heavily in arguing that the byzantine abortion law abridged the Canadian constitution. The "most publicized and controversial case in the Charter's brief history," as F.L. Morton characterized it,[21] lasted almost a week, although judgment was reserved for fifteen months. Manning argued that the Criminal Code on abortion violated sections 2 ,7, 12, and 15 of the Charter, but the crux of the case lay in how the Court would interpret section 7. Worded broadly, section 7 guaranteed "life, liberty, and security of the person." Did that extend to an unwillingly pregnant woman's decision to abort? It was a gnarly legal question, since it required the Court to consider what it most dreaded doing: whether to uphold — or possibly — abolish an article of legislation.

Far from the Supreme Court, most members of CCCA were unaware that the Steering Committee had not printed or released the August issue of the *Newsletter*. I did not learn of this until late September. As part of the plan to publicize news about a clinic widely, a version of my editorial for the CCCA *Newsletter* appeared in the September issue of *Kinesis*.[22] In late August, I volunteered to represent CCCA at the BCTF Status of Women Committee's networking session with other women's groups, held at UBC. On my way to the campus, I stopped at Norah Hutchinson and Nelson Savein's spacious house on the west side to pick up a box of booklets and pamphlets, which I spread on a table and sold at the conference. Later, I returned the box of literature. No-one answered the bell when I arrived, so I left the box by the front door and phoned Norah later to tell her it was there. Both the *Kinesis* article and the box of literature became matters of furious dispute within CCCA that did not end until the new year.

On September 13, 1986, to the surprise of most CCCA members, the

Vancouver Sun ran an article headed "Abortion clinic slated for city in '87":

> Norah Hutchinson, a spokesman for the Concerned Citizens for Choice on Abortion, said although her group won't be responsible for the actual construction of the clinic, "we'll be organizing the political support for it."
>
> "We certainly envision a clinic within the next 12 months. But it will depend on the medical personnel stepping forward," she said. ...Hutchinson said her group, which does not yet have financing for the clinic in place, is aiming for a fully insured clinic, not a 'fee-for-service' facility.[23]

Anti-abortionists George Carruthers and Betty Green expressed outrage at this possibility.[24] In the next day's *Sun*, attorney-general Brian Smith "warned...he would not hesitate to close down a free-standing abortion clinic, if one were established in BC." To which Norah Hutchinson replied, "We would advise Mr. Vander Zalm and Mr. Smith to sit back and take some lessons from what's happening in other provinces in the country," adding, "You won't find a jury in Canada that would convict a physician of performing an abortion in a safe, free-standing clinic."[25]

But despite that proud assertion, police, judges, and governments could, and had done, a great deal of harm to physicians working in clinics and women who used them. The truth was that, as regularly as juries acquitted Morgentaler, governments appealed the verdict and charged him again. Hutchinson's fierce warning to the Socreds came when the groundwork for a clinic in Vancouver had scarcely begun. It seemed a bit early for her to be so cock-sure.

Immediately, there was considerable buzz about clinics, and Norah Hutchinson, Dr. Nelson Savein, and Marva Blackmore appeared on BCTV. Nonetheless, the CCCA Steering Committee saw fit to censure me for the article I had submitted to *Kinesis*, charging that it was "misleading and incorrect," and that "the potential repercussions of that article...could have posed a serious problem for CCCA."[26] Later, I was informed the offending line in my article read, "So far, one doctor who is prepared to work in the clinic has come forward and is working closely with CCCA." No doctor's name was mentioned. But given that Dr Nelson Savein had written about a clinic in the CCCA *Newsletter*, and that he did not refuse to be interviewed on TV, it seemed an overreaction to blame me for possible suspicions that Norah Hutchinson's husband might work in CCCA's clinic. It was then that she informed me that the August issue of the *Newsletter* had not yet been released, in order to "protect" her husband.

That was only the beginning. A month after the BCTF meeting to which I had taken a box of CCCA literature, Hutchinson claimed it was missing. When I reminded her I had left it on her doorstep and notified her of that, she developed the belief that it had been stolen. The thought was terrifying. She had young children. Prowlers on her property could not be tolerated.[27] I was held to be responsible for the missing literature, and a list of titles was phoned to me to be ordered post-haste from CARAL and Catholics for a Free Choice. I put in a rush order to Toronto and to Washington, DC. Then I was smugly informed that the Steering Committee expected me to pay for the $200 worth of pamphlets I had just ordered.

Despite this unpleasantness, I was cheered that steps toward a clinic were finally getting underway. The semi-public planning meeting, decided on in July, had become a tour by three leaders of the movement from Toronto: Carolyn Egan, a principal figure in the Ontario Coalition for Abortion Clinics, Norma Scarborough, president of CARAL, and Dr. Nikki Colodny. A highlight of their five-day visit in mid-October was an all-day conference to plan a clinic for Vancouver, to which women's groups and selected others were invited. An expanded version of the CCCA *Newsletter*, written for release in August, was re-dated October, 1986, featured a photo of Nikki Colodny on the cover, and made available at the conference.

It was opened by Penny Tilby, who told the twenty-six women present that CCCA's decision to proceed toward a clinic was spurred by locating 'a doctor who is interested in working in a clinic.'[28] That same phrase had brought censure on me, and I was being ostracized by most CCCA members. The three visitors described the Morgentaler and Scott clinics in Toronto and then took questions. Norah Hutchinson then summed up her view that a local clinic planning committee would be 'parallel' to CCCA, and that it would not be 'accountable on every little thing to CCCA.' That was to spare people from unnecessary meetings. Nikki Colodny gave qualified acceptance to this 'parallel' structure, but emphasized the need for communication between the clinic group and the political-movement-building group, which she felt should be broader than CCCA. When we re-assembled for the closing plenary session, there was dissatisfaction from some that the meeting wasn't forthwith electing a steering committee for a broad coalition, 'rather than leaving it all to CCCA.' Hutchinson promised to invite everyone back to another meeting in the new year. That wasn't felt to be sufficient, and, in the end, it was agreed to form a planning committee on the spot, that would organize a January 1987 founding conference for a clinic coalition.[29]

Was that what the CCCA leadership had in mind? It was difficult to tell. Hutchinson's concept of a clinic and, especially, of what she called the "nuts and bolts" of opening it — dull work in her description, but full of excitement in most others' eyes — was very vague. It seemed to leave out altogether the hard fact that free-standing clinics were illegal in Canada. On the issue of whether or not there were doctors ready to risk life imprisonment for opening a clinic in BC, both Hutchinson and Nelson Savein were coy. Depending on who she was talking to, Hutchinson said both 'yes,' there was a doctor, and 'no, no, no.' And where would the money come from? As for the political support which she agreed would be necessary and which she expected CCCA to do, there was little sense that Hutchinson anticipated the kind of massive opposition that had developed wherever Dr. Morgentaler had opened a clinic. In BC, we would have to outwit the police, the courts, the anti-abortionists, and the provincial and federal governments. That job would take more than the small group which came to the October 18 conference at Langara — especially if it were seen as no more than an occasional outfit that would turn out at three-month intervals to get the word from CCCA.

After the uproar over my *Kinesis* article and the sly shenanigans about the "missing" literature, I was not only angry but quite worried about whether a clinic would succeed, given the confused politics and elitism that had developed within CCCA. I wrote up my concerns and discussed them in confidence with two feminists not active in CCCA. The statement went no further, but one of the women I had shown it to in confidence passed it on to a member of CCCA whom she knew was hostile to me. My uncirculated statement was condemned as the ultimate betrayal. I was barred from attending further CCCA meetings, except for one in which I was to explain myself. The date for that showdown was set for January 20, 1987.

Abortions continued to dominate the news across the province. Plucky gynecologist Dr. Peter Goeritz of Powell River accused the local hospital's TAC of discriminating against poor women who could not afford to leave town to get an abortion. The number of procedures performed in Powell River had declined steadily from 55 in the 1978-79 fiscal year to only 14 in 1983-84. "Word has probably gone around town that it's not even worthwhile to go to a doctor here, so women go directly to Vancouver," said Goeritz.[30] During the fall of 1986, the hospital board election in Vernon erupted over the abortion issue, followed by a medical staff vote to withdraw its services from administrative committees. Nonetheless, a re-constituted TAC refused to approve any applications it received, after adopting stringent new guidelines in late October.[31] And in Vancouver, St. Paul's Hospital, run by Catholics although funded publicly, announced it would ban tubal ligations for women who desired to be sterilized. It partially rescinded this policy after a public outcry.[32]

A second announcement of an immanent Vancouver clinic was made in October, by Norah Hutchinson, with Dr. Nikki Colodny at her side. Reported the *Sun*, "Vancouver will have an abortion clinic within one year, backed by money from community groups and staffed by doctors willing to risk arrest, a pro-choice group says."[33]

Days later, Bill Vander Zalm and the Socreds won in a landslide. The outcome of the October 22 election was declared only seventeen minutes after the polls closed. A perpetually grinning Vander Zalm ingenuously told reporters that being premier was "a piece of cake."[34] Buoyed by his sunny disposition and by six months of EXPO, the electorate seemed to think it charming when Vander Zalm explained why his wife was not campaigning at his side: "She's washing socks, ironing shirts, and getting me ready for next week. I always wear a clean shirt, thanks to Lillian...We're equal partners in everything," he drawled.[35] That summed up his concept of a woman's role.

In November, planning for the January founding of a clinic coalition got underway. A dedicated group of about twelve met weekly for two and a half months. Four or five of its members came from Fraser Valley CARAL, despite the long trip in from Langley and south Surrey. In the beginning, six members of CCCA attended meetings, over which Lynda Raynard, of the CCCA Steering Committee, kept a close eye. In addition, two longtime feminists who were momentarily unaffiliated with a group participated: Jackie Ainsworth and Janet Vesterback. Even though I was unwelcome at meetings of CCCA itself, no attempt was made to bar me from the conference planning committee. Approximately 1200 notices went out to every kind of social action group. The agenda was carefully planned. Jackie Ainsworth and I met at La Quena coffeehouse on Commercial Drive to draft a series of motions that would take the conference, step by step, through the process of adopting a basis of unity, establishing a coalition, and electing a steering committee.

Four days before the momentous conference took place, I was expelled from CCCA. It was a tense and hostile meeting. The charges against me were that I'd been censured in September because of submitting an article to *Kinesis* that the Steering committee later objected to, that I had failed to pay for the lost literature I had been commanded to re-order, and that I had authored a statement "which may jeopardize CCCA's credibility in the community," even though I had shown it to only two people. The CCCA constitution had been revised expressly to provide for expulsion. There were amusing aspects to the meeting, because, in their fury, many members became inchoate and could scarcely talk, and the chairing was completely inept. Nonetheless, I was voted out, ending nine years of work in a group I had helped to found and to which I had given my all. In the snarling atmosphere, most of CCCA seemed to believe that my personality was the main issue: what obtuseness that I would stay on, when I wasn't wanted! Yes, but — couldn't they see that we hadn't won the battle yet? To me, the issue was winning legal, safe abortions — and a BC clinic, if possible. I was willing to compromise on almost anything but a clearheaded pursuit of our politics.

The year closed with another attack from the premier. In December, Vander Zalm proposed cutting the fee paid to doctors for abortions, as a bid to reduce the number performed in BC. He got the idea from Alberta, where doctors were paid only $89.75 for the operation, as opposed to an average of $104 in BC. CCCA called the idea "ludicrous." NDP MLA Joan Smallwood, who may have been the only candidate in the October election to run on an openly pro-choice platform, charged that Vander Zalm was aiming to put the province back in the "dark ages."[36] Dr. John O'Brien-Bell, president of the BC Medical Association, was also opposed: "You don't change society's views on abortion by pressuring doctors and turning abortions into a marketplace commodity," he advised.[37]

The premier, who'd floated his proposal off the cuff on a radio talk show, got a new idea. First he instructed health ministry officials to review all abortions in BC to determine whether or not they were being performed frivolously. Then he announced the government would promote adoption, by matching abortion applicants with couples who wished to adopt. "That's going to cost money," said Vander Zalm. "That doesn't matter; it's a priority."[38]

And that was the premier's Christmas Eve gift to BC. He liked to see himself as Santa Claus, among other roles, and during his 'reign' he starred as "Sinter Klaas" in a Dutch language movie. A few months after being elected, he and Lillian paid $750,000 for a replica of a Dutch castle, which had been sent over to commemorate Vancouver's one-hundredth anniversary. They hauled it from a downtown corner to Fantasy Gardens, installed a moat and drawbridge, and moved in. At a flea market, they snatched up a velvet Elvis Presley portrait to decorate its walls.[39] When asked by reporters what he thought about the propriety of the head of government living in a phony castle in a theme park for paying visitors, Vander Zalm replied, proudly, "I think it's neat."[40]

CHAPTER 13

FOUNDING THE BC COALITION
FOR ABORTION CLINICS

The conference that founded the BC Coalition for Abortion Clinics (BCCAC) on Sunday, January 25, 1987, ratcheted the local women's movement up a notch or two. There was electric tension among the nearly 200 people there (including a few men). Here was a tangible goal — opening a clinic — that combined the promise of a needed service for women with excitement, glamour, and power! Many of those who came intended to have a major say in the process. What separated this feminist gathering from others over the years were the number of conflicting secondary agendas in the room and the emergence of raw political combat.

It was four months since the first of CCCA's public announcements about an abortion clinic had appeared in the *Vancouver Sun*. Vander Zalm briefly abandoned his sunny belief that everything in BC was "Faaaantastic!" There would be no abortion clinic in his province; he said he would close any such thing down. "We can't allow people to go around breaking the laws just because they think they're in the right," said the premier,[1] who, days later, told a group of anti-abortionists, "you can't go too far wrong if you believe that what you are doing is right. I think I'm on the right course."[2] The anti-abortionists agreed and presented the premier with a brief entitled "Fulfilling Your Mandate." They were of the view that Vander Zalm's "moral" position on the abortion question was what got him elected.[3]

Some members of the electorate disagreed and sent letters to the *Sun* about it. "Mr. Vander Zalm's proposal makes me furious. I was wondering when his simplistic, pig-headed approach to controversial issues would link up the inadequate government adoption system and his vendetta against abortions," wrote a woman from Maple Ridge.[4] Three Vancouver women co-signed a letter saying sternly, "[Vander Zalm is] not going to force women into the back alleys of butchers again. History has changed."[5]

Somewhat surprisingly, the local press lined up behind the pro-choice movement. Despite the large pro-choice majority shown in numerous public opinion polls, we were still depicted in the media as fly-by-night extremists representing almost no-one. But Marjorie Nichols titled her January 16th column in the *Sun*, "Vander Zalm's BC: it's anti-abortion...but hates kids."[6]

Two days later, the *Province* editorialized, "The reality is that whatever the Supreme Court decides [in the Morgentaler case], the vast majority of Canadians favour free choice on abortions. Parliament will eventually have to allow women to decide for themselves. It's only a matter of time."[7]

The best support came from Dr. John O'Brien-Bell, president of the BC Medical Association, who stated "Abortions should be performed in clinics and not in hospital operating rooms."[8] The *Province* described this as coming "out of the closet, so to speak...Dr. O'Brien-Bell is in effect supporting the Concerned Citizens for Choice on Abortion (CCCA) who want a 'free-standing' abortion clinic in Vancouver." The doctor did not, however, offer to join the clinic's staff.

I almost lost heart and didn't go to the conference on January 25. The distemper and double-think that had seized CCCA dismayed me. Although I believed my time in the pro-choice movement was ended and that CCCA would block my participation in the new coalition, I went to the conference after all. I arrived at the Vancouver Indian Centre on Hastings Street, as it was called then, in time to squeeze in between the TV camera people, who were asked to leave as soon as the meeting began. Planning for an illegal clinic had to be done out of the spotlight.

A cross-section of pro-choice supporters and the women's movement — the Vancouver Women's Health Collective, Rape Relief, Women Against Violence Against Women, the Vancouver Status of Women, and *Kinesis* — was there, as was the well-known midwife Gloria Lemay. These groups had strong political views and they were especially critical of the medical establishment. They believed fiercely that women could rely only on themselves to get honest and satisfactory care. Fraser Valley CARAL members came, excited about the proposal for a clinic but as vague as most of us about how to get one. Apart from being pro-choice, the politics among other groups was diverse. The crowd was dismayingly Caucasian, although Marjorie White and Doreen Manual from Urban Images for Native Indian Women replied to the RSVP and and they were there.

More than 150 people had registered when a bloc of forty women from the NDP arrived. We learned later that they had met together twice to plan for the conference, and they had a brisk and determined manner as they strode into the hall.[9] Since the NDP Women's Rights Committee (WRC) had split away from planning the Morgentaler tour of 1980, few NDP women had mingled with CCCA. Suddenly, this conference attracted the leadership of the WRC, a sizable number of its members, and even three NDP Members of the Legislative Assembly. Heading the group was Joan Smallwood, MLA from Surrey, closely followed by Darlene Marzari, MLA from Point Grey in Vancouver, and Anita Hagen, MLA from New Westminster.

The meeting was called to order, and Marva Blackmore of CCCA gave the keynote speech: why an abortion clinic was needed in Vancouver. The next speaker was Marcy Bloom, co-ordinator of the feminist abortion clinic in Tacoma, Washington, who supported us all the way. But Bloom reminded everyone that, despite the advantages of clinics, they did not solve every problem. They did not guarantee access to abortion for women in small communities. They were exposed to anti-abortion opposition and sometimes to violent attacks. She closed with:

> Remember the women. Remember ourselves.
> Remember coat hangers and back alleys.
> Out of the back alleys and into the clinics is
> a really good motto to keep in mind.

When we broke for coffee, the NDP women pulled their chairs into a circle in the middle of the floor and conferred. It was the old Open Caucus technique, in which a minority opposition refuses to withdraw into a back-room and, instead, proudly plots in the open. During the mid-seventies, an Open Caucus flourished within the BC NDP itself, convening on the floor of provincial conventions at breaktimes, running opposition candidates for the party executive (and routinely capturing a third of the vote). I sat on the steering committee of that Open Caucus for two or three years, helping to organize day-long conferences across BC, and taking the technique to the federal NDP convention in Winnipeg the year Ed Broadbent defeated Rosemary Brown for the leadership. But what were the NDP women cau-cusing about in the midst of this conference to found an abortion clinic coalition in BC?

During the small-group discussions — 'workshops' — that followed, I began to find out. There were four workshop topics; I joined a group on political strategy that drew, among others, Joan Smallwood and others from the NDP; Melanie Conn, founder of the Vancouver Women's Health Collective; socialist feminists like Cynthia Flood and Jackie Larkin; as well as Kate Braid and Karen Kilbride whose allegiance was to the labour movement. These were strong-minded women.

The NDP women argued that opening an abortion clinic would play right into Vander Zalm's hands. It would be closed forthwith. Better to con-centrate on the long-cherished NDP proposal for a province-wide network of community care centres. Such centres, offering a full range of reproduc-tive health care services — not just abortions — would appeal to a broad range of BCers and would qualify for public funding. Of course! The plan of the Foulkes Report, adopted by the provincial convention in 1974. I'd worked to get that policy adopted at the Peachland convention, too. It had its roots in the Women's Caucus and the Women's Liberation Alliance. But I thought there was an unspoken message behind what the NDP women were now saying. It was: 'Wait sisters. Put this clinic talk on hold until the NDP wins an election and is in charge of BC.' The party wanted to avoid being linked with what would inevitably be an illegal clinic. NDPers had been featured in too many pro-choice rallies, conferences, and media announcements to extricate themselves from this project — in the minds of party members and of voters, and in the accusations of the Socreds. These NDPers were afraid that a clinic opened by a women's coalition might cost the NDP at election time.

After lunch, a plenary session got down to business. Debate opened on the major proposal, written by Jackie Ainsworth and me, to form a coalition and move toward two goals. The immediate one was to establish "an abortion clinic in Vancouver, separate and apart from hospitals." The longer-term goal was to establish "women's health clinics around the province...these clinics would provide comprehensive health services, including abortion, to women."

The second goal was essentially the same as the NDP's. Predictably, a motion was made to switch them around, so that an abortion clinic would be created only after there were full-service clinics around the province.

A fierce debate ensued. There was no way the radical feminist organizations — the Health Collective, the Status of Women, the rape crisis centres, the midwives, those who worked with battered women, etc. — would agree to that. Nor would the women from left-wing groups. They wanted a clinic now. For a time, it seemed that both the coalition and an abortion clinic might founder and the conference come to naught.

Then, with canny skill, Hilda Thomas proposed an amendment that saved the day. A long-time social democrat, she had contributed greatly to the NDP, both in BC and in the federal party. But her loyalty had an independent bent. Her proposal was to accept the reversal in the order of priorities, so that the long-term goal of a provincial network of clinics would come first. But, she moved, "*in the interim*, we establish and support the ongoing operation of an abortion clinic in Vancouver, and that we demand this service be funded by" the provincial health care plan. How could the NDP delegation argue against that without betraying feminism? They couldn't. Thomas's amendment was adopted overwhelmingly.[10]

So we had a basis of unity, and the conference rapidly voted to establish a coalition and select an interim steering committee. Departing from the script — the proposal drafted by Ainsworth and me was for a steering committee of 7-9 members (we didn't expect so many people at the conference) — the CCCA chairwoman called for up to twenty volunteers. With a shock I realized this opened a space for me, and I joined the crowd gathering at the front of the room. My days in the pro-choice movement weren't to end, after all.

So eager were the participants to get started on a clinic that twenty-two women came forward or were nominated for the interim steering committee. It was agreed to accept them all. A brief announcement was given to the media, which was waiting just outside the doors. The new group would be known as the BC Coalition for Abortion Clinics (BCCAC).

Later, I read over my notes. The opposition from the NDP women and how it had been neutralized loomed large in my evaluation. But another sub-agenda had existed, also, and veiled references to it had been made by various CCCA members. I wondered how many understood what they'd meant. The majority at the conference, and certainly those who'd planned it and the representatives of the radical feminist organizations, assumed, of course, that the clinic would be opened and controlled by the new coalition itself. It wasn't until the second meeting of the interim steering committee that CCCA revealed it had a different kind of clinic in mind. Sparks began to fly at once. In March, when the second general membership meeting of the coalition was held, this conflict was the central issue of debate.

Elsewhere, the war against feminism was in full gear. Bernard Nathanson released an eight-minute sequel to *The Silent Scream,* which focused on second trimester abortions and was shown throughout the Senate Office Building in Washington, DC. Boston *Globe* columnist Ellen Goodman reviewed the new video and found it puzzling that "the central character" — the pregnant woman whose womb was being evacuated — "keeps disappearing." She was not identified, except as "'the murderess.'" Where did Nathanson find a woman who would agree to her abortion being filmed for his purposes, and how could he justify performing an abortion at all, despite the propaganda element? Goodman raised several ethical and medical questions about Nathanson's motives and claims.[11]

In Canada, women seemed to vanish from the body politic just as easily. By mid-1986, abortions were almost as scarce in Nova Scotia as they were in PEI and Newfoundland, where they'd disappeared altogether. In other provinces, the procedure was equally unavailable unless the applicant lived in a major city and was lucky enough to find a doctor with credentials at a hospital that would grant its approval. In the 18th year of being semi-legal, access to abortion services was increasingly on decline.[12] Three-quarters of the abortions in Canada were done at the 15 per cent of hospitals that offered "reasonable" access to the procedure. The *Vancouver Sun* published an article in March, 1987, revising its 1985 survey on the number of BC hospitals with functioning abortion committees. It had dropped from 51 out of 115 hospitals in the province to 38.[13]

In the midst of an uproar about abortion fees in Alberta, a 16-year-old from Medicine Hat made legal history with a valiant fight to end her pregnancy. One of eight children in a Mormon family, whose 14-year-old sister was also pregnant, the teen was prevented from getting an abortion by a court injunction issued to her parents. They argued that their daughter had no legal right to make such a decision on her own. But on December 31, 1986, the Alberta Court of Appeal ruled that the only issue was whether the young woman had the capacity to make a decision involving moral and emotional issues, and the court found that she did. "She has sufficient understanding and intelligence to make up her own mind," declared the judges.[14] Because of the two-month delay caused by the injunction and appeal, the young woman had to undergo a 16-hour second trimester abortion — exactly the sort, and probably the same age-group, that Nathanson was targeting in his new video. Teens frequently waited longer to come to terms with the irreversible aspect of pregnancy, out of fear, lack of support, and societal pressure, and studies showed they were more likely to undergo late abortions. The spunky Albertan told an interviewer: "That was probably the hardest thing I'll ever have to do — but I'm glad I did it and I hope it will make things easier for other teenagers who have the same problem."[15]

An important report was published in Ontario: a review of hospital abortion services by Dr. Marion Powell. Commissioned by the provincial Liberals and released in January 1987, the report was a damning indictment of the system. Powell identified numerous inadequacies and cases of injustice and chicanery. At the same time, the doctors she interviewed "felt strongly that abortion should be removed from the Criminal Code and...be a decision between a woman and her doctor."[16] Powell recommended multi-purpose, regional women's clinics "not necessarily located in hospitals," as well as many other reforms. "Area abortion centres urged for Ontario"— in other words, clinics — reported the *Vancouver Sun*.[17]

During this period, Ottawa achieved a mixed report card. On the one hand, secretary of state David Crombie turned down a request for operational funding from R.E.A.L. Women, on the grounds the group did not advance the cause of equal opportunity.[18] On the other hand, PC backbencher Gus Mitges (Grey-Simcoe, Ontario) dropped a motion into the Commons to amend the Charter of Rights to guarantee life, liberty and security for the "unborn."Although such private member's bills seldom get to the floor in parliament, this one did. It was discussed for four hours in November, 1986 and was scheduled for a second discussion in January 1987. CARAL in Toronto counted a total of 52 MPs who held anti-abortion views, including seven from BC. All but one (Ontario Liberal John Nunziata) were Tories. Earlier, Mitges had demanded the death penalty for women who have abortions.[19] A constitutional upset was avoided after an emotional debate that culminated in a vote on June 2, 1987. Mitges's proposal was defeated 89-62. Immediately afterwards, justice minister Ray Hnatyshyn declared the vote was close (although it was defeated 3-2) and said it reflected the lack of a firm consensus on the issue within Canada. John Reimer, Tory MP for Kitchener, then called for removing the word "health" from the Criminal Code section on abortion. That would have blocked the availability of abortion in almost all cases, requiring a woman's life to be in danger in order for her to obtain one. The motion died on the order paper after being debated on June 15.[20]

In British Columbia, the explosive issue of hospital abortion committees moved to the Okanagan centres of Vernon and Kamloops that spring. At Jubilee Hospital in Vernon, the doctor's strike that had begun in December, 1986, continued. A solution would almost be reached, and then the board would put its foot in it again. This went on nearly all year, and at the AGM in the fall, all the candidates elected were against abortion.[21]

The Kamloops battle became, not only ugly, but a province-wide scandal involving, again, a teen-ager. In January 1987, the anti-abortion majority on the board of Royal Inland Hospital ruled its pro-choice chair, Ms. Gus Halliday, could not vote or debate any issue on the agenda. The hospital's lawyer said that was illegal, but the board ignored him and changed the structure of the TAC. This had the active support of health minister Peter Dueck.[22] The new, anti-abortionist TAC caused 70 out of the 130-member medical staff to vote non-confidence in the trustees.[23] Sandy Mallory, alderman and new chair of the hospital board, explained the need for opposing abortion: "We get ladies who say they want an abortion because they have an ingrown toenail."[24]

Then it was discovered that one of the many applicants turned down in Kamloops was a pregnant 14-year-old. She had been referred by Dr. David Gilmore from her hometown in Dawson Creek, and he was surprised the Royal Inland board had rejected the request. In Dr. Gilmore's opinion the girl's health was at risk if the pregnancy continued — a view echoed by several other physicians. "I am amazed, because I think a pregnant 14-year-old is a pregnant child," said a Kamloops gynecologist. The girl's father said that his wife and daughter spent two weeks and "$3000 that we couldn't afford" in a Kamloops motel, waiting for the TAC's decision. Board chair Mallory said, "I wouldn't be surprised if someone planted that as false information...there are people who are trying to keep stirring this issue up." Health minister Dueck defended the ruling on the teenager: "If that's the decision they made, I'd have to say they made it properly." The father described his daughter as a good girl, who got pregnant the first time she had sex. "She's never been into drugs or alcohol or anything like that. It was just bad luck." Finally, as she entered her fifteenth week of pregnancy, the Dawson Creek teen managed to get an abortion in Vancouver.[25]

At the June 18 AGM, all six vacancies on the Royal Inland hospital board were won by pro-choice candidates. All obtained at least 500 more votes than their opponents. Approval of abortions at the Kamloops hospital resumed shortly thereafter.[26]

The eleventh annual skirmish for control of Lions Gate hospital board, on June 24, elected four trustees. Had anti-abortionists won these seats, they would have been only one vote short of a majority. But they didn't win. Lions Gate remained pro-choice.[27]

Less than a week after the January 25 founding conference, the interim steering committee of Vancouver's new clinic coalition, BCCAC, met for the first time. Thirteen members attended. Elaine Bernard summed up the immediate task: to develop a proposal for structuring the coalition, which would be presented to the next general membership meeting, and to make the coalition a "very open and flexible organization." Then confusion arose about CCCA and the role it planned to play. Neither of the two CCCA members present was in the 'in-group,' and they could not answer the question put by a representative from the Vancouver Status of Women: 'Is the coalition going to open the clinic — or are we meant to be merely a support group?' Most speakers were adamant that the clinic *would* be opened by the coalition.[28]

At the next meeting, CCCA turned out in some force. Five of the fifteen people present were from that group. Norah Hutchinson presented CCCA's position, which was little different from the view she'd held since the previous June. CCCA, she said, supported the formation of a Committee to Establish an Abortion Clinic, (CEAC), which would be a separate working body, not a sub-committee of the coalition. Its members would be any and all doctors and nurses willing to work in the clinic, two lawyers, and two members of the Vancouver Women's Health Collective. Of course, the clinic coalition could send two representatives to liaise with CEAC. The CEAC's eight to twelve members would be responsible for finding a location for the clinic, securing staff, etc. As the Minutes put it, "CEAC to be responsible for the medical facility," while the coalition would serve as political backup. Until such back-up was needed, BCCAC would be kept on ice.

Astonished BCCAC members argued forcefully that the founding conference vested responsibility for opening and maintaining a clinic with the coalition. One woman, whose father was a doctor, said, 'I am absolutely definite about what I want for the coalition,' which was that control should stay with the body formed in January. She described doctors as human beings with particular skills. They would make a special contribution to a clinic, but she was opposed to a hierarchical arrangement that would put doctors in charge over the coalition.

As they tended to do when they met opposition, the CCCA leaders spoke with soothing condescension. One said she could see no reason why doctors wouldn't work with the coalition, but they would certainly have to control the medical procedures. Another reminded us that doctors 'are very conservative;' therefore, we would just have to wait to see what they wanted. But what did they want? And which doctors out there were interested in the clinic? A motion carried that the next interim steering committee meeting hear a report from Physicians for Choice. It was followed by the question: why aren't the doctors here tonight?

Because, said Norah Hutchinson, they hadn't formed their group yet.

Because, she explained, nobody, certainly not the members of CCCA, knew which doctors were ready to join, or even whether there were any. She knew of only three who were possibly interested: her husband, Dr. Nelson Savein, a gynecologist; Dr. Ingrid Pacey, a psychiatrist — who had already represented herself to the media as a spokesperson for Physicians for Choice — and one other doctor. There was no Physicians for Choice. Therefore, it was plain to her, plans for a clinic were on hold. 'Until they [doctors] meet and adopt a Basis of Unity, who knows?'[29]

"It was clear the issue was not going to be resolved tonight," read the Minutes. The absurdity of the situation seemed to escape the notice of those in CCCA. For nine years, Concerned Citizens for Choice on Abortion had led the pro-choice fight, always on the basis of including everyone it could reach. On January 25, 1987, most participants assumed that the coalition formed that day was initiated by CCCA and that CCCA would continue in a leading role. Not until three weeks later did Norah Hutchinson reveal that she planned a clinic with other groups in mind, and with only a sideline role for the coalition. But, she admitted, apparently without awareness that it cost her the clout she presumed to monopolize, the doctors she was waiting for and counting on just weren't there.

Perhaps not, but the women's movement was. Unaware the CCCA was withholding its blessing, Vancouver feminists' commitment to the coalition formed in January was already unstoppable.

The next BCCAC general membership meeting took place on March 22, at Heritage Hall on Main Street. TV cameras pressed against the windows from without, since they were not allowed inside. That evening, the local news showed ordinary people calmly re-arranging chairs and moving about in Heritage Hall, while reporters gasped out that plans for an illegal abortion clinic were apparently going ahead.

The morning session hammered out a structure for the coalition: general membership meetings every six months, at which elections to the Steering Committee would take place; the majority of the 20-member Steering Committee must be "women representatives of feminist groups and groups whose main goal is reproductive choice;" and both individuals and members of groups could sit on the Steering Committee. With a sense of achievement, the approximately fifty attendees broke for lunch.

That afternoon, the main debate was on who would have charge of the clinic. Because the CCCA delegation did not return from lunch on time, the two proposals — which had been mailed out with the agenda — were read aloud. Mouths gaped as the import of CCCA's resolution sank in. The first volley came from Hilda Thomas, who cited the laboriously-constructed statement of purpose adopted in January and was astonished that it should now be contested by the group she had believed was the coalition's sponsor. 'Let's get these differences out in the open and no pussy-footing around.' Similarly, Elaine Bernard described CCCA's proposal as 'waiting around until some doctors come forward.' If that's the plan, she said, then 'we don't need a coalition;' just phone me when you get your act together.'[30]

Norah Hutchinson had arrived and she then spoke up, taking responsibility for resolution #2, whereby the coalition would focus its work "around the building of the community and political support and endorsement necessary for the establishment of a free-standing clinic." It was not as divisive as people thought, she said.

But without exception, every person present who was not involved in CCCA, opposed that idea. Eventually, Dr. Ingrid Pacey rose and spoke about Physicians for Choice, which she declared herself to represent. The group had not yet met, she informed us, but 35 doctors agreed with its basis of unity, which was to oppose the law and call for a free-standing clinic in BC. The doctors were waiting to know whether there was a broad-based coalition behind them. They also needed a legal team and a war chest. After all, she said, the doctors are the only ones at risk of being arrested, so it would be imprudent for them to be too open about their plans as yet.

Are you asking for deferment of a clinic until a doctor is ready, asked a member of Fraser Valley CARAL. Yes, was the reply. No way, said speaker after feminist speaker in BCCAC. Hilda Thomas again broke the impasse. 'This morning, we voted you couldn't even be a member of this coalition unless you agree to the basis of unity, which calls for *establishing a clinic*,' she said. Surely there are pro-choice doctors who will work with this coalition. The meeting burst into applause. Resolution #1, which extended the basis of unity adopted at the founding conference of BCCAC, was approved overwhelmingly. There were no votes opposing it, although there were three recorded abstentions. Norah Hutchinson did not vote.[31]

CCCA then played a trump card, announcing that Dr. Morgentaler, Dr. Nikki Colodny, and Carolyn Egan of OCAC would come to BC in early April. A leaflet had already been printed and was handed around at Hillcrest Hall. Why did it list only CCCA's name, when BCCAC had been invited to co-sponsor the tour? 'Just an error,' shrugged CCCA.

That afternoon, the first official Steering Committee was elected. It included representatives from Fraser Valley CARAL, the Women's Health Collective, Vancouver Rape Relief, the NDP Women's Rights Committee, the Congress of Canadian Women, the Feminist Women's Counselling Centre, and seven unaffiliated individuals. Officially, only one member of CCCA was elected, but, in fact, three to five of the individuals elected were actually members of CCCA. The other individuals on the Steering Committee were Elaine Bernard and me.

Premier Vander Zalm's report on abortion practices in BC, titled "The Prevention and Handling of Unwanted Prenancies," was released on schedule at the end of March. Many at the January founding conference of BCCAC had urged that a counter-report be prepared from the pro-choice view, but that proved to be impossible. We were too new and wary about working together, and our resources were nil. Like CCCA, the coalition had no office, no staff, no phone or filing cabinet, and was in debt for expenses of the March 22 general meeting.

The Vander Zalm report was light-years behind the call for improved abortion services, and even clinics, made by Ontario's Powell Report. But it found that, in BC, the few provincial hospitals performing abortions were doing so ethically, within the guidelines of the Criminal Code. Hospitals had not become abattoirs, as the anti-abortion movement frequently charged. Furthermore, the report made it clear that women were not using abortion as a form of birth control.[32] Pro-choice doctors and hospital administrators felt exonerated.[33] Yet the report showed, again, how acute the crisis of access was in BC, which had the highest rate of abortions per-live-births in the country. Eighty per cent of abortions in the province were done at a mere ten of the 115 publicly-funded hospitals. Seventy-seven hospitals approved no abortions at all. The premier drew his own, predictable conclusion: "Basically," he growled, "what we have in BC...is abortion on demand." He called for tighter guidelines on granting approvals.[34]

The Morgentaler tour of 1987 attracted less media attention than usual, perhaps because the province was convulsed again by draconian Socred labour legislation. The entourage from Ontario arrived on Friday, April 3, and its appearances were handled entirely by CCCA. At a press conference shortly after he de-planed, Dr. Morgentaler said, with characteristic bluntness:

> ...most people opposed to abortion are religious fanatics or zealots who do not respond to reason...who are so rigid and convinced of the rightness of their views that they do not take into consideration very important democratic principles, such as freedom of religion and conscience.[35]

Indeed, the *Globe and Mail* made more or less the same assertion in a story featured on page one just two days earlier. York University sociology lecturer Lorna Erwin's study of more than 800 members of anti-abortion organizations found that "Religion is the central focus of their lives." The Christian religion, of course. Seen as threats to the "pro-life/pro-family cause" were feminism, homosexuality, pornography, sex education, and above all — rated by 99.8% as dangerous — abortion.[36]

Dr. Henry Morgentaler spoke to a large crowd at John Oliver Secondary School on Saturday, April 4, 1987. The circus of 1985 did not manifest itself again. Later, he and Nikki Colodny met privately with eight or nine BC physicians, pitching the importance of volunteering to open a Vancouver clinic. No doctor responded.

There was also an information-sharing session at Britannia community centre for the feminists from Toronto and Vancouver. Again we heard how Toronto got its clinics, which was fine, but it didn't fit the situation we were facing. Toronto had almost a surplus of clinic doctors. During discussion, CCCA accused BCCAC of being hostile to physicians. When the session ended, no-one's enthusiasm for a clinic was dampened, but the wariness between the different Vancouver factions was intact.[37]

The BC NDP convention in April voted to establish a free-standing abortion clinic, funded by medicare, "immediately upon forming the government."[38] A new leader was elected — Mike Harcourt.

Teachers shied away from endorsing the call for an abortion clinic in BC. A resolution to that effect had been submitted to the BCTF AGM in March, but an illegal clinic was too much for many. Even some teachers on the left shied away from it.[39] And anyway, the BCTF was almost wholly consumed with fighting the new Socred labour laws, Bills 19 and 20, and didn't have time for feminism — especially when Vander Zalm announced he "would not be afraid to block support by the BC Teachers' Federation for free-standing abortion clinics."[40] The premier who wanted students to "write good" didn't like teachers meddling in social issues.

After the Morgentaler-Colodny-Egan tour, BCCAC activists got down to business. Although the coalition had an elected Steering Committee, meetings were open, and non-elected women often attended with full voice. Votes were seldom needed to reach a decision. BCCAC continued to operate in the preferred feminist way, of ignoring hierarchies and including everyone who showed interest. The Steering Committee met every two weeks, and sub-committees met in between. Leaflets were produced, requests for donations were mailed out, the media was kept informed. There was lots of participation, and goodwill came from many sources. But no money and no doctors appeared.

Suddenly, unexpected proof of public support dropped into our laps, when results of a poll commissioned by the NDP were leaked to BCCAC. The May 1987 Omnibus Report asked, "Some people now are proposing to establish free-standing abortion clinics in BC...not governed by a hospital board. Do you oppose or support [such clinics]?" 59% were in support.

At last, on June 14, 1987, a founding meeting for a local Physicians for Choice group was held. BCCAC, of course, was not invited, but we learned later that eight doctors came, six of them women. They set themselves one activity — that of making personal contact with other doctors about the issue. It was clear that BC Physicians for Choice was prepared to act only as a support group and was not ready to provide medical staff for a real clinic.

So by late summer, the BCCAC clinic sub-committee decided to conduct its own search for a doctor.[41] A letter, introducing the clinic coalition and its goals, was sent to the now somewhat-outdated list of pro-choice doctors that had been contacted so many times before. Around the same time, feminist lawyers from the Legal Education and Action Fund (LEAF) and the Vancouver chapter of Women and the Law (VAWL) sat down with BCCAC. They offered to research various legal situations we might face.

After Steering Committee elections at the general membership meeting of October 3, a vigorous sub-committee, headed by Janet Vesterback, waded into planning a march and rally for October 18. It was to be a National Day of Action, sanctioned by CARAL in Toronto. A number of women, not otherwise active in the coalition, participated: Hilda Thomas and Sandra Bruneau of the NDP Women's Rights Committee, Linda Ervin, a United Church minister, Gabriella Moro of Co-op Radio, and others. At noon on the appointed Sunday, about 175 marchers stepped off down Georgia Street from the Art Gallery, and, by the time they reached the rally site, First United Church at Hastings and Gore, the crowd had swelled to 400. Speakers included Val Carey from Kamloops, Maggie Thompson of BCCAC, and representatives from a number of BCCAC member groups.

One of the speakers, Dr. Ingrid Pacey, sounded cautious and worried. "No doctor has yet stepped forward to work in a free-standing clinic," she told the rally. "To do so is to put their life and work on the line."[42] Pacey told reporters, "There isn't money for legal defence or for the clinic," arguing that a doctor would not come forward until a war chest of $800,000 had been amassed.[43] This was news to the clinic coalition.

On the same day, 100 marchers had turned out in Edmonton, 500 in Toronto, 1,000 in Québec City. Contrasting with the supposed need for $800,000, the collection in Vancouver was $1,330, which matched expenses and left BCCAC with only a couple hundred dollars in the bank.[44] A fund-raising dance on December 11 was only a moderate success.

Questions about money hung over our heads — money for premises, for equipment, for salaries, for a legal defence fund. Tension between the two pro-choice groups grew. Eventually a meeting was arranged to iron things out. But on December 9, Dr. Nelson Savein made it clear he would not work in a clinic that doctors did not control. BCCAC was told it was inappropriate for us to attempt contact with Physicians for Choice.

As best we could, BCCAC stayed in touch with pro-choice groups such as OCAC, CARAL, and the National Action Committee on the Status of Women (NAC), scraping funds together to send representatives to meetings in Toronto and Edmonton. We wanted to be ready to join in a co-ordinated response to the Canadian Supreme Court decision on the Morgentaler case — expected from week to week, but not yet announced. We'd heard the decision had been arrived at in October and had been sent to the transla-tors. What would the outcome be? We weren't very optimistic.

Hard as we'd worked, the year 1987 was closing. The deadline for a clinic "in twelve months" trumpeted by CCCA in September 1986 was long past, and there was little concrete progress toward a clinic for BC. At least BCCAC had swelled its membership, consulted with legal advisors, municipal planners, and nervous doctors. If CCCA had moved ahead, there was little evidence of it. But the caution advised by some CCCA members certainly hadn't rubbed off on the coalition. We regretted it was taking so long, but our faith that a clinic would open in BC was undimmed.

Members of Abortion Caravan circle the Centennial Flame at Parliament Hill, Ottawa, May 1970.

[Photo by Barb Hicks]

Margo Dunn (far right), on the
steps of Parliament, 1970.

[Photo by Barb Hicks]

A woman pleads for an abortion from white-coated and masked doctors
in an Abortion Caravan skit in Edmonton, 29 April 1970.

[Photo by Barb Hicks]

Cartoon by Robert Krieger
from *The Province*,
14 September 1981.

Dr. Henry Morgentaler, Vancouver, April 1985.
[Photo by Karen Kilbride]

BC Coalition for Abortion Clinics meeting at Rape Relief Centre 10 September 1988, planning to announce purchase of clinic later that day.

L-R: Anne Hamilton, Marg Panton, Janin Wear, Janet Vesterback.

[Photo by Ann Thomson]

Anti-abortion protestors swarm onto the street across from Everywoman's Health Centre (not shown in photo), Vancouver, 4 November 1988.

[Photo by Katherine Kortikow]

Hilda Thomas, opening
ceremony of Everywoman's
Health Centre, Vancouver,
4 November 1988.
[Photo by Katherine Kortikow]

Betsy Wood, opening
ceremony of Everywoman's
Health Centre, Vancouver,
4 November 1988.
[Photo by Katherine Kortikow]

Dr. Robert Makaroff, opening
ceremony of Everywoman's
Health Centre, Vancouver,
4 November 1988.
[Photo by Katherine Kortikow]

Security volunteers during opening ceremonies of Everywoman's Health Centre,
Vancouver, 4 November 1988.

Fund-raiser Elaine Bernard
instructs in "brolly semaphore."

Opening Rally at Hotel
Vancouver for Everywoman's
Health Centre, 5 November 1988.

L-R: Janet Vesterback (Rally
Chair), Elaine Bernard, Robin
LeDrew (NAC Representative).

Opening Rally at
Hotel Vancouver for
Everywoman's Health Centre,
5 November 1988.

L-R: Elaine Bernard, Margaret
Mitchell (NDP MP),
Janet Vesterback (Rally Chair),
and Dr. Lorena Kanke,
(Clinic Medical Director).
[Photo by Ann Thomson]

Joy Thomspon (far right)
holding son Owen during IWD
rally, Vancouver, 1989.
[Photo by Karen Kilbride]

2,500 marchers surge down Howe Street in Vancouver during 1989 IWD rally.

BCCAC rally: Canadian day of action on theme "No New Law",
Sunset Beach in Vancouver, 14 October 1989.

CHAPTER 14

MORGENTALER WINS, VANDER ZALM LOSES IT

Suddenly came victory! Sixteen months after it heard the case, the Canadian Supreme Court reported its decision on Drs. Morgentaler, Scott, and Smoling. By a 5-2 majority, on January 28, 1988, the justices found that section 251 of the Criminal Code was, indeed, unconstitutional. This scrapped the 'reform' of 1969, and all its clauses. It meant hospital thera-peutic abortion committees were out, and free-standing clinics were legal. The doctors' acquittals on charges of opening the Toronto clinic were upheld. Twenty years of dogged fighting were vindicated: Dr. Henry Morgentaler had won!

It was a breathtaking achievement that left Canadians reeling, unable to absorb it all at once. A jubilant Henry Morgentaler was swept outside the Court chambers to face a shouting mass of reporters. "Bravo for the Supreme Court of Canada! Bravo for the women of Canada! Justice for the women of Canada has finally arrived!" he called out, as he flashed the V-for-Victory sign.[1] His closest supporters and the pro-choice movement across the country were delirious with joy.

Moving quickly, CCCA set up a rally that Thursday evening in Vancouver. By noon on the momentous day, BC health minister Peter Dueck had announced the province would not comply with the court's ruling. He suspended medicare for any abortion in BC that was not approved by a now-unconstitutional hospital therapeutic abortion com-mittee. Dueck grudgingly acknowledged the Supreme Court had struck down TACs, but, he said, "We do not believe that taxpayers' dollars should be used to fund abortions on demand...to be funded by the taxpayer [an abortion] should be medically required."[2]

About 170 people gathered at the Unitarian Church to celebrate the victory and serve notice to the BC government. They heard from Norah Hutchinson of CCCA, Anglican Minister Barbara Blakely, Pamela Cooley of the Downtown Eastside Women's Centre, and Dr. Ingrid Pacey. Pat Brighouse of CCCA demanded that Vander Zalm reverse the curtailment of abortion funding and scrap TACs within 24 hours, or else resign. Pro-choice groups would fight the government "in every way we can," announced Brighouse, and, echoing the Women's Caucus and the Abortion Caravan, she said, " We are declaring war."[3]

Lawyer and then-former judge (she later resumed the bench) Nancy Morrison warned that parliament would swiftly pass a new law to re-criminalize abortion. "I think it is premature to rejoice too much. I think the new struggle is just beginning," she said.[4] Which was exactly the plan announced in the House of Commons by Tory justice minister Ray Hnatyshyn, immediately upon hearing of the Court's ruling.[5] But it turned out to be harder than expected to reach consensus among parliamentarians, anti-abortionists, the Catholic Church, and others considered to have a valid interest in the matter. Women were not consulted about it.

"Abortion law scrapped; women get free choice," blared the *Globe and Mail*,[6] and the Court's decision indeed centered on women. More than a narrow legal interpretation of the Charter of Rights, the landmark ruling established that the Charter had teeth, and that its freedoms extended to all women; in this instance, particularly, to unwillingly pregnant ones. Because, the justices said, the abortion law was unfair and discriminatory. Even so, the triumph hadn't come easily. Four different judgments were written — three in favour of women and one supporting Section 251 — and the three supportive judgments argued the case differently before coming to the same conclusion.

Excerpts from the majority judgments were printed in newspapers across Canada. But, recognizing the need for convenient copies of the complete texts, BC's Shelagh Day and Stan Persky edited and published a paperback of *The Supreme Court of Canada Decision on Abortion* in May, 1988.[7] Before that, Svend Robinson, NDP MP, rushed from Ottawa to Vancouver with the text of Justice Bertha Wilson's remarks and walked into a BC Coalition for Abortion Clinics' meeting to deliver it. His gesture was much appreciated.

Chief Justice Brian Dickson and Antonio Lamer concurred that Section 251 was unconstitutional, while Justices Jean Beetz and Willard Estey agreed on slightly different grounds. The men on the male-dominated court finally came around.

Still, the value of having Canada's first woman justice on the court bore extraordinary fruit, for the unflappable Bertha Wilson's judgment, legally unimpeachable, placed the issue in the realms of both the personal and the political. She phrased it as a question of liberty, self-respect, and human dignity, and she found that the Charter guarantees "the right to make fundamental personal decisions without interference from the state.[8] She wrote that the decision to terminate a pregnancy...is one that will have profound psychological, economic and social consequences for the pregnant woman.

> The circumstances giving rise to it can be complex and varied and there may be, and usually are, powerful considerations militating in opposite directions. It is

a decision that deeply reflects the way the woman thinks about herself and her relationship to others and to society at large. It is not just a medical decision; it is a profound social and ethical one as well. Her response to it will be the response of the whole person.[9]

Most amazingly, she acknowledged the power of the women's movement in demanding choice on abortion, placing it within "the history of the struggle for human rights from the eighteenth century on." Prior to that time, it had been men "struggling to assert their dignity and common humanity against an overbearing state apparatus."

> The more recent struggle for women's rights has been a struggle to eliminate discrimination, to achieve a place for women in a man's world, to develop a set of legislative reforms in order to place women in the same position as men. It has not been a struggle to define the rights of women in relation to their special place in societal structure and in relation to the biological distinction between the sexes.[10]

Thus, in a stroke, Justice Wilson ruled out potential future charges that reproductive rights were 'reverse discrimination' or unwonted 'affirmative action.' They were, instead, matters of fundamental justice to women.

Like Dickson and Lamer, Bertha Wilson stated explicitly that women are not "passive recipients of a decision made by others" as to whether their bodies are to be used "to nurture new life."[11] Section 251's primary purpose, in her view, "must be seen as the protection of the foetus,"[12] and with that principle she vigorously disagreed. Quoting from British Professor C.E.M. Joad of the University of London, she rejected the argument that the individual should be subordinated to the interests of the state. Instead, she made it clear that women have an innate individual and legal worth and ought not to be forced to accept the bearing of children as their sole function or duty to society. "'This is the doctrine of eternal sacrifice — 'jam yesterday, jam tomorrow, but never jam today,'" wrote Joad in dissmissing the states' rights view[13] and Justice Wilson made his ethics on that score a part of Canadian law.

So thoroughly were the legal precedents examined in scrapping the 1969 abortion law that the Morgentaler decision remains today beyond appeal. Nor, it turned out, could justification be found for a new abortion law that would withstand challenge before the Canadian Supreme Court — although Ottawa tried mightily to craft one.

The most frequently printed photo of Dr. Henry Morgentaler, in the immediate wake of the ruling, showed him fondly cradling his two-and-a-half week old son, Benjamin. At age 64, he had begun a new family — this Auschwitz survivor whom anti-abortionists tried so hard to label a baby-killer. Although he unquestionably relished the spotlight, Henry Morgentaler also gave his all to the cause of justice, not for himself, but for women. The victory he won in the Supreme Court seemed to re-energize him, and with hardly a pause, Morgentaler went on to fight for access to abortion wherever it was denied. Over the next decade, he withstood every pressure from provincial governments and anti-abortionists of every stripe, and, using his own money, he opened clinics across Canada, from Alberta to the Maritimes.

Every province was now forced to consider how to carry out the about-face that the January 28, 1988 court ruling required. All were hostile to abortion. At first, most provinces simply froze the status quo. Why change, when parliament would surely adopt a new law post-haste? Some pundits expected that to happen within days.[14] As spring progressed, most provinces did make changes — negative ones, that amounted to a backlash.[15] The best outcomes were in the provinces, indeed in the cities, that already had Morgentaler clinics — Montréal, Toronto, and even Winnipeg. Those clinics had begun the long process of winning acceptance by the people, the medical establishments, and the governments. But in the Maritimes and in the western provinces, there was revolt against the court ruling. As in BC, the governments of Saskatchewan and Alberta announced that hospital TACs were to remain in place and that provincial guidelines would thenceforth prohibit abortions. In every province, uproar ensued, and nowhere was it louder or more divisive than in British Columbia.

What pro-choicers didn't fully realize when CCCA gave Vander Zalm 24 hours to submit to the Supreme Court's ruling or else resign, was that Bill and Lillian weren't in BC. They were part way through a two-week vacation in Hawaii, and they stayed on in Honolulu, even though they didn't get much further time in the sun. Our outraged premier was kept indoors and on the phone to his office in Victoria. Although he was away, it was Vander Zalm who crafted the policy that Dueck announced: no abortions without a TAC's approval, no payment for abortions unless doctors deemed them "medically" necessary. Obviously, it was not a policy drafted in conjunction with the Socred caucus or party — not when it was made thousands of kilometres from BC. It was pure Zalm-mania.

Vander Zalm and his coterie of anti-choice advisors — his assistant David Poole, health minister Peter Dueck, and attorney-general Brian Smith — were bent on making BC an abortion-free zone. But hospital abortions were only one of the brush-fires they had to battle. "Dueck Fights Clinics," headlined The *Province's* initial story on the court ruling, with "Morgentaler Wins Historic Case" in much smaller type.[16] The seventeen-month old story of a clinic in BC was transformed from a non-starter to a matter of intense public interest. Pat Brighouse of CCCA now told the press, off the cuff, that a BC clinic might open as early as June, or even in four to six weeks. Dr. Ingrid Pacey added that doctors who were "too scared before" no longer had reason to hang back.[17] Reporters began phoning the spokeswomen of both BCCAC and CCCA at all hours and arriving on their doorsteps with vans full of cameras, lights, and microphones. When will a clinic open, was their incessant query. Despite what Brighouse and Pacey said, no pro-choice group had any of the necessaries at that point: no money, no place to operate, no doctor.

The absent premier's announced stance was immediately opposed by the BC Medical Association. Its new president, Dr. David Jones, said the government was interfering with the doctor-patient relationship. "What the government would be asking doctors to decide is whether the procedure should be paid or not. That is not our role."[18] Doctors voted unanimously not to sit on the now-illegal TACs. However, attorney-general Brian Smith told reporters that the Supreme Court had struck down the abortion law, but it "hasn't struck down committees."[19] Had he, the province's top lawyer, read the decision? NDP leader Mike Harcourt and MLA Joan Smallwood charged Smith with advising Dueck "to commit an illegal act"by tightening medicare and requiring TACs to remain in place.[20]

Dueck back-pedaled somewhat. He said hospitals could call the committees by another name than TACs. "It can be a medical advisory committee. We're asking the hospital to have a mechanism to 'prove' that an abortion is 'medically required.'"[21] Later, he spoke of a "second opinion" that would verify the "necessity"for performing an abortion. An exasperated Herme Crewson, of the BC Health Association which represented hospitals, complained the government had announced at least three positions in the first days after Morgentaler's win. But the health minister continued to bluster that, despite the BCMA's opposition, he could find doctors to serve on hospital committees. And a planned $1.5 million media blitz on "alternatives to abortion"would go ahead.[22]

At last, nine days after the Supreme Court ruling, the premier returned to the province. On Saturday, February 6, a tanned and toothyVander Zalm de-planed and addressed the media in the airport terminal. "I will recommend to cabinet tomorrow that the government no longer pay for any abortions, save those in emergency situations," he said. "Abortions diminish society's respect for human life."[23] The next afternoon, before the caucus met, a reporter asked whether the ban on paying for abortions would apply to pregnant victims of rape and incest. Replied the premier, "There will be no exceptions."[24]

Thus was launched a two-month battle fought with escalating shrillness that saw Bill Vander Zalm refuse to budge despite opposition from women, the media, the medical profession, the courts, public service professionals, and, increasingly, members of his caucus and the Social Credit party. His evangelical stance turned voters against him, split his party, and can be said to have brought down the government — although that didn't happen immediately. If it would it not offend his Roman Catholic sensibilities, one might compare Vander Zalm's blind course to that in a 'pagan' Greek drama.

200 pro-choice supporters rallied in the rain at Robson Square in Vancouver on Saturday, February 6. They blasted government policy that had, so far, been articulated only by the health minister. Dueck's assertion that women sought abortions for cosmetic reasons, as if they were tummy tucks, inspired picket signs saying he needed a "tongue tuck."[25] Letters for and against the government flooded onto the pages of local newspapers.

A two-day meeting of the Social Credit caucus began in Powell River on Sunday night. Until then, only Dueck and Smith had been privy to Vander Zalm's thinking or had any opportunity for input. But with The *Province* headlines screaming about the premier's stand on rape and incest victims, the issue of abortion opened the morning session on Monday, February 8. Vander Zalm and Dueck briefly informed the caucus that their personal views were now government policy. Abortions would be paid for only if the woman's life was endangered by her pregnancy. That was necessary to prevent "abortion on demand,"shuddered the premier, who "had to" devise his policy to "end the killing."[26] Reportedly, caucus members asked no questions. Silence fell and the issue did not arise again during the caucus meeting.[27]

Outside it, however, reporters continued to query Vander Zalm. "What about a fourteen-year-old girl who is raped in a park and becomes pregnant? What if she has no money to pay for an abortion? Are you saying you won't provide funding for her?" Reiterating that "there can't be any exceptions" to his policy, Vander Zalm squeezed his eyes shut and covered his ears with his hands. Onlookers gaped at this method of fending off the implications of his position. "Don't ask me those questions. I don't want to hear them," the premier said, backing away with his ears still covered. David Poole, Vander Zalm's principal secretary, stepped forth and drew him off. Describing the scene in their book, journalists Gary Mason and Keith Baldrey wrote, "The room had grown much quieter and a few party supporters stared into their glasses, looking embarrassed."[28]

Mischievous reporters hit on another idea. Why couldn't a pregnant rape or incest victim have her abortion paid for by the BC Criminal Injuries Compensation program? After all, that law offered various forms of restitution to victims of crime. The premier was startled by this wrinkle, especially when the administrator of the Compensation Office, Larry Timoffee, said he thought it was reasonable. Muttered Vander Zalm, "I would be disturbed if...another arm or agency of government was using another piece of legislation to do what we wouldn't normally do."[29]

Abortion now dominated the news in Victoria and Vancouver, nearly pushing aside stories about the Calgary Olympics, the faltering Meech Lake constitutional accords, the rat-a-tat march toward a free trade agreement, and even US televangelist Jimmy Swaggart's sexual peccadilloes and conviction on extortion charges. The Vancouver dailies routinely ran six to eight items per day on the issue, including news stories, editorials, columnists' views, and letters to the editor. "Abortion policy mocks justice," editorialized The *Province* on February 8, opening its piece with "The king of the castle has returned from his vacation...[with]...a brain-addling enunciation of policy."[30] The bloom was gone from the gardener-premier's rose.

While the government caucus met, tumult broke out in many other quarters and just kept on boiling. The premier disappeared. Five days after they returned from Hawaii, the Vander Zalms packed up their smug moral consciences and flew off to Europe. For more than two weeks, only David Poole was in touch with them, and even he did not always know where to reach the premier.[31]

Peter Dueck said the dictate announced in Powell River — "Abortions will not be funded — period"— went into effect immediately, but he didn't think hospitals would have any trouble coping with that.[32] Herme Crewson said Vander Zalm's hard line must have been taken without benefit of legal advice.[33] But, he said, hospitals could be ready within days to perform abortions outside the medical plan, for women who paid in cash.[34] By Tuesday, February 9, the two Victoria hospitals stopped performing abortions, and Dr. David Jones of the BCMA said they were directing their patients to clinics in Bellingham, Washington, where an abortion cost about US$350.[35] A day later, the Greater Victoria Hospitals Society announced a fee schedule: $205 for hospital daycare (rising to $456 if an overnight stay was needed), plus a $50 anesthetist's fee, plus the doctor's fee, for a minimum of $355.[36] Vancouver General Hospital announced its fee schedule on Thursday, February 11 — a minimum of $455 — and was considering requiring a second medical opinion for those few abortions to be charged to the medical plan.[37]

In those days, federal vigilance was keen against two-tier health policies. Normally, BC's clear violation of the publicly-funded Canadian health care system would have led to a cut off in federal transfer payments. But just then, everything was up in the air. Passing a new anti-abortion law was all that Ottawa politicians talked about.[38]

That ancient horror, the backstreet abortion, loomed again over most of Canada and certainly over BC, just when it should have been banished. Hemorrhaging, sepsis, permanently damaged wombs, agonizing pain, fear, expense, loneliness, and shame — uncounted numbers of women suddenly had no alternatives. At that moment, a pre-teen from Victoria appeared, needing an abortion. "This is a 12-year-old girl who is 12 weeks' pregnant, who has gone through the difficult decision to have an abortion only to suddenly have the rug pulled out from under her," said Dr. Rick Hudson, who described her as a victim of the premier's new abortion policy. Hudson said the young woman's family didn't have the $350-$400 it would cost for the procedure.[39] It was an extremely anxious time for BC women.

Before leaving for Europe, the premier announced he would accelerate plans for his 'alternatives to abortion' program and double its funding to $2.2 million. Intended to "strengthen family life," the wide-ranging program was to include a provincewide network of homes for expectant mothers.[40] "That just smacks of the '50s and unwed mothers' homes," objected Norah Hutchinson. Maggie Thompson, spokesperson for BCCAC, said Vander Zalm was playing God and that his policy "certainly gives us much greater incentive to open our clinic as soon as possible."[41]

In the roaring confusion, *Province* columnist Mike Tytherleigh spoke clearly and bluntly. His piece on Wednesday, February 10, was titled "Premier shows hostility to women." Tytherleigh wrote: "Despite the smile, this humorless, vindictive and stubborn man might be portrayed as a woman-hater out to control their reproductive rights, keeping them as chattels of men and second-class citizens."[42]

Just as the Powell River caucus meeting wrapped up, the BC Civil Liberties Association announced it would challenge the government in the courts. Feminist lawyers in the Legal Education and Action Fund would join in. BCCLA's Dixon said Vander Zalm had left "British Columbians in an insufferable position in which the provincial government has put in place a policy that is 180 degrees opposed to the spirit of the decision of the Canadian Supreme Court."[43]

Reporters Kim Bolan and William Boei, and columnists Vaughn Palmer and Nicole Parton, all of the *Vancouver Sun*, separately began marathon defences of women's right to choose. Bolan and her colleagues continually found new angles to cover and frequently penned several articles on abortion per day. *Province* reporters Holly Horwood and Olivia Scott did the same. Parton, a Socred, was particularly acerbic. Her Thursday, February 11 column was titled "A dangerous man surrounded by simpering sycophants." She asked, in shock:

> Can it really be that each and every one of the 17 ministers in the Socred cabinet marches in perfect lockstep with the premier? That not a single man or woman has the slightest niggle of concern that this man's extreme and odious views on abortion will be imposed on every BC woman of childbearing age?

Parton went on: "It was quite a sight — a sight I shall never forget, this past Tuesday night on the TV news — to see cabinet aspirant Kim Campbell do a crablike scuttle from the television reporter who asked if her opinion on abortion coincided with the premier's."[44] The next day, Parton wrote that she'd received more calls from readers than at any time in her 17 years with the newspaper, and that "the silent majority has awakened like an angry, roaring giant." "Welcome to the backlash, Mr. Vander Zalm. Is this what you want for the Social Credit party?" One person who phoned her was Social Credit MLA for Point Grey, Kim Campbell. More than three days after the premier simply told his caucus what the abortion policy would be,

Campbell ventured to oppose Vander Zalm through Parton's column.[45]

Of course, her defection was also the lead story on page one, especially since Campbell said other Socred MLAs agreed with her pro-choice views.[46] By the next day, three more were willing to publicly state that they disagreed with the government. Langley MLA Carol Gran, Cliff Serwa of Okanagan South, and Ivan Messmer of Boundary-Similkameen called for funding abortions for rape and incest victims. Gran said, "I'm not a dissenter. I'm a person who has to be honest and I can't help but feel there's a better way." She was upset that the caucus was not told about the premier's stance toward rape and incest victims and said she hadn't learned about it until two days after the meeting in Powell River. The *Sun* story revived the call for the Criminal Injuries Compensation Act to fund abortions for rape and incest victims.[47]

The *Vancouver Sun's* editors took an extraordinary position: "A citizen's arrest is the only route:" "When people in power set themselves above the law as Mr. Vander Zalm has done, they must be pulled down — as quickly as possible. The question is, who will bell the cat? The premier's cabinet will not do it...So it must be a citizen's arrest." By "citizens," the *Sun* meant the BC Civil Liberties Association, whose suit "should be mounted as quickly as possible, before Mr. Vander Zalm returns and causes any more damage...No effort should be spared to put Mr. Vander Zalm in his place — in compliance with the Charter of Rights."[48]

The hospitals, which changed to accommodate the 1969 reforms at a glacial pace, now turned on a dime. Vancouver General and the two Victoria hospitals now required a second doctor's approval for both the rare provincially-funded abortion and those paid for in cash. Government policy did not require them, although Dueck said second opinions "are always a good idea." The BCMA, which had previously advised doctors not to participate on TACs after the court decision, now warned against second opinions: "We would advise doctors to be very careful, if not refuse entirely to get involved in that."[49] Dueck finally agreed to meet with the BCMA executive, which had been shut out of government offices til then. He also met with representatives of six pro-choice groups, but they were unable to get him to change his mind.[50] By the following week, a replay of the bad old days began when the Richmond hospital board voted to end all abortions.[51] Vernon Jubilee Hospital followed suit.[52] A day later, Vancouver General began demanding cash up front from abortion patients.[53]

In Montréal, Dr. Henry Morgentaler told the press that Vander Zalm was "an absolute religious fanatic," whose response to the Supreme Court decision was "ayatollah-like." He said he'd promptly written to the health ministers in Manitoba, Newfoundland, British Columbia and Prince Edward Island, offering to open clinics in those provinces. He wrote to

Peter Dueck, "The imposition of your dogmatic religious beliefs on a pluralistic society is outrageous and unacceptable."[54] He was right, of course, but Dueck and Vander Zalm were not persuaded.

By Monday, February 15, the BCMA had completely caved in. After meeting with Dueck, its president Dr. David Jones said his members would comply with the guidelines and make no political statements about the funding policy. "It is not our place to be happy with the policy. It is our place to provide medical care," he said. But an unexpected development was that a high-profile member of Dueck's own medical ethics committee, who had not been consulted about the new policy, now objected to it strongly. Dr. Eike-Henner Kluge of the University of Victoria said, "Ethically what is required is that you don't erect a two-tier health care system." He promised to tell the health minister so when the ethics committee met with him in the next week.[55]

The pregnant 12-year-old in Victoria, whose parents were on welfare, managed to pay for an abortion through donations collected with the help of a pro-choice group and Dr. Mary Conley. The child had to travel to Vancouver, however, because she was then in her second trimester and would have been delayed even longer in her home town.[56]

A CBC television opinion poll taken Monday, February 15, received the highest number of calls ever in response to the question: "Should the government pay for abortions for rape and incest victims?" The results were 2,901 yes, 496 no. Executive producer Helen Slinger said there'd been callers of all ages and both sexes and said "several (who said yes) even identified themselves as a Socred family."[57]

As he filed for a court injunction against the Socred's policy, BC Civil Liberties Association president John Dixon said, "Real people are really hurting." Attorney-general Brian Smith was served with a subpoena Monday, February 15, but he refused to comment to the press.[58]

Norah Hutchinson said CCCA unanimously endorsed the BCCLA's action. In concert with pro-choice women in Victoria, CCCA conducted a petition drive and raised funds to pay for poor women's abortions.[59] The Vancouver Women's Health Collective sought donations to cover interest-free loans to women who needed money for an abortion. The loans were to be repaid "when and if they can."[60]

The dike of Socred solidarity cracked further. A fifth Socred MLA, Dave Mercier of Burnaby-Edmonds, distanced himself from the premier's policy. He supported most of the anti-fundiing decree, but he thought the "rape and incest part of the policy" should be reconsidered.[61] Then Madam Social Credit herself, economic development minister Grace McCarthy, said she would support "taking a second look" at the policy, "but I certainly would leave [doing] that to the leadership of the premier." She was echoed by MLA Howard Dirks of Nelson-Creston.[62]

From deep in the absent premier's office came a piteous snuffle that was detected at once by the media. Okay, okay, it said, let rape and incest victims collect from the Criminal Injuries Compensation Fund. Almost no-one was satisfied with that. Anti-abortionists were angry. Norah Hutchinson and Dr. Ingrid Pacey pointed out it only meant women would have to justify themselves before another kind of board.[63] The *Sun's* editors were especially disgusted that the policy shift came from the premier's deputy, David Poole, who had been elected by no-one.[64] An eighth elected Socred, Cliff Michael of Shuswap-Revelstoke, joined the rebels. Regarding Grace McCarthy's "gingerly opined" position, Nicole Parton was unimpressed. "Now *that's* gumption. Hot damn!" she wrote and expressed keen disappointment in the silence of attorney-general Brian Smith.[65] The Federation of Medical Women, charging the government showed utter contempt for women, also objected to the beginning of a two-tier health-care system, to the penalizing of women with no responsibility for the male partner, to cutting funds for birth control education, and to "the unrealistic notion" that women would carry their pregnancies to term and give the babies up for adoption if there were unwed shelters available to them.[66]

Someone was impressed with Vander Zalm's policy, however — the Tory premier of Saskatchewan, Grant Devine. He cut medicare funding for abortions except in life-threatening situations. Saskatchewan's doctors objected. Alberta hospitals minister Marv Moore announced women seeking abortions would have to be physically examined by two doctors, both of whom must approve it if the province were to pay for the procedure.[67] That was also the policy in New Brunswick.[68]

All this within two weeks of the Canadian Supreme Court's ruling.

It was Kamloops's Royal Inland Hospital that objected to the cash-up-front policy other hospitals were adopting. VGH now demanded approximately $500 from each abortion patient before she was admitted. With Royal Inland's restored pro-choice board, hospital spokesperson John Forrester pointed to Section 4 of the provincial Hospital Act, which held "No hospital shall refuse to admit a person on account of his indigent circumstances." He said it was against the law to demand cash in advance.[69] Dueck said flatly that hospitals allowing women to get away without paying for their abortions would have the amount deducted from their global budgets. He said his officials "may have to look at that section" of the provincial act quoted by Forrester to make sure the no-abortions policy was enforced. Pro-choicers and the NDP were appalled to find further social guarantees under threat.[70]

From every Catholic pulpit a two-page letter was read out to the faithful from Vancouver Archbishop James Carney on Sunday, February 21. "We must express our views to the provincial government; we must work to defend life," it said. The provincial government was way ahead of the

Archbishop, so the bulk of the missive urged the city's 300,000 Catholics to demand a new federal anti-abortion law. A similar commitment was pledged by the approximately 40,000 Pentecostal believers in BC. However, Rev. Jim Elliott of the United Church stood by the adopted position of a woman's right to choose.[71] Responded the *Vancouver Sun*, in an editorial on March 2: "Cardinal Carney's letter is a dangerous piece of goods: it advocates overriding the Constitution, denying what Canadians are guaranteed under their Charter of Rights and Freedom. The church, which he claims to speak for, does not have this divine right."[72] Still, "BC is the most secular place in North America," a UBC professor told the *Sun*, and several of his colleagues agreed.[73] Most had no religious reason to heed the Archbishop or the Pentecostals.

The crisis drew many new activists to the BC Coalition for Abortion Clinics, and almost as many turned out for its February 21, 1988 general membership meeting as the 200 who attended its founding meeting thirteen months before. Among the plans made for supporting women in the present moment were to escort abortion patients into VGH through anti-abortion picket lines. Most of the resources needed for a clinic were still lacking, but there was renewed dedication to finding them. A canvass of doctors turned up volunteers to perform abortions in the interim. Between 30 and 40 doctors were "willing to offer an afternoon a month for free because of the incredible crisis that exists in BC," said BCCAC spokesperson Janet Vesterback. The group supported whatever solutions could be found: abortions performed in doctors' offices, clinics that might open wherever possible.[74]

The BC legislature resumed sitting on Tuesday, February 23, and the Socred caucus held a four-hour meeting on the Monday. Half of its time was taken up with the issue of abortion. Apparently, David Poole's announcement that about Criminal Injuries Compensation Fund satisfied most of the dissenting MLAs. Caucus chair Carol Gran announced there was "unanimous" support for the government's no-abortion policy. Contradicting her, Kim Campbell told reporters she still didn't support it. "I've been very candid about my views and I don't change them," she said.[75]

As the MLAs assembled, more than 2000 pro-choice demonstrators rallied on the legislature lawn. NDP leader Mike Harcourt called Vander Zalm a hypocrite, out to make women "second-class citizens" and to remake the health care system into "one for the rich and one for the poor." One sign read: "Vander Zalm: Stay out of peoples' privates." Many sported the button "The moral majority is neither." Well to the back of the crowd, about 200 anti-abortionists tramped in a quiet circle.[76]

Vander Zalm made contact with the *Vancouver Sun* from London, England, denying any lack of communication since he went away. In an emergency, "I think David [Poole] could have tracked me down," he said, adding that his secretary had acted correctly in speaking for the government on abortion.[77] The next day, in another transatlantic call, he labeled women who sought abortion funding under the Criminal Injuries Act as "cheaters." He said none of the criticism had convinced him his abortion policy was wrong.[78]

That was too much for Nicole Parton, who headed her February 24 column "Resign, gentlemen, resign." She concluded that "Dueck and Vander Zalm are personally vindictive and are prepared to do anything to circumvent not only the will of the court, but the will of the people...they are despots."[79] Columnist Vaughn Palmer, ever a critic of sitting governments, noted that Socred MLAs were "far from united" on the abortion policy and, while they remained in the house during question period, "I have seen more persuasive displays of enthusiasm at funerals."[80]

Returning to BC at last, Vander Zalm again used a media scrum at the airport as a policy-making vehicle. He rejected any federal government attempt to withhold health-care transfer payments because of his abortion stand. He also promised to block an abortion clinic. "It would need to be licenced and controlled and investigated and monitored vigorously. It's impractical, given the controls we'll insist on," said the premier, who admitted the Canadian Supreme Court ruling cleared the way for clinics. "What kind of regulations is he talking about? He's not the king," said Norah Hutchinson. Said Janet Vesterback of BCCAC, "Of course it [Vander Zalm's statement] concerns us but it's not going to stop us."[81]

Re-appearing in the legislature on Monday, February 29, the premier said he was ready to go one-on-one with Harcourt on the abortion issue.[82] And the premier did indeed go one-on-one, not just with the NDP, but with the whole province. That very day, he gave a fifteen-minute speech on abortion that horrified the opposition and voters, and flummoxed many in his own party. "Remember," he began, "when I am accused...of exaggerating or overstating or using words too strong, that the same thing was first said about those who described the Holocaust."

Then, without benefit of medical knowledge, Vander Zalm insisted — twice — that "Abortions at an advanced stage require the dismemberment of the baby without as much as a baby aspirin for the victim...without so much as an anaesthetic being given to the baby. A process without an anaesthetic to remove the pain and suffering that's inflicted. No one here can imagine such suffering, and no one ever lived to tell about it." That argument had been thoroughly discredited following the debut of Bernard Nathanson's video, "*The Silent Scream*." It was not medical practice to perform "late" abortions, whatever cutoff the premier had in mind. For medical and ethical reasons, abortions were done whenever possible in the first trimester. Prestigious doctors had proved that, before the brain and nervous system develops at about five months, the fetus is incapable of feeling pain. BC physicians responded to Vander Zalm's speech by underlining that message. "It is impossible for a fetus to cry at 20 weeks," was Dr. Garson Romalis's statement in an interview in the *Vancouver Sun*.[83]

It was a fact, however, that, for millennia women had been forced to undergo abortions without anesthetic, and the scale of their suffering was truly unimaginable.

Vander Zalm went on, "An abortion clinic is where people work for profit, big profit." Then he told a sob story. It concerned "a happy couple" who learned early in pregnancy that their baby would be born with no skull and, if born alive, wouldn't live long. That couple was to serve society as a prescriptive model, according to the premier, for they devoted themselves to the severely handicapped infant for the three weeks of its life. The greater part of Vander Zalm's speech centered on the "almost supernatural" love the couple experienced for their son, Christian, a love that blessed "the doctors, the nurses, and neighbors and friends" as well, and, indeed, "touched everyone."[84]

In their book on the Vander Zalm years, *Sun* writers Gary Mason and Keith Baldrey reveal that the model father in his speech was the Vander Zalm's "unofficially adopted son."[85] The story was deeply touching, but the hagiography the premier cast over the couple was not universally applicable to people facing problem pregnancies.

Speaker after speaker fired questions at the premier after his speech. He replied to the seventeen questions with short, single sentences, or deferred to his ministers. NDP MLA Joan Smallwood of Surrey-Guildford-Whalley was expelled from the legislature for the day when she said Vander Zalm's stand was "unconscionable" and called him a "coward." Asked about the incident later, the premier said, "When you consider the source, I'm not too surprised."[86]

And he refused to be surprised by the storm the speech caused across the province. A telephone poll on the evening he had spoken showed that almost two out of three respondents believed the government should pay for abortions.[87] Official and unofficial polls had shown the same results for months, and in their constituency offices, Socred workers knew it.[88] Vander Zalm excoriated those who would have him govern according to polls. "Would they cut off welfare if a poll showed most people were opposed to welfare? Have they no courage to govern except for political expediency?"[89]

The columnists were scathing. Denny Boyd said that Vander Zalm spoke as from a "fiery pulpit, delivering a gore-reeking declamation of abortion techniques that seems lifted from The Texas Chainsaw Massacre script." Nicole Parton dubbed the speech "unforgivable ignorance" and reissued the stern call: "Resign, sir. Resign."[90]

Initially, only a few Socreds were willing to publicly distance themselves from the premier. One was MLA Russ Fraser, who buttonholed
Vander Zalm for fifteen minutes on the legislature floor after the astonishing speech. Another was the president of the Vancouver East Socred
constituency association, who told the *Sun* that Vander Zalm's hard-nosed
policy damaged his ability to lead the party.[91] Dr. Marco Terweil resigned
from the executive committee of the Socred's Dewdney branch and told
Vaughn Palmer, "I like the man personally, but this time he's gone too
far...He has never seen an abortion and he doesn't know what he is talking
about." The physician added, "I don't see women coming in asking for
abortion on demand. I see women who are really up a creek and don't
know where to turn or what to do. We ought to be granting abortions on
the basis of medical necessity."[92] By the end of the week, eight Socred constituency associations had publicly criticized the premier's abortion policy.
Not all were in the lower mainland. They included Yale-Lillooet, Prince
George North, Prince George South and Comox. Dueck suggested legislation to outlaw clinics, and he warned grumbling caucus members to either
shut up to get out of the party.[93]

In Ottawa, an eight-hour long meeting of the Tory 'national caucus' —
MPs plus senators — failed to reach a consensus on whether a new anti-
abortion law was needed. PM Mulroney had to say something, so he told
the media scrum that he was considering a free vote on the issue in the
Commons.[94]

Fittingly, BC Chief Justice Allan McEachern ruled on the Civil Liberties
Association's suit against the Socreds on March 8, International Women's
Day. He declared the funding cut to be "invalid and of no force and effect."
However, his decision was based on a technicality, and McEachern pointed
a way out of the impasse. If the Socreds just dropped their requirement
that a funded abortion must be "medically necessary," and simply ruled
that abortion was not an insured service under the medical plan, they
would be within the law, he said.[95] Vander Zalm and Dueck admitted temporary defeat while vowing to fight on. But attorney-general Smith recommended against appealing the judge's decision.[96]

Nicole Parton's comment was: "Never let it be said that Premier Bill
Vander Zalm's convictions are carved in stone...His record clearly shows he
is flexible: he has been a Liberal and a Conservative, and he ran for mayor
of Vancouver under the Non-Partisan Association banner..." She recalled his
claim to have "some sort of guiding hand" — ("Ah! Divine intercession,"
noted Parton), that he relied on his wife's "special powers of ESP and intu-
ition" and that his horoscope was one of his touchstones. It was time, wrote
the columnist, that he recognize the force of the law and the courts.[97]

The slow-to-learn premier summoned his cabinet to draft a new
anti-abortion policy — but they produced no decision.[98] However, a low-

profile member of the health ministry announced that women who had paid for their own abortions during the funding ban would be reimbursed. No-one would say how many women that might be, but Vancouver General Hospital admitted collecting about $500 from 97 women, and Dr. Mary Conley of Victoria planned to forward a number of receipts for reimbursement.[99]

Despite McEachern's ruling and the funding ban's end, there was too much high feeling in the province for the abortion issue to fade quietly. The premier went to Prince George, usually a right-wing bastion, and was blasted at what the *Vancouver Sun* called "by far, the most anti-Vander Zalm town-hall meeting since he became premier." When the raucous meeting ended, he admitted to reporter Keith Baldrey that "his strong personal views on abortion" could not be translated into government policy without being struck down in court.[100] Then the premier escaped on a holiday to Alaska.[101]

Meanwhile, it turned out that the vaunted Alternatives to Abortion program — which was variously described as costing $2.2 million, or $4.4 million[102] — would feature TV spots promoting marriage as a life-long commitment. A health ministry official said that couples should prepare for marriage as carefully as they did for pre-natal classes and births. Countered the pro-choice movement: a substantial percentage of abortions had always been done at the request of married women.[103] The NDP derided the suggestion that marriage could serve as an alternative to abortion.[104]

Anti-abortionists' hopes were pinned on the federal government's promise to make abortions totally illegal. Vander Zalm awaited this with bated breath. But the new law was difficult to design. Federal justice minister Ray Hnatyshyn and his provincial counterparts met for two days in Saskatoon to discuss abortion, but the meeting ended in disarray.[105] Leaks about the possibility of setting time limits — for example, outlawing abortions only after sixteen weeks of pregnancy[106] — met with explosions of anger from anti-abortionists. They demanded a complete ban. But majority opinion was clearly pro-choice, and Mulroney would soon have to call a federal election. His advisors were casting about for the best way to avoid alienating voters. Liberal leader John Turner was equally nervous and refused to discuss his party's position on abortion.[107]

BC Coalition for Abortion Clinics' spokesperson Janet Vesterback said the group opposed any federal legislation that would restrict access to abortion for women. "We don't need a law; it's a red herring. Women are able to make their own moral decisions."[108] The same position was taken by an informal national coalition that combined trade unions, doctors, lawyers, and women's groups. As it assembled in Ottawa, a spokesperson for the Planned Parenthood Federation of Canada, which was part of the coalition, agreed that no law on abortion was needed.[109]

Socred attorney-general Brian Smith returned from the Saskatoon conclave persuaded that a federal abortion law would be introduced within a month or two, so the BC government put its promised new policy on hold.[110] Nonetheless, the Civil Liberties Association, dissatisfied with the technicality that triggered McEachern's ruling, announced it would return to court to get any provincial funding ban ruled out of order.[111]

Richmond General Hospital, meantime, continued to behave as though nothing had changed. Its board voted to suspend abortions. As usual, the medical staff condemned the decision, and the hospital was picketed by pro-choice advocates. But anti-abortionists retained their control at the June AGM.[112] For months, many other BC hospitals sidestepped providing abortions. A backlog developed at Vancouver General Hospital, and its vice-president of medicine, Dr. Derek Gellman called for help. "Frankly, I think if there is a demand for this medical service in the community, they (hospitals) have an obligation to provide it."[113]

When it was finally launched, on April 5, Vander Zalm's Alternatives to Abortion program was worth $20 million. Only three months before, it was to cost $1.1 million, but that was before the Canadian Supreme Court decision. The pro-choice public knew what it wanted. CCCA handed over a petition containing 17,500 names to NDP MLA Joan Smallwood, who submitted it to the legislature just as the premier was announcing his bloated family fund. If Vander Zalm were really interested in strengthening the family, Smallwood said, he should help women cope with economic realities by providing pay equity, social housing and food for hungry kids.[114]

So proposing $20 million to promote adoption was what Vander Zalm had to settle for. He could not ban abortions, order hospitals or doctors around, or re-write the rules on medical funding. Reporter Gary Mason asked the premier how disappointed he was, and he got a more-than-candid reply. Trying for nonchalance, Vander Zalm said, "I was mostly disappointed that my colleagues didn't have the moxie to fight alongside."[115]

Who *"didn't have the moxie?"* As the insulting story ran on the *Sun's* front page, the premier faced an angry cabinet for the daily briefing. When he later emerged, to face exploding flashbulbs and pointed questions from reporters, he did something unprecedented: he walked tight-lipped away from the media he liked to believe adored him. Wrote Vaughn Palmer, "I hesitate to predict permanent damage to a political institution (the Social Credit Party) whose demise has been announced prematurely every year since it took office in 1952..."[116] But Palmer wasn't alone in hearing the bell begin to toll.

CHAPTER 15

A SUMMER OF EXCITEMENT

Vander Zalm's mulishness put BC on tilt for the first months of 1988, but the BC Coalition for Abortion Clinics (BCCAC) kept its focus on opening a clinic. A name was selected — Everywoman's Health Centre — and the lengthy processes of registering as a society and becoming incorporated were begun. We hoped that registering under the provincial Societies' Act would help us obtain status as an official charity, so that tax receipts could be issued to donors. We needed to incorporate so we could enter into legal financial transactions, when the time came.

New Steering Committee members were elected in February. Only one was a woman of colour; all but one, who was retired, had day jobs, and most had husbands and children. They were also involved in other women's rights' organizations, which sent them as delegates to BCCAC. These were busy women before they volunteered their time to open an abortion clinic.

Only two members had any medical training, as we began this venture of opening a medical facility. Lucille Wood, a nurse, had been occasionally active since the previous year. She dropped off the Steering Committee in June 1988 but continued to help out through the summer.

Bettie Scheffer was a nursing instructor and medical personnel officer. BCCAC was her first foray into feminist politics. It had, she recalls, "an enormous agenda," and marched toward it steadily despite having "no real experts in the provision of health care around the table."[1] Many discussions presumed an experience with feminism that were difficult for a new-comer to follow. Laughing, she recalls it was "very much a challenge to feel part of that group...I certainly felt shut out lots of times."

She was distressed to hear descriptions of painful and demeaning treatment by doctors. A greater shock was the group's rejection of the 'medical model' — a clinic controlled by its doctors — and the "clear mistrust of anyone who was a health professional." Feeling awkward because she wasn't an east-sider, she went home thinking, "you know, it's too bad that they don't recognize that there's such a common core for women, no matter where they happen to be." In fact, most Steering Committee members did recognize that common core to women's experience, and they'd dedicated years of fighting to ease it. What pained Scheffer was probably the sometimes-savage establishment of a pecking order, which took place despite all protestations against hierarchical systems. That unacknowledged process caused me a lot of pain, as well. To Scheffer's credit, she refused to take the jibes personally, hung in, and made important contributions.

Another newcomer was Anne Hamilton, who came to the coalition by a unique route. A young business woman, she had joined a personal therapy group when "Vander Zalm opened his mouth."[2] Hamilton saw him as "so irrational" that "I couldn't stand the thought of another man manipulating and controlling my life in that way." The group, which didn't see itself as feminist, wasn't sure what to do but decided to call an information meeting on the abortion issue. They invited the media and all the pro-choice groups they could find out about, made a publicity effort, and — "two people came!" Actually, there were about thirty in attendance, but most were connected to the therapy group or the media. The speakers were Joy Thompson of BCCAC and Norah Hutchinson of Concerned Citizens for Choice on Abortion (CCCA).

Hamilton was invited to attend BCCAC meetings by Thompson and Hilda Thomas, who told her therapy group, "we need people like you, [who] have this kind of energy." With a friend, Hamilton made her way to Commercial Drive, where the Women's Health Collective was located. It was a small office, and the fifteen or so at the BCCAC meeting were "all crowded in and sitting on top of the photocopier." The discussion felt over her head to Hamilton, but when a *Province* reporter came, wanting an interview, she was "intrigued...that this group was actually being heard." The next week she went again, alone, listening intently, impressed by these women who had incredibly strong opinions, could debate with each other, and certainly weren't letting themselves be manipulated or controlled. She began to understand "the real scope of the issue, and the real impact of politics and women's health." And she liked the women of the coalition. Eventually, she began to speak in meetings, and she felt she was being heard. "So it was the environment [of the meetings], more than the issue, that prompted me on."[3] In a sense, she had an opposite experience to Bettie Scheffer's.

Joy Thompson, a petite and modish dynamo from England, took over from Maggie Thompson (no relation) as the representative to BCCAC from the Women's Health Collective. The mother of two boys, a pre-teen and a toddler, Joy had recently separated from their father. While she had no medical training, Thompson was a community member of the board at Reach Clinic, a non-profit medical centre on Commercial Drive, and was its vice-president for six years. She identified herself as a socialist feminist, felt experienced as an abortion counsellor, and brought to the BCCAC

Steering Committee a "well-developed philosophical alternative to the 'medical model'" of service. In February 1988, she "almost literally stepped into the role that Maggie had played," joining the media committee and becoming an elected spokesperson.[4] At ease on camera, she had a forthright manner and tended to inspire confidence when she spoke.

Hilda Thomas has already appeared in this history. Passionate about feminism and a stalwart of the NDP, Thomas was known for thinking quickly, bringing a wealth of experience to political matters, and for brooking no rivals or opposition to her views. An instructor in English at UBC, she had a distinctive voice that commanded an audience for her ideas and her music; with her husband Phil, she was a founder of the Vancouver Folk Song Society. Hers was a take-charge personality, and she joined the BCCAC Steering Committee after the Supreme Court victory. She saw it "as a place where I could put my hand on the lever, as it were...for something that I believed in and that I thought was very important at that moment."[5] She and Joy Thompson became the best-known of the several elected spokespersons for the coalition and were its public personae.

Having worked in the office of her general practitioner father, Marg Panton brought valuable skills to BCCAC. She had been active since its founding as an individual member. Now, with the opportunity to open a legal facility, Panton focused intently on finding out what equipment would be needed, locating medical suppliers, and other administrative concerns.

Fraser Valley CARAL made Pat Katagiri its representative to BCCAC. She, too, had been active since before its founding in 1987 and drove to Steering Committee meetings from her home in Langley. With a son just entering high school and a husband with an automotive shop, Katagiri's skills as a bookkeeper found their niche in Everywoman's Health Centre when it opened.[6]

Like Katagiri, Drena McCormack had a long history of political activism. An SFU grad, she worked on campus and played a role in establishing the first union of SFU staff. By 1988, her two children were high school age, and her partner was busy with his own union and political work. McCormack was a committed member of the Rape Relief and Women's Shelter collective. She took the place of Nicole Kennedy as its representative to BCCAC and joined the Steering Committee in February 1988.[7]

The difficult years of trying to form a stable lesbian group bore fruit with the establishment of Vancouver Lesbian Connection, which then ran a resource and social centre on lower Commercial Drive. Its representative to BCCAC, Mary Murphy, a librarian, was valued for her warmth and wit. She served on the steering and media committees and later handled a tricky job for the clinic. The NDP Women's Rights Committee was not comfortable with the plans to open a clinic, but it gave Ruth Houle the okay when she volunteered to represent it on the BCCAC Steering Committee. Houle had years of experience with left-wing and women's groups, and was known as a reliable and thorough campaign worker. She was recently retired, her husband had his own activities, and her children were grown. Houle's quiet competence and dedication proved invaluable when procedures for making appointments needed to be developed.[8]

Janet Vesterback had been active in the NDP WRC, but she joined the Steering Committee as an individual member. An elementary teacher in Vancouver, Vesterback had the asset of speaking French, and she was the coalition spokesperson who dealt with Radio Canada and French-language TV. She often brought students' work to mark during meetings, while taking an active part in discussions.

Sharon Hager, an active feminist since Women's Caucus days who had devoted all the years since then to pro-choice and left-wing causes, was usually in attendance at Steering Committee meetings.[9] She and Jean Rands, a Women's Caucus founder, provided continuity with the movement's Vancouver origins. In 1988, Rands worked for the BC Teachers' Federation and was president of the Union of Teachers' Federation Employees. She attended BCCAC Steering Committee meetings when her time allowed, as an individual member — not as the representative of a group.[10]

Carol Todd, of the United Fishermen and Allied Workers' Union (UFAWU) was our union representative over the summer of 1988. Jackie Ainsworth made clear-sighted contributions at meetings, but health problems kept her away much of the time. UBC student and representative from the campus pro-choice group, Janin Wear, was an eager member of the BCCAC Steering Committee from February, 1988, through the summer. Marje Stretten served as the representative of the Feminist Counselling Association until late in the summer of 1988. Donalda Greenwell (then Viaud), active in BCCAC since 1987, continued as the representative from the Canadian Congress of Women, but did not always attend Steering Committee meetings. Elaine Bernard continued on the Steering Committee from 1987 until she was elected president of the BC NDP. Ann Thomson — the author — was away from BC during the tense months when the Socreds stood with fingers in the dike against the Constitution. I was re-elected to the Steering Committee in my absence in February, but dropped off during the summer, while still attending its always-open meetings. In September, I was elected again. This, then, was the active core of the BCCAC Steering Committee. CCCA now had the same status as all other member groups of the Coalition. It had a seat on the Steering Committee, which was filled by whomever was assigned to come on a particular night. Sometimes, CCCA sent a delegation of four or more.

These women dedicated most of their waking hours to the clinic over the next eighteen months, and several stayed active for years. Equally committed were the volunteers, especially those on the Security Committee that was established in the fall of 1988, and those who became known as the "phone crew" after the clinic opened. In fact, hundreds and possibly more Vancouver citizens played some active role in launching Everywoman's Health Centre.

In January, just prior to the momentous Supreme Court decision, BCCAC had about $1900 in the bank.[11] Finances hovered in that range throughout the spring months. We were a nickel and dime organization, as pro-choice groups had always been. Ineligible for government grants because we had political goals, we always had to plead for donations from individuals, supportive groups, and from unions.

A positive sign was the interest beginning to be shown by two or three doctors. All were female, and all understood the need for a free-standing clinic. Most came from out of province and had not yet established a practice here, nor did they have a BC billing number to collect from the medical plan. In no position to open a clinic of the traditional "medical model," themselves, these doctors made tentative inquiries into the two pro-choice groups in Vancouver, BCCAC and CCCA.

Then at the May 4 Steering Committee meeting, we were jolted by sudden news. Dr. Robert Makaroff was planning to open an abortion clinic with Dr. Nelson Savein, possibly within a month. So that was why reporters were hovering near the doors. They'd come on a tip or a hunch: the news was not made public.

Okay. So, did that mean BCCAC needn't continue to plan for Everywoman's Health Centre? Pat Katagiri couldn't believe we would even consider retreating. For her, it was beyond question that BCCAC *would* plow ahead, and, after a serious discussion, the other members agreed with her. BCCAC was ready to welcome any non-profit abortion clinic, and if a medical model clinic was in the works, there was still a need for a clinic run by and for women.

Since Dr. Savein was Norah Hutchinson's husband, BCCAC members wanted to know how CCCA members planned to relate to this doctor-controlled clinic. That night the answer was that CCCA no longer wanted to establish a clinic. The need now was to prevent a new federal law, through education and lobbying. That, and its fund-raising work meant that CCCA could spare little time for BCCAC in the future.[12] In fact, CCCA members couldn't stay away from our meetings.

BCCAC members had also been talking to Dr. Makaroff, and we knew that, despite his strong moral commitment to helping women get abortions, he was uncertain about his own role. He hadn't practiced medicine for nearly twenty years and felt a little rusty. So Joy Thompson made a dinner date with Dr. Makaroff. In the restaurant, she asked if he really planned to go ahead with a private clinic. Why don't you take a less significant personal and financial risk and support BCCAC's plans for a clinic, she suggested. The normally shy doctor liked the plan. He'd been scorched by the spotlight in the past and wasn't eager to go through that experience again. Thompson left with a four-figure cheque and a suggestion that more might be forthcoming. No Makaroff-Savein clinic came about.

BCCAC threw itself into fund-raising. Anne Hamilton put together a list of people known to make large financial donations. A barrage of appeals went out to lawyers, doctors, academics, other professionals, and those philanthropists we'd managed to identify. But the effort didn't get much cash.

Some BCCAC members had been quietly looking for a rental location, and they had no luck, either. So in late May it was decided, in violation of all the rules for non-profit fund-raising, to find a building for sale — and then beat the bushes for money to buy it. Four women contacted a realtor. They were vague when asked what use was planned for the building. Hilda Thomas remembers being taken to view a former veterinary clinic in Kitsilano: "the stench was overpowering," especially since it was a boiling hot day. That location got thumbs down.

Meantime, Pat Katagiri had another idea. From her kitchen in Langley, she read through the 'properties for sale' ads in the *Vancouver Sun*. She found a notice about a medical clinic for sale off Victoria Drive, which sounded promising, so she phoned Thomas with the address. The search committee went to take a look.

And they knew at once it was the perfect place. Built of concrete, with no windows, it was like a bunker. Inside was 3000 square feet of space, with a large reception area flanked by two wings of offices. It was already zoned for medical use, was on a bus line and near a row of medical laboratories that could provide back-up services. Four doctors had practiced there; some were retiring, others were re-locating. The asking price was approximately $250,000. Anne Hamilton remembers wandering through the building and remarking on how suitable it was. The BCCAC members struggled to keep blank faces so the realtor wouldn't guess they had scarcely a dime in the bank Regrettably, the coalition was in no position to make a bid to purchase it.

Around that time, Anne Hamilton read a newspaper article about a woman in Alberta, whose late husband had left her a sizable fortune. She was the largest single donor to the federal NDP that year. Knowing nothing further about her, Hamilton sent a short description of our project to this complete stranger, figuring we had nothing to lose. The woman's name was Irene Dick. A few weeks later, Marg Panton returned from our postal box with the mail and handed Hamilton a personal, hand-addressed envelope. It had been slit open, causing shivers of apprehension in the two women. Who was monitoring our mail? Inside was a brief letter, and a cheque for $10,000!

On her next visit to the postal outlet, Panton met the man whose box was next to ours. Apologizing for mistakenly opening the letter from Irene Dick, he said he'd found it in his box and opened it without checking the address. Then he'd turned it over to the postal officials and it had come, in time, to us. Astonishing. Of course, he must have seen the cheque. Who knows what undercover agency may have sent him?

Full of deep thanks to this generous Alberta widow, to whom we could not even offer a tax receipt, BCCAC fund-raisers felt their hopes rising. Maybe the crazy idea of opening a clinic was not impossible.

It was July now, and, on checking, the Search Committee found the building at Victoria and 44th Ave. was still on the market. When BCCAC members showed up to look at the place again, the doctors pressed harder for information about our purposes. When they learned what we meant to do, it came out that one of the doctors was Catholic. This caused them to debate long and hard among themselves about whether they would sell to BCCAC, even if we came up with the money.

Bob Makaroff was invited to tour the building and advise us on whether it would work as the clinic we wanted. Hamilton and the doctor made an inspection, and she was so adept at real-estate jargon by then — which she'd picked up from her many discussions with the realtor — that, afterward, she and Makaroff had a laugh. "He thought I was the real estate agent," she recalls, and I said, 'No, no. I'm one of the [search] committee.'" Doctor Bob thought the building looked just fine. He mulled it over for awhile and then offered to invest some money, if negotiations for the purchase looked promising. He was willing to put up several thousand dollars.

With approximately $35,000 in hand and in promises, a financial prospectus was put together, and we set out to look for a mortgage. VanCity Credit Union, whose board members were from the NDP and which was proud of supporting community efforts, seemed like the place to start. Hilda Thomas, with Pat Katagiri, Lucille Wood, and Anne Hamilton, paid a visit on Bob Williams, former MLA and now the central figure at VanCity. No, he said, the credit union could not advance us any money. Further, the Loans Department would not meet with BCCAC without approval from the board of directors. So an appointment was made and a delegation went off to meet with the VanCity board. Hamilton presented our prospectus. "I remember sitting at the head of this table with all these people around it [who looked] very stern and non-committal. All sitting back in their chairs with arms folded. And we proceeded to tell them all about ourselves and make a proposal to them."

The board said, "'very nice, good luck, goodbye.'" Two weeks later, we finally got their verdict. No dice. They insisted on judging our request solely on the basis of financial risk. They did not consider its political merit at all, despite the long-standing NDP policy of supporting choice on abortion. BCCAC turned next to the smaller community credit union, CCEC. We were offered some funds, but not enough to make a down payment, on the (reasonable) basis that we had no collateral, nor even an account with CCEC.

By that time, after the entire Steering Committee had inspected the building, BCCAC had made an offer of $230,000 for it. A counter-offer was made, and the following Monday, July 25, we offered $237,000, with $40,000 down. The vendors were considering it, and also thinking about taking out a second mortgage for which they would charge us 10.5% interest. It was a tense and giddy moment.

The next morning, July 26, Nicole Parton of the *Vancouver Sun* broke a scandalous story on page one. "Former A-G [Brian] Smith admits pro-choice group spied on; Detectives worked undercover," ran the headline. A photo of Smith, with a bulldog-set to his jaw, was printed above a photo showing members of CCCA, "the organization...that was infiltrated." Twice the size of these was a photo of the now highly-respected Dr. Henry Morgentaler.

The spy scheme was triggered by Vander Zalm's fear that CCCA would open an abortion clinic — as the group had announced it would do in September, 1986. Shortly after the October '86 election that clinched his tenure in the premier's office, Vander Zalm's attorney-general had gone to the prominent law firm of Farris, Vaughn, Wills, and Murphy, and directed it to set up the spy operation. The lawyers hired a recently-formed security company called Newcombe and Associates. Reported Parton:

> At least four private investigators, working undercover, posed as pro-choice supporters and joined Concerned Citizens for Choice on Abortion...The detectives say they taped private conversations that took place during CCCA meetings and strategy sessions and obtained copies of financial records, as well as names and addresses of donors to pro-choice causes. They obtained copies of membership, mailing, and telephone lists. Everything they collected was forwarded by Newcombe and Associates to Farris and Co. Smith says he launched the operation — which lasted from January to July 1987 — to prepare an injunction aimed at preventing the opening of a free-standing abortion clinic in BC.[13]

Parton cited some of the more than 150 organizations whose endorsement of CCCA had been obtained in the early '80s. She took care to give the pro-choice group a squeaky-clean image. The story ran across Canada and won an award. It remained on the front and editorial pages in Vancouver for a week, and was still news in late August.

In a later interview with me, Nicole Parton described how she came to learn of the spying operation. An anonymous phone call to her office one Thursday, from a very angry man, gave her the briefest of summaries. Then the man hung up. Parton launched an intensive search, and she was able to find the caller. He was a bartender, whose romance with the woman spy had soured. Parton found the woman spy, too, and discovered she was one of four detectives hired by a law firm to infiltrate the pro-choice movement.[14] The spy Parton met was "not someone I would have chosen for the job," she told me with discretion. Perhaps the firm of Farris, Vaughn still associated abortion with the sleazy underworld, and they went to that milieu to find their investigators.

To identify the detectives, Parton contacted Norah Hutchinson of CCCA, who was horrified to learn what had happened. Hutchinson showed Parton photographs of people who'd come to a social function during the Morgentaler tour in April, 1987. Recalls Parton, "I looked at all those pictures very closely and tried to commit them to memory. Because later, when I met the detective...I did recognize her. I had already seen her" in the photos, and "I could quickly put two and two together."

Newcombe and Associates consisted of just two women, so they had joined forces with another private firm, called MPI Security. Parton contacted its principles, Larry and Marzena Banks, who reluctantly gave her "only minimal facts.""Eventually, I traced the hiring of these people up the ladder in government, and directly to the attorney-general of the day, who was then Brian Smith."Brian Smith had, in fact, resigned from cabinet on June 28, only weeks before this story broke, presumably because he knew Vander Zalm and his friend, Peter Toigo, were being investigated by the RCMP. They were suspected of influence peddling in the sale of the Expo lands. Smith said nothing of that at the time.[15] The Socred Party was shredding. Other cabinet ministers, including Grace McCarthy herself, resigned in that period.[16]

Parton confronted Smith, told him, "Look, I already know what happened, and I want your confirmation of it...and also your side" of the story. She persuaded him to let her tape the discussion, because it would protect him from being misquoted.[17] Smith stood by his rationale that the spying was to prevent commission of a crime. He claimed he'd received only a few verbal reports from his close friend, Jack Giles, a senior partner at Farris, Vaughn, and they were "usually the same — that this abortion clinic isn't going to get off the ground."[18]

Possibly that was because the spies infiltrated the wrong pro-choice group. It was the BC Coalition for Abortion Clinics that would open a clinic, not CCCA. During the time they were snooping, however — before the Supreme Court made abortion clinics legal — prospects didn't look good for BCCAC either.

Parton found it particularly significant that Smith insisted "the premier, Bill Vander Zalm, was fully aware of the action," even though Vander Zalm denied it. Reports from Newcombe traveled to the law firm, then to Smith, and he recalled passing the information to the premier through his secretary David Poole. Poole had just taken a fall for the premier and had been "fired" from his job in Vander Zalm's office.

The day after the story broke, photos with capsule comments ran above the page one headline. Vander Zalm, smiling genially, said, "I would never condone it. I would never stand for it and Mr. Smith knows that." David Poole said, "I had absolutely no knowledge that he'd authorized a private investigator to infiltrate the pro-choice movement." Captioning a photo of Brian Smith was the quote: "I don't see where you get this trampling of rights. Why does someone have a right to open an illegal clinic?" Later in the story, Smith was said to admit "the 1987 operation was an invasion of privacy," while he still maintained "the premier's office was aware of the investigation."[19] Letter-writers to the local press recalled Smith's writ of seditious conspiracy against workers who rebelled against anti-labour Bill 19 in 1987, and the former A-G's call for re-instating capital punishment, by firing squad.[20]

Public accounts showed the provincial government paid Farris and Company $145,337 for all work done for it in 1987. Brian Smith said he would "be surprised" if the spy operation had cost taxpayers more than $12,000.[21] $12,000 would have covered all expenses for about three years in any pro-choice group I ever worked with! It also came out that the Socreds had used the same law firm to send spies into the Solidarity movement of 1983.[22]

At a press conference, Norah Hutchinson said CCCA was considering legal action against the government. "We're a 10-year-old, very public group and we want to know why we were being investigated...These people were in our meetings, they were in our homes..."[23]

"Abortion caper a very bad joke" editorialized The *Province*, next to a cartoon in which whisperers suggested labels for it: "Snoopergate? Pro-Choicergate? Phone-tapping-A-G-Rapping-Zalm-Zapperingergate? Here-we-go-again-ergate!"[24] The *Sun's* editors said Parton "unearthed a particularly loathsome pit of sly intrigue for which the government shelled out public money. To what purpose?...Mr. Smith's justification rings spurious." The *Sun* could not believe Vander Zalm was not in on the scam.[25] NDP Leader Mike Harcourt demanded "an apology for this sleazy, shady operation," and his A-G critic Moe Sihota was characteristically irreverent and shocked. BC Federation of Labor president Ken Georgetti and MP Svend Robinson added their denunciations.[26]

As the story unraveled, it came out that the three women investigators had sat at a CCCA table during the 1987 BC NDP convention, at which Harcourt was elected leader. They had collected signatures on a petition, talked to delegates, and taken donations. Before that, investigator Marzena Banks had registered attendees at the BCCAC general meeting at Heritage

Hall on Main St. in March, 1987. Newcombe and a woman who wouldn't give her real name to the press, calling herself Gloria Howells, had volunteered to drive Dr. Morgentaler's luggage from the airport to Vancouver during his 1987 visit.[27]

"To me, it sounds a bit ridiculous — like a tale out of some banana republic," said Henry Morgentaler, contacted at his Toronto clinic by the *Sun*. He pointed out that pro-choice groups across the country were open and above-board, so that anyone could easily get information about them without disguising themselves. "It shows the anti-abortion people for who they are — they have no respect for democratic institutions. Most people who are against abortion are doctrinaire, dogmatic...they do not have an understanding of what it means to have freedom of conscience," said the doctor. His luggage had contained only his personal belongings.[28]

Smith argued that he'd been pressured by many, including members of the cabinet, to prevent the opening of an illegal clinic. He'd chosen to go to the law firm rather than work through the police. But now both the RCMP and the Vancouver police said they wouldn't have "bothered to infiltrate the pro-choice movement to gather information." "I couldn't see it on something like that," RCMP chief superintendent George Powell told the *Sun*. "You save that for serious stuff." Added deputy Vancouver police chief Ted Lister, "in the total context of crime in Vancouver, it certainly wouldn't be at the top of the list." Police procedure would have been to contact CCCA and advise it of the law, and of the penalties for committing an illegal act. The police saw no point in spending thousands on undercover detectives.[29]

The BC Civil Liberties Association called on the province to release reports of the investigation and demanded the provincial ombudsman look into the case. "People need to understand how serious an infringement this is," said Phil Bryden, vice-president of BCCLA. By the end of the week, BC ombudsman Stephen Owen announced he would indeed start an inquiry into the spy incident.[30]

Nicole Parton gave the spies themselves space to answer their critics, and they had many complaints. "'We were pawns in a bigger game,'" Larry Banks was quoted as saying. In his view, the NDP was behind the uproar. "Mike Harcourt is trying to use the government pro-choice spy scandal for his own political gain, say three of the private detectives who took part in the operation." The woman known as Gloria Howells said, "'All I can remember of the entire [NDP convention] is that it was a big bore...I'm not the political type.'" The Banks's were adamant that their most highly prized assets were "'unflagging confidentiality and a good reputation.'" Both were former police officers with degrees in criminology. They said the furore put their careers at risk, but since the newspapers had already published the story, they were willing to go on record because "'we have nothing to hide.'" "'We did not do anything illegal, immoral or unprincipled in the activities that we have engaged in.'" This claim rested largely on Marzena Banks's use of her real name and address, and the fact that she drove her own car to meetings. Also, she did not sign the membership card she was given at her first meeting, which asked for her agreement with CCCA's Basis of Unity. Therefore, in Mrs. Banks's view, she had not disguised herself or engaged in "'any other kind of deception'" of CCCA.[31]

A month later, Stephen Owen issued his report. He declared the government had used poor judgment in sending spies into the pro-choice movement but had done nothing illegal.[32] Case closed.

While British Columbians were pre-occupied with the spy scandal, abortion was also top news in Ottawa. Seven months after the Supreme Court nullified Canada's long-standing laws that made abortion all-but-a-hanging offence, the Tories had been unable to draft new legislation. The male-dominated Commons was filled with MPs who knew no stronger creed than that God, or at least their personal sense of manliness, demanded that men make women knuckle to them, especially when it came to reproductive issues. But there were enough MPs, women of every party, a few Liberals, and almost the entire NDP caucus, who were adamantly pro-choice. That made the chances dicey for getting a creditable anti-abortion vote.

Parliament was scheduled for summer recess, beginning the end of July. It could not adjourn without somehow addressing the abortion issue. There were repeated threats from the powerful anti-abortion lobby that MPs who did not heed them would lose their seats in the upcoming election. But what was put before the Commons on Tuesday, July 26, was not proposed legislation, but a vaguely worded motion, satisfactory to no-one. The motion called for eventual legislation that would straddle the division in views. Its text sounded very like the deleted Section 251.[33]

After two all-night sessions, the motion was put to a (straw) vote on Thursday, July 28. It failed dramatically: 147-76. News photos showed glum faces all around, with captions such as "Waste of time."[34]

The absence of an anti-abortion law created a particular problem for Joe Borowski. At last, he had a date to put his argument before the Canadian Supreme Court — October 3, 1988. At every prior stage of the case, Borowski had argued that section 251 of the Criminal Code violated the Canadian constitution. But nine months earlier, the court had struck down Section 251 for reasons opposite to those argued by Borowski. Now the Manitoban health food store owner, who had withheld his taxes, gone on a hunger strike and to jail, and stumped the country preaching his gospel, had no law to denounce. His supporters in the Commons pressured for a delay in the court proceedings until new legislation could be adopted,[35] but Chief Justice Brian Dickson "curtly dismissed" the request on July 19.[36]

By August 2, the BCCAC Steering Committee was in strike-force mode. We had taken a nearly irreversible step by bidding to purchase the building on East 44th Ave., and we still hadn't the money for it. Anne Hamilton laid it out: we had two weeks to raise $40,000 for the down payment, and three weeks to raise the first mortgage payment. After that, we'd need money to hire staff and equip and supply the clinic. Again, we reviewed the lists of potential donors we had culled from many sources, and divided into pairs to contact them.

We also considered how and when to reveal our coup, that a site for the clinic had been found. It was tricky. We hoped the announcement would bring in donations. But we needed to keep the location of the building a secret from our anti-abortion foes as long as possible. We began planning for a meeting in September.

Drena McCormack and I used phones at Rape Relief House to plead for donations. It was my job to contact Dr. Henry Morgentaler, and my messages got an early reply. Dr. Morgentaler regretted that he was so much in debt to his attorneys he could not make a financial donation. But he would and did send us a vacuum aspirator machine — at first, on loan; later as a gift. Dribbles of cash and promises of a bit more came in from this concerted phone campaign.

A disturbing development began in upstate New York, where a used-car dealer, family man, and self-declared preacher named Randall Terry found he could whip up anti-abortion activists by appropriating the tactics of the earlier civil rights movement. He called his concept 'Operation Rescue.'

Operation Rescue aimed to close down abortion clinics. Rather than using arson or firebombs — which remained staples in anti-abortionists' armouries — Randall Terry worked in the open air, with large crowds that used their bodies to blockade the entrances to clinics. Women with abortion appointments were verbally harassed and prevented from getting inside. During a week of vigils and blockades in New York City in May, 1988, 1,664 'rescuers' were placed under arrest.[37] "'Everyone here is committed to being arrested, said Terry.'" Joseph Scheidler, a sort of dracula look-alike from Chicago's 'Pro-Life' Action League, was inspired and pledged to do a 'rescue' in his home town.[38] New York was not amused. A federal district court judge levied fines of $25,000 per day for each day Operation Rescue blocked access to medical clinics.[39] Randall Terry skipped town without paying.

1988 was an election year in the United States. Ronald Reagan's term as president was ending. Despite his cordiality toward and frequent public promises to the anti-abortion movement, nothing much had changed for them. *Roe v. Wade,* the 1973 case that made abortion a US constitutional right, was intact. True, access was scarce, and cutbacks to medicare made abortion out of reach for women on welfare, but those had been enacted before Reagan's time. The 'Gipper's' anti-abortion bias had, perhaps, its greatest effect on US foreign aid, which was routinely refused to any nation that permitted contraceptives and abortion to be so much as mentioned to its citizenry. That hardly mollified the crowd at home. One might say that a misogynist zealot scorned is apt to become a hellion.

The Operation Rescue roadshow turned out in force in Atlanta, Georgia, in late July. The Democratic Party convened there to nominate Michael Dukakis and Jesse Jackson as its candidates for the White House. The Democrats omitted opposition to abortion from their platform, in contrast to the Republicans' and George Bush, Sr.'s prayerful allegiance to it. Some 'rescuers' in Atlanta blockaded medical clinics, while larger crowds swarmed about in the parking lots outside the convention hall. They clutched bibles and sang, "We Shall Overcome." Terry's assistant, Joseph Foreman, told reporters with paradoxical pride that 'rescuers' were the kind of folk who "don't know anything about civil disobedience except that they were against it when blacks did it."[40] To foil police officers trying to grab and arrest them, many scuttled about on their hands and knees, which made for startling images on TV news.

The total arrested was less than in New York in May, but in Atlanta a canny ploy kept the 'rescuers' in the news. They concealed their identities and went to jail under the names of 'Baby John' or 'Baby Jane' Doe. Those who gave their correct names were released on $500 bonds, but those who insisted on anonymity were held in jail. If they failed to appear for their court dates, police could not track them, without their names. At least 60 were still in jail when the Democratic convention ended, so Operation Rescue stayed on in Atlanta for months, wreaking whatever havoc they might. 'Moral Majority' leader Jerry Falwell became an enthusiastic convert and told his followers, "This is a departure from anything I've ever preached...The only way is nonviolent civil disobedience."[41] In Vancouver, BCCAC activists sensed it was an omen of things to come.

Sheer grit raised the money BCCAC needed to purchase the building we wanted. One Steering Committee member mortgaged her home; CCEC Credit Union backed others in taking loans with their RRSPs as collateral. The few BCCAC members who had any, donated their life savings. An anonymous local angel gave another hefty amount. Donations from our persistent pleas to potential supporters came in, in dribs and drabs.

Anne Hamilton remembers it as "an incredibly intense time...That summer, and on into the fall, I was putting in thirty-five-hours a week on my regular job, and then another fifty hours for the clinic. Literally there til midnight." Hamilton and Marg Panton talked to the vendors about leaving fixtures behind. "And in the end, they did leave quite a lot of stuff. Counters. Those large, four-drawer medical filing cabinets. So they came around and were very co-operative, and actually quite supportive, through to the closing of the deal."[42]

With no other option open, Pat Katagiri and Anne Hamilton went to a non-bank mortgage broker. They obtained a three-year, conventional mortgage at 12.5% interest — two per cent above the bank rate. The monthly payment would be approximately $1720. Bettie Scheffer found an agency that offered us fire and physical damage insurance. Our concrete-bunker building impressed them. But then the agency backed out, and we had to keep looking.[43] Expenses were mounting, and we had yet to find money for the necessary renovations, for equipment and supplies, for hiring medical staff. Whenever anxiety levels threatened to explode, I remember Anne Hamilton re-assuring us all that we could do it. An interim purchase agreement was finally signed, with a closing date of September 30.[44] Jubilation vied with exhaustion.

Money-wise we were hanging by our fingertips. We booked the Biltmore Hotel at Kingsway and 12th for September 10. That was when we'd announce that we had a site for a clinic, and we were counting on it to bring in additional donations. The media would be admitted at the beginning, to hear what we were prepared to make public. After a break, BCCAC members would re-convene for a general membership meeting. Our chief fear, then, was that anti-abortion vandals would locate the building and do damage before the deal was final. That didn't happen. But the September 10th meeting turned out to be a bombshell in a way we didn't expect.

CHAPTER 16

EVERYWOMAN'S HEALTH CENTRE OPENS

Bettie Scheffer had exciting news for the 135 women attending the British Columbia Coalition for Abortion Clinics' meeting at the Biltmore Hotel on September 10, 1988. It was that we were ready to purchase a building, and the long-awaited clinic would truly open soon. Of course, the building's location was confidential, but to prove we were not bluffing, three photos of the interior were shown. They revealed nothing that might identify where the building was.

Scheffer's announcement was met with cheers, and a motion to approve the purchase was eagerly adopted. It was a surprise to see three or four hands waving emphatically to vote '*nay.*'

Spokespersons Joy Thompson and Hilda Thomas repeated our news to the press. The clinic was to be community-based and run by women; it was wheelchair and ambulance accessible, close to major hospitals, and could be secured against violent attack. A mortgage was already arranged, but donations were still needed to cover start-up costs. And we would definitely bill the provincial medical plan for costs related to the abortions done at Everywoman's Health Centre.[1]

When we re-convened, *sans* media, for the quarterly general membership meeting, an unexpected opposition revealed itself. Three women from CCCA sat grouped around NDP MLA Joan Smallwood. Angrily, they challenged the BCCAC Steering Committee's authority to take on so much debt. The financial burden we were assuming was enormous, irresponsible, and could not be met. The member groups of BCCAC would become liable for the money owed, and they would be ruined by it. The enthusiasm in the room was undercut by doubt. BCCAC speakers assured the members that we were not acting foolishly, and that none of the 35-40 groups in the coalition would be financially jeopardized by our debts. But the meeting ended in stunned confusion, not in the triumph we expected.[2]

The Socreds immediately warned against charging abortion patients for the clinic's non-medical operating costs. The government had learned the hard way not to threaten doctors, so doctors' fees for abortions would be paid. But if the clinic charged patients anything more, that "would be considered extra-billing," and penalties would apply.[3] Of course, until we won provincial funding, we would have no choice but to charge fees for our services.

Distinguishing between CCCA and BCCAC was understandably diffi-cult for the media. CCCA had been active in Vancouver since 1978 and had figured prominently in the news during the summer, so it was presumed to be the dominant group. Yet it was newcomer BCCAC that was now announcing the opening of a clinic. CCCA was only one member group of the coalition. To her credit, despite her angry charges at the Biltmore, Norah Hutchinson made no public announcement against BCCAC. She told the *Sun* that "although her group doesn't operate abortion clinics, it is committed to getting public funding for them."[4] The *Province* strongly endorsed abortion clinics, with an editorial that listed four clear reasons why they were preferable to hospital procedures.[5]

Within days, the NDP Women's Rights Committee scheduled a special meeting of its table officers and summoned BCCAC to attend. It demanded we submit any papers we had signed to the WRC for perusal. Hilda Thomas and Janet Vesterback went for the BCCAC Steering Committee. Also attending were two MLAs, Joan Smallwood and Darlene Marzari, as well as Norah Hutchinson from CCCA, and Elaine Bernard. Bernard had become president of the BC NDP and was no longer active with BCCAC. But she ended the sniping by relaying advice she'd got from lawyers — that only the Steering Committee, acting as trustee for the clinic, was liable for any arrears run up by BCCAC. In the end, the NDP women passed a motion of support for Everywoman's Health Centre.

Little by little, money came in. On September 12, Anne Hamilton reported that $64,000, in cash or pledges, had been raised over the past five weeks. Nearly $3000 was donated by women attending the meeting at the Biltmore, and $400 came from the Vancouver local of the postal workers' union.

Finding money was not the only delicate matter we faced. Another essential was the need for a medical director, as required by the College of Physicians and Surgeons. Through her job placing medical personnel, Bettie Scheffer had made discreet inquiries, and she found that a particular name kept coming up. The person was a woman, pro-choice and knowl-edgeable in reproductive medicine, who had 'peerless credentials.' Scheffer announced she had offered this doctor the job, and the doctor was taking a week to think about it.

Immediate debate broke out on the Steering Committee. We had worked so long for a clinic run by and for women, not by doctors. Did this doctor understand she would not have veto power over the Steering Committee, or the board of directors that would eventually replace it? Terms of employment for the medical director were drafted at once, and Scheffer relayed them to her candidate.

We also needed legal advice. Indeed, a dozen lawyers eventually donated *pro bono* time to the clinic, for, however one looked at it, our medical service was at the same time a legal and political insurgency. Extraordinary amounts of time were given by lawyers David Mossop and Don Crane, and by others as time went on. There was no stopping BCCAC now.

As chair of the outreach committee, I negotiated with the BC Federation of Labor until, finally, a letter went to all its affiliated unions on September 15, over the signature of president Ken Georgetti. It was an urgent appeal for donations to the Everywomen's Health Centre Society.[6] Six months later, that letter figured in a crisis within the labour movement.

On September 14, Nicole Parton, who had been a guest speaker at the Biltmore the previous Saturday, gave us generous support in her column:

> It is a very brave thing the BC Coalition for Abortion Clinics is doing, establishing a site for the province's first free-standing abortion clinic. It is brave because there remains vast ignorance among many people who do not understand why such a clinic is important: no more kitchen table abortions, no more self-mutilation and deaths, no more protracted pleadings to terminate unwanted pregnancies, no more abortions in a costly hospital setting that is better reserved for those who are ill.[7]

Trouble was brewing in the Vancouver Right to Life Society. Within a week, seven members of its board resigned, including vice-president Brenda Montgomery, who told the *Vancouver Sun* that members were 'dropping out left, right and centre." At issue was president Betty Green's leadership style: her public comment that CCCA should be billed for the thousands of dollars the Socreds spent to spy on it, and the charge that health minister Peter Dueck was "afraid" to pursue his anti-abortion principles in the courts. Montgomery said that if Green "will attack a strong pro-lifer like Peter Dueck and a pro-abortion faction with the same vigor, I'm in the wrong group."[8] Sissy von Dehn, a long-time anti-abortion activist, and several others, including the president of Vancouver Christians for Life, followed Montgomery out. Betty Green waved away their complaints — which included her hiring a lawyer for $200,000, without the board's knowledge, to defend her against charges of slander by Dr. Nelson Savein. Her explanation was the ex-board members were "inexperienced."[9]

After she had reviewed our job description, whereby the medical director would "work in collaboration with the members of Everywoman's Health Centre Society and staff," Dr. Lorena Kanke accepted our offer to become medical director. Our idea was that the medical director would function, more-or-less, as a figurehead. The reins of the clinic would remain in its founders' hands. It was, indeed, a strong endorsement of us that Kanke accepted, for she was an established and respected member of the medical community. On staff at both Vancouver General and Grace hospitals, she was also on the medical school faculty at UBC. Kanke was to prove content to lend us her name and let us solve our own problems, but the name she lent us gave Everywoman's Health Centre new respectability. She agreed to an honorarium for a one-year appointment, with a review after three months. Steering Committee members spent a rare social evening around the fire in Bettie Scheffer's gracious living room, getting acquainted with Lorena Kanke. She told us she accepted the Basis of Unity, and she thought it would be exciting to work as a member of a team.

Later, Dr. Kanke recalled some of her reasons for accepting the position with Everywoman's Health Centre. She grew up in the lower mainland and went to medical school at UBC. "I know women came into the hospital bleeding," she says of that period. "And a certain percentage of them would have had some instrumentation [to end pregnancy] done by someone else, whether it was a physician or not." She recalls "there used to be a lot of so-called spontaneous miscarriages, the rate of which fell dramatically after legal abortions became available." Doctors knew, even though the woman denied it, when a clandestine abortion had been attempted.[10]

After UBC, Kanke spent a crucial three years in Chicago, where she interned and did two years' residency at Cook County Hospital. Cook County served Chicago's vast ghetto. When Kanke went there in 1967, contraceptives were illegal, and unwanted pregnancies were frequent. As a resident, Dr. Kanke put in twenty-four-hour shifts, during which "I would get maybe ten to twenty women who were in various stages" of emergency, due to botched abortions. The patients would arrive bleeding and sometimes infected.

> Sometimes those infections could be life-threatening, and sometimes they were fatal. Women would go into septic shock and die. The kidneys would shut down, the livers would fail. The heart would fail, because of the toxins. And then they'd die.

So many women suffered in this way that one of the hospital's four large obstetrics-gynecology wards was reserved for post-abortion patients: Pathological OB, Ward 41. Antibiotics were routinely administered because of rampant infection, and many incomplete abortions had to be finished in the hospital. Dying women were sometimes pressured by police to name their abortionists. "Patients almost uniformly refused to inform," says Kanke. Those who survived might be sterile, due to a puncture of the uterus, damage to the fallopian tubes, scarring, or infection.[11]

Another Vancouver doctor who does abortions, Dr. Garson Romalis, did part of his training at Cook County Hospital, too. His experiences on the same 40-bed obstetrics ward led to his commitment to help women terminate their pregnancies: "I'll never forget the 17-year-old girl, brought in on a stretcher by ambulance, with six feet of small bowel protruding from her vagina," Dr. Romalis told the *Vancouver Sun* — after the second attack on his life by a presumed 'pro-life' killer in July 2000. "It's like Holocaust-remembrance stuff...You have to keep reminding people that these things really happened, or else they're liable to happen again."[12]

The double squeeze of raising enough money in time to meet the payments had everyone tense. Pat Katagiri and Marg Panton drew up detailed budgets and passed them around to the Steering Committee. Start-up capital expenses were projected at $73,400, most of which was already in hand. But we would soon run up a deficit of $11,000 for operating expenses. They predicted, optimistically, that even with a modest beginning schedule, doing eighty abortions on twelve operating days per month, the fees we would be forced to charge the patients should be sufficient to retire the deficit after four months. Until we succeeded in getting the funding due to any medical facility from the health care plan, such fees were unavoidable. As back-up, we had obtained a $35,000 line of credit and a possible loan from CCEC credit union. Nonetheless, CCCA's representative on the BCCAC Steering Committee, who appointed herself as our auditor, was distressed. She was insistent that BCCAC raise an additional $50,000 before opening the clinic.[13] What could we do but politely hear her out, then get on with business.

Mary Murphy obtained a business licence for the clinic. It was issued promptly, and we believed City Council was sympathetic to us. But, Murphy warned, it was a public document, and the location of the clinic would be discovered soon. Just before that happened, the Canadian Supreme Court opened its October 3 hearing on the suit of Joe Borowski.

Borowski contended that the fetus is a person with a constitutional right to life. Without consulting his lawyers, he arrived at the Supreme Court in Ottawa with two large glass jars containing fetuses. He showed them to reporters and earnestly explained that he wanted the justices to see them and "pass them hand to hand."[14] But the seven justices were in such confusion about whether they had jurisdiction in the case that more than half of them expressed public doubt about the wisdom of making a ruling on it at all. Neither the constitution nor the Charter of Rights mentions the fetus. After some debate, the Court decided to hear Borowski's appeal.[15] It held over its decision for five months, then announced that the case was made moot by the decision on Morgentaler in January, 1988. Therefore, the Court refused to address the question of whether or not the fetus is included in section 7 of the Charter of Rights.[16]

The clinic's whereabouts was front page news in both Vancouver dailies on Friday, October 7. Sissy von Dehn, "a former member of the Vancouver Right to Life Society," immediately plastered the neighborhood with anti-abortion leaflets. They warned "disruptions will occur from [anti-abortion] protesters."[17] BCCAC responded by taking an Open Letter door to door and found we had a largely friendly response from area residents.

At the same time, Operation Rescue launched what it called a "four day siege" of Atlanta. 700-800 demonstrators from across the U.S. converged there, because, as one said, "God told me to." They zeroed in on three abortion clinics in midtown, where they tried to break through police barriers and block the entrances.[18] More than 400 people were arrested, and busloads of reinforcements kept arriving.[19] The idea spread, and after a month of protests, more than than 2000 Operation Rescue demonstrators were arrested in 32 US cities on the weekend of October 28-29. The uproar spread to Toronto, where 39 protesters were arrested outside the Morgentaler clinic.[20] Curiously, the only newspaper in Canada to carry these stories was the *Calgary Herald* — in a city that neither had an abortion clinic nor expected one to open anytime soon.

The moment came when two members of our anti-hierarchical group were struck off to drive to the lawyers' and realtors' offices to sign papers as 'President' Drena McCormack, and 'VP' Joy Thompson of the Everywoman's Health Centre Society. Joy Thompson remembers:

> As we were driving down there, we had such a chuckle. Here's two relatively low-income women, who've been feminists for as long as they can remember, never had two pennies to rub together, never bought property in their lives and probably never will, who were going off to purchase what was then a significant piece of real estate!

Wiping the grins from their faces, the women signed the papers, "did the seal and all the rest of it", took the deed and shook hands with everybody involved. And as they walked away, they exchanged a look and agreed, "We really should have called the society 'The Feminist Army' or some such."[21]

By October 12 the Everywoman's Health Centre Society owned the building at 44th and Victoria. The Steering Committee greeted the news with applause. It was a relief, especially for the three women who had spent months negotiating the deal, all the while fending off inquiries about how much money we had, where we did our banking, where our funds came from, etc. It is true that, by mid-October, 1988, BCCAC had received more than $80,000 in donations,[22] but the suspicions of CCCA were partly right. No other group was in financial danger because of our efforts, but BCCAC had bid to buy the building when we had less than half the amount needed, and when the outcome of our fund-raising wasn't yet known. Thinking back to the many tight corners the building-purchase team got past, Pat Katagiri says, laughing, "Sometimes when I think about it now, I get even more afraid than I was then."[23] But turning back was not an option. It was as though this clinic was meant to be. With the first mortgage payment due on December 1, the pressure was on to open up and begin generating income.

No sooner were the phones installed than they began ringing off the hook. The volume of calls was astonishing. At least ten per cent were from out of province. An additional 15%-20% came from outside the lower mainland, where legal abortions were still almost impossible to obtain.[24]

Ruth Houle and Pat Katagiri put in long hours answering the phones, sometimes with help from Women's Health Collective members and other volunteers. They tried to spend as much time as needed with each caller, listening to and re-assuring her about the procedure.

The great advantage of a legal clinic is that women can refer themselves; they don't need to see a doctor before coming in for their abortions. Still, it was necessary to determine how advanced each woman's pregnancy was, and whether she had any medical condition that might put her at risk. It had to be explained why we must charge fees for an abortion, and that we would use a local anesthetic, so that women were conscious during the procedure. Some found that prospect unsettling. They felt easier when they learned the operation lasted less than ten minutes and that, after resting in the recovery room, a woman could leave within a few hours of her arrival — with a friend, or alone, as she preferred. For many callers, maintaining confidentiality was a big concern. So a code was devised. If it were necessary for the clinic to phone a client and someone other than herself answered, we would say that 'Sara' or some such name was phoning, and the woman could call us back.[25] Houle trained volunteers to help with the phones, despite our strong belief that staffers should be paid — even if we couldn't afford to pay what they were worth. From the first, the clinic depended on two types of volunteers: those who worked on the phone-lines, booking appointments, and those who served as security persons at the clinic doors. Both were essential, and many served faithfully for years.

We took occupancy of the clinic immediately, and the Steering Committee held its evening meetings in the waiting room from October 19 on. It was very exciting, but steady nerves were called for. With only a few weeks to get ready, we had still to hire staff, renovate the building, bring in equipment and supplies, and see to it that the clinic was secure.

Four hiring committees were quickly formed and drew up job descriptions for, respectively, physicians, nurses, counsellors, and office administrator. Notices were placed inviting applicants, and, despite our lack of a track record, and the hurry forced upon us, some came in. All applicants were contacted and interviewed.

In the end, two of the positions were filled with women from the BCCAC Steering Committee. Marg Panton was the obvious choice for clinic administrator; she was already carrying out that job. The job description provided for sixteen hours per week, at $15 an hour. It wasn't humanly possible to do the job in sixteen hours per week, but Panton had to admit the budget didn't allow for more than that. Seven women applied for the counsellor's position, but the recommendation was to hire Joy Thompson. She happily declared, 'When I first walked into this clinic, I felt that a job had been waiting for me here for seventeen years.'[26]

There was only one choice for a physician. Dr. Kanke was a member of that hiring committee, but our arrangement did not commit her to perform abortions at the clinic. Dr. Karen Hossack was the only serious candidate. For months, she had been commuting weekly between Port Moody and Winnipeg, where she did abortions at the Morgentaler clinic. She was committed to the pro-choice movement, and after many discussions about women-controlled, vs. doctor-controlled care, a contract was signed with her to perform abortions on a part-time basis.

Finding nurses with operating room experience was more difficult. It was not until after the opening ceremonies that two nurses were hired part-time, and agreements were reached with three others to work on-call.[27]

Hilda Thomas took charge of writing to Dueck, requesting what he had already rejected in the press — that Everywoman's Health Centre be designated as a medical facility and thus eligible for government funding. He replied in the negative, on the grounds that the clinic would not offer a full-range of medical services.[28] We laughed at that weak excuse. After all, we would perform abortions, do nursing, some laboratory work, and full abortion and birth control counselling. X-rays were obtainable just down the street. The only service Dueck mentioned that we would not have was a full-scale emergency ward. But then, we planned to use local anesthetics, much less dangerous than general anesthetic, and patients would remain conscious during the procedure. Emergency services weren't likely to be needed. If they were, hospitals were nearby. The Socreds never did include Everywoman's Health Centre under the medical plan.

We began renovations at once. The interior of the clinic was astonishingly grimy — the previous occupants apparently had bachelors' standards about cleanliness. Lysol, pails, and scrub brushes were among our first purchases, and we rolled up our sleeves and set about cleaning up. The community was excited about the clinic, and volunteer electricians, drywallers, and carpenters were found with ease. Many came from the building-trades unions that had, partly through the urging of Peter Norris, partner of Marcy Toms, long endorsed and donated to the pro-choice movement. The principal needs were to build a secure and fire-proof operating room, enlarge former offices into a recovery room, install extra toilets, reinforce the outside doors with metal cladding, and build a partition between the glass front door and the waiting room. Many supporters helped paint the premises. Furnished comfortably, but inexpensively, the interior of the clinic was designed to be warm and soothing.

Orders were placed for equipment and supplies. Dr. Kanke heard of a used ultrasound machine for sale, and we bought it at a bargain price. She contacted the College of Physicians and Surgeons and reported that its approval was not required before the clinic opened. Later, after we'd had time to get up and running, a delegation would inspect us. However, to our astonishment, the College disapproved the name we'd chosen!

"Everywoman's Health Centre" was "too all-encompassing." Dr. Kanke told us the College had the right to regulate the name under which any group of doctors might practice,[29] but it was too late now. We had no intention of modifying the clinic's name.

When the Fire Department came to inspect the clinic, they greeted us as though we were celebrities. "They were just absolutely thrilled to meet people they'd seen on television," recalls one staff member. Telephone installers, insurance inspectors, and delivery persons tarried to shake hands, congratulate us, and share their personal stories about reproductive crises.

Dealing with the police was another critical task. Our electronic security system had an emergency button that would connect us with them directly. To persuade them to link up with us, a small delegation paid a call on the officers of Section 5, in whose jurisdiction the clinic lay. Articulate, neatly-dressed, and thoroughly rational, the BCCAC women presented themselves to a very wary group of lawmen. The suspicion that abortion-rights activists were somehow linked to the mafia may have lessened somewhat since clinics became legal, but the police still viewed us with great suspicion.

Reluctant agreement was given to our plan for opening ceremonies on November 4. It was explained that we would recruit marshals ourselves and equip them with rented walkie-talkies. While we expected the police to be there, it was agreed that we would only call on them in the case of a bomb threat. We asked for wooden barricades and got approval for our security marshals to arrange them as they saw fit. The next day, we learned how little we were accepted, when police showed up unannounced at the clinic and demanded to make an inspection tour and take photos.

Joy Thompson went to lengths to equip herself for a second visit to the police. A close contact at Pacific Press supplied her with printouts about Operation Rescue's antics in the US, from every major news network. She had a guide on Operation Rescue put out by the US-based National Abortion Federation, to which the Morgentaler clinics also belonged. It included photos of potential troublemakers. "I remember the police being absolutely astonished that we were...willing to share this information, and that we were so damn organized," recalls Thompson.[30] She was also armed with the clinic's business licence, and inspection reports signed by city officials. Slowly, the police understood they would be called upon to co-ordinate with the fire department, ambulance services, and other agencies, because Everywoman's Health Centre was legitimate.

Meanwhile, a start was made on recruiting and training a volunteer security force to guard the clinic. Thompson explained this to the police, as well. They were nervous, at first, thinking we planned a vigilante squad, but that fear was laid to rest. Throughout her discussions, Thompson remembers, she was conscious that "if the tide turned and clinics were outlawed," she was speaking to the "self-same people who would arrest us off the streets and drag women off operating tables." Eventually, two officers from Operation Auxiliary Services (OAS) — the riot squad — both named Brian, were assigned to the clinic. They came to appreciate and respect the women running it. Just after we held opening ceremonies, these officers informed us that Operation Rescue was expected to arrive in two weeks.[31]

Despite the rush to get ready, finding and training a squad of security volunteers could not be postponed. Lots of people had helped with this at marches and rallies over the years, and an initial training session was held in borrowed space on Commercial Drive. At later sessions, volunteers were asked for references. Helene Wisotzki, who stuck through clinic security for the next few years, recalls what the training was like. First, it was explained that anti-abortion protests would be more forceful than at most past demos and that security volunteers must be disciplined. As always, protesters should never be touched. Whatever happened, we did not want to open the pro-choice side to a charge of committing assault. In addition, security volunteers were cautioned against speaking to or answering questions from protesters. There should be no interaction. No response to taunts, nothing that might distract the clinic volunteers' attention. Then video clips were shown of Operation Rescue in Atlanta. It was Wisotzki's first view of grown people crawling around on their hands and knees, but she realized it was a slick maneuvour that made the protesters hard to catch. In fact, that tactic was not used at Everywoman's Health Centre.

Then small groups of the volunteers practiced forming a ring to isolate a protester and, without touching, move him or her away from the crowd. This was important practice and, also, helped identify who was suited for the role. "You need an awful lot of patience" to be a security volunteer, affirms Wisotzki, who, along with Hilda Thomas, Jackie Brown, and Will Offley served on the clinic security committee. People who were bothered by the jibes and jabs of protesters "might as well go home for the day."[32]

Opening Day! November 4, 1988, a drizzling Friday afternoon, was upon us all too soon. Invitations had been sent to a crowd small enough fit into the clinic waiting room. We'd invited Premier Vander Zalm, Peter Dueck, and NDP leader Mike Harcourt,[33] but no-one was surprised when the Socreds didn't show.

As Steering Committee members rushed to install the final ceiling tiles and make sure the bathrooms were clean, volunteer marshals arrived and donned makeshift insignia made of garbage bags with holes cut for the head and arms. These were useful against the weather, but truth was, we could afford nothing more. Standing close together around the entire exterior of the building, the security marshals set up wooden police barricades to separate them from the crowd of noisy protesters. Uniformed and plainclothes police stood at a distance, watching indifferently.

No-one else there was relaxed. Pushing, chanting, sometimes screaming, 300 anti-abortionists crowded into the half-block of 44th

Avenue in front of the clinic. They were, it seemed, from a 20-group coalition that included Campaign Life, Betty Green's crowd, churchgroups from the Fraser Valley, and teachers and students from the forty Catholic schools in the Vancouver area. And there was another element: a few protesters reminded us of the biker types that had ringed John Oliver School when Dr. Morgentaler spoke there in 1985. Nearby residents and businesspeople came to check out the commotion. Most, including a 68-year-old Catholic man, and Nick Baily, owner of the bowling alley next door to the clinic, told reporters they were more upset by the protesters than by having an abortion clinic in the neighbourhood. "If you are going to have an abortion, you should be able to have one in a safe place, and not on someone's kitchen table," said one resident.[34] Hilda Thomas gave the media the longstanding pro-choice response: "As long as people are protesting peacefully, we respect their right to picket."

Inside, the clinic looked lovely. The soft colours and lighting were accented by bouquets sent by supporters to congratulate us. I especially remember the gift from Vancouver Rape Relief: a large, low-slung basket made of glazed bread, in which a sheaf of red roses was heaped. Bread and Roses, the emblem of feminism.

Pleurisy, brought on by the intense exertions of the past weeks, threatened to fell Joy Thompson. But she was the designated speaker for BCCAC and nothing could keep her from the opening. I had been nominated to introduce the speakers. Dr. Robert Makaroff said a few shy words. City Council member Libby Davies spoke for COPE mayoral candidate Jean Swanson, who could not attend. MLA Darlene Marzari delivered greetings from Mike Harcourt and paid her own tribute to the clinic. Only when the door was buzzed open to admit another guest did the wailing outside penetrate the concrete walls. Finally, glasses were raised and a cheer rang out, as Anne Hamilton stepped forward to cut the ribbon that Mary Murphy held across the door.

The next day, our victorious march through downtown streets took place in rain so torrential it broke all records to that date — nearly 53 mm. fell on Vancouver in only twelve hours. The organizers, of which I was one, conferred on whether or not to dispense with the march and proceed to the indoor rally. As in 1982, the rally was held at the Hotel Vancouver, but hotel officials were less anxious this time around; we'd proved very peaceful and capable before. While we wondered what to do, marchers began arriving. Hundreds of them. Mere rain couldn't deter their joy in helping to inaugurate Everywoman's Health Centre. Placards were soon soggy, but nearly 300 people chanted and marched along the winding route that began at the far end of Georgia St. and ended at the hotel.

In the warm and dry inside, hundreds more well-wishers crowded in until it was standing-room only in the hotel ballroom. Janet Vesterback rose to call the rally to order. Robin LeDrew of the National Action Committee

(NAC), who had flown in from Vernon, was the first speaker, followed by brief greetings from two of the three women candidates in the federal election, then underway. Both were from the NDP: Margaret Mitchell, the incumbent for Vancouver East, and Johanna den Hertog, one-time founder of Rape Relief, who was running in Vancouver Centre against Kim Campbell. Campbell had been invited, but she didn't show. After breaking with Vander Zalm over the issue of abortion only months before, she had jumped the provincial ship and became a candidate for the Progressive Conservatives — but apparently she felt the issue was too volatile to raise in her federal campaign. Still a small group of women carrying signs that said "Tories for Choice" had joined us on the march.

A loud and long ovation greeted Dr. Lorena Kanke, who spoke shyly, for less than a minute. She reminded us that abortion is always a difficult decision for women to make, "and I think they need all the help they can get." She made a plea for the safety of the clinic's clients. Well-loved songstress Shari Ulrich provided a warm touch with her voice and guitar. Anne Harvey, an executive council member, delivered heartfelt greetings from the BC Federation of Labor.

Then to cheers and laughter, Elaine Bernard reprised her role as fundraiser. With many references to singing in the rain, Bernard gave a short lesson in "brolly semaphore." Pushing open her still-dripping umbrella, she waved it wildly to signal, "I can't believe we've actually opened the clinic!!!" Still waving, she said, "This means, 'I lean to the left.' This means, 'Gale force wind from the right.'" Then she upended the umbrella so that it became a basin. "This means, if you can fill this umbrella with your contributions, we can beat that gale from the right." More than $1300 was poured into the collection buckets.

Finally, Hilda Thomas rose to speak for the BCCAC and Everywoman's Health Centre. As steam rose from the participant's wet clothing, she said the march had been tremendous: "just as though we were washing away years of pain and struggle, and celebrating our victory in the rain." She read a brief passage from Anne Collins's book, *The Big Evasion*, in which the timidity of Canadian politicians is chastised: "'They change controversial laws carefully, years after public practice has made them obsolete. Such change is then touted as reform and thrown as a bone to the unruly individuals who demand change.'"[35]

"But I don't want to think of those men, today. I want to think about the women. I want to think about the unruly women," said Thomas, to cheers and applause. She recounted the Persons Case, won in 1928; it was "only by going to the British Privy Council that five unruly women got our sex recognized as persons in Canada." She recalled Dorothea Palmer, a pioneer fighter for birth control, who was tried and acquitted in Ontario in 1937. She described the press conference held by the arrogant Trudeau on his return from Asia in 1970, when Women's Caucus members tried in vain to get the chair's attention, so they could ask the PM questions. "And you know what they did? They just took over that press conference...And I still remember a woman standing there and shouting, 'We're talking about *women's lives!*'" The applause mounted as Thomas paid tribute to Henry Morgentaler, and to the women of CCCA, of CARAL, the women who fought the hospital board elections, and for the repeal of the Criminal Code. "And that led to our year of victory!."[36]

Unleashed joy swept through the audience, which rose to its feet in applause.

Standing at the back, so that I could survey the entire room, I found myself shouldered aside by a very angry man. He was quickly surrounded by our security volunteers, who recognized Jim Demers from photos. This was the man who, in 1985, stole the vacuum aspirator from the hospital in Nelson. From under their coats, two other men pulled out gory fetus photos, but they were sufficiently intimidated by the cheering and good-will that neither uttered a word.

A congratulatory moment for ourselves was all the Steering Committee could afford, for an enormous number of tasks still faced us. Reluctantly, we drew up a fee schedule: $150 maximum for women who had medical insurance, for whom even the Socreds would pay the physician's fee; $250 maximum for women who had none. Dr. Hossack would rebate part of her fee to the clinic. But, emphasized the Minutes of the November 9 meeting, "This fee schedule [is] to be under continual review and development"— until, we hoped, it was eliminated because we got provincial funding. Finally, a tentative, beginning schedule for performing abortions at BC's first free-standing clinic was set, and the first appointments were quietly made for late November.

On the evening of the first day abortions were performed, we were faced with yet another, and quite extraordinary crisis. Our physician, Dr. Karen Hossack, announced she was resigning. She had many complaints, ranging from a need for more nurses and a change in the process of hiring them, to better equipment, to a greater respect for her medical authority. And she questioned our financial competence. A stunned Steering Committee responded carefully, at pains not to become defensive or unclear. Nonetheless, an emotional Dr. Hossack fled the room in tears, followed by the visiting Dr.Ingrid Pacey — who had done the same thing more than a year before.

Indeed, five members of CCCA, an unusually large number, had arrived for the Steering Committee meeting that evening. Again, they raised many questions about the finances of the clinic and our attitude toward doctors. We skirted the question that night, since it was not central, but the fact was that women merely wanted trust from doctors in return. The discussion continued until a late hour, and although some of the distress receded, reconciliation was not achieved. The only agreement reached was that three nurses would be on duty on each procedure day.

It seemed that no sooner did we bridge one crevasse than the next tried to engulf us. At an in-camera emergency meeting, the Steering Committee came to the sober realization that we had not adequately introduced our vision of a woman-run clinic to the medical staff. We were so engrossed in our concept of a non-hierarchical structure that we presumed it was self-evident, and that the newly-hired staff understood and accepted it. We were breaking new ground and had been forced to go from zero to speed in an incredibly short time. But also, we discovered too late that the effort to paint us as financially-irresponsible, wild-eyed doctor-bashers had scored close to home, and that Dr. Hossack had been drawn in by it. Dr. Kanke said she could not tell us how to set up the kind of clinic we apparently wanted. She believed we were committed to succeeding, but success would depend on attracting doctors to work with us. Dr. Hossack was adamant about using a particular drug that was administered intravenously, and our nurses did not have the required training for it. Dr. Kanke persuaded us to arrange for them to get that training.[37] We formed a crisis management committee to work toward resolution of staff concerns.

Two days later, at the regular Wednesday night meeting, the number of CCCA visitors had grown to seven — almost equal to the number of Steering Committee members present. As a clinic spokesperson, Hilda Thomas raised an disquieting issue. She had been deluged by the print and electronic media about an 'unconfirmed financial crisis' at the clinic, and about rumours that Dr. Lorena Kanke had resigned. She stressed the importance of confidentiality, while saying that the source of these rumours was unknown. CCCA members believed Thomas must be responsible for the leak.[38]

An invited member of CCCA had attended the clinic staff meeting that day and came away impressed. She reported that the staff was working well together, although inundated by details, and that a staff development day was being planned. Hilda Thomas gave a more substantial report on where things stood. Two Steering Committee members had met with Dr. Hossack. They reviewed the Minutes of the past months with her, to respond to her questions about where our money came from and how it was being spent. That clarified some matters, and although Dr. Hossack had not withdrawn her resignation, she intimated she might come back to the clinic after she'd had a holiday. We had been in contact with two doctors on whom we could fall back. Dr. Hossack's departure would not leave us in the lurch.

On this chastened note, Everywoman's Health Centre edged into December. 1988 had been an extraordinary year — indeed, a friendly *Sun* reporter told us more stories had been written on abortion that year than on any other issue. What we didn't know was that another explosion would hit us the very next day.

CHAPTER 17

CLINIC BLOCKADES

The next day, the blockades began.

Early on Thursday, December 15, 1988, a group began assembling in the dark along East 44th Avenue in front of Everywoman's Health Centre. When the first clinic staffers arrived around eight o'clock, they found a crowd of 80-100, forming a human wall half a block long. They sang hymns as they jammed shoulder to shoulder behind a large sign that said "Rescue in Progress." They wore cards around their necks saying "Baby Jane Doe", or "Baby John Doe." Operation Rescue was in town and the Vancouver clinic blockade season had begun.

We knew they'd come sooner or later, but the sight of them was definitely chilling. It was obviously impossible to enter the clinic, and the staff did not attempt to cross the picket line. Joy Thompson went to the pay phone on the corner and called 911. Two police officers in an unmarked car nearby made no move to identify themselves to her, and they continued sitting there throughout the morning.

To get help, Thompson and Marg Panton crossed Victoria Drive to the upstairs offices of city outside workers, CUPE local 1004. Without hesitation, the local freed telephones for them, and for hours its offices served as a warm 'safe house,' with coffee in the pot and no questions asked. Ten women were scheduled to have abortions that day. Panton began phoning to describe the situation and give them the option of re-scheduling. Most wanted to come anyway and were willing to wait until the blockaders were gone, although no-one knew when that might be.

Clinic escorts, whose green bibs were on order, donned yellow garbage bags for identification and were stationed at the bus stops and the corner of East 44th Avenue. They watched for clients who could not be reached because they were already on their way. But two women were not reached at all. One had come from Alberta, and we lost contact with her. For another, December 15 was the last day of her first trimester — the last day on which she could have had an abortion at Everywoman's Health Centre.[1]

A blockader who refused to give her name boasted to the *Vancouver Sun*, "We have our sources. And we are aware that they are planning to do some [abortions] today."[2]

She was right. For precisely that reason, about twenty security volunteers were expected. Many had already arrived, and a general call for help went out that drew about forty more people. Some came from the campuses, some came from BCCAC member groups, and quite a few came from union offices, responding to a summons from Kim Zander. Zander had come to her first Steering Committee meeting, as a visitor, only the night before. The contacts she offered proved very useful. This sizable show of support was enough to defend the clinic, but it was a smaller force than that of the blockaders. We did not want a counter-demonstration or anything that might suggest we sought confrontation. Our volunteers showed superb discipline. Not one word or gesture invited a blockader's attack.

The blockaders, on the other hand, loudly harassed anyone associated with the clinic, whom they could not tell from passersby. They waved picket signs, indulged in name-calling, and sent spotters to watch for clinic clients. Women they suspected of coming for an abortion were chased down the street with hysterical cries, ranging from 'Jesus loves you' to '*murdering bitch!*' Some clients ducked into shops or restaurants, only to be followed inside by the blockaders. Dr. Karen Hossack took some of the women to a coffee shop to wait it out. They were relieved to be with the doctor, although it was a long wait. The women had not eaten and were obliged to continue fasting from solids until the local anesthetic used in the operating room had worn off. Karen Hossack was furious. According to Joy Thompson, Hossack scribbled an angry letter to the mayor on a serviette, objecting to being forced to sit with her patients for six hours, waiting to get inside the clinic and provide the medical service they'd come for.[3]

Despite repeated calls, the police did not show up for hours. The blockaders were trespassing on a legitimate business, that practiced entirely legal medicine, but the few plain-clothes officers on site told Joy Thompson they didn't have authority to remove the anti-abortionists. They were waiting to hear from 'upstairs' — that is, from the mayor's office, in consultation with crown consul and the provincial attorney-general.[4] Thinking of the effort spent in educating the police about the clinic and about Operation Rescue, Thompson could only groan.

Towards noon, police vans finally arrived. The officers held discussions with all sides. Blockaders were warned they could be arrested and charged with committing mischief. When they would not leave, police read out their rights and opened the doors of the paddy wagons. At this, the blockaders slumped limply to the sidewalk and refused to stand or walk. Taking care to inflict no injuries, a group of officers lifted each blockader onto a stretcher and carried him or her to a police van. It took nearly three hours for 24 officers to arrest 70 blockaders. Until their turn came, the protesters pressed tightly into all three doorways, prolonging control of the clinic as long as they could. "Don't do it," one of them yelled. "Don't kill your baby. Your husband wants that baby."[5] High-profile blockaders Betty Green of the BC Pro-Life Society and Langley-based John Hof of Campaign Life stepped to the periphery and escaped arrest. Most of the blockaders were strangers to the clinic, although Jim Demers was among those arrested.

At last, the seven abortion clients who'd sat out the long wait were surrounded by a flying wedge of yellow-garbage-bag clad escorts and conducted into the clinic. The women hid their faces with scarves or purses, forced yet again to shield themselves from humiliation for choosing a legal right. It turned out that glue had been poured into the locks, delaying the opening of the doors until a locksmith could arrive. Inside, staff found further vandalism: the phone was out of order and the heating system was damaged.

By a fluke of timing, the vacuum aspirator, the machine used to evacuate the womb, had been sent out for repairs the day before. When it was returned by tradesmen, security volunteers intercepted it and kept it out of sight until most of the blockaders were gone. Then it, too, was disguised with yellow garbage bags and, surrounded by a phalanx of similarly-clad volunteers, it was wheeled through the front door into the clinic. None of the blockaders realized what was going on. It seemed to be just another client. Once safely inside, the aspirator's escorts collapsed with laughter.

By mid-afternoon, all was in order and the staff set briskly to work. It was past 10 pm when the last client left, and the staff could sit down with the legal team and review the day. Their statements and those of some of the clients were prepared as affidavits.

In fact, the blockaders had been driven downtown and then released without charge. After the ordeal they put us through! During the long day, clinic spokeswomen and one of our volunteer lawyers held discussions with the police, with regional crown council Bob Wright, and with Boris Tyzuk of the attorney-general's office. Lawyer Bill Coller recalls that these officials "were stone-faced in response" to requests that criminal charges be laid against the blockaders. Tyzuk explained their reasoning — it was, in their eyes, a "'political' or 'civil dispute,' not a criminal one.'"[6] Agencies of the law would not take responsibility for dealing with this or future blockades. They emphasized that the police would only act if ordered to do so by the judiciary, reported Coller. The only option allowed to us was to apply for a civil injunction against further blockades.

That forced the clinic into a tight corner. Onus was placed on Everywoman's Health Centre for getting rid of the blockaders, without help from the authorities. At the same time, police and the A-G issued a very stern warning: should there be any violence during a protest or blockade, the pro-choicers would be held at fault. Our volunteers and staff would be immediately arrested, because the police were washing their hands and placing all responsibility on the clinic for what might happen.

As for why it took so long to turn up at the clinic, police cited lack of man-power and moaned about the expense of tying up so many officers in the arrests of blockaders. We thought about the stretchers, about the ever-so-gentle handling of each blockader, and compared that to the quick-and-dirty arrests of strikers in a recent labour dispute. Had it been a sawmill or logging site that was blockaded, the picketers would have been quickly sacked for criminal trespass on private property. Police also said, straight-faced, that they did not want to appear to favour the pro-choice point of view.

Coller remembers how well he thought the clinic representatives han-dled themselves at this meeting. In the face of such mendacious stone-walling, they stayed cool and were articulate and insistent in protesting the brutal effect the blockade had on the clients. Each day, or even hour, that their pregnancies advanced, the more dangerous their situation became. Somewhat familiar with left groups in the city, Coller remembers "thinking that there were a lot more 'together' women in Vancouver than there were men."

Trevor Lautens, columnist for the *Vancouver Sun* and a member of its editorial board, admired the blockaders. In a sophomoric tone, he wrote about "Consorting with criminals", to whom he and his wife served coffee and cookies in their living room, while they listened to the blockaders' plans.

> When they finished I asked: "How soon are you going to do this?" John Doe glanced at his companion, Jane Doe, and then at me. 'What are you doing at six o'clock tomorrow morning?" he said.
>
> I was there at 6:04. Serious business lay ahead for Operation Rescue.

If this sounds like pulp fiction, wait a moment. Lautens turns high-brow a few paragraphs on, quoting a penetrating thinker of the mid-twentieth century: "Hannah Arendt, writing of Nazi Germany, made famous the phrase 'the banality of evil.' She overlooked the banality of goodness, too."[7]

From that point on, a sort of 'second front' to the clinic struggle opened in the courts. While women received counselling, abortions, recovery, and follow-up care at the clinic itself, hearings, trials, and appeals continued in BC courtrooms for months — even years — to come. Clearly, we were going to need a lot of legal help. Bill Coller began contacting lawyer friends of his and — in addition to other lawyers who were helping us in various ways — a group of four began holding meetings to discuss strategies, cases, and arguments regarding blockades. I sat in on as many of these early meetings as I could, having been assigned by the Steering Committee to be its legal liaison. We usually met in the office of John Steeves'. He and Laura Parkinson had experience in union-side labour law; Bill Coller was starting out with a downtown firm, and Star Rosenthal had been called to the bar only days after the first clinic blockade.

The legal situation was tricky. To begin with, civil law usually entails one party or individual's complaint against another individual. But there were many blockaders, and the clinic itself was also multi-faceted, since it was run by a coalition of groups.

More to the point, injunctions were established as anti-labour and anti-civil liberties' law. There was the possibility that broadening the target in the clinic's case might set an undesirable legal precedent, one that would rebound on the very clients in the labour movement that Parkinson and Steeves usually served. But because the authorities had restricted the clinic to the civil law arena, an injunction was the only remedy we could seek. The procedures for getting one were well-defined, and civil injunctions had a history of effectiveness in stopping unwanted activity. The first step would be to persuade a judge to order future blockaders to cease and desist. Laura Parkinson had the most experience in this area, and she worked late, researching cases and extracting language from them, so that the injunction sought by the *pro bono* team would fit its wish list. Her comment was, "We were taking established legal principles, commonly applied in labour disputes, and turning them to our advantage."[8]

At an emergency meeting of the BCCAC Steering Committee on Sunday, December 18, John Steeves outlined the many steps involved in obtaining a civil injunction. To stop a wildcat strike, the process would be steamlined. But we were not the sort of mutinational corporation that usually made such applications, and for us it was a process so lengthy and involved it resembled the drip-drip of water torture. An injunction, Steeves explained, is a court order restraining some illegal activity. It must be obtained from a judge, on the basis of legal arguments made to him in a courtroom. Since the case law usually involved worksites, the acceptable arguments would hinge on proving the clinic was a legitimate business. We should show that our revenue was jeopardized by a blockade, and we would also have to show that the threat to the clinic was not frivolous, but serious enough to lead to a court trial. These arguments — not arguments about women's rights — would have the best chance before a judge. However, should the injunction be set aside by the court at the time of the trial, we — the plaintiffs — would have to pay the court costs, and might be liable to a counter-suit from the anti-abortionists.

And that was only the beginning. We later found out just how complex it was to prove a blockade was taking place. We must be able to identify at least some of the blockaders; prove they had received notice of the judge's order to disperse and had not obeyed it; that, therefore, an enforcement order was required; that the enforcement order was received by the police, and that they carried it out by making timely arrests. At the time the process was explained to us, there wasn't much emphasis on how to get it enforced.

The Steering Committee was reluctant to seek an injunction. It was a 'tool of the bosses.' An injunction would, we knew, place the clinic in conflict with many of our allies, and certainly with the labour movement — which may have been one of the outcomes intended by the authorities who left us with no other choice. Also, we were adamant that peaceful picketing by anti-choice protesters was their constitutional right, and we refused to curb their freedom of speech. At the same time, we could not allow the clinic's clients to go through the agony of uncertainty and hunger they had endured on December 15 again. After a very long discussion, a vote to file papers in court for a civil injunction carried.[9]

The police made one concession to us. Although the blockaders had all been released, the clinic was given a list of the names and addresses of those arrested. Three of the suspected leaders were from the US.

Two days later, Bill Coller accompanied Joy Thompson and Hilda Thomas to the court registry office on Smithe Street. They filed a writ that would allow our lawyers to seek an injunction immediately, in case of another blockade.

We taped photocopies of this writ to the front door and outer walls of Everywoman's Health Centre. Geared up though we were, we got through December with frequent picket lines outside the clinic, but no further blockades. That was good, because there were internal problems enough to deal with. The staff was still adjusting to our concept of 'non-hierarchical decision-making,' and also to the skimpy paychecks of our part-time operating schedule. We simply didn't have the resources to perform abortions every day, particularly since our operating funds were based on unpredictable generosity. After a month of performing abortions, the income from our clients had barely begun to accumulate. We still needed the base of donations.

It was only after the clinic opened — and before abortions began — that drafting the medical protocols to standardize and govern its work was undertaken. That was unavoidable, but undesirable. There was such intense pressure — from the need to meet mortgage payments, from the media, the women's movement, the community, and especially from the Steering Committee itself — to get the clinic up and running, that everything had to be done at racing speed. We had a political obligation to open that clinic, and, had we been unable to pull it off, it would have meant demoralization beyond thinking about. So, after gathering the protocols used by Dr. Morgentaler and other clinics, this abundant raw material had to be tailored to our needs. Our nurses had never drafted nursing protocols; it had never been required of them. So further long and difficult staff meetings were necessary to hammer these out.

In retrospect, Joy Thompson regrets these protocols were not adequately developed before the clinic opened. Designing them while simultaneously dealing with the anti-abortionists, the media, the police, the intense pressure of an unsure financial base, and with medical staff that had not gone through the development phase and were, naturally, less focused on the political aspect of the clinic project, put a great deal of pressure on her and Marg Panton. Those two staff members' dedication to Everywoman's Health Centre was all-consuming. In addition to their jobs, they shouldered whatever tasks were left over at the end of the day. Writing those protocols ended up taking months, and Thompson believes the misunderstandings that led to Dr. Karen Hossack's departure were partly due to the lack of them.

We located two doctors to fill the position of Dr. Hossack, who left after Christmas instead of at the end of January. In addition, Dr. Lorena Kanke came in to perform abortions at the clinic during December, which was not part of our agreement with her, but which helped greatly in supporting our finances. One of the new doctors was a newcomer to Canada, who had spent months getting a licence to practice in BC. The other was from Québec, Dr. Lucie Lemieux. Dr. Lemieux turned up in one of those uncanny coincidences that signaled Everywoman's Health Centre was meant to survive. She had met Maggie Thompson of the Vancouver Women's Health Collective at a conference in the east some time before, and the two had kept in touch. Later, Lemieux, whose experience went back to the heady days when her friends put out the McGill Birth Control Handbook, and who had worked in a Québec abortion clinic, moved to Kaslo, BC. Bearing her infant son in tow, she visited Maggie in Vancouver, learned about our clinic, and soon agreed to fly in at intervals to work at Everywoman's Health Centre.

If not blockades, there were picketers outside the clinic every day. In all weathers, they tramped in circles and sang their hymns. Their numbers varied. The crowds were largest on the 28th of each month, the anniversary of the January date on which the abortion law had been struck down. On December 28, there was a large anti-abortion picket line, but we'd expected it and no abortions were scheduled for that day. Further training sessions were held for the many people who wanted to volunteer for security duty. Helene Wisotzki told them to think of their security shifts as a job. Be on time; phone ahead if you can't make it; be disciplined. And they were. The security volunteers were essentially reliable, and their commitment was invaluable to making the project work. Their training was expanded to include collecting data that would stand up to examination in court. Thus, on advice from our legal team, security volunteers began carrying small notebooks in which they jotted down descriptions of known or of especially hostile picketers, as well as the dates and times at which they appeared. Sometimes, Polaroid cameras recorded the presence of certain protesters, because the photos would be needed in court.

And so the eventful year 1988 ended. Beginning with the Canadian

Supreme Court ruling in favour of Henry Morgentaler, which struck down the Criminal Code on January 28, through to the notice that Everywoman's Health Centre would seek an injunction against blockaders, the issue of abortion had been a lead story every week of the year.

1989 was little different.

In mid-January, Operation Rescue spent three belligerent days in Toronto, harassing abortion clinics. However, they did not succeed in blockading the clinics nor in preventing abortions, which were conducted as usual. After a fractious first day of protests, the Toronto police were polite toward the demonstrators, but they took action faster and more res-olutely than in Vancouver.

Simultaneous protests were held in several US cities while Operation Rescue was in Toronto. But outside Everywoman's Health Centre, there was only the daily picket line. We were braced for another blockade, but when would it come? Not until a week after "O-R" departed Ontario.

On Saturday, January 21, with ten women scheduled for abortions, Vancouver staffers were greeted by nearly 200 chanting, jeering, hymn-singing "Jane" and "John Does" at the entrance to the clinic. It was the largest blockade we endured, the longest and most trying, and the moment to put the application for a civil injunction to the test.

The day was grey and drizzling. Clinic supporters came to observe and stood in damp clumps across the street, to which the occasional yellow leaf was plastered. The security volunteers were cool and practiced now, and, since CUPE 1004 was closed on Saturday, a safe house was found at the Tenants' Rights Action Coalition offices on East 43rd. Volunteer escorts met each arriving bus and car and efficiently identified the clinic's clients, although neither group had met each other before. The women would see the green bibs with "Escort" in white letters, and "of course, we all looked like reasonable people," as Helene Wisotzki puts it. "So, more often than not, these women would come up to us and ask, 'Are you from the clinic?' And they'd be scared, of course. So we'd say, 'Yeah, we are.' We'd just take them away for coffee." The escorts' calm attitude "made a world of differ-ence to these women," providing re-assurance for them in the chaotic and noisy stand-off.

A Saturday procedure day had been scheduled partly to accommodate working women clients, and partly in hopes that blockaders would not expect it. However, by showing up on a weekend when the courts were closed, Operation Rescue meant to outwit us. The volunteer legal team of Coller, Parkinson, Rosenthal, and Steeves, augmented by articling student Kyong-Ae Kim, was ready. "We all had our assigned roles," recalls Coller. They busily collected evidence that could be turned into affidavits. Witnesses described vans delivering fresh laundry that had been turned away by the blockaders, to show loss of "business." A couple that parked near the clinic was spotted by anti-abortion "sidewalk counsellors" and was chased down the lane. The woman and her boy friend tried to escape by ducking into a café, but a clutch of the monomaniacal protesters surrounded their table. Star Rosenthal managed to get a statement from the woman's boy friend about this harassment, but as the long day wore on and on, the client herself agreed to give testimony that the lawyers then turned into an affidavit. We were grateful for her willingness to be publicly identified at such a private moment.

Meanwhile, other members of the legal team waited at Bill Coller's nearby apartment to turn the evidence into legal documents. Accustomed to having secretaries in their work-a-day world, and short on typewriters, the lawyers laughingly recall that these affidavits were cut-and-paste jobs, with some hand-written corrections in the margins.[10] They did not have the polished look considered standard for the courts. Star Rosenthal remembers gathering the affidavits and rushing to the East End Food Co-op to make photocopies of them, in the hope that would conceal the paste. "It was a very *ad hoc* kind of effort," a fast and furious one, she laughs.[11]

Because it was Saturday, Coller explains, "We had to employ a special rule to have the courthouse opened and a judge brought down from his home in Shaughnessy to hear the clinic's application for an injunction." The blockaders arrived about 6a.m., but it was noon before Mr. Justice Lloyd McKenzie opened his courtroom on the injunction matter. Lawyers for the blockaders and the city of Vancouver rushed to the court as well, and Justice McKenzie permitted all sides to present their arguments. The clinic team's case was that the blockade was illegal and was harming a legitimate business. We requested an order that would require the blockaders to stop, and we requested police action should they refuse to leave. Joy Thompson and a clinic security volunteer took the witness stand, as did a police officer, and their responses to questions from Parkinson and Steeves described for the judge what was happening at Everywoman's Health Centre.

Appearing for the blockaders were Humphrey Waldock, a venerable member of the bar, and Paul Formby, an anti-abortion activist and lawyer. They called Betty Green, president of the Vancouver Right to Life Society, to the stand. She looked every inch the prosperous and formidable Point Grey matron that she was. Her testimony, however, rather countermanded her bid for respectability. Coller recalls that Green "told the judge that abortion was bad — against a *higher law*, God's law — and that if parliament wouldn't stop it, then she and the others had every right to do so themselves."

Such an argument may seem a peculiar, even insolent, one to make before a judge of the BC Supreme Court. Nonetheless, it was the essence of the anti-abortionists' beliefs and legal arguments, and it was proclaimed again and again in Vancouver courts in the months ahead.

This lengthy hearing was inconvenient for everyone. But, in Coller's account, "to his credit (Justice McKenzie) recognized...that there was no legal excuse for the blockaders' actions. The image of over a hundred people making noise in a residential area, on a Saturday afternoon, and preventing access to and from a legal establishment, was too much for him." The judge came to his decision and issued an interim injunction. It ordered all named defendants along with anyone else, "not to watch or beset at the clinic; not to impede, interfere, block or obstruct; not to disturb or interrupt; not to conspire to injure the clinic; not to trespass; not to intimidate; not to cause a nuisance; and not to attempt to do any of those things," recalls Coller.

That was not the end of the court session, however. There were two other points to be decided. The judge asked if the clinic wanted an order limiting the number of picketers and protesters, and our lawyers said no. The clinic did not want any curb on freedom of expression and was willing to tolerate peaceful protests. Then there was the matter of getting the injunction carried out. Terry Bland, counsel for the city of Vancouver and the police department, argued against both an injunction and, when that failed, against any order requiring police to arrest those who disobeyed it. To disobey a civil court order is in itself a criminal offence, but Mr. Bland convinced the judge that "police officers don't wish to become involved in the political issue...it [is not desirable] for the police force to be seen as siding with any particular party."[12] Never mind that refusing to arrest defiant blockaders put the police clearly on the anti-abortion side. No enforcement order was made.

All that while, the stand-off on East 44th Avenue continued. The wet and frustrated staff and anxious, hungry clients had no choice but to wait it out. By the time our lawyers returned from the courthouse, it was late afternoon. The next step was to serve the injunction on the blockaders, and Bill Coller took the task in hand.

> "I remember striding in amidst the front door blockaders, with TV cameras rolling, microphones stuck under me...and reporters and clinic security members to my sides and behind me. I started reading the injunction out loud word for word. At that point, the leaders began singing 'Oh Canada.'...I...could see...smirks on several of their faces. As I read, a couple of the blockaders signaled the others to sing louder."

None of the blockaders would take the paper from Coller, "so I touched several with it and dropped copies at their feet."

Clearly, the blockaders were not going to leave. That meant the lawyers had to summon the judge once again and return to court. They brought photos and snide comments that had been caught by a tape recorder as evidence that the blockaders were in contempt of the injunction. Nobody in the courtroom was happy. Indeed, the most experienced members of the clinic's legal team, Parkinson and Steeves, drew the line at this point. They declined to participate in arguing for police action against the disobedient blockaders, fearful of setting a precedent that could be used against the labour movement. Injunctions had been invoked for centuries, but the law on arresting those in contempt was much narrower. Our lawyers' loyalties were in conflict there.

As the hours wore on and the blockaders remained crowing from the doorways, Hilda Thomas and Joy Thompson climbed into the back of a van and discussed giving up on the police and taking matters into their own hands. Why not just force their way in? The famished clients couldn't wait much longer. The whole principle of women's right to choose was at risk. But, indignant though they were, the reality was that our side was out-numbered, and we were the ones liable to be arrested for what would surely turn into a brawl. Still, they were so angry that, in the aftermath, they made a somewhat rash announcement to the media:

> Everywoman's Health Centre may bypass the courts in future and ask sup-porters to physically prevent demonstrators from denying access to staff and patients, clinic spokesman [!] Hilda Thomas said Sunday.[13]

That comment brought condemnation from all the powers-that-be and caused embarrassment to the stoically well-behaved security volun-teers. It was a minor part of the whole story, but the media delighted in headlining it.

Bill Coller and Star Rosenthal returned from the courtroom well after dark with the enforcement order. And finally, at nearly 9 pm, a half-dozen squad cars pulled up and police officers began walking slowly toward the crowded clinic doors. In response, the blockaders walked unhurriedly away. No effort was made to catch or arrest them. Their victory seemed complete. They'd shut down the clinic for fifteen hours, and they simply escaped into the night.

Without dwelling on that, the weary staff and clients entered the clinic and the work scheduled for the day began. One woman had come from out of town and waited hours for her abortion. The work went on until nearly dawn. In spare moments, the lawyers collected further statements and wrote more affidavits. The late-evening enforcement order applied only to the events of January 21. We were all sure that blockades would continue, and it would be necessary to use the injunction tool again.

As it happened, a BCCAC General Membership meeting was sched-uled for the next day, Sunday, January 22, 1989. It was time for new Steering Committee elections. On very little or no sleep, we trooped to the Holiday Inn on West Broadway and checked the names of more than a hundred registrants. Two or three aroused suspicion. When they refused to say they were committed to the pro-choice side, they were asked to leave.

Bettie Scheffer gave a progress report, and, despite everyone's awareness of the previous day's ordeal, she accurately sensed the mood in the meeting room. The focus was not on what we were doing right, but on accusations that we were up to no good. When Scheffer took her seat, four or five CCCAers, who seemed to be that group's entire active membership, rose one after the next to attack the BCCAC Steering Committee. Their charges were that we were financially incompetent and that we alienated doctors. Karen Hossack strode angrily to the front to announce she was leaving the clinic. Since she had already left a month before, one wondered why she was still kicking the cat. The meeting grew worried and restless.

As a result of these outbursts, there was a call for investigating the Steering Committee, although what infractions might be uncovered no-one knew. It did not pass. Steering Committee elections were put off for a few weeks, at the request of a confused membership.

The 'Strategy Report' was the last item on the days' agenda. I presented it, as the chair of the outreach committee. It outlined two needs — to continue opposing a federal law to re-criminalise abortion, and to continue demanding funding from the province. During the previous week, a delegation from Everywoman's Health Centre had met, at last, with health minister Dueck, who gave a flat "no" to our funding request.[14] That meant we must continue charging for abortions. I proposed we respond to Dueck and to the blockaders with a rally the following Saturday, which was January 28, the first anniversary of the Canadian Supreme Court victory. In addition, I assured everyone I had checked carefully and found that there were no plans in the works for International Women's Day that year. The usual IWD Committee had temporarily run out of steam. Therefore, I proposed that the BC Coalition for Abortion Clinics hold the annual march and rally, to take place on the Saturday before International Women's Day, March 4, 1989.

These upbeat suggestions were welcomed by the anxious meeting. Still, I wasn't sure what she planned to say when Hilda Thomas spoke from the back of the room. Visibly and understandably weary, she said, 'I don't know where you get your energy, Ann,' and then endorsed my motions. Plans for the demonstrations were adopted enthusiastically, and as participants rose to leave, there were even strained smiles on some faces.

In the next week, the police did issue warrants for the arrest of eleven people identified in the enforcement order, and for "other persons unknown" who had defied the injunction.[15] The persons unknown were asked to turn themselves in. "All I can tell you is, it's not going extremely well," said Constable Jim Szekeres of this call for voluntary surrender. "We don't normally get involved in civil suits. Consequently, it's difficult for us to know the rules." Was there something the police academy had neglected to teach them — a secret hand signal, perhaps, or a unique twist to the cuffs, to be used when arresting people under civil law?

Two protesters did turn themselves in, and Betty Green was actually arrested at her home. By the end of the week, a total of ten blockaders had been taken before Justice McKenzie. All were undoubtedly eager to appear in court. Despite loud claims that they didn't recognize the law's authority, they badly wanted the opportunity of a trial. It was the arena in which they would rip the wraps off abortion and expose its evil to the world, finally and at last. And, whatever the verdict, they saw it as a stepping-stone to overturning leniency on abortion, by carrying the case to the Canadian Supreme Court.

Mr. Justice McKenzie exacted a reluctant promise from nine of these people not to block the clinic's doors until a court hearing scheduled for February 6. They were released without bail. McKenzie managed only a weak objection when the blockaders announced that, despite the injunction and despite the promises just given, all ten would attend the January 28 demonstration outside the clinic. Vincent John Hawkswell, a priest and editor of *The BC Catholic,* refused to promise to honour the injunction. He announced that he would not stop protesting in front of Everywoman's Health Centre until it stopped "killing babies." The judge looked kindly on the reverend and waved his threat away.[16]

The *Vancouver Sun* felt called on to editorialize. "Talk of vigilantism to protect Vancouver's independent abortion clinic from demonstrators is inappropriate," it began, chastizing the clinic's spokeswomen. Nonetheless, the editors found an opening to continue their campaign against the premier, and, on that score, they found themselves disturbed that the blockaders had "been allowed to get away with it...Just why that has happened is not clear, but the suspicion that politics is involved cannot be entirely discounted in view of the Vander Zalm government's strong opposition to abortion."[17] We had the same suspicion.

So on the first anniversary of Morgentaler's and women's victory in the Supreme Court, two demonstrations took place in widely separated parts of Vancouver. Supposedly, nearly 600 anti-abortionists paraded for two blocks along East 44th Avenue.[18] About half that number showed up for the hastily-called pro-choice rally downtown.

The law had been struck down, but there was little progress in making abortion accessible during that year. Most provinces had tightened purse strings to reduce the availability of hospital abortions. New provincial regulations restricted access, often with encouragement from the colleges of physicians and surgeons. Only four new clinics had opened in that year — two in Toronto, one in Winnipeg, and one in Vancouver. "I'm very disappointed," said Dr. Henry Morgentaler.[19]

CHAPTER 18

CIRCUSES IN COURT AND INTERNATIONAL WOMEN'S DAY

Operating Everywoman's Health Centre took nerve, energy, and ingenuity. There were no nearby Canadian models for the service we provided; we had to make it up as we went. The absence of any law opened the way to that long-sought goal, abortion on demand. Women could refer themselves. Once they phoned us, each woman got an appointment for counselling — non-judgmental and open-ended — and her decision was treated with respect. We were ready to help the woman who might go to the brink and then choose adoption. But that seldom happened; women with too few choices came to the clinic with abortion in mind. A nurse or even her partner literally held the woman's hand and gave soothing encouragement during the actual procedure. Family or friends might stay with her in the recovery room. Caring, comfort, and follow-up were the clinic's watchwards. All this on a miniscule budget. We weren't mismanaging money. We simply didn't have much.

Relying on donations for operating expenses, we managed. Our donors came through and made the clinic possible; it was as much theirs, as much Vancouver's, as it was the founders' clinic. The shortage of funds for staff and supplies meant that abortions were performed only part-time, which was difficult for clients and the rest of us. For a long while, it was necessary to juggle payments to understanding suppliers and pray we could meet the mortgage and the payroll. Stretching pennies was mandatory, until, at last, the clinic eased into being open more days and hours. For well over a year, the non-medical staff did the janitorial work and washed the clinic's laundry at home. We could not accommodate all the women who phoned us for appointments, due to lack of operating funds, so our phone crew became a *de facto* information and referral agency that served the province, and, indeed, all western Canada.

There were few exceptions to the loyal support shown us. One day, a clean-cut security volunteer was phoned about scheduling his next shift, and his mother helpfully mentioned he was in class at Trinity Western University. This evangelical Christian school in Langley often sent busloads of protesters to parade outside Everywoman's Health Centre. Realizing his cover was blown, the fellow didn't turn up again until he came with an anti-abortion sign. It was tricky for a spy to show genuine commitment to protecting the clinic, and the Trinity Western student may have been the only one to try it. We may never know.

For clients, the language of flowers had a role to play. The Vicway, a cramped diner at Victoria and Kingsway, became a favoured rendezvous during blockades and heavy protests. An abortion client would wait at the counter, holding a single flower in her hand. It would identify her to the escort who met her there. Over coffee, escort and client would discuss the ordeal of getting through the mob in front of Everywoman's Health Centre. If the Vicway serving staff, or the police who ate in the back room, realized what these meetings were about, they never let on. Then the women would drive the nine blocks to the clinic and leave the car a short distance away. A protective force of security volunteers would surround the client and shepherd her through the crowd and into the clinic. Escorts also cleared the way when the woman left, arranging for a friend's car or a taxi to stop in the lane, then ushering her out the side door to safety.

The fact was, apart from the dispute with Dr. Karen Hossack, the clinic had okay relations with doctors. It's true that only a handful showed interest in performing abortions with us. Years of knock-down battles over hospital board elections and provincial policies made most BC doctors weary and wary of the issue. Still, many GPs referred women to us, and they were glad enough that the clinic existed to help deal with the demand. We were not going to replace Vancouver General Hospital any time soon — it continued to perform the greatest number of abortions in the province — but we made a difference.

New doctors were in negotiations with us. We were not anti-doctor, as Karen Hossack, Ingrid Pacey, and CCCA charged, but neither were we a doctor-run clinic. This novel concept required getting used to by everyone. Our non-hierarchical ideal was eventually modified, but feminists control the clinic to this day. There were also obstacles that were beyond our control. For instance, because medical schools provided no training in performing abortions, one MD found herself required to assist at many, many procedures at VGH before she could get admitting privileges — medically necessary in order for her to work at Everywoman's Health Centre. Should an emergency develop that we were not equipped to handle, the clinic's doctors would need admitting privileges to a hospital in order to transfer a patient there. Another MD, new to Canada, had to battle for acceptance of her credentials and for a billing number in BC. These doctors eventually did abortions, part-time, at the clinic.

Dr. Lucie Lemieux understood our vision and had experience with feminist-run clinics in Québec. She was a perfect fit for Everywoman's Health Centre, joining the roster of clinic doctors in late 1988 and becoming medical director when Lorena Kanke stepped down in April 1989. Lemieux attended BCCAC general membership meetings — she was there, distressed but not discouraged, when Karen Hossack trashed the clinic's founders in January, 1989 — and she marched with the masses on International Women's Day.

On the plus side, our feminist model meant the doctors' identities were shielded. Apart from the attention showered on Dr. Kanke when she became medical director, our doctors had no public image. So neither the media nor the anti-abortionists harassed them at home or their own medical offices. Other local doctors had no such protection. In early July, 1989, the Shaughnessy and Belmont Avenue homes of doctors at Burnaby General and Grace Hospital were ringed with picketers carrying signs and chanting "Baby Killer." They knocked on the doctors' doors to announce they'd come to "expose and humiliate them." "You can't kill people at the office and go home and be a happy family man," picketer Brian Young told a reporter. Horrified neighbours supported the doctors and were offended by the invasion of privacy, calling the picketers "conceited and selfish" because "they think they have to force you to live the way they do."[1] The same anti-abortion tactic was used in Calgary and in Toronto. But during Everywoman's Health Centre's many days in court, no doctor had to take the witness stand. The anonymity they enjoyed was "vital," in Joy Thompson's view, to encouraging doctors to work with us.

Demand was high. On 'procedure days,' every appointment slot was booked. Whatever worries, tensions, internal squabbles or outside protests had to be dealt with, they had little or no effect on patients. Evaluation forms filled in by clinic clients showed nearly unanimous gratitude and satisfaction with the service.

Unlike the doctors, clinic staffers were soon identified and constantly challenged by the protesters. But everyone involved was also energized by the extraordinary electricity of making history. What a high!

By the end of January, 1989, residents and businesses near 44th and Victoria had had enough. Evelyn Napodi, representing her neighbours' views as well as her own, phoned police to complain when anti-abortionists swarmed the street on January 28. What if somebody needed an ambulance; how could it get through such a crowd? She wanted to protect her granddaughter from the frightening images of blood and gore on the protesters' picket signs. Napodi told the *Vancouver Sun*, "I don't mind them protesting at the clinic, that's their business. But to protest in front of my house, that's my business."[2] A large photo in the *Sun* showed Nick Baily, owner of the Victoria Drive Bowling Centre just around the corner. We already knew him to be a sweetheart; he often drew volunteers and clients inside, offering them refuge and coffee. On January 28, he complained, "Nobody could get in any of the stores down here. They couldn't get in the bowling alley and they couldn't get out. It was just terrible." He blamed the protesters, not the clinic's operators.[3] Ever since the clinic opened, nearby residents had occasionally pressed small bills into the hands of security volunteers.

Late in January, International Women's Day plans got underway. A dozen people, many of them newcomers, came to the first outreach committee meeting. We sketched out plans to march through the downtown, and rally in front of the art gallery on Georgia St. We would co-ordinate the rally with a conference called for the same day by women in the labour movement.

Then at the second meeting a week later, a woman stood up and announced we'd been replaced by an "IWD Committee" formed that afternoon by a half dozen clinic security volunteers. This self-appointed group felt forced to halt the outreach committee's work because three of its participants were men, and 'men have no place in organizing International Women's Day.' The males at the meeting were guilted into voting to dissolve the outreach committee. Most of the twenty people in the room hurried away and did not come back.

Negotiations with the 'IWD Committee' were carried out by other members of the BCCAC Steering Committee. I was kept out of them and no report was given me until, at week's end, a clinic staffer phoned to say that the 'IWD Committee' would organize the action for March 4, but that I would be allowed to participate in its meetings. I was too angry to trust myself to speak, and so I did not make an issue of it.

To this new committee's first meeting, with less than three weeks and only seven people to do the work, I was able to bring a mock-up of a poster for the event. Before the appearance of the 'IWD Committee' I had contacted Dugg Simpson, and he had donated the design for an arresting poster. The 'IWD Committee' liked it and decided to have it printed in magenta ink on cherry-pink paper. Thus, the date, time, and form of the action, as spelled out on the poster, became *ipso facto* what was planned, and we were spared wrangling about that. Much of the evening was taken up in discussing how many copies to print, and who would poster where. Postering remained the focus for most on this inexperienced committee, which left the bulk of the organizing to me. It was difficult, because I had little time during the workday to make phone calls, but it got done.

On the same day as our demonstration, the BC Federation of Labor Women's Rights Committee was holding a conference for women union members. It would be the last event presided over by outgoing chair, Anne Harvey, then of Office and Technical Employees Union (OTEU), local 378. She was a vice-president of the Federation and sat on its executive council. Harvey was very much in favour of co-ordinating the lunch break for her conference with our rally, so that the women unionists would have time to join in the last part of the march and stay to hear the speakers in front of the art gallery. Well aware of the delicate situation caused by the clinic's use of an injunction, I was equally eager to involve the Fed's Women's Committee. Anne Harvey and I agreed on the value of linking the organizing skills of the labour movement with the issues raised by feminists outside it. And we agreed it was crucial to heal any rift between Everywomen's Health Centre and the labour movement.[4]

And rift there was. In fact, abortion was a highly inflamed issue within the BC Federation of Labor at that moment, and not merely because of the clinic's use of an injunction. To explain why, it's necessary to sketch in the story of Mervyn Lavigne.

Lavigne, an otherwise nondescript instructor at the Haileybury, Ontario School of Mines, linked up with the wealthy, far-right National Citizens Coalition (NCC) to launch an anti-union court case in 1984. He refused to join the union that negotiated for his salary and benefits, the Ontario Public Service Employees' Union (OPSEU). But under Rand Formula law, authorized by the Canadian Supreme Court, he had to pay union dues anyway. Lavigne sued OPSEU, charging that the miniscule portion of his dues donated by the union to the NDP, to abortion rights groups, and to the nuclear disarmament issue, violated his freedom of association under the Charter of Rights. Of the $1000 in union dues that he paid between 1983 and 1985, a total of $1.36 had been donated to seven causes he objected to.[5]

But this was far from a penny-ante case, because it tested the still-new Charter on the weight given to individual versus collective rights. It became known as the "labour trial of the century."[6] The Ontario Supreme Court ruled in Lavigne's favour in 1986, which had the effect of suspending part of organized labour's legitimacy. This was challenged by the combined forces of OPSEU, the Ontario Federation of Labor, and the Canadian Labor Congress. In a hearing before the Appeal Court in mid-June, 1988, OPSEU's lawyer pointed out that union contributions to the pro-choice movement benefited women workers and fitted in with union campaigns for day care and pay equity. "All members of the unit benefit from equity in the workplace, union members or not," he said.[7]

That ball was still in the air, and the Ontario Court of Appeal had not delivered its verdict, as 1988 came to an end. Fast forward to January 17, 1989. Four days before Operation Rescue's largest and longest blockade of Everywoman's Health Centre, an ad appeared in the *Chilliwack Times*. Headed "An Urgent Message to All Union Members," it read, in part:

FACT: The BC Federation of Labor has taken a pro-abortion stand.

FACT: Your union money is being used to support this cause.

FACT: The radicals in the BC Federation of Labor could end up destroying the labour movement.

DOES THIS CONCERN YOU?

A coupon was attached, addressed to the Chilliwack Pro Life Society, and union members were asked to send it in if they wished to "...halt the direct or indirect funding of pro-abortion causes with my union fees."[8] The parallels with the NCC-Lavigne case were eerie, and as coupons forwarded from Chilliwack flooded into the Fed's offices, its leaders were, indeed, scared. They sought an opinion from their legal advisors — who said that, based on Fed president Ken Georgetti's letter to affiliates in September, 1988, calling for union donations to Everywoman's Health Centre, the labour body could be considered "pro abortion," and not merely "pro-choice." This semantic nicety apparently suggested the BC Federation of Labor might be severely diminished, or even demolished, in a court of law. At a hastily-called officers' meeting, there was bitter language denouncing feminists and their nasty clinics. Anne Harvey and Joy Langan, two of the vice-presidents of the Fed, stood up for women and clinics, but they felt the men weren't listening.

The BC Teachers' Federation was facing a similar threat from an anti-abortion couple who taught in North Vancouver. They launched a case before the BC Industrial Relations Council, arguing that their religious opposition to abortion forbade them being members of an organization that had pro-choice policy. The outcome of the IRC's ruling was not yet known. But the BCTF's legal status as a closed-shop union stood to be undermined. Should this couple win the right to withdraw from the union without losing their jobs, who knew how many of the numerous, vocal, anti-abortionists heard every year at BCTF AGMs, might follow. Teachers began retreating from the pro-choice stance. The Surrey Teachers' Association executive committee struck a resolution supporting clinics from the agenda of an important December, 1988 meeting. In March, 1989, the 700 teachers in Abbotsford went on strike to support 18 of their members who wanted to drop out of the union because of BCTF's pro-choice policies.[9] At the BCTF AGM in 1989, mention of abortion was taboo, and I found myself a pariah. Although some of these events had not yet been played out, anticipation of them contributed to the nervousness within the labour movement, as International Women's Day drew near.[10]

Added to all this was the ongoing whisper campaign that Everywoman's Health Centre, which was forced to charge its clients for abortions, was a 'private' facility and a threat to public health care. The civil injunction against blockaders was just one of the issues leading labour leaders to back away from supporting choice on abortion, only months after the Fed's November 1988 convention adopted policy indirectly supporting clinics. While each of us worked on International Women's Day plans, Anne Harvey and I consulted one another on the phone at the end of long, tiring days. She filled me in on the raging debate at the Fed's headquarters on Boundary Road, and she organized a blitz of labour support for Everywoman's Health Centre.

In the nick of time, on January 30, 1989, the Ontario Court of Appeal ruled that OPSEU had not breached Mervyn Lavigne's constitutional rights.[11] The BC Federation of Labor did not sigh with relief until it heard from its legal advisors, but Lavigne's loss took the heat off. After much argument by feminist officers at the Fed, approval was given for the women's conference to adjourn for lunch and join our march, and for Anne Harvey to speak at the BCCAC IWD rally.

At the blockade in January, we got a better look at the people of Operation Rescue. A handful had come up from the US. Some were Catholics. A few, including some of those jailed in early February, were from other parts of BC — the Okanagan, the Kootenays. But most were stalwarts from the Fraser Valley and the southeast suburbs of Vancouver — Surrey, Delta, Langley, Abbotsford — known as BC's 'bible belt.' They were family-minded people who attended the predominantly evangelical and pentacostal valley churches.

But some were of a different breed. Their T-shirts bore neo-Nazi slogans. One apparent loner had a 6-inch knife stuck in his belt beneath a black leather jacket. Another frequent picketer was discovered to be the brother of the Ku Klux Klan organizer for Aldergrove. The Klan popped up in small but menacing numbers throughout BC in the 1980s. The first time he was noticed on East 44th Avenue, in December, 1988, this man was flashing a sawed-off hockey stick beneath his jacket. During the clinic's first year of operation, he regularly distributed *Life Gazette* to the other picketers, a misogynist and white-supremacist paper. These elements later made their presence felt more strongly.

Mr. Justice McKenzie began hearing the case against the ten blockaders netted after the January 21 blockade on Monday, February 6. The blockaders freely admitted to defying the injunction but said they were justified because "there were babies about to be killed." Gearing up to take over the court and become stars instead of defendants, anti-abortion lawyers Paul Formby and Robert Culos called Fraser Valley West Tory MP Bob Wenman as a witness. Wenman had not been at the blockade. His exhortation on why and how soon parliament would pass a law to protect the "unborn" was cut off by the judge, who had no intention of allowing the court to become a forum for either side. John Steeves' submission for the clinic was scheduled for the following day.[12]

But at 6 am the next morning, 105 anti-abortionists blocked the doors at Everywoman's Health Centre, clearly demanding to be included in the showdown at court. Justice McKenzie angrily ordered their arrest, saying the February 7 blockade was a "blatant defiance of [the] earlier court order." When police arrived, the anti-abortionists sat down on the sidewalk and began singing. Again, they were lifted one at a time onto stretchers and, three hours later, were all in the sheriff's van.[13] That evening about fifty anti-abortionists held a candlelight vigil at the courthouse, while the blockaders spent the night in jail. They were taken before Justice McKenzie the next day.

Vincent Hawkswell, of the *BC Catholic*, told the judge that the injunction "puts us in a situation where we have to break it."

> "I, as one individual, am pledged to do everything I can to stop it (abortions) regardless of whether there is an injunction or not."
>
> Justice McKenzie told him: "What you are saying is that, according to your own conscience, you can choose which laws you obey and which laws you won't...I suggest to you, if all citizens do that, it is not the rule of law. The result is anarchy."

Hawkswell replied that "If it forces society to a situation (where it breaks the law) then it is not society that is wrong, but the injunction that is wrong."[14]

This placed the blockaders at odds with the courts of law, not merely with feminists and their clinics. The justices were irritated. Hawkswell's assumption that the blockaders were equal to all of "society," did not persuade Justice McKenzie to invalidate the injunction. Still, most of the blockaders did produce identification and pledged to stay away from the clinic until their sentencing date, February 23. Forty-five of them refused to pledge and chose jail instead. Many were still claiming to be 'John' or 'Jane Doe.' They were sentenced to serve fifteen days on successive weekends.

A contempt trial was then held for the twelve blockaders who had refused to apologize to the court. Their leaders were identified as Rev. Vincent Hawkswell, Rev. Donald Spratt of Surrey, supermarket clerk John Hof of Langley, and Right to Life Society president Betty Green. The twelve were sentenced to 24 days in jail — on alternate weekends — and were also ordered to pay all of the clinic's legal costs. That was an unexpected triumph for us — politically, if not financially. Their lawyer Robert Culos said the anti-abortionists would pay "not one cent to the abortuary, not a cent." Hilda Thomas replied, 'We are very pleased (at winning costs). When we first sought the civil injunction in December, we had no idea it was going to occupy hours and hours of legal time."[15]

The blockaders had offended enough people that calls to change the civil charges into criminal ones were rising from many sources. One was the blockaders themselves, who wanted to open the door to a challenge to the Charter of Rights. They seemed confident that the Vander Zalm government would support their cause.[16] Another was Supreme Court Justice Lance Finch, to whose courtroom some of the hearings had been routed because Justice McKenzie couldn't handle them all. Finch declared it was unfair to require the clinic operators to keep the blockaders in line, and he sternly called on attorney-general Bud Smith (who had succeeded Brian

Smith) to assume prosecution of the case.[17] The Socreds, of course, were pretending the situation was no concern of theirs, even though solicitor-general Angus Ree had said, as early as January 23, that the blockaders' defiance of the injunction posed a threat to law and order. "I may be sympathetic to the people who are demonstrating. I am not sympathetic to the method, or them breaking the law, in no way, shape or form," said Ree[18] Justice Finch addressed Boris Tyzuk, who was observing from the back of the courtroom and seemed to hope for anonymity, and urged the attorney-general's assistant to get his boss to take over the prosecution. The conduct of the blockaders, said Finch, was a classic case of criminal contempt and "'would tend to bring the courts into scorn and abuse.'"[19] The *Vancouver Sun* chimed in, with an editorial titled "A-G should police abortion contempt."[20]

A-G Bud Smith remained deaf to the court's invitation. Vander Zalm, returning from 23 days in Europe, made a fervent plea for parliament to make abortion illegal again.[21]

During their stay in jail, the female anti-abortionists made such a ruckus that other inmates, serving on unrelated charges, went to court to complain. Three of them asked to serve their sentences on weekdays instead of weekends, so they could avoid the anti-abortionists. "From morning to night, it's the same thing. They [the anti-abortion inmates] pray, they talk about fetuses and how noble their cause is. They talk about nothing else but their cause," one inmate told a reporter. She and her cell-mate had gone without eating so they could avoid the anti-abortionists and the pictures of bloody fetuses posted around the jail. "They're putting pictures up of unborn kids, saying their mothers are killing them. I don't need to see this," she said, explaining she felt harassed and made to suffer mental anguish by the pictures.[22]

The court was thronged when it convened again on, Thursday, February 23. The more than 100 defendants themselves took up most of the seats, leaving dozens of spectators in the hall outside.[23] Riding the escalator to the courtroom behind clinic opponent Lane Walker, a security volunteer noticed the hair on Walker's head was cut very short, with the shape of a cross shaved into the center of his crown. In his leather jacket and biker regalia, he seemed a strange cohort of Betty Green.

In the overheated air, there were a number of surprises. Under the direction of Chief Justice Beverley McLachlin, the full court authorized the new presiding justice, Josiah Wood, to convert the civil case to one of criminal contempt. If the attorney-general wouldn't do it, the justices would and did.

As a result, Crown prosecutor Joe Arvay took over from the clinic's legal team. Justice Wood refused to hear a statement from Bud Smith, saying, "Why should this court give a forum to the attorney-general to state his views? He was invited by the court to take part in the process and he chose not to. That should be the end of the matter."[24]

Those who felt left out mounted a fourth blockade of Everywoman's Health Centre. In a bid to get in on the action, more than 100 anti-abortionists kept the clinic closed for five hours the next day, Friday, February 24, 1989. City police refused to make arrests. Their lawyer, Terry Bland, insisted they still needed a specific order from the courts, just as when the matter was a civil case.[25] Clinic lawyers were forced to re-enact the scenario from January 21 — rousting a judge from Saturday leisures, proving the need for an enforcement order in a court hearing, etc. By the time that was done, the blockaders melted away again. No arrests were made. Arrest warrants issued for three blockaders by the Court were not acted on by the police.[26]

On the Monday, Justice Reginald Gibbs banged his gavel and said, "There is a clear pattern of organized and systematic victimization of citizens of this city."[27] Betty Green *et al* had already told the court that the blockades were spontaneous and had no leaders. She could not explain how the crowds arrived at the same place, at the same time, and any coordination of the blockades at Everywoman's Health Centre mystified her. This unlikely claim was meant to provide escape from what was happening in the US. A March 4, 1989 ruling by an appeal court in Philadelphia held Operation Rescue liable for more than $100,000 in damages and lawyer's fees, under racketeering laws. In support of an abortion clinic there, the court said, "The center pleaded and proved that defendants embarked on a willful campaign to use fear, harassment, intimidation and force against the center...Employees testified that they were even harassed at their homes and that their children were afraid."[28] What irony that abortion-providers, long accused of being thugs, were now legal, while their opponents were being arrested for their thuggery. Anti-racketeering laws were not invoked against blockaders in Vancouver, however.

The criminal contempt trial of the 105 charged in the February 7 blockade got underway on Monday, February 27. Proving himself capable of stealing from Henry Morgentaler as well as from the US civil rights movement, anti-abortion lawyer Paul Formby proposed to use the defence of necessity. "The defendants had no legal alternative," with the injunction in place, but "to hinder women from securing abortions at the clinic," argued Formby. He said he would introduce witnesses to testify "that unborn babies are human beings and that abortion is the direct killing of these human subjects." He also wanted to show the video *The Silent Scream* in court. Formby did not represent Jim Demers, who acted as his own lawyer and requested a jury trial.[29] Justice Wood would not allow either the defence of necessity or a jury trial, taking great care to cite justification in law. The court took pains to protect against future charges that it had acted incorrectly, or failed to deal fully with the issues.

The blockaders' defence rested on a paper presented by counsel Humphrey Waldock. He said it showed that abortion was contrary to ancient Christian common law and the feudal system, whereby the strong protected the weak. This argument did not go down well with the judge. Justice Wood chided both Waldock and Formby, pointing out that common law was superseded in Canada when the Criminal Code was enacted in 1892. Waldock also argued that the medieval common law was unaffected by the 1988 Canadian Supreme Court decision which held that the abortion law was unconstitutional, an argument that Wood found "novel." Of Waldock's presentation, Wood told the press, "With the greatest of respect, it's not a legal submission."[30]

Nor, ruled Wood on March 1, did the anti-abortionists' honest belief it was their Christian duty to "prevent what they perceive as the killing" of fetuses justify their unlawful conduct. They were found guilty of criminal contempt for violating the injunction. Wood rejected the claim that the anti-abortionists were following a "higher law" and were therefore justified in disobeying secular law.[31]

Their lawyers, it seems, didn't get it. After their clients were convicted, defence lawyers Formby and Culos still wanted to show *The Silent Scream* to the court. They had to be reminded by Justice Wood that "The moral issue of abortion is not before the court, either for adjudication or for debate. I will not permit this court to become a platform for either side in this debate." The lawyers requested sentences of community service, not jail time. Again, the judge reminded them that their clients were already serving jail time, which they choose to do rather than to promise not to continue blockading the clinic. Finally, the lawyers told the judge that 90 of their clients, sprawled throughout the courtroom in the jury and witness boxes, as well as the public gallery, wished to make personal testimonials when sentenced. In a conciliatory mode, the judge agreed to that.[32]

For two days, then, the BC Supreme Court was, in the words of *Vancouver Sun* writer Larry Still, "transformed...into a religious forum," as one by one, the convicted anti-abortionists "invoked God's word to justify their defiance of a court order." Many carried bibles, and most of them chided parliament's failure to re-criminalize abortion and provide their actions with a cloak of legality.[33] Justice Wood listened quietly, even when one convicted protester told him he had "blood on his hands." He said he would pronounce sentence the following Monday.[34]

As they paraded before the bench, excerpts from training tapes produced by Randall Terry, founder of Operation Rescue, were published in the *Vancouver Sun*. These advised blockade organizers on all aspects of shutting a clinic down, and on dealing with the police, courts, and the media. Recruitment was best done through church groups, and arrests should be sought in order to "put abortion on trial by delivering the anti-abortion message in court.""The courtroom is in enemy hands"was part of the message, and the judicial system is "a power behind the forces that kill." Anti-abortion leader Donald Spratt denied having heard the tapes, sticking to the story that the blockaders came together by chance. But Brenda Montgomery, the estranged former vice-president of the Vancouver Right to Life Society, said the tapes had been circulating in local anti-abortion circles since the previous October.[35]

Justice Wood sentenced the blockaders to three-month prison terms. Gasps of shock and disbelief filled the courtroom. Then the judge suspended the sentences for twelve months. If the convicted obeyed the law and the court injunction for that time, the sentence would be discharged and they wouldn't have to go to jail again. The gasps turned into giddiness. Wood warned that anyone who didn't take the sentence seriously and who blocked access to Everywoman's Health Centre again would face a stiffer penalty. Cameras whirred for twenty minutes, recording the convicted blockaders emerging from court to cheers and hugs from other anti-abortionists. They had a dazzled look and insisted that God had moved the judge to release them. But Wood announced, "this court does not apply the law of God...the court applies the law of the country."[36]

Nonetheless, it became apparent that these church-going folk were shamed by their experience in jail, and they did not want to risk it again. They had jobs, mortgages, and families to look after, and their consciences had been assuaged by the testimonials made before Justice Wood. The truth was, the injunction and the courts broke the back of Operation Rescue (now called Rescue Canada). Small blockades did occur at times through the summer, but none of them was as large as those on December 15, January 21, February 7, or February 24. As the number of participants dwindled, the blockades became increasingly bizarre and tinged by implicit violence from the anti-abortionists.

So, the evangelicals got what they wanted and thought they were winning. They'd tied up the courts and created an unholy uproar all over town. Best of all, they'd been convicted of a criminal offence. This — hooray — opened the door to an appeal and, one day, they expected to strike down the constitution in the halls of the Canadian Supreme Court.

Then it was International Women's Day, and IWD was commemorated with a bang. 2500 marchers tramped along the downtown streets. It was the largest women's demonstration in Vancouver to that date, and the triumph of my eighteen years' work in the pro-choice movement. TV cameras, mounted on top of the Hotel Georgia across from the art gallery, showed the crowd surging down Howe Street and swelling over the lawn — an inspiring sight — and I whooped with joy at the coverage. The crowd was jubilant. Speakers at the rally included city councillor Libby Davies,

Jyoti Sanghera of the India Mahila Association, Anne Harvey of the BC Fed, Hilda Thomas and Joy Thompson. Pay equity and an end to sex tours in Asia were demanded, along with no new law on abortion. Pat Davitt and the Euphoniously Feminist and Non-Performing Trio led us in song. And when United Church minister Linda Ervin raised her arms and shouted, "Let's celebrate our day!" the crowd roared with one voice *"Women! United! Will Never Be Defeated!"*

Two pro-choice marshals briefly forgot discipline and tried to prevent a CBC cameraman from filming the two counter-protesters who showed up at the art gallery. A minor scuffle ensued and was, of course, featured prominently in the media[37]

When the collection buckets were emptied by a dazed Anne Hamilton, sitting on the steps beneath the stone lions, she found the crowd had donated more than $4000 to Everywoman's Health Centre. It was more than we'd received in months. As I knew it would, Vancouver had taken the clinic to its heart. We had active participation from hundreds, and support and sympathy from thousands. We would not be defeated.

It was a satisfying moment, but the challenges kept coming. As the wind sifted out of the blockaders' sails, a rather dispirited Joe Borowski came to town in April. The Canadian Supreme Court had dealt him a knock-out blow on March 9, 1989, when it ruled that his case was moot. The justices decided not to rule on Borowski's 'challenge'— his claim that the fetus had rights the law was denying it — since Canada had no abortion law, and a fetus had no legal standing. In desperation, Borowski stumped the country, calling for more blockades. At a day-long demonstration on East 44th Avenue on April 7, he called the Vancouver blockaders "heroes," and models for the rest of Canada. No longer did he refer to himself as a hero, and his scornful threats of the past were absent. "At least you've got Vander Zalm, God bless him," Borowski shouted to nearly 300 supporters, who responded with applause[38] — but not with blockades.

Soon afterward, a more sinister element appeared. Supporters of right-wing US extremist Lyndon LaRouche set up a table outside the clinic at the April 28 protest. Their leader was serving a 15-year prison term for fraud. His followers hawked pamphlets in which Larouche was declared to be a victim of Satan and claimed that a conspiracy between Lucifer and the US government had framed him up. Protesters were invited that same evening, April 28, to the Croatian Cultural Centre on Commercial Drive for a public meeting titled "Satanism and Bolshevism." Among the meeting's numerous purposes, stated the leaflet, was resisting "the extensive use of racketeering and organized crime statutes against pro-life activists."[39]

At the risk of being discovered, a couple of clinic security volunteers slipped into the meeting and took extensive notes. These were distributed as widely as possible and became the basis of an article in the *Vancouver Sun*.[40]

Speakers ranged from LaRouche apologists to anti-Communist crusaders to — of greatest interest to the pro-choice movement — Peggy Steacy, President of 'R.E.A.L. Women' BC. Her appearance among the racists and kooks rather exposed her group's pretensions to represent core, middle-class Canadian values. R.E.A.L. Women had received a substantial federal grant in March, while pro-choice groups were consistently barred from receiving such funds on the grounds that we were 'political.'

Altogether, ten speakers represented far-right and anti-abortion groups. Wayne Poley, speaking for the neo-Nazi publication *Life Gazette*, reportedly said that Satan was staging a comeback through pro-choice women in parliament. Calling on God to demolish Satanism and Communism, the Christian Heritage Party's 1988 candidate in Delta, Keith Gee, told the meeting that the worldwide peace movement was a "Soviet pawn to lull the West into slaughter." Dan Wray, speaking for a group called "Canada First," charged that Trudeau was a socialist, that the UN was controlled by atheist Russia, and that the Nazis were blamed for Soviet atrocities.[41]

Dan Wray's brother Barry was Everywoman's Health Centre's most consistent picketer. He was there almost every day, distributing *Life Gazette* on East 44th Avenue. His unabashedly fascist views were featured in an article called "Men Who Love to Hate"by Terry Gould, in *V Magazine*, May, 1989. Gould identified Barry Wray as a trucker for Pacific Press. At a January 1989 public meeting of a virulent white-supremacist group, Wray had excitedly called for the release of Ernst Zundel. Zundel, the anti-Semite and Holocaust denier, was then in prison in Ontario. Days later, Wray entered a meeting of the local Aryan Nations affiliate with a cry of "Seig Heil!" One theme of that evening's meeting, reported *V Magazine's* Gould, was planning violence against homosexuals during the upcoming Gay Games in Vancouver.[42]

No wonder Hilda Thomas told the *Vancouver Sun* the BC Coalition for Abortion Clinics was "worried that anti-abortionists and extreme right-wingers may be forming an alliance."[43]

The *V Magazine* story described Scott Graham bursting through the door on that January 1989 evening. Graham soon made a name for himself as the representative of the Ku Klux Klan. His recruiting efforts at Surrey high schools stirred opposition, and he was pushed eastward to Abbotsford, where he operated for awhile and managed to infiltrate the Canadian armed forces base in Chilliwack. When this was exposed, public pressure forced him to move on.[44] At the clinic, we recalled the uproar when a white-robed klansman joined a rally of the Calgary Coalition for Life the year before. Some Calgary anti-abortion leaders objected and told the media it was "unethical...for the KKK to use us to further their inappropriate ideology."[45] But the president of the Alberta Pro Life Alliance said he welcomed KKK members in the fight against abortion.[46] No white robes appeared in front of Everywoman's Health Centre, although those were years of white-supremacist and Klan activity throughout the lower mainland and the Pacific Northwest.⁴⁷ In southern US states like Florida and Texas, the Klan did form a significant part of the active anti-abortion movement.⁴⁸

Occasionally, church-going protesters held prayer services around the dumpster in our lane. The products of abortions were not, in fact, discarded there. But complying with the legal and medical requirements for disposing of this tissue wasn't easy. We persuaded the provincial laboratory which, by law, examines medical waste, to add Everywoman's as a client, but it would not send a truck to collect our specimens. So, for many months, Marg Panton and Joy Thompson tucked the canisters into their cars and dropped the medical waste off at the lab on their way home.

Her high visibility and daily presence at the clinic made Joy Thompson a special target of anti-abortion harassment. Understandably protective of her privacy, Thompson was unable to avoid bringing her three-year-old son with her to the clinic one afternoon. Security volunteers remember the faces of the protesters that day. Could the woman they demonized as a murderer, witch, and child-hater have children? Certainly. So did most of the other founders of the clinic.

When the courts began handing out jail sentences to blockaders, someone retaliated with a death threat against Joy and her two children. It came in mid-April, 1989, through a message left on CCCA's phone line, and it was chilling: a string of obscene epithets, and the warning "I know where you live...You're going to burn, you're going to burn...all you bitches." Because it was delivered via an answering machine, the call could not be traced, but several staffers believed they recognized the man's voice. The police did not take the death threat seriously, conducted no investigation, and offered Thompson no protection. Later, when abortion providers began being gunned down, Thompson regretted not demanding more of the police at the time.

Meantime, there was still much to do to get the clinic truly off the ground.

CHAPTER 19

THE STRUGGLE CONTINUES...

"Want One! Like on TV!" read a mocking message sprayed across a wall on Commercial Drive, about this time.

A petulant spirit descended on BCCAC meetings between February and May, 1989. Feminist observers crowded into weekly Steering Committee meetings all spring. Any member of the Coalition could attend with voice, but not vote. Smelling blood, a clutch of women began showing up after they heard CCCA and Dr. Karen Hossack attack the clinic's founders at the January 22 BCCAC general membership meeting. They came ready to believe that the Steering Committee alienated doctors and mismanaged clinic money.

Since they had no evidence to support the whisper campaign against us, the observers held few cards. Unmistakably, they believed that they were worthier than the Steering Committee to run the clinic. The Steering Committee was pressed to speed up elections for a board of directors, as stipulated by the BC Societies Act, under which the clinic was now registered. The newcomers clearly meant to capture the seats on this board. With an ironic twist on the anti-consumer slogan of the graffito, these women were grabbing for Everywoman's Health Centre. They'd seen the clinic on TV, and they wanted it, or at least the camera spots, for themselves.

Stampeded from all directions as the clinic was, the founders hung tough. At last, all preparations were finished for turning responsibility over to the registered Everywoman's Health Centre Society. The original BC Coalition for Abortion Clinics, which had opened the clinic, would not dissolve, but its managerial duties would be supplanted by a board of directors to be elected May 7, 1989. Notice was given, and the campaign was on. When the meeting opened at the Justice Institute, then still located at Jericho Beach, there were two opposing slates of candidates — those who were clinic founders, and those with animosity towards them. Nominees walked to the front, and as each identified herself, a few catcalls were heard. The tension was strong, and when the ballots were counted, four women from each side had been elected.

Among the founders — members of the BCCAC Steering Committee — there was Hilda Thomas, Anne Hamilton, and Ruth Houle. Joining them was Margaret Birrell. From the opposition, there was Jessica Gossen and Kyong-ae Kim, two of the volunteer lawyers for the clinic, Penny Tilby of CCCA, and Jackie Brown, a security volunteer. Kyong-ae Kim resigned at the first board meeting, and her place was taken by runner-up candidate, Colleen Glynn. I was more interested in the political job of fighting against a new abortion law than in service-work at the clinic, and I did not stand for the new board.

Would the conflicts of the past few months continue? In an unguarded moment, one new board member boasted that the opposition had staged a "takeover." The truth was that the women with the greater political and feminist experience — from the former Steering Committee — succeeded in drawing the newly-elected oppositionists into the board's work and integrating them well. The newcomers soon realized there had been no basis for the hostility they'd carried — indeed, they were rather awed by the competence of the founders — and, now that their ambitions had succeeded, everyone got down to the hard work of running the clinic.

Meanwhile, in Kamloops, Langley and Richmond, battles to control the hospitals went on just as if abortion were still illegal.

Then, suddenly, the issue was tossed to the courts again and tumult reappeared.

The Reagan-stacked US Supreme Court retreated somewhat from the sixteen-year-old principle of women's right to choose abortion. On July 3, it released a split decision that allowed Missouri, and other states, to pare down the availability of the procedure, by banning abortions in publicly-funded clinics. Hundreds of thousands rallied across North America, on both sides of the issue. Randall Terry, of Operation Rescue, gleefully predicted that "*Roe [v. Wade]* is going to fall."[1] He was wrong. The Justices hacked at the law, but it was not overturned.

As it happened, a pro-choice fund-raiser was already in the works for Thursday, July 6, 1989, at the Commodore Ballroom in Vancouver. The timing was fortuitous, for not only did the US Supreme Court decision threaten the future of abortion rights in Canada, but a Toronto judge had just stirred a hornet's nest. He stopped 22-year-old Barbara Dodd from going ahead with an abortion by granting an injunction to her former boyfriend. The fetus was thereby made a ward of the court, exciting those who argued that the unborn should be protected by the Charter of Rights.[2]

The popular Commodore Ballroom was licenced for a crowd of 1000 people — so filling it was a challenge, especially on a weeknight. The job of making the event work was shared by Brent Kane, a programmer at Vancouver Co-operative Radio, and me. Drew Burns, then the sympathetic owner of the Commodore, offered us the room for free, with the house to take the proceeds from the bar, and Brent lined up a hot list of performers. He taped a terrific carte, or sound ad, which was played frequently over Co-op Radio, a co-sponsor of the evening. I took on selling the tickets, which I farmed out in blocks to dozens of supporters — and, at $10, they must have offered one of the cheapest nights' dancing on the famous sprung dance floor ever available.

Angered by the injunction against Barbara Dodd and by the attack on *Roe v. Wade, Province* editor Patricia Graham penned a column urging readers to go to the fund-raiser. Feminists had, at last, battled their way into positions of clout at Pacific Press, and the pro-choice movement was no longer dismissed as marginal. Graham's column was publicity we had no budget for — and it worked. People poured through the door, a near-capacity crowd, to hear sultry singer Amanda Hughes, girl-band The Dots, and another band, The Nyetz. It was a terrific evening. Halfway through, I went onstage to thank all those who had made the event happen, and gave a special mention to Patricia Graham. Then I introduced Joy Thompson. Her brief remarks were heartfelt and she asked the crowd to attend a rally planned for that weekend. Hilda Thomas brought out her guitar and got the audience to join in new lyrics to the old song, 'If You Wore A Tulip...' In Hilda's version, it went

So, you wear a condom, a big rubber condom,
And I'll wear a Great Big Smile.

Later, a small woman pushed through the crowd on the dance floor and introduced herself to me as Patricia Graham. She took her own advice about attending the fund-raiser.

After expenses, including paying appreciative amounts to the performers, we came away with nearly $5000 for the clinic. Money was tight, as always. A few months later, one of the new directors of the clinic board of directors, Jackie Brown, heard of a fund-raising method being used in the US. It was a great idea and was put into practice here at once. The new campaign was called "Pledge a Protester," and a good number of amused donors signed up. Each day, the clinic kept tabs on the number of protesters parading around outside, and sent out the total number at the end of the month. Subscribers might pledge, say, twenty cents per protester, and if the tally was 120 that month, they would donate $24 to the clinic. There were enough pledges to create a basic monthly income, which helped, although the clinic remained in the red. In the end, it took a court battle for Everywoman's to win charitable status and be able to send its donors tax-deductible receipts. That did not come about until the end of 1991.[3]

Back in Toronto, in July, 1989, feminists rushed to support Barbara Dodd. The judge who awarded the injunction against her was revealed to be an anti-abortion campaigner.[4] A week later, an appeal court overturned the ban, and Dodd had an abortion. Later, she regretted it, joined the anti-abortionists and, eventually, married the man who had taken her to court.[5]

It wasn't a new tactic, but suddenly banning individual abortions by court order was being tried all over. It didn't work for a Winnipeg man, who was turned down by the judge when he asked for an injunction against his former girl friend. He rushed from the court to the hospital, where he tried to bully the woman into continuing her pregnancy. "She looked upset but she wasn't crying," the man told the media later, and he admitted that the abortion had gone ahead.[6] It was all for spite, said the unnamed woman. "He's not trying to save the life of a human being. It's a revenge to get back at me because I left him."[7]

Chantal Daigle wasn't so lucky. Her ordeal had all of Canada holding its breath for over a month, for not only did a judge grant her former boyfriend guardianship of the 18-week fetus she carried, but the Québec Superior Court upheld the injunction. An unnamed woman phoned the *Montréal Gazette* to offer Daigle $25,000 to carry through with the pregnancy, adding that she wanted to raise the child. "No, she is not going to get the baby," responded Jean-Guy Tremblay, the boyfriend. "I'm going to get the baby." His mother would raise it, he said[8] He admitted in court to having assaulted Daigle. Campaign Life paid Tremblay's legal fees, and his lawyer asked the Superior Court judge to have the fetus put in an incubator rather than to permit it to be aborted. Just how that might be done, he didn't say. The proposal met with incredulity from spectators in the packed courtroom in the northwestern mining town of Val D'Or.[9] Through it all, 21-year-old Daigle maintained her dignity. Others were furious. The president of Planned Parenthood of Montréal said, "This is a court becoming a pregnancy enforcer...This is worse than what's going on in the United States."[10] Two days later, the now 20-weeks-pregnant Daigle won permission to take the injunction further, to the Québec Court of Appeal.

But the Court of Appeal turned against her and ruled she must continue the pregnancy because, it declared, the fetus was protected under Québec's Charter of Rights.[11] Explosive anger met this pronouncement. Ten thousand people poured into the streets of Montréal to support Chantal Daigle.[12] In Toronto, Judy Rebick told a spontaneous rally, "If every woman who gets pregnant has to fear that her boyfriend, her husband, her ex-boyfriend, even a stranger can go to court and get an injunction and plaster details of her personal life all over the newspapers, women have no equality." "For the first time in Canada, the courts are forcing a woman to give birth or go to jail," said a statement from the Metro Toronto Labour Council.[13]

Daigle then turned to the Supreme Court of Canada. The court agreed to interrupt its summer recess and consider her case, which, by now, was a *cause célebre*. Doubtless alarmed lest separatist Québec's Charter of Rights outweigh the federal Charter, the court convened on August 8 and heard pro- and anti-choice arguments. The federal government itself — reliably anti-abortion for the previous century — tried, weakly, to stay out of it, while simply stating it had the right to legislate on abortion. But, as F.L. Morton points out, Ottawa's "failure to legislate for the [previous] eighteen months was a principal cause of the whole [Daigle] affair."[14] By then it was nearly a month after the July 17 injunction had been granted, and time had run out for Chantal Daigle. She went in disguise to Boston to have her 22-week pregnancy terminated, even though she had no legal permission to do so. Tremblay, her ex-boyfriend, who was dismissed from his job for unsatisfactory performance, threatened to pursue her for defying the injunction. She said nothing publicly until mid-August, then explained to the press that she'd broken off with Tremblay after seeing his "other side." "I wasn't going to stay with a man who was violent, insanely jealous and wanted to control all aspects of my life," she sensibly said.[15]

News of Daigle's trip to Boston reached the Canadian Supreme Court just as it assembled to consider the case. But instead of finding her in contempt, the justices needed less than two hours to agree unanimously on overturning the initial injunction.[16] Although the Court vindicated Daigle in August, it did not release its legal rationale until November, 1989 — again, at a fortuitous moment.

As they lost round after round, anti-abortionists taxed themselves to up the ante. Fifteen blockaders chained themselves to one another and to the wire-mesh outer door at Everywoman's Health Centre in April. It took a blasé police force four hours to arrive and cut the chains, but Justice Wood was not as laid-back. He sentenced most of the blockaders to sixty days.[17] On July 4, following the US Supreme Court's upholding of Missouri's restrictive law, two people lay down before the door with bicycle locks connecting their necks to a large block of concrete. Acetylene torches were needed to cut the locks away.[18] In a bizarre hoax less than a week later, another anti-abortionist lay chained to a pipe that went around her neck, which she claimed was filled with gasoline. 'Cut this away and there'll be a massive explosion and death,' threatened her supporters. When city workers arrived with cutting torches, the bluff was called and a key was produced to set the blockader free. Joy Thompson saw this as a "terrorist action" against the clinic's clients, while Hilda Thomas told the press, "The hostility, anger and hysteria of these people is escalating and the attempt to frighten the staff is getting more intense."[19]

Meantime, the pro-choice movement chose October 14 for a 'National Day of Action' against any attempt to re-criminalize abortion. The Mulroney government kept hoping the issue would die; it had even won re-election without introducing a new abortion law, but right-wing hounding was incessant. After each embarrassment — Borowski's defeat, the Supreme Court decision on Daigle, etc. — a new promise would be made to make abortion illegal again. The outreach committee of BCCAC, which I continued to chair, began planning for October 14, strengthened by a dozen new members, women politicized by the Dodd and Daigle cases. Still lacking office space, the outreach committee met at the Britannia community centre, passing the hat to pay the rent for each meeting.

Organizing was not smooth. The new members would enthuse about details and lose track of the main task. But with the clinic more-or-less on its feet, former skeptics renewed their support. For example, NDP leader Mike Harcourt's office phoned me at home with his request to speak at the rally — Dr. Morgentaler's victory before the Canadian Supreme Court had wiped out the NDP's grousing that caused Harcourt to shun his tour of Vancouver in 1985.

On October 14, the action in Vancouver was a great success. Everywoman's Health Centre was a source of enormous pride for thousands of Vancouver and BC residents, and, standing on a bench to count the passing crowd as I always did at a demo, I was satisfied that 2000 people came out. For once, the print media got it right. "2000 join pro-choice action rally," was the headline in the *Province* — but, astonishingly, CBC-TV set the turnout at 4000, and BCTV said there were 5000 marchers. TV coverage included full-throated chants of "Choice now!" and clips of United Church minister Linda Ervin declaring that women are "wise moral decision-makers, and we do not need new laws to control our bodies." Harcourt promised that an NDP government in Victoria would give funding to Everywoman's Health Centre, and he outlined the ideal of full-service, community-based clinics that had been party policy since adoption of the Foulkes Report.[20]

"Don't Lose the Right to Choose" was the theme that drew out more than 17,000 people in at least 31 cities in Canada for that National Day of Action.[21] They ranged from Victoria, where more than 200 rallied on the lawn of the legislature, to St. John's, Newfoundland. Toronto's rally drew 2000 as well, if the *Globe and Mail's* coverage was accurate.

Nonetheless, one day short of the first anniversary of Everywoman's Health Centre, on November 3, 1989, the Mulroney government introduced Bill C-43. Its terms prohibited abortion at all stages of pregnancy unless the pregnant woman's health was in danger. Only one doctor would be required to declare the woman at risk, but if he were challenged on his judgment, both doctor and patient would face two years in jail.

The Tories claimed this was a moderate position, but the slim exception made for the woman's health drove the anti-abortion movement to hysteria. Heather Stilwell, long one of the most extreme of her kind in BC, told the *Province* that the bill allowed "abortion on demand for nine months of pregnancy." Fervent anti-abortion MPs Alex Kindy and Gus Mitges, who claimed 110 MPs shared their views, vowed to vote against the bill. Linda Ervin, a new spokeswoman for the BC Coalition for Abortion Clinics, pronounced it "devastating," and said "We don't need any law which controls women's bodies."[22] Doctors saw they were to be damned no matter what they did, and women saw their choice disappearing. "Within hours of its introduction," reported the *Globe and Mail*, "groups from the entire spectrum of the abortion debate were lining up in Ottawa...to denounce the government's proposed abortion legislation."[23] Opined the *Vancouver Sun*, either the "Commons or court will kill the bill."[24]

Pro-choice supporters in Vancouver rallied twice outside the federal Health and Welfare Department offices at Sinclair Centre, 200 on November 4, abut 400 on November 6.[25] Ottawa and Toronto also rallied against Bill C-43. An Environics poll commissioned by CARAL found that Canadians across the country opposed the bill by more than two to one.[26]

It was at this point that the Canadian Supreme Court released its reasoning in the Daigle case. A fetus is not a human being, it ruled, and individual men can't stop women from having abortions. The Tories insisted the court's opinion would not affect passage of the proposed abortion bill, but editors of the *Vancouver Sun* labeled that claim "wishful thinking."[27]

However, federal justice minister Doug Lewis said he was "personally happy" with the bill and he hoped it would be adopted by Christmas. Tories were told to vote in favour of it, or else. No 'free vote' this time. Which may explain why Barbara McDougall, then minister of employment and immigration, and a long-time pro-choice advocate, rose to speak in support of the bill. Apparently, her desire to remain in cabinet won out over her principles. On November 27, Bill C-43 was approved on first and second readings by a vote of 164-114.[28] The entire NDP caucus of 40 voted 'No,' in defiance of parliamentary protocol: this was tantamount to voting against putting the bill on the floor for debate.

Hearings before an all-parliamentary committee got underway in early 1990 and continued through February and March. Dawn Black, rookie MP for New Westminster-Burnaby, was the committee's lone NDP member, and she readied herself to butt heads with the Tory majority. Her office in Ottawa became headquarters-central for the pro-choice campaign against the bill. She recalls striding into her first committee meeting armed with an 'A', a 'B', and a 'C' list of pro-choice groups to be invited to present their views. Perhaps anti-abortion committee members, like Benno Friesen, MP for Surrey-White Rock, were complacent about victory, at first. But after Black succeeded in getting intervenor status for her entire 'A' and 'B' lists, he was visibly appalled by her competence.[29]

As the hearings progressed, Dawn Black had to deal with threats of harm to her children, and threats of violent death to herself from such shadowy groups as "Commandos of the Unborn." She was once physically attacked at the entrance to the House of Commons. Her back-bench amendment to eliminate all reference to abortion in the Criminal Code was defeated, as were all other amendments to the bill.

At the end of February, Canada got its first female justice minister, when Mulroney tapped Vancouver's Kim Campbell for the role. A cynical move. Campbell had ridden on her pro-choice reputation for years, and many came to see her sudden, new appointment as a sop to women that would absolve the government for its bill to re-criminalize abortion. Ms. Campbell, however, picked up the gauntlet and strove mightily to get Bill C-43 adopted.

Her efforts to wave away well-grounded suspicions of the bill only undercut her credibility. If anything, Bill C-43 was harsher than the law thrown out by the Canadian Supreme Court in 1988. Doctors did not buy Campbell's assurances that it would guarantee "an explicit national entitlement" to abortion. Instead, the CMA, the BCMA, and other medical bodies opposed the bill strongly. They saw jail and ruined careers ahead. Accessibility to abortion began drying up immediately, and more than half of Canadian obstetricians announced they would stop performing the procedure if Bill C-43 became law.[30] Campbell called the bill "useful and the best possible," a view that seventeen law professors publicly dubbed "surprisingly uninformed" and "legal nonsense."[31] Nonetheless, she said, the bill "is talking about good medical care. I'm very comfortable with it — I think doctors will be very comfortable with it."[32]

The Mulroney government promised full debate, until all MPs had had their say, before the third and final reading. So many wanted to speak that an all-night session was scheduled for May 24. It coincided with a glittering state dinner attended by most of the Tory cabinet. Dawn Black recalls how the House was nearly vacant late that evening, except for NDP MPs who were waiting their turn to speak. Midnight passed, and not a Tory nor a Liberal was to be seen. Cautiously, lest their faces betray their plan to the parliamentary cameras, Dawn Black and Joy Langan (Mission-Coquitlam) wrote out a motion and sent a page to carry it to the speaker. In a casual monotone, Black rose and said, "Mr. Speaker, I think you'll find in the House at this time there would be unanimous agreement to withdraw this legislation." The speaker was reading the motion aloud — when a backbench Tory MP hurtled through the gold curtains into the chamber in time to yell out "NO."

"But he just made it, without even seconds to spare. We came very, very close to having the legislation withdrawn," recalls Black. There was still one option. With only five or six MPs in the House, Joy Langan rose to call quorum. Without at least twenty members present, no business could be conducted. This last-ditch motion precipitated near panic; the bells rang for thirty minutes to call the members to their seats. One arrived still tucking his shirt into his pants.[33] Tory house leader Harvie Andre ran over to the NDP lobby and just "exploded," remembers Black. He bellowed that the granting of an all-night session involved a deal that there should be 'no surprises.' The NDPers present were all rookies, and most of them were women. The ruling party had underestimated them. "And I remember watching Kim Campbell storm back into the House of Commons, absolutely furious! Because, of course, this was her legislation and *we* [the NDP] had almost got it dropped right off the parliamentary agenda! Oh, she wasn't the only one who was steaming, believe me," says Black. The next day, Black was unrepentant as she told the media, "This government has a nerve to talk about breaking deals." Then she reeled off a list of unkept election promises on women's issues.[34]

Bill C-43 was passed in the House of Commons with only nine votes to spare — 140 to 131 — on Tuesday, May 29, 1990. Incredibly, the bill no-one claimed to want was adopted. The prime minister led the way in defeating all 12 amendments to it. Anti-abortion MPs were rounded up with a last-minute threat that if Bill C-43 didn't pass, "it will be years, even decades," before any government got another chance to restrict abortion.[35] Liberal Party leader John Turner made yet another turn-around and voted for the bill.[36] So did perennially anti-abortion Tories like Benno Friesen and Ross Belsher (Fraser Valley West). Their supporters were confused. "I couldn't understand it," said BC Campaign Life spokesman Ralph Stewart.[37] The point was that Mulroney wanted to put an end to the controversy and silence the matter.

But the opposite happened. Howls of defiance arose from all sides, since, no matter how the votes were counted, neither the pro-choice nor anti-abortion forces wanted Bill C-43. The battle raged on, right up to the vote in the Senate, in January 1991.

Much happened in between. In Vancouver, fourteen months after it opened, Everywoman's Health Centre was toured by inspectors from the College of Physicians and Surgeons. The upstart clinic was put under the microscope. And lo and behold! In early February, 1990, it was awarded the highest accolade the College could bestow: accreditation for three years. Vancouver General Hospital, far longer established, although a more complex facility, had to renew its accreditation every twelve months. It was a stunning tribute to the quality of care and the careful preparation by the clinic's staff and directors.

Just two weeks earlier, Bill Vander Zalm had gone on TV to quell dissent in his caucus and stroke the electorate, and, for the first time in his career, he admitted he had made mistakes. Particularly about abortion. The premier hinted he'd been wrong to freeze funds for abortion in 1988, said he was sorry for any "honest" mistakes he'd made. But he continued to insist he'd never tried to impose his moral views on British Columbians.[38] Nonetheless, when the clinic won accreditation, his government still refused to fund its operating expenses.[39]

Then at noon on Sunday, February 25, vandals smashed through the double glass doors at Everywoman's Health Centre and destroyed key equipment with a crowbar. They were in and out in minutes, obviously familiar with the clinic's layout and knowing exactly what they were after. Narcotics supplies and patients' records were not disturbed. But the diagnostic ultrasound machine, and the clinic's only aspirator, the machine used to perform abortions, were ruined. Witnesses saw men rushing away from the clinic, and a bus driver volunteered to testify. Police claimed they responded quickly to the electronic alarm, but their investigation of the abundant evidence was feeble and no arrests were ever made.

It was a disaster. The clinic's directors met it with the resilience they'd shown in every crisis. The centre was operating on a full-time basis, by then, and clients coming in on the next day had to be re-scheduled. But, by Tuesday, another aspirator had been found and abortions were resumed. Here's how it happened.

No hospital in the region could be persuaded to loan an aspirator to the newly-accredited clinic. Still, by Monday afternoon, an aspirator had been located in northeastern Washington state. A feminist-run clinic there was sympathetic to the predicament of Everywoman's Health Centre — which was great, except it was 600 km away. Staffers Joy Thompson and Marg Panton were struck off to go get it. Thompson put on her cowboy boots, arranged baby-sitting for her kids, and the two set out in a borrowed van around 6 pm on Monday, February 26. Clients would be coming in the next morning at nine o'clock, so they had about fifteen hours to make a fourteen-hour trip. With only one pit-stop, they pulled up at the home of the Yakima clinic's director about 2am. She was waiting with the aspirator. None of them had ever met before, and the Vancouver women were full of gratitude that the Yakima women would hand over their precious spare aspirator, on faith. They rigged a plywood ramp and pushed the aspirator up it into the van. Then, after brief and cheery good-byes — 'send it back when you're done with it' — the hell-for-leather drive back to Vancouver began.

The tricky part came at the border. Before they'd left, the advice of Canada Customs had been sought and it was that, even though the aspirator was only on loan, it must be declared at the border and duty for it paid. When the van got there at a dark, blear hour, there were two cars in the line ahead of it. 'If we declare the aspirator,' Thompson and Panton agreed, 'then we'll have to unload it for inspection, fill out forms in triplicate, and blahblahblah.' There wasn't time for that. Should they just not say anything? The problem was, it wasn't a small machine. It was noticeable in the back of the van, a large metal contraption with bottles and tubes attached. 'Got anything to declare, girls?' asked the Customs officer. They explained they had no purchases, but the fellow could see the aspirator just behind the driver's seat. 'Well, yes, we have a piece of medical equipment here, but it's just on loan.' He could tell they didn't mean a bandage or syringe. Taking a deep breath, Thompson explained about the break-in at

Everywoman's Health Centre and the lucky find of an aspirator in Washington state. She didn't actually ask to be waived through, but she described the roster of clients waiting for them in Vancouver. Incredibly, the tough-guy said he'd heard about the break-in and he thought it was dreadful. Then he said something like, 'Well hurry up and go on then. But *don't do it again.'*[40]

The van sprinted through the border and arrived at the clinic with minutes to spare. A blanket was thrown over the aspirator and it was wheeled in past the protesters and through a waiting room full of clients. The break-in closed the clinic for only one day.

The Commons' passage of Bill C-43 led almost at once to tragedy. Access to the procedure shrank even further. Within two weeks, a 16-year old in Kitchener suffered injury when she turned to an unqualified practitioner for an abortion. Then came the death of 20-year-old Yvonne Jurewicz in Toronto, who tried to abort herself. A grieving and angry Carolyn Egan of the Ontario Coalition for Abortion Clinics blamed Bill C-43, even though it had not yet passed into law. "The fact that the bill has yet to go to the Senate escapes most people," she told the *Globe and Mail* on June 14, 1990. Doctors had already stopped doing abortions at some hospitals, she pointed out,[41] and the horrors of the back alley were already leaping into the gap.

Physicians from Calgary to Halifax announced they would no longer perform abortions for fear of being sued under Bill C-43.[42] At its annual meeting in August, the Canadian Medical Association called on Kim Campbell to withdraw the bill before it reached the Senate. Anxiety rose as anti-abortion groups announced they would recruit women to lay charges against doctors who aborted them.[43]

In Vancouver, the day arrived when Concerned Citizens for Choice on Abortion set up a clinic of its own. Nearly two years after Everywoman's Health Centre opened its doors, Norah Hutchinson and her friends christened their clinic after Elizabeth Bagshaw, a pioneer woman physician. Learning from the trials of the first clinic, they located Elizabeth Bagshaw in a medical office tower on a street with heavy traffic. Protesters appeared outside on the narrow strip of sidewalk, but no-one could tell which of the many people streaming through the buildings' doors was going in for an abortion. Vander Zalm, embroiled in scandal and facing revolt from his party — again — meekly allowed he could do nothing to prevent the new clinic opening in September, 1990.[44]

Then came the great court case — the long anticipated anti-abortionists' appeal of the injunction that had been granted to Everywoman's Health Centre in January, 1989. Jessica Gossen, who had a practice in family law and who was now a board member and the financial officer of the clinic, led the defence. She was assisted by Kyong-ae Kim, from the office of Rush, Crane, and Guenther. Both these women had done *pro bono* work for the clinic since its early days, and Gossen had been active in the women's movement since the period of the BC Federation of Women.

Gossen believes she was "just absolutely, incredibly lucky to have been there at that time. It was an incredible honour to be representing the clinic." The appeal trial made history. It was also time-consuming and a lot of hard work, since the research and documentation had to be done after hours.

It turned out that the case was heard before a panel of the top judges in BC. First, Chief Justice Allan McEachern, whose specialty was injunction law — "the kind of law that the Court of Appeal absolutely adores dealIng with; there's just a ton of case law that relates to injunctions," says Gossen. Also, Justice Mary Southin, "very outspoken, very clear in her opinions, and a legal historian of some note," in Gossen's description. And to add a neutral, but scholarly tone, newly appointed Justice Harold Hollinrake.

By the time the case was heard, in October, 1990, it was twenty-two months since the injunction against blockading Everywoman's Health Centre had been granted. The appellants, the blockaders of February, 1989, were again represented by Humphrey Waldock, Paul Formby, and Charles Lugosi, who was brought in at the last minute and allowed, by the court, to file his factum only two weeks before the hearing. These three divided the case into arguments on injunctions, the Charter of Rights, and — God.

In Gossen's view, "they got away with behaviour that no litigant that I've ever come across would have gotten away with." Chiefly, that their arguments had no basis in the law. The judges thought the same. As described in the *Vancouver Sun*, "The court told Waldock they had been unable to discern any point of law in his presentation, saying it was filled 'with philosophy and morality that you would impose on others.' That isn't law." The Chief Justice told him, "You have a duty to outline the points of law on which you base your appeal."[45]

However, because of the notoriety of the case, and no doubt to settle the matter and prevent its being taken to higher courts, the three judges allowed Waldock, Formby, and Lugosi to take up four and a half days of court time. The crux of their case was handled by the passionate and enormously dignified Humphrey Waldock. He was also colourful. To court, he wore a cape of fine black wool lined with red satin. Gossen says, "Humphrey Waldock [was] an English barrister in the finest tradition of English barristers. He spoke with a very deep English accent and wore tweeds and smoked a pipe. He should have been born during the time when wigs were allowed..."

Despite their reservations about his prepared case, the justices permitted Waldock to present thirty grounds for why the injunction (and abortion) was an outrage to God. He argued that the common law was based on "duty to thy neighbor," and was therefore founded on the teachings of Jesus Christ. He referred to Charlemagne. He argued that the 17th century English Bishops had made the church the head of state, and therefore, all law must be acceptable to the Christian God. For proof, he held up an American dime, on whose rim is the motto, 'In God We Trust.'

As it happened, Justice Mary Southin knew a lot about the Bishops, and in the reasons for judgment, she wrote that the appellants were, regrettably, wandering in "a nether world, half philosophy and half history" but "not the world of law." Justice McEachern pointed out that Canadian law is based on tradition that was considerably evolved and developed beyond the era of the Bishops.

Justice Southin, not usually regarded as a feminist, asked some penetrating questions in the courtroom. She asked Mr. Waldock whether he was seriously arguing that women should go back to the Bishops' times (and later) when women simply died of exhaustion after giving birth a dozen times or more. Was that what the 'wisdom' of the Bishops amounted to? She also asked Waldock whether he was saying that a thirteen-year-old who becomes pregnant through rape should be forced to bear a child. The clinic's lawyers were surprised by "the kind of grass-roots identification and the knowledge that she had about that particular issue."

Gossen and Kim, sitting with their cases of notes, waited their turn with some trepidation. Where to begin? How to counter these wildly irrelevant arguments? But when the anti-abortionists' case rested, Chief Justice McEachern waved his hand and said the court didn't need to hear from the Crown — that is, from the counsel for the clinic. After all that preparation, Gossen and Kim did not address the court. McEachern dismissed the appeal and upheld the injunction. The anti-abortion appellants had failed to "raise any point of law that could persuade the court", as the *Vancouver Sun* put it.[46] Nor, indeed, had the anti-abortionists developed a case they could appeal to any higher court.

Further, the judges awarded costs to the clinic's side. Not only costs, but the newly introduced measure of Special Costs. This meant that the anti-abortionists were to pay an additional amount, on top of all the expenses for preparing the clinic's case. It was meant to penalize Waldock, Formby, and Lugosi for wasting the court's time. Special Costs were awarded very rarely.

The bill for costs presented by Gossen and Kim reflected the help they got from the clinic's longstanding legal team of Laura Parkinson, Star Rosenthal, and Bill Coller. Gossen estimates that a big law firm might have charged between $100,000 and $200,000. But, socially conscious as they were — "It just isn't in our nature to over-bill," says Gossen — they submitted a bill for about $48,000.[47] The anti-abortionists refused to pay. It took more than three years to get the money out of them, and $45,000 was finally paid only because the clinic's legal team placed liens on the houses of seven leading anti-abortionists, including John Hof and Betty Green.[48]

The outcome did not deter anti-abortionists from swarming around Everywoman's Health Centre, stalking its staff,[49] and threatening violence. At length, after the election of the BC NDP in 1992, and the nearly-fatal shooting of Dr. Garson Romalis in 1994, a law was enacted creating "bubble zones" around the Everywoman's and Bagshaw clinics, doctors' offices and homes. Protesting is not allowed in these areas. Bubble zones have been repeatedly violated by anti-abortionists. They were partially struck down by a court decision in January, 1996, as infringements on freedom of expression, but were restored to full force by the BC Court of Appeal in October of that year. In 1998, bubble zones were extended to include Vancouver General Hospital.

The governance of BC hospitals was changed from elected to appointed boards by BC health minister Joy MacPhail in April, 1997.

In 1991, abortion was again on the agenda in Ottawa. The Senate showed its mettle here. It debated Bill C-43 thoroughly and, finally, on January 31, 1991, while most of the world focused on the bombing of Iraq in the Gulf War, the Senate scrapped abortion from Canada's lawbooks.[50] New Democrat MP Dawn Black found it ironic that Bill C-43 was defeated by 43-43 — a vote in which the affirmative failed to reach a majority, and thus lost. The first Tory Senator to rise and call out her vote was BC's Pat Carney, formerly the powerful trade minister in Brian Mulroney's cabinet. She was in Vancouver, getting treatment for her arthritis, when the moment came to vote on the abortion bill. "There was no doubt as to how I would vote," Carney says in her memoir, *Trade Secrets*. She was pro-choice. Boarding an all-night flight back to Ottawa, she cast her vote against Bill C-43. But first she went to her office and took a call from her relative and successor as MP for Vancouver Centre, Kim Campbell. "'Kim said [vote for the bill] or [she'd] hang me out to dry in the riding," my black book records."[51] The threat was made good when, days later, Carney was removed from a committee struck to consider amending the constitution — an appointment she had a keen interest in.[52]

Since that day, Canada has been unique among liberal western nations. It has no federal laws for or against abortion. Some time later, after her short-lived and humbling try at being prime minister, even Kim Campbell publicly boasted about the advantages to Canada of having abolished its abortion laws.

Access to abortion is, still, another matter. Despite the monumental, decades-long struggle by feminists and Dr. Henry Morgentaler, hospital abortions are still governed by often hostile by-laws, tight quota systems, provincial opposition, and diminishing budgets. Most Canadian women are still unable to get abortions in their own communities, and fear and shame still beset many of those who do. Dr. Morgentaler plowed ahead and opened clinics in Alberta, Saskatchewan, and the Maritimes, using his own funds and defeating all the opponents he'd met before in other provinces. It required court challenges and new laws, sometimes a change of government, to clear the way for him and the women his clinics serve. Nonetheless, only a handful of free-standing clinics exist in Canada, and, as the 21st century began, Dr. Morgentaler undertook another campaign to force governments in the Atlantic provinces and elsewhere to fund his clinics.

British Columbia has five abortion clinics, as of this writing. One in Kamloops, established only in 2000, and four in Vancouver. All of these were opened by women from the pro-choice movement: Everywoman's Health Centre (1988), the Elizabeth Bagshaw Clinic (1990), and the one located within BC Women's Hospital, designed by Joy Thompson and Barb Hestrin. Dr. Ellen Wiebe has worked ceaselessly to defeat obstacles to using the drug RU-486, which, taken early in pregnancy, causes women to abort, and, while the drug is not always available for Canadian women, her practice is considered here as an abortion clinic.

When Bill Vander Zalm crashed to the ground and was forced to resign as premier, the immediate cause was his acceptance of a $20,000 gift from the buyer of his theme park, Fantasy Gardens. In return for the money, the Zalm is alleged to have used his office to get Petro-Canada to throw its adjacent property into the deal. It was the final sleazy chapter in a long history of scandals, and it destroyed the Social Credit Party as well as the premier. Still, there is wide-ranging agreement that the lynch-pin in Vander Zalm's downfall was his extraordinary arrogance on abortion. The public and his own party began to divide when he insisted on bucking the 1988 Supreme Court ruling that made abortion fully legal in Canada. In April, 1991, pro-choice activists took satisfaction in knowing that many pundits agreed with them: abortion toppled the BC government.

The BC NDP ousted the Socreds from office, in October, 1991, and the promise to fund abortion clinics was, in time, carried out. Everywoman's Health Centre and Elizabeth Bagshaw Clinic joined together to negotiate with the ministry of health. They were awarded contracts for operating expenses on a year-by-year basis in 1992. With the defeat of the NDP in 2001, this funding base became uncertain.

But one more delicious story remains to be told about Everywoman's Health Centre. It is the story of how a shy, big-hearted benefactor saved the clinic from impending financial chaos.

One busy day in 1991, the clinic received a phone call from an apparent prankster. From someone who talked about donating a lot of money. His call was shuffled from one staffer to another, and the caller grew miffed.[53] Eventually, he managed to contact the financial officer, who was board member and legal counsel for the clinic, Jessica Gossen.[54] He identified himself as a lawyer, and she recognized his name. A tirade ensued about the rudeness dealt to his earlier call. Gossen apologized in her most professional tone. It developed that the lawyer represented a donor who insisted on maintaining the strictest anonymity. A donor who offered to pay off the clinic's mortgage.

Swallowing her astonishment, Gossen kept up her lawyerly demeanor while her mind raced. Despite the brave front always presented to the public, Everywoman's Health Centre was in financial distress. It was juggling two mortgages, on which it managed to pay only the monthly interest. The principal of the debt remained untouched. Payroll was met with difficulty, and the roof leaked. It had been damaged in the February, 1991 break-in, and repairs could no longer be delayed.

The unknown donor demanded a professional undertaking from Gossen to reveal nothing of the transaction, not even to the board of directors on which she sat. She had to ask the board to trust her and to ask no questions. It was a distinctly odd situation to be in. As financial officer, she came up with a figure for the amount needed to clear the clinic's debts, and she conveyed this to the go-between.

At last came the transfer, in a scene reminiscent of a noir-genre movie. Gossen was allowed to take her law partner into confidence, so that there would be an independent witness. The two women waited in the lobby of their office building to meet the lawyer-go-between. This person arrived by cab, handed the women a sealed box, and sped off again. The two women, laughing with astonishment and delight, took a taxi directly to the bank. They were escorted to a back room, and the box — which bore the label of 'Dom Perignon' champagne — was opened in the presence of bank officers. It was found to contain, not wine, but careful stacks of used twenty-dollar bills. $180,000 in all. What a class act, recalls Gossen. The ironies of using an expensive label to conceal the gift, and of depositing it in one of the poorer neighborhood bank branches in town, at Kingsgate Mall, still amuse the grateful recipients from Everywoman's Health Centre.

The gift was used to pay off the clinic's mortgages, repair the roof, and improve the ambiance for clients by buying a stereo to relieve anxiety in the waiting room. And, at last, machines were purchased so that the clinic's laundry could be done on site. The wonder of it has not diminished with time. Praises are still sung to this thoroughly unknown donor, to whom the women of Vancouver and BC owe so much.

Thus concludes this tale. "Past is prologue," Shakespeare tells us, and Marshall McLuhan pointed out that, while we are unavoidably rooted in the legacy of the past, that which is immediately behind us lies in the blind-spot of our collective rear-view mirror. It is easy to be ignorant of, or to have forgotten, these struggles conducted so recently. But the fight for women's right to choose on pregnancy is not ended. This book is meant to illuminate the fights of the 1970s and 1980s, in hopes of aiding the coming battles. The reader has seen how, what is accepted by many today as self-evident, that the woman who is pregnant should make the decision about whether or not to continue her pregnancy, arrived like a tsunami wave that sucked in virtually every sector of society — some of whom thought they were indifferent on the matter, while others were passionately partisan to women or ferociously opposed to change.

But the enemies of abortion, the 'fetus-fetishists' in Henry Morgentaler's memorable phrase, are still very active. To their warped minds, being 'pro-life' gives them a licence to kill, and to date, nine abortion-providers in North America have been assassinated. Vancouver's Dr. Garson Romalis was stalked and badly wounded — twice — and doctors in Ontario and Manitoba have also been shot by a sniper. A notorious internet list of clinics and their doctors directs future killers to their prey, and court judgments have been ineffectual in getting it removed from the 'net. In certain ways, the furious contests recounted in this book represent only the initial stages of the battle. The struggle continues...

ENDORSERS OF CHOICE ON ABORTION

Concerned Citizens for Choice on Abortion (CCCA) actively sought written endorsement from organizations and individuals, who were also its donor base. To show the breadth of support for our demands, the Endorsers List was published widely. Based on it, we were able to claim that more than 500,000 people in BC were pro-choice. The version below, taken from the back cover of the January, 1987 CCCA Newsletter, shows this support at its height.

Women's Rights Organizations
Argenta Women's Group
Ariel Books
BC Federation of Women
Canadian Association of Sexual Assault
    Centres
Coalition of Rape Crisis Centres
Cranbrook Resource Group
Downtown Eastside Women's Centre
Euphoniously Feminist &
    Non-Performing Quintet
Federation of Medical Women of Canada
Feminist Counselling Association
Howe Sound Women's Centre
Images Collective
Ishtar Transition House
Lesbian Information Line
Lesbian Show — Co-op Radio
Maternal Health Society
National Action Committee on the
    Status of Women (NAC)
Nelson Women's Centre
North Island Women's Resource Centre
North Shore Women's Centre
Northwest Women in Crisis
Okanagan Women's Coalition
Organized Working Women
Port Coquitlam Women's Centre
Press Gang Publishers
Regina Women's Community Centre
South Surrey — White Rock Women's
    Place Association
Third World Women's Group
Upper Fraser Valley Transition Society
Vancouver Association of Women and
    the Law
Vancouver International Women's Day
    Committee, 1985
Vancouver Rape Relief
Vancouver Status of Women
Vancouver Women's Bookstore
Vancouver Women's Health Collective
Women Against Imperialism
Women Against Nuclear Technology
Women Against Violence Against Women
    (WAVAW)
Women in Focus
Women in Need
Women in Trades Association
Women's Equal Rights Association
Women's Research Centre

Labour Organizations
Association of University and College
    Employees – Provincial & Locals 1,2,6
British Columbia Federation of Labor
BC Provincial Council of Carpenters
BC Teachers' Federation
Canadian Association of Industrial,
    Mechanical & Allied Workers, Local 14
Campbell River, Courtenay & District
    Labour Council
Canadian Brotherhood of Railway Transport
    & General Workers, Local 326
Canadian Farmworkers' Union
Canadian Union of Public Employees
    (CUPE), Local 402
Canadian Union of Postal Workers
    (CUPW), Vancouver Local
Capilano College Faculty Association
Cement Masons, Local 919
Hospital Employees' Union, Local 180
IWA Locals 1-357 & 1-405
Letter Carriers Union of Canada, Local 12
Marine Workers' and Boilermakers' Union,
    & Local 1
New Westminster & District Labour
    Council
Service, Office & Retail Workers' Union of
    Canada (SORWUC), National & Local 1
Teamsters Union (Canada), Local 464
Telecommunications Workers' Union,
    BC & Local 10
United Bank Workers, BC Section
United Fishermen & Allied Workers' Union,
    Locals 2 & 8
UFAWU Women's Committee
    United Brotherhood of Carpenters &
    Joiners, Local 452
Vancouver & District Labour Council
Vancouver — New Westminster Newspaper
    Guild, Local 115
Vancouver Municipal & Regional
    Employees' Union, & Local 2

Pro-Choice Organizations
Canadian Abortion Rights Action League
    (CARAL), Victoria
Chilliwack Citizens for Choice
North Shore Association for Choice on
    Abortion (NORSACA)

Community Organizations

BC Civil Liberties Association
BC Psychologists for Social Responsibility
Canadian Rights and Liberties Federation
Collective Resource & Service Workers
  Co-op
Community Alternatives
IDERA
Isadora's Co-operative Restaurant
Men Against Rape
Mental Patients Association
Pulp Press
Single Parents' Association of Nanaimo
Smithers Indian Friendship Centre
Unitarian Church Social Responsibility
  Committee
Vancouver Gay Community Centre
YWCA

Student Organizations

Langara Student Society
Langara Women's Centre
SFU Student Society
SFU Communications Students' Union
SFU English Students' Union
SFU Women's Centre
SFU Women's Studies Students' Union
UBC Alma Mater Society
UBC Graduate Students' Association
UBC Women's Committee

Political Groups

Alliance for Socialist Action
BC New Democratic Party & constituencies:
  Capilano
  Maillardville — Coquitlam
  North Island
  North Vancouver — Seymour
  Point Grey
  Richmond
  Surrey — White Rock
  Vancouver Centre (federal)
  Vancouver East
  Vancouver Little Mountain
  Vancouver South (provincial)
  Victoria
  Repeal 251 Committee
  Women's Rights Committee
BC Women's Liberal (Party) Commission
Communist Party of Canada
Revolutionary Workers League

Other Endorsers

Rosemary Brown, NDP MLA
Eileen Dailly, NDP MLA
Pauline Jewett, NDP MP
Ms. Susan Mendelson
Dr. Henry Morgentaler
Harry Rankin, Vancouver Alderman
Svend Robinson, NDP MP
Bob Skelly, NDP Leader of the Opposition
Ms. Hilda Thomas

Notes for Chapter 1 — Feminism Arrives at SFU

[1] Wasserlein, Frances J. "'An Arrow Aimed at the Heart": The Vancouver Women's Caucus and the Abortion Campaign, 1969 — 1971." (master's thesis, Simon Fraser University, 1990), 33.

[2] Bernstein, Judy, Peggy Morton, Linda Seese, Myrna Wood. "Sisters, Brothers, Lovers...Listen..." Reprinted in *Women Unite!* Toronto: Canadian Women's Educational Press, 1972. 31-39.

[3] Wasserlein, 34.

[4] Wasserlein, 57.

[5] Wasserlein, 33-34.

[6] Wasserlein, 57.

[7] *The Peak.* Wednesday, July 3, 1968. 1.

[8] *The Peak.* Wednesday, July 10, 1968. 8.

[9] Toms, referring to a discussion with Margaret Benston and Brenda Morrow. In Wasserlein. 58.

[10] Wasserlein. 56.

[11] Brief biographies of major figures in the Women's Caucus appear in Wasserlein, 30-54. The information here draws on her research.

[12] Woodsworth, Ellen. In Wasserlein. 44-45.

[13] Benston, M.L. "on abortion." *The Peak.* September 25, 1968. 16.

[14] Maggie Benston is greatly missed since her death from cancer in 1991.

[15] Hoffer (as Davitt was then known) to L.N. Wilson, Dean of Student Affairs. Undated. Letter in Women's Caucus files.

[16] Lader, Lawrence. *Abortion II: Making the Revolution.* Boston: Beacon Hill Press. 1973. viii

[17] Ibid.

Notes for Chapter 2 — Background To Change in Law

[1] *Criminal Code of Canada,* Chapter C-34, Section 237 (adopted 1892). *See also* Morton, F.L. *Morgentaler v. Borowski: Abortion, The Charter, and the Courts.* Toronto. McClelland & Stewart. 1992. pp. 17-19.

[2] The precedent may have been set in 1937 when Ontario nurse Dorothea Palmer was acquitted of violating the Criminal Code sections banning dissemination of birth control. Even though the law remained on the books until 1969 and using birth control was not invasive, as abortion was, there seems to have been a societal relaxation on these sexual matters afterward, at least regarding the middle class. See Collins, Anne. *Abortion: The Issue That Won't Go Away.* Toronto. Lester & Orpen Dennys. 1985, p. 13.

[3] See Collins, pp.15-16, for a description of abortions performed in hospitals before 1969, and for the debate that led to reforming the law.

[4] Estimates of illegal abortions done in Canada vary wildly. In 1922, the Canadian Medical Association *Journal* estimated abortions at "somewhere between 7 and 14 per cent of live births."Vital Statistics for BC put the annual maternal death rate from abortion at 13.3 per cent in the 1930s. These were of women who died in hospital of botched backstreet procedures; countless other abortion-related deaths went uncounted. See McLaren, Angus and Arlene Tigar McLaren. *The Bedroom and the State: The Changing Practices and Politics of Contraception and Abortion in Canada, 1880-1997.* Second edition. Don Mills. Oxford University Press. 1997. pp. 44-53.

[5] Collins. pp.17-18

[6] Morton. 21. *The Globe and Mail*, December 20, 1967, 1, gives other figures: it says the Committee began hearings in June, 1967, held 17 meetings, received 18 briefs, and heard 49 witnesses. Collins, p. 16. Collins says the National Council of Women had 500,000 members.

[7] The British Columbia CMA adopted this position in 1961. See Collins, pp. 15-19 for a full account of the discussion of a new law before 1969.

[8] de Valk, Alphonse. 'Abortion in Canada, 1960 — 66.' In Kremer, E.J. and E.A. Synan, Eds. *Death Before Birth*. Toronto: Griffin House. 1974. 21-23.

[9] Dunphy, Catherine. *Morgentaler: A Difficult Hero*. Toronto: Random House of Canada. 1996. 62-65.

[10] Many sources. For example, see Pelrine, Eleanor Wright. *Abortion in Canada: The Reform that Hardly Was*. Toronto: new press. 1972.

[11] United Church of Canada. Proceedings of the 19th General Council, 1960. *Toward a Christian Understanding of Sex, Love, and Marriage*. Kindly lent to the author by Rev. Jim Manly, former NDP MP.

[12] Editorial. 'Hypocrisy and Abortion." *Vancouver Sun*. Wednesday, August 23, 1961. 4.

[13] Editorial. "B.C.'s Abortion Industry." *Vancouver Sun*. Thursday, August 24, 1961. 4.

[14] Ardies, Tom. "Even Dogs Fare Better." *Vancouver Sun*. Friday, August 25, 1961. 1.

[15] Ibid.

[16] McLaren, Angus and Arlene T. McLaren. *The Bedroom and the State*. 2nd ed. p. 136.

[17] Gifford Jones, W. *On Being a Woman: The Modern Woman's Guide to Gynecology*. Toronto. McClelland & Stewart. 1969. p.82. (The origin of this claim was in a 1960 series on abortion in *The Saturday Evening Post*, by John Bartlow Martin; it was also quoted by Tom Ardies in the *Vancouver Sun* in August 1961. 'W. Gifford-Jones,' cited here, is the pen name of Dr. Kenneth Walker of Toronto, whose syndicated column on health appears in publications across North America.)

[18] Barbara Hestrin, interview by author, August 4, 2000, Vancouver, British Columbia, tape recording.

[19] Ibid.

[20] Dr. Marion Rogers and Dr. Roger H. Rogers, interview by author, January 6, 1996, Vancouver, British Columbia, tape recording.

[21] Ibid.

[22] Ibid.

[23] Ibid.

[24] Ardies. *Vancouver Sun*. Monday, August 28, 1961. 8.

[25] 'Prosecutor Raps Doctors for Silence on Abortions." *Vancouver Sun*. Thursday, August 24, 1961. 1.

[26] "Abortion Probes Not Doctor's Duty." *Vancouver Sun*. Friday, August 25, 1961. 10.

[27] Ardies. *Vancouver Sun*. August 25, 1961.

[28] Ardies, T. and John Arnett. "Abortion Law Relaxation Urged." *Vancouver Sun*. August 30, 1961. 1-2.

[29] Morton. 20.

[30] de Valk. 15.

[31] "Vancouver lawyers to ask probe of abortion laws." *Vancouver Sun*. September 12, 1961. p.1

[32] Biographers Stephen Clarkson and Christina McCall state that Trudeau's remark was "borrowed directly from an editorial written by Martin O'Malley that week for the *Globe and Mail.*" *Trudeau and Our Times.* Vol. I, "The Magnificent Obsession." Toronto: McClelland & Stewart. 1990, p. 107.

[33] de Valk, Alphonse. "Abortion in Canada, 1960-66." p.64

[34] de Valk, Alphonse. "Abortion Politics, Canadian Style." In Sachdev, Paul, Ed. *Abortion: Readings and Research.* Toronto. Butterworths. 1981. p.8

[35] Ibid.

[36] McNeil, Gerald. "Bishops to be heard on abortion measure." *Vancouver Sun.* December 30, 1967. p.46

[37] de Valk. "Abortion Politics, Canadian Style."

[38] Morton. 26-27.

[39] "Abortion Clauses Emerge Unscathed After Debate." *Vancouver Sun.* Saturday, May 10, 1969. 33.

[40] Pelrine, Eleanor Wright. *Abortion in Canada.* p.31

[41] Pelrine. 34.

[42] Pelrine. 35.

[43] Ibid.

[44] Ibid.

[45] *Vancouver Sun.* May 10, 1969. 33.

[46] "Commons Legalizes Abortion; Criminal Code Filibuster Folds." *Vancouver Sun.* May 14, 1969. p.1

Notes for Chapter 3 — The Abortion Information Service

[1] Cohen, Marcy and Jean Rands. "A Report Back to the Simon Fraser Left on Women's Caucus Summer Organizing." September 1969. Mimeograph. Copy in Women's Caucus files.

[2] "Women's Caucus — A History and Analysis." Mimeograph. (no author cited; probably written in November 1970.) In Women's Caucus files.

[3] "Women's Caucus Program." Spring 1969. Mimeograph, in Women's Caucus files.

[4] Betsy Wood, interview by author, August 24, 1994, North Vancouver, B.C., tape recording.

[5] "Human Rights...but not for women." "By a B.C. Civil Servant." *Pedestal.* Fall (actually August) 1969. 1,3.

[6] Mary Stolk, lengthy personal communication (written interview), February 23, 1995.

[7] Donna Liberson, interview by author, October 24, 1994, Vancouver, B.C. tape recording.

[8] Ibid.

[9] Ibid.

[10] "Women's Liberation Demonstrates Here." *Georgia Straight.* October 22-29, 1969. 17.

[11] Wood interview.

[12] Stolk, Mary. "abortion information now available to all." *Georgia Straight.* December 3 — 10, 1969. p. 11. *Also* "Women's Group Seeks Abortion Law Change." *Province.* Thursday, December 11, 1969. p. 22. *Also* "'Butcher Abortionists' Target for Women's Group." *Vancouver Sun.* Thursday, December 11, 1969. p. 8.

[13] Stolk, interview.

[14] Ibid.

[15] Stolk, Mary. "Abortion Campaign." *Pedestal.* Winter 1969. p. 1.

[16] Liberson, interview.

[17] Helen Potrebenko, interview by author, Dec. 10, 1994, Burnaby, BC.

[18] Ibid.

[19] Stolk,Mary "Abortion Campaign." *Pedestal*. Winter 1969. p.1

[20] Potrebenko, interview.

[21] Helen Potrebenko, unpublished article, no date.

[22] Stolk, interview.

[23] Gray, Gratton. "Abortion, North American Style." *Georgia Straight*. December 31, 1969 — January 7, 1970. 2,3,5.

[24] Potrebenko, interview.

[25] Dr. Marion Rogers and Dr. Roger Rogers, interview by author, January 6, 1996, Vancouver, B.C., tape recording.

[26] Potrebenko, interview. Stolk, interview.

[27] Potrebenko, interview.

[28] Ibid.

[29] Liberson, interview.

[30] Ibid.

[31] Stolk, interview.

[32] Ibid.

[33] Liberson, interview.

[34] Reinholz, Mary. "Abortion clinic busted — doctors seek arrest to test law." *Georgia Straight*. April 1 — 8, 1970. 3.

[35] Helen Potrebenko. unpublished article, no date.

[36] Ibid.

[37] "The Abortion Clinic: Six Months Later." *Pedestal*. July 1970. 16.

[38] Helen Potrebenko. unpublished article, no date.

[39] "The Abortion Clinic: Six Months Later." *Pedestal*. July 1970. 16.

[40] Ibid.

Notes for Chapter 4 — Going Through the Proper Channels

[1] Betsy Wood, interview by author, 24 August 1994, North Vancouver, British Columbia, tape recording.

[2] Unsigned article the *Pedestal*, February, 1970.

[3] Moore, Diana. "Guerrilla theater." *Pedestal*. March 1970. p. 3.

[4] Unsigned. "Hundreds Protest Abortion Laws." *Pedestal* March, 1970. p. 3.

[5] Mitchell, Jeannine. "Abortion March a Success." *Georgia Straight*. February 18-25, 1970. p. 2.

[6] Ibid.

[7] Ibid.

[8] "Hundreds protest abortion laws." *Pedestal*. March, 1970. An undated letter from Women's Caucus member Alice James (in the Women's Caucus files) to a correspondent from the Unitarian Church credits Dr. Foulkes with directing the women to the most recent figures on abortion from the Dominion Bureau of Statistics: 100,000 illegal abortions in Canada per year, with 2000 deaths and 2000 more in hospital facing disability or death.

[9] "General Meeting Report — February 1970." Mimeograph in Women's Caucus files.

[10] Article by Vancouver Women's Caucus. "Trudeau Surprised." *Georgia Straight*. April 1-9, 1970. p. 1

[11] Rands, Jean, for the Women's Caucus. "Open Letter to Mary Lynn Hinston, Policewoman." *Georgia Straight*. March 25 — April 1, 1970. p. 8

[12] With bureaucratic ponderousness, the old and new abortion laws were later amalgamated, and the old parts were removed from the Criminal Code. The law was re-titled 'Section 251.'

[13] Letter from Vancouver Women's Caucus, M. Hollibaugh and B. Meadley [Wood] to Prime Minister Trudeau and the Ministers of Health and Justice, 19 March, 1970. Copy in Women's Caucus files. Printed in the *Pedestal*, April 1970. p. 8

[14] Weppler, Dodie to Health Minister Loffmark. Handwritten text in the Women's Caucus files.

[15] Wrotnowski, Dorothy. "Caucus Plans Protest on Abortion Practice." *Victoria Daily Colonist*. March 25, 1970. p. 24.

[16] Wood interview. *Also*, Alet McLeod, interview by author, Vancouver, BC, March 19, 1995, tape recording.

[17] 'Strangers in the House." *Pedestal*. April 1970. pp 1-3. *Also* 'Women Confront Loffmark."*Pedestal*. April 1970. p. 3.

[18] Ibid.

[19] "Strangers in the House.' *Pedestal*. April 1970. p. 1

[20] Mitchell, Jeannine. "Loffmark: 'some would be offended.'" *Georgia Straight*. April 1-8, 1970. p. 1

[21] Wood interview.

[22] 'They want simple change in law: get rid of the damned thing." *Vancouver Express*. Saturday, April 11, 1970. p. 4

[23] Beckman, Bonnie. "Trudeau Passes the Buck."*Pedestal*. April 1970. p. 2

[24] A copy of the telegram is in the Women's Caucus files.

[25] Mitchell, Jeannine. "Women Ordered from College." *Georgia Straight*. April 15-22, 1970. p. 3.

[26] Ibid.

[27] Ibid.

[28] Ibid.

[29] 'They want simple change in the law: get rid of the damn thing." *Vancouver Express*. April 11, 1970. p. 4

[30] Rogers, interview.

[31] Liberson, interview.

Notes for Chapter 5 — The Abortion Caravan

[1] Unsigned article. "Munro Agrees to Talk; Sask. women demonstrate for safe abortion." *The Pedestal*. May 1970. p. 2

[2] Photos. *The Pedestal*. May 1970. p. 1.

[3] Cynthia Flood, interview by author, tape recording, Vancouver, B.C., December 31, 1994.

[4] Margo Dunn, interview by author, tape recording, Vancouver, B.C., March 15, 1994; Mary Trew, interview by author, tape recording, Berkeley, California, July 30, 1995; Betsy Wood, interview by author, tape recording, Vancouver, B.C., August 24, 1994.

[5] Unsigned article. "B.C. Government Discriminates." *The Pedestal*. April 1970 p. 4.

[6] Betsy Wood, interview.

[7] Margo Dunn, interview.

[8] Wasserlein, Frances Jane. "'An Arrow Aimed At the Heart:' The Vancouver Women's Caucus and the Abortion Campaign, 1969-1971." (Master's Thesis, Department of History, Simon Fraser University, 1990). n. p. 87.

[9] Margo Dunn, interview.

[10] Unsigned article. "These Women Understand the Democratic Procedure." *The Pedestal*. June 1970. p 6.

[11] Jean Rands, interviewed by Wasserlein, Frances Jane. "'An Arrow Aimed At the Heart.' p. 94

[12] Margo Dunn, interview.

[13] Ibid.

[14] Mary Trew, interview; Betsy Wood interview.

[15] Margo Dunn interview.

[16] Rach, Lynne. "Abortion Caravan on Move." *Calgary Herald*. April 29, 1970.

[17] "Pregnant Women's Dilemma Depicted." *Calgary Herald*. April 19, 1970.

[18] 'Women's protest dramatizes horror of illegal abortions." *Edmonton Journal*. April 30, 1970.

[19] Ibid.

[20] Ibid.

[21] Margo Dunn and Mary Trew interviews. "These Women Understand the Democratic Procedure." *The Pedestal*. June 1970, p. 6.

[22] *Pedestal*, June 6, 1970, p.6.

[23] Margo Dunn interview.

[24] Betsy Wood interview.

[25] "Abortion caravan visits city." *Saskatoon Star-Phoenix*. May 1, 1970. p. 3.

[26] "Abortion group meets hostility."*Vancouver Express*. May 5, 1970. p. 21.

[27] Ibid.

[28] "Nixon surprises: orders troops into Cambodia." *Saskatoon Star-Phoenix*. May 1, 1970. p. 1

[29] Photo and story in *Georgia Straight*. April 22-29, 1970. pp.1-2.

[30] Mary Trew interview.

[31] Margo Dunn and Betsy Wood interviews.

[32] Weiers, Margaret. "Feminists demand no restrictions on abortions." *Toronto Star*. May 6, 1970.

[33] Vedan, Barbara. "Abortion Campaign Not Whole Story." and "An Open Letter to the Prime Minister." *Winnipeg Free Press*. May 4, 1970. p. 16.

[34] Letter to "Dear Dawn and Sisters" from Joan Baril, April 26, 1970. In the Women's Caucus files.

[35] *Women's Liberation Newsletter.* Thunder Bay. Undated. Copy in the Women's Caucus files.

[36] Mary Trew interview.

[37] "*Women's Liberation Newsletter*."Thunder Bay. Undated. Copy in the Women's Caucus files.

[38] Rajnovich, Nan. Letter bearing the imprint of the *Sault Daily Star*, to Betsy Meadley [Wood], dated April 20, 1970. Copy in Women's Caucus files.

[39] Margo Dunn interview.

[40] Trew, Mary. "On the caravan: How We Differ." *The Pedestal*. June 1970. pp. 1, 8-9.

[41] Margo Dunn interview. Dunn's memory is almost exact. The head line in *The Sudbury Star*, May 5, 1970, p. 1, read "Guardsmen Shoot Four Students; U.S. Swept by Wave of Protest."

[42] Margo Dunn interview.

[43] Mary Trew interview.

[44] Cathy Walker, interviewed by Wasserlein, Frances J. "'An Arrow Aimed At the Heart.' n. p. 93. Since the 1960s and 1970s, formerly sealed files have occasionally been made public, and it is no longer a secret that many branches of the police spied on feminist, left-wing, labour, and student groups, including the BC NDP government of 1970-73. An example of such an admission was Beeby, Dean. "RCMP spied on women's committee." *Vancouver Sun*. October 12, 1993. A10. Beeby wrote: "Intelligence officers began the 269-page secret file on the ground breaking [federal Status of Women] commission in 1968 and kept it open for four years, the documents indicate."

[45] Weiers, Margaret. "Feminists demand no restrictions on abortion." *Toronto Star*. May 6, 1970.

[46] "Abortion cavalcaders will attend meeting — will PM?" *Globe and Mail*. May 7, 1970.

[47] "300 expected to join abortion march on Ottawa." Toronto *Telegram*. May 7, 1970. p. 75.

[48] Weiers, Margaret. "Feminists demand no restrictions on abortions." *Toronto Star*. May 6, 1970.

[49] "300 expected to join abortion march on Ottawa." Toronto *Telegram*. May 7, 1970.

[50] Mary Trew interview.

[51] Margo Dunn interview.

[52] Mary Trew recalled these lyrics, interview by author.

Notes for Chapter 6 — Invading Parliament

[1] Wasserlein, Frances J. "'An Arrow Aimed At the Heart.' n. p. 97.

[2] "Birth control and abortion services in Canadian provinces vary from West Coast to East." *Globe and Mail*. October 9, 1970.

[3] Gillespie, John. "Where abortions are easier." *Globe and Mail*. June 24, 1971.

[4] Kreps, Bonnie. "Radical Feminism I." In *Women Unite!* Toronto: Canadian Women's Educational Press.1972 p.74

[5] Wood interview. All references to views of, or quotes from Betsy Wood are taken from the author's interview of her, August 24, 1994.

[6] O'Leary, Veronique and Louise Toupin. *Québecoise Deboutte!* Tome 1, *Une anthologie de textes du Front de liberation des femmes (1969-1971) et du Centre des femmes (1972-1975)* Montréal. Les editions du remue-menage. 1982. p. 71. The French text is quoted in Wasserlein, Frances J., *n.* p. 101. *See also* "FLF won't be along, but backs English." *Montréal Star*. May 8, 1970.

[7] Photo. *Toronto Star*. May 11, 1970.

[8] Telegram from Richard D. Hayes, Executive Assistant for the Minister of Justice, to the Women's Caucus. No date. Women's Caucus files.

[9] McCook, Sheila. *Ottawa Citizen*. Monday, May 11, 1970. p. 25. *Also*, Fisher, Douglas. "This noise of women gags voice of reason." *Vancouver Sun*. Tuesday, May 19, 1970.

[10] McCook, Sheila. *Ottawa Citizen*.

[11] "Angry Feminists Cry Out for 'Free Abortion' Laws." *The Ottawa Journal.* Monday, May 11, 1970.

[12] Power, Doris. "Statement to the Abortion Caravan, May 1970." In *Women Unite!* Toronto: Canadian Women's Educational Press. 1972. pp. 121-124.

[13] McCook, Sheila. *Also* Siggins Maggie. "Abortion law protesters take coffin to PM's home. Toronto *Telegram.* Monday, May 11, 1970.

[14] Pelrine, Eleanor Wright. *Morgentaler.* Scarborough, Ontario. Signet Books. 1976. pp. 64-76.

[15] Margo Dunn interview. References to the views of and quotations from Dunn are from the author's interview of her, March 15, 1994.

[16] Keate, Kathryn. "Out From Under, Women Unite." *Saturday Night Magazine.* July 1970. pp. 15-20.

[17] McDowell, Stan. "Abortion backers dump coffin at PM's door." *Toronto Star.* Monday, May 11, 1970.

[18] Becker, Susan. "Abortion Caravan sits in at 24 Sussex." *Montréal Star.* Monday, May 11, 1970.

[19] Keate, Kathryn. *Saturday Night Magazine.* July 1970. p. 17.

[20] "FLF won't be along, but backs English." *Montréal Star.* Monday, May 11, 1970.

[21] Dolan, Sandra. "Women seek abortion right on Mother's Day," and "Pressure abortion boards, doctor tells women's group." *Montréal Star.* Monday, May 11, 1970.

[22] Janz, Susan. "Coffin carried to protest abortion deaths." *Winnipeg Tribune.* May 11, 1970.

[23] "Marchers urge special clinics for abortions." *Edmonton Journal.* May 11, 1970. p. 22.

[24] Photo. *Georgia Straight.* May 13-20, 1970. p. 3.

[25] Margo Dunn and Betsy Wood interviews.

[26] Keate, Kathryn. *Saturday Night Magazine.* July 1970. p. 19.

[27] McKenna, Brian. "MPs study ways to curb disruptions." *Montréal Star.* Tuesday, May 12, 1970.

[28] Sanger, Clyde. "Angry women halt sitting of Parliament; Demand free abortions." *Globe and Mail.* Tuesday, May 12, 1970. p. 1

[29] Ibid.

[30] Ibid.

[31] Canada, House of Commons *Debates.* May 11, 1970. 6793.

[32] House of Commons *Debates.* May 11, 1970. 6796. The 'Hansard' record was also quoted by Sanger, Clyde. *Globe and Mail.* Tuesday, May 12, 1970. A2.

[33] Pape, Gordon. "Women yelling for abortion halt Commons." *Montréal Gazette.* Tuesday, May 12, 1970. pp. 1-2.

[34] Sanger, Clyde. *Globe and Mail.* Tuesday, May 12, 1970. pp. 1-2

[35] Tierney, Ben and Peter Calamai. "'Free-Abortionists' Bring House to Halt.' *Calgary Herald.* May 11, 1970.

[36] Sanger, Clyde. *Globe and Mail.* May 12, 1970.

[37] McKenna, Brian. "MPs study ways to curb disruptions." *The Montréal Star.* Tuesday, May 12, 1970.

[38] Sanger, Clyde. *Globe and Mail.* May 12, 1970.

[39] Pape, Gordon. *Montréal Gazette.* May 12, 1970.

[40] McKenna, Brian. *The Montréal Star.* May 12, 1970.

[41] Ibid.

[42] MacDonald, Wayne. "Protective shield urged for MPs, after women's 'invasion.'" *Vancouver Sun*. Friday, May 15, 1970.

[43] Connolly, Greg. 'House screams to a halt; Pro-abortion protest."*Calgary Herald*. May 11, 1970.

[44] Mackie, Victor. "Protesters Force House to Adjourn." *Winnipeg Free Press*. May 12, 1970.

[45] Ibid.

[46] Connolly, Greg. *Ottawa Citizen*. May 12, 1970.

[47] McKenna, Brian. *The Montréal Star*. May 12, 1970.

[48] Sanger, Clyde. *Globe and Mail*. Tuesday, May 12, 1970.

[49] Tierney, Ben and Peter Calamai. *Calgary Herald*. Monday, May 11, 1970.

[50] Sanger, Clyde. *Globe and Mail*. May 12, 1970.

[51] Ibid.

Notes for Chapter 7 — The Early 1970s

[1] Hobbs, Lisa. "Amateur abortions a large part of Toronto's everyday life: doctors; Figure may be hundreds a week."*Globe and Mail*. May 18,1970. p.1

[2] "Little Rise in Abortions: RC's, Québec, Small Hospitals Hesitate." *Victoria Times*. March 11, 1970. p 6.

[3] *Pedestal*. June 1970. p 1.

[4] Ablett, Dave. "Shouting abortion reformers get message from Pierre."*Vancouver Sun*. Saturday, May 30, 1970. p B3.

[5] Ibid.

[6] Gillen, Mollie. "Why Women Are Still Angry Over Abortion." *Chatelaine Magazine*. October 1970. p 34.

[7] Walker, John B. "Abortions in 1970 tripled to 11,200."*Province*. April 17, 1971.

[8] "Strategy."*Pedestal*. June 1970. p 2.

[9] Gibbs, Bev. "The Alternative Within Women's Caucus; the majority reply [to the splitters]."*Pedestal*. July-August, 1970. p 8.

[10] Flood, interview.

[11] Former Prime Minister Kim Campbell cannot remember attending the conference but considers the views attributed to her to be authentic, and she believes it must have been she who made them. Personal communication to author, June 15, 1999.

[12] "The Young Socialists' Position."*Pedestal*. July-August 1970. p 9.

[13] Ibid.

[14] "Where Are We Going? Strategy Conference, June 20, 21."*Pedestal*. July-August 1970. p 7.

[15] This slogan was later abandoned by feminists, because it was equally useful to anti-abortionists. It was replaced by the call, 'Repeal the [anti]Abortion Laws.'

[16] "Abortion death protested."*Vancouver Sun*. June 26, 1970. p. 28

[17] Curtin, Katie. "another woman dead: FREE ABORTION ON DEMAND." *Pedestal*. July-August, 1970. p 12

[18] Pat Davitt, interview by author, October 22, 1995, Vancouver, B.C., tape recording.

[19] MacDonald, Wayne. *Vancouver Sun*. November 24, 1970.

[20] "CMA says issue personal matter."*Vancouver Sun*. June 8, 1970.

[21] Pelrine, Eleanor Wright. *Morgentaler*. Scarborough. Signet, New American Library. 1976. p.64ff.

[22] "Abortion law attacked." *Vancouver Sun.* June 12, 1970.

[23] Angus, Don. "Thousands join New York women's parade." *Vancouver Sun.* Thursday, August 27, 1970. p 12.

[24] Trask, Peter. "Pastor admits abortion aid: Doctor Made $300,000 in Year." *Vancouver Sun.* Friday, September 18, 1970. p 21.

[25] Ibid.

[26] Ibid.

[27] Ibid.

[28] Quoted in "Abortions," *Georgia Straight,* September 23 — 30, 1970. p.6

[29] "Abortions." *Georgia Straight.* September 23 — 30, 1970. p 6.

[30] Trask. *Vancouver Sun.* September 18, 1970. p 21.

[31] "Dr. Makaroff Jailed." *Georgia Straight.* September 30 — October 9, 1970. p 9.

[32] 'Dr. Makaroff fined, jailed for abortions." *Vancouver Sun.* September 25, 1970. p 17.

[33] Ibid.

[34] "Abortions." *Georgia Straight* September 23 — 30, 1970. p 6

[35] Government of Canada. *Report of the Royal Commission on the Status of Women in Canada.* Florence Bird, Chair. 1970. pp. 281-286.

[36] Douglas, Mares, Cruikshank. 'The Abortion Campaign." *Women's Liberation News.* [published monthly by the Women's Liberation Alliance.] March, 1971. p. 3

[37] Cynthia Flood interview

[38] Heather Johnson, Carol La Bar and Gail Riddell, interview by author, November 18, 1995, Vancouver BC, tape recording.

[39] Perry Millar [formerly Becker], interview by author, July 8, 1995, Vancouver, BC, tape recording.

[40] Betsy Wood interview.

[41] Small item in *Women's Liberation News.* No date, but undoubtedly May, 1971. pp. 1-2. The six women who left later gave their reasons in an article: "Trot-Trot-Trotsky, Goodbye." *Georgia Straight.* June 1-4, 1971. p. 8.

[42] "Spaying may be only solution, Borowski suggests, as abortion controversy escalates in Winnipeg." *Globe and Mail.* August 18, 1971. p.9

[43] *Spokeswoman,* published by the Canadian Women's Coalition for Abortion Law Repeal (Toronto) in April-May, 1972 — citing statistics for 1969 given in an editorial in the *Globe and Mail.*

[44] Angus, Lis. "New goal: 100,000 signatures." *Spokeswoman.* Summer, 1972. p. 3.

[45] Taylor, Gwen. "International week of actions May 1-6" *Spokeswoman.* Summer, 1972. p. 4.

[46] For further information on Dr. Morgentaler in this period, see Collins, Anne. *The Big Evasion: Abortion the Issue That Won't Go Away.* Toronto. Lester & Orpen Dennys. 1985. *Also* Dunphy, Catherine. *Morgentaler: A Difficult Hero.* Toronto. Random House of Canada. 1996.

Notes for Chapter 8 — Hospital Board Elections: I

[1] McCarthy, Colman. "Abortion — and woman's soul." *Vancouver Sun.* April 2, 1971. p.29.

[2] Oberlyn, Ros. "Organized anti-abortionists to take lead in desperate fight for life." *Vancouver Sun.* June 24, 1978.

[3] Cuneo, Michael W. *Catholics Against the Church: Anti-Abortion Protest in Toronto, 1969-1985.* Toronto: University of Toronto Press. 1989. pp. 5-9.

[4] Francke, Linda Bird. *The Ambivalence of Abortion.* New York. Random House (Dell). 1979. pp.24-27.

[5] Mohr, James C. *Abortion in American: the Origins and Evolution of National Policy.* Oxford University Press. 1978.

[6] Gordon, Mary. *New York Review of Books.* No date. Back-cover blurb on Mohr's book.

[7] "Baby buying group defends actions." *Vancouver Sun.* October 20, 1977. A14.

[8] McLean, Bruce. "Money-for-babies ad was a premature ploy." *The Province.* October 30, 1977. p.37. The same tactic was tried again in Prince George: "Baby-cash ads drive moves to Prince George." *Vancouver Sun.* February 28, 1978. C1

[9] "Baby snatch advised." *Vancouver Sun.* June 30, 1979.

[10] B.C. Federation of Women Health Sub-Committee. *1977 Abortion Handbook for British Columbia.* Author's copy.

[11] "Hospital limits abortion zone." *Vancouver Sun.* October 5, 1970, p. 1. *Also* "Hospitals restrict abortions." *The Province.* October 6, 1970. p. 1

[12] Sarti, Bob. "2000 sign up for new fight over VGH abortion policy." *Vancouver Sun.* March 19, 1977.

[13] Volkart, Carol. "Anti-abortionists lose VGH election battle." *Vancouver Sun.* April 21, 1977.

[14] Moya, Miguel. "VGH faces glut of members." *Vancouver Sun.* July 8, 1978.

[15] Ibid.

[16] Ibid.

[17] "Abortion issue stalls VGH meeting." *Vancouver Sun.* August 21, 1978. A1.

[18] "Pro-lifers win in Powell River." *The Province.* June 16, 1978. p. 41.

[19] "Anti-abortionists hail cancellation of VGH meeting." *Vancouver Sun.* August 22, 1978. B1

[20] Trueman, Mary. "Specially equipped regional centres best places for safe abortions, Badgley report says." *Globe and Mail.* February 10, 1977. F3. *Also*, Nichols, Marjorie. "Abortion — a bad law lingers." *Vancouver Sun.* February 11, 1977. p.4

[21] BC Federation of Women Health Sub-Committee. *The 1977 Abortion Handbook for British Columbia. Also,* Alsop, Kay. 'Controversy over therapeutic abortion." *The Province.* March 2, 1978. p. 6. *and* Sarti, Bob. "Women's group hits arbitrariness in abortion policy." *Vancouver Sun.* March 4, 1978.

[22] *ICAR Newsletter and Manifesto.* 1978. Author's copy.

[23] "100,000 women join in massive protest." *Vancouver Sun.* April 3, 1976. *Also* Shuster, Alvin. "Italy in a Political Crisis over Abortion." *New York Times.* April 3, 1976. *Also* "Italy: Abortion Law OK'd." *Vancouver Sun.* January 22, 1977. And "Italy legalizes virtual free abortion on demand." *Globe and Mail.* May 19, 1978.

[24] Frankfort, Ellen and Frances Kissling. "Investigation of a Wrongful Death." *Ms. Magazine.* January 1979. pp. 66-82.

[25] See "We demand the right to choose." *Kinesis.* April/May 1979, p. 11. *Also* "Celebrating 20 years." *Kinesis.* March, 1994. P. 11. *Also.* Thomson, Ann. "Our work in the Vancouver abortion rights movement: CCCA". *Kinesis.* March 1994. p.3.

[26] Reid, Malcolm. "Life in Québec: Abortion-performing clinic exists uneasily in Québec." *Vancouver Sun.* December 17, 1979. A6.

[27] Roberts, Anne. "Second recount needed in vote between BC abortion factions." *Globe and Mail*. June 22, 1979. *Also* Houle, Ruth. 'Pro-choice plays catch-up.' *Priorities*. October, 1979.

[28] Padmore, Tim. 'Heroin act doomed, abortion reviewed, Mair says." *Vancouver Sun*. January 10, 1980.

[29] "Abortions becoming harder to get in smaller hospitals." *Vancouver Sun*. January 10, 1980.

[30] Still, Larry. "Abortion: Doctors walk tightrope on 'health' needs." *Vancouver Sun*. October 10, 1980.

[31] "VGH 'follows Criminal Code directives.'" *Vancouver Sun*. December 3, 1979.

[32] "Women's fed attacks Mair." *Vancouver Sun*. January 15, 1980. A18. The BC Federation of Women, the Vancouver Status of Women, the Coalition of BC Rape Crisis Centres, and CCCA are quoted in this article.

[33] Ibid.

[34] 'Sex education favoured by Mair over abortion." *Vancouver Sun*. January 16, 1980.

[35] "Victoria hospital rejects most abortion requests." *Vancouver Sun*. January 18, 1980.

[36] Maitland, Andrea. "Debate of women frays council tempers." *Vancouver Sun*. March 5, 1980.

[37] Reid, Gayla. "The night they crucified VSW at Vancouver City Hall." *Kinesis*. June 1980. *Also* Oakes, Jim. 'Status of Women: Paying the price for being pro-choice." *The West Ender*. March 27, 1980. p. 6.

[38] "CCCA escalates defence of abortion rights." *Kinesis*. April 1980. p. 24.

[39] The Revolutionary Workers League (RWL) resulted from a 1977 merger of Canadian Trotskists, including the League for Socialist Action, the Red Mole Group, and groups in Québec.

[40] "Mair sponsors abortion study." *Vancouver Sun*. May 30, 1980.

[41] Editorial. "Starting at the middle." *Vancouver Sun*. June 7, 1980.

[42] Thomas, Hilda. "Right to choose: 200 protest Mair's attacks on abortion rights." *Priorities*. July-August 1980. p.12

[43] Hunter, Dr. Marlene. "Abortion: an unwinnable battle." *Vancouver Sun*. September 4, 1980. p. 5. *Also* Volkart, Carol. "A bitter pill for some..." *Vancouver Sun*. June 7, 1980. B6. *Also* Bishop, Mary F. "Prevent unwanted pregnancies or arguing on abortion." *The Province*. July 2, 1980. B2.

[44] Gainor, Chris. "Pro-lifers win vote for Surrey hospital." *Vancouver Sun*. September 18, 1980.

[45] Gainor, Chris L."Mair 'won't interfere' in Surrey abortion fight." *Vancouver Sun*. September 25, 1980. A1

[46] Birrell, Margaret and Dixie Pidgeon. "WRC strategy for abortion law repeal." *Priorities*. July-August 1980. p. 13.

[47] Gainor, Chris. "Surrey hospital board votes to end abortions." *Vancouver Sun*. October 3, 1980.

[48] Gainor, Chris. "Surrey abortion showdown set." *Vancouver Sun*. October 7, 1980. A1

[49] Cohen, May. "Therapeutic Abortion and the Law." *Canadian Women's Studies*. Vol.2, No.4, 1980. pp. 94-96.

[50] "Surrey Compromise Fails: MDs stand firm in abortion crisis." *Vancouver Sun*. November 14, 1980. A9.

[51] "Gainor, Chris. L "Surrey abortion fight a step nearer solution." *Vancouver Sun*. November 25, 1980.

[52] Hossie, Linda. "Cityside" column. "It's not a matter for church or state." *Vancouver Sun*. December 1, 1980. The Sun also carried a four-column photo and story on the rally by Rob Klovance, on p. A3, while the December 1 *Province* devoted most of page one to its article and photo of the rally.

[53] Dr. Morgentaler's speech is reconstructed from several sources: the author's notes at the rally, and media articles including Hossie, Linda. "It's not a matter for church or state." and Klovance, Rob. "'Pro-life' supporters 'fanatical busybodies.'" *Vancouver Sun*. December 1, 1980. '*Province* Staff Reporter:' 'MD calls for abortion on demand." *The Province*. December 1, 1980. Klingenberg, Felicia. "Campaign launched to repeal abortion laws." *Globe and Mail*. December 4, 1980. T4.

[54] "Abortions continue to climb." *Vancouver Sun*. Dec. 17, 1980.

Notes for Chapter 9 — Hospital Board Elections: II

[1] Doris Anderson gives the figure of 1300 in *Rebel Daughter*, p. 244. On March 5, 1981, the *Vancouver Sun* reported 1200 at the conference, while the *Globe and Mail*, on February 14, 1981, p. 16, reported "600 to meet in defiance of [cabinet minister Lloyd] Axworthy."

[2] Anderson, Doris. *Rebel Daughter*. p. 245.

[3] Morton, F.L. *Morgentaler v. Borowski*. p. 110-111.

[4] Ibid., pp.112-116.

[5] "Resolution introduced: Ban abortions, Congress told." *Globe and Mail*. January 23, 1981. p.15

[6] Cuneo, Michael W. *Catholics Against the Church: Anti-Abortion Protest in Toronto, 1969-1985*. Toronto. University of Toronto Press. 1989. p. 47.

[7] G. Emmett Cardinal Carter. 'Charter of Rights." *Catholic Register*. April 4, 1981. Quoted in Cuneo, p.49.

[8] *Toronto Star*. April 11, 1981.

[9] "Anti-Abortionists Write Pope to Condemn Carter." *Toronto Star* April 30, 1981. p. 1

[10] Letter from Campaign Life (signed by members of the Toronto and national executives) to His Holiness John Paul II, May 12, 1981 Quoted in Cuneo, pp. 49-50.

[11] Cuneo, Michael W. *Catholics Against the Church*. p.54

[12] *The Interim*. September 1983. Quoted in Cuneo, p. 57.

[13] 'Nielsen ponders doctors' plea: abortion issue at Surrey Memorial." *Vancouver Sun*. June 9, 1981. A1

[14] Ibid.

[15] Ferry, Jon. "Surrey doctors boycott Pro-Life hospital board." *The Province*. July 15, 1981. A4.

[16] "Chairman raps abortion charge." *Vancouver Sun*. July 16, 1981.

[17] "Abortion row 'not serious.'" *The Columbian*. Monday, June 22, 1981. p.1

[18] "Hospital Abortion Dispute: Surrey trustees up in air." *Vancouver Sun*. June 24, 1981. A16.

[19] Emi Yoshida, a Richmond pro-choice activist, in phone call to author, June 29, 1981.

[20] The *Vancouver Sun* ran two photos of the scuffle on page 1, June 30, 1981. Accompanying a lengthy story by Ted Alden, "Pro-lifers grab hospital board," the *Richmond News* also ran a photo of three guards holding back the cowboy on July 8, 1981. p. 1.

[21] Alden, Ted. "Pro-lifers grab hospital board." *Richmond News.* July 8, 1981. pp.1 & 10.

[22] Kieran, Brian. "Peacekeeper tackles task at Surrey Memorial Hospital." *Vancouver Sun.* August 13, 1981.

[23] 'Surrey OKs abortions; Trustees, MDs agree." *The Province.* February 7, 1982. A5.

[24] "Anti-abortionists lose out." *Vancouver Sun.* September 3, 1981.

[25] Townsend, Ted. "Abortion groups clash at Surrey hospital." *Vancouver Sun.* September 10, 1981. A3

[26] "Two factions still arguing about anti-abortion rally." *Vancouver Sun.* September 12, 1981.

[27] Ibid.

[28] Krieger, Robert A. Letter to the editor. *The Province.* September 23, 1981. B2.

[29] Gainor, Chris. "Anti-abortionists win at Victoria hospital.' *Vancouver Sun.* September 11, 1981.

[30] "Pro-abortion groups rally." *Vancouver Sun.* September 14, 1981.

[31] "'Fight for your rights,' abortion rallies told." *The Province.* September 13, 1981. p. 1

[32] 'Abortion issue boiling." *Vancouver Sun.* August 25, 1981. A12. And "'Pro-Lifers' Defeated." *Vancouver Sun.* September 24, 1981.

[33] 'Anti-abortionists join another hospital board." *Vancouver Sun.* October 16, 1981. G8.

[34] 'Pro-lifers re-elected to board." *Vancouver Sun.* October 10, 1981.

[35] 'Abortion foes focus on Victoria election." *The Province.* November 20, 1981. p. 7

[36] "RGH adopts abortion compromise: decision reached secretly." *Richmond Review.* February 26, 1982. p.1

[37] "Surrey OKs abortions; Trustees, MDs agree.' *The Province.* February 7, 1982. A5. *Also* "Tighter abortion rules see decline in Langley." *Vancouver Sun.* September 22, 1982. A3.

[38] "Hospital board, doctors tangling over abortions." *Vancouver Sun.* February 27, 1982.

[39] 'Hospital ruling reserved." *Vancouver Sun.* October 14, 1982.

[40] "Anti-Abortion suit fails: ex-directors hit Lions Gate." *Vancouver Sun.* May 17, 1983. A15.

[41] "Borowski 'very weak;' anti-abortion fast continues." *Vancouver Sun.* July 18, 1981. *Also* "Anti-abortionist calls off fast." *Vancouver Sun.* July 20, 1981. A16.

[42] Dickens, Bernard M. "Abortion: 2. Fetus status and legal representation." *Canadian Medical Association Journal.* Vol.124, February 1, 1981, 253-254. (Dr. Dickens was on the Faculty of Law at the University of Toronto.)

[43] Nikiforuk, Andrew. "Ready to start illegal abortion clinics across Canada, Morgentaler states." *Globe and Mail.* April 26, 1981. pp. 1-2.

[44] "Women need ready access to safe medically-insured abortions." Full-page ad in the *Globe and Mail,* sponsored by the Ontario Coalition for Abortion Clinics. November 12, 1982.

[45] Landsberg, Michele. "Women's group behind plans for abortion clinic." *Toronto Star.* November 4, 1981. *Also* Roseman, Ellen. "Abortion clinics: the battle is on." *Globe and Mail.* November 8, 1982. *Also* Sabia, Laura. "Her Decision." *Toronto Sun.* November 9, 1982.

[46] Morgentaler, Henry. *Abortion and Contraception.* Toronto. General Publishing. 1982.

[47] Kome, Penny. "Free-standing abortion clinics," in 'Woman's Place' column, *Homemaker's Magazine* March 1983. 72D-72I

[48] Morgentaler. *Abortion and Contraception.* pp.146.

[49] Morgentaler. p.143-144.

[50] Eddy, Kathleen. "When Does Life Begin? Does Science Have the Answer?" *CCCA Newsletter.* February 1982. pp. 8-9

[51] 'U.S. Senate defeats Anti-Abortion Bill." *CARAL Newsletter.* Toronto. Fall, 1982. p. 14.

[52] Ibid.

Notes for Chapter 10 — Dr. Morgentaler Fights Back

[1] The figure of 4000 abortions in the US for Canadian women in 1981 came from the Alan Guttmacher Institute in New York. Statistics Canada's total for legal hospital abortions in Canada that year was 65,053, which did not include the number performed in Québec clinics or done clandestinely. Nolte, Judith. "Canadian abortion statistics aren't complete." *News-Nouvelles; Journal of Planned Parenthood Federation of Canada.* Vol. 4, No. 1, 1983. p.11.

[2] Reagan, Ronald. *Abortion and the Conscience of the Nation.* Nashville TN. 1983

[3] Greenhouse, Linda. "High Court Clears Up Any Doubts on Abortion." *New York Times.* June 19, 1983. E7. Reprinted in the September 1983 *CCCA Newsletter,* p. 17.

[4] Collins, Anne. *The Big Evasion.* p. 63.

[5] Morton, F.L. *Morgentaler v. Borowski* p 156.

[6] Ibid.

[7] *Montréal Gazette* December 1, 1982. Cited in Dunphy, Catherine. *Morgentaler: A Difficult Hero.* p. 205.

[8] Collins, Anne. p. 61.

[9] *Globe and Mail.* May 7, 1983. Quoted in Morton, F.L. p. 155.

[10] Morton, p. 159.

[11] Morton, p. 160.

[12] Morton, p. 159.

[13] Collins, p. 82.

[14] Dunphy, Catherine. pp.216-221.

[15] Dunphy, p. 218.

[16] Lamb, Jamie. "Fondness for past plagues the NDP." *Vancouver Sun.* July 2,1983.

[17] The text of these resolutions was reprinted, with several other articles about the embattled clinics in Winnipeg and Toronto, in *Priorities,,* August 1983. pp.11-15. NDP women continued to be hostile to CCCA, but they firmly called for repeal of the abortion law.

[18] Collins, p. 83.

[19] Douglas, Karen and Joan Newbigging. 'Defend Winnipeg abortion clinic!" *Socialist Voice.* May 16, 1983. pp. 6-7.

[20] Leona Gom gave CCCA permission to re-print her poems in its December, 1983 *Newsletter,* pp. 12-13. She also authorized including a poem in this book.

[21] *Vancouver Sun.* October 3, 1983. A12.

[22] Morton, F.L. pp.131-153.

[23] Ochs, Karen. 'Northern BC women denied choice for abortion." *Kinesis.* November 1984. p.3

[24] *CCCA Newsletter.* November, 1984, p. 9. *Also* Trotter, Maureen. 'Quesnel Transition House: Woman Fights Anti-Choice Clause." *Kinesis.* February 1985. p. 17.

[25] "Anti-Abortion group probed." *Vancouver Sun.* October 10, 1984.

[26] Cronin-Wohl, Lisa. "Antiabortion violence on the Rise: How Far Will it Go" *Ms. Magazine.* October 1984. p. 138.

[27] Cronin-Wohl, Lisa. *Ms. Magazine*. October 1984. p. 135.

[28] Ibid.

[29] Ibid. *Also*, Thomson, Ann. "Firebombed Everett Clinic Re-Opens with Rally.' *CCCA Newsletter*. April 1984. .

[30] Peterson, Ron. "New Right Takes Aim at Abortion." *CCCA Newssletter*. April 1984.

[31] CARAL National Office leaflet, "Summary of the Constitutional Challenge Decision, July 20, 1984." p.5

[32] Callwood, June. "Strange Judicial Reasoning." *Globe and Mail*. July 27,1984. p14.

[33] "Anti-abortion Leader blasts Campagnolo," *Vancouver Sun*. August 1, 1984.

[34] Photocopies of three Campaign Life leaflets, given to the author by Svend Robinson.

[35] *Montréal Gazette*. August 18, 1984 B1

[36] All quotes are from "Turner says posterior-patting is part of his political style." *Globe and Mail*. July 21, 1984. p. 1

[37] Cruikshank, John et al. "Issue of trust left hanging after debate." *Globe and Mail*. August 16, 1984.pp 1,4.

[38] Windsor, Hugh. "Trust question cuts through words." *Globe and Mail*. August 16, 1984. p.2

[39] Robertson, Heather. 'Women vs. The Pope." *Chatelaine*. September 1984. pp.62-62, 158-166.

[40] "A Diversity of Opinions Regarding Abortion Exists Among Committee Catholics." *New York Times*. Sunday, October 7, 1984. E7.

[41] Sisters of Notre Dame Patricia Hussey and Barbara Ferraro (no relation to Geraldine), who signed both ads, eventually left their order. Their book, *No Turning Back: Two Nuns Battle with the Vatican over Women's Right to Choose* (New York. Poseidon Press. 1990) documents the movement of dissenting American nuns and the church's ferocious determination to silence them.

[42] Makin, Kirk. "Canada's complex abortion laws cause delays, danger, court told." *Globe and Mail*. October 27, 1984. pp. 1-2.

[43] "Women enslaved by abortion law: witness." *Vancouver Sun*. October 31, 1984.

[44] Makin, Kirk. "Long abortion delays are recounted at trial." *Globe and Mail*. October 26, 1984. pp.1-2.

[45] 'Morgentaler on the stand." *Vancouver Sun*. October 31, 1984. A11.

[46] Makin, Kirk. "Anarchy foreseen if Morgentaler freed." *Globe and Mail*. November 3, 1984.

[47] Butters, Brian. "U.S. abortion supporters outraged by bombs." *Also*, "Bombings 'gift to Jesus.'" Both in the *Vancouver Sun*. Friday, January 4, 1985.

[48] Woodward, Kenneth and Mark D. Uehling. "The Hardest Question.' *Newsweek*. January 14, 1985. p. 29.

Notes for Chapter 11 — A Big Year in Vancouver

[1] "Operation unavailable in some areas." *Vancouver Sun*. January 12, 1985. A1, A10.

[2] Bohn, Glenn and Larry Still. "Abortion: Weekend Special." *Vancouver Sun*. January 12, 1985. A1,A10,A11.

[3] "Abortion equipment damaged." *Vancouver Sun* Tuesday, January 29, 1985. A3. *Also* "Court Orders restitution over abortion equipment." *Globe and Mail*. October 12, 1985. D10. *Also* Moir, Rita. "Nelson polarized by abortion battle." *Globe and Mail*. November 4, 1985. H3.

[4] Horwood, Holly. 'Abortion article causes uproar." *The Province*. Saturday, February 26, 1985.

[5] Communication from A. Keamarden, author's files.

[6] "Abortion battle rages: demonstrator splatters doctor with catsup." *Vancouver Sun*. January 16, 1985. A13.

[7] "Choice under attack." *Kinesis*. February 1985. p. 1.

[8] Read, Jeanie. "Questions, no answers." *The Province*. April 14, 1985. p. 49.

[9] Long, Wendy. 'Morgentaler now plans BC clinic in four months." *Vancouver Sun*. April 13, 1985. F18.

[10] Ibid.

[11] Ibid.

[12] 'Anti-abortion protest urged." *Vancouver Sun*. April 3, 1985. A12.

[13] 'One Man's 16-Year Crusade." *The Province*. April 7, 1985. p. 27.

[14] "3 abortion foes arrested at rally: no charges laid." *Vancouver Sun*. February 22, 1985.

[15] Ferry, Jon. "3000 hurl abuse." *The Province*. April 14, 1985.

[16] Ibid..

[17] Ouston, Rick. "'I won't kill my baby,' pregnant teen insists." *Vancouver Sun*. April 15, 1985. A10.

[18] Baldrey, Keith. "Abortionist wants clinics in BC: Morgentaler plans to ask Victoria for aid." *Vancouver Sun*. April 15, 1985. A10.

[19] Ibid..

[20] Author's copy of April 20, 1985 letter to Chief Constable R.J. Stewart, Vancouver Police, from Janet Shaw for CCCA.

[21] Author's report to CCCA of Maguire's speech to the CARAL AGM, April 18, 1985.

[22] Maguire, Marjorie. "Personhood, Covenant, and Abortion." *American Journal of Theology and Philosophy*. Vol. 6, no. 1. January 1985. pp. 28-39.

[23] Quotes from Gardner, Rebick, and Morgentaler are taken from a "succinct summary of the minutes from the bi-national strategy meeting held during the CARAL AGM on May 5, 1985," prepared by OCAC. In author's files.

[24] Adams, Michael, Donna Dasko and Yvon Corbeil. "Majority in survey want better access to legal abortions: the *Globe*-CROP Poll." *Globe and Mail*. June 17, 1985. p.15. In the US, a poll by ABC News in January, 1985, found that 53% of Catholics were in favour of "abortion on demand"— higher than the 52% of all Americans with that view.

[25] "Priest convicted in attack on abortion clinic." *Vancouver Sun*. May 1, 1985. F12.

[26] "Anti-abortionists elected at hospital." *Vancouver Sun*. June 27, 1985. A14.

[27] "MDs called upset over vote." *Vancouver Sun*. September 27, 1985. A13. The hospital board election meeting in Vernon was held on September 22.

[28] Conn, Heather. "Catholic feminists fighting for choice." *Kinesis*. September 1985.

[29] Thompson, Joey. "Sterilized in error." *Province*. June 4, 1985. p. 5

[30] "Women's Health & Family Planning." *Telus — Journal of Planned Parenthood Federation of Canada*. Spring 1985. p. 10.

[31] Coalition for Reproductive Choice. 'Abortion is a Woman's Choice." Winnipeg. 1984. p. 11. In author's files.

[32] Morton, F.L. *Morgentaler v. Borowski*. pp. 211-213.

Notes for Chapter 12 — Take-Over of CCCA

[1] Testimony of Suzanne Arundel-Ross, quoted in Fisher, Barrett. "Choice group puts abortion laws on trial." *North Shore News* Friday, January 24, 1986, pp.9-10. Print media reports on the Tribunal appeared in the following: O'Brien, Jan. "Abortion stories." *The Province*. Friday, January 24, 1986, p.54. *Also* Middleton, Greg. "Laws are a crime." *The Province*. Sunday, January 26, 1986. *Also* "Women's tribunal 'convicts' abortion law in mock trial." *Vancouver Sun*. Monday, January 27, 1986. *Also* 'Love on trial.' *The Democrat*. February 1986, p.8. *Also* Lang, Gretchen. "Speaking out for choice." *Kinesis*. February 1986, p.8. — On the other hand, *The Province* ran a full-page story with photo by "Staff Reporter" called "One couple's story of abortion trauma" on January 19, 1986, p.4, about a young woman who believed her abortion was "the most tragic mistake of her life."

[2] Herman, Lisa. "Abortion abuse cited by Rogers.' *Vancouver Sun*. March 29, 1986. A1, A2.

[3] Mason, Gary. "Bennett faulted by Skelly." *Vancouver Sun*. Friday. April 4, 1986. A1.

[4] "Bennett won't demand Nielsen's resignation." *Vancouver Sun*. February 1, 1986. A13.

[5] "US abortion victory." *Kinesis*. July/August 1986. p.13.

[6] Ibid.

[7] Typed statements: "Goals for the next 6-12 months," "CCCA Steering Committee Proposal for the Establishment of a Free Standing Abortion Clinic Planning Committee," and typed Minutes of the June 17, 1986 CCCA meeting. In author's files.

[8] Quotations are from the author's detailed notes of the July 3, 1986 CCCA Clinic Planning Committee meeting, as well as from the official Minutes of that meeting. Blackmore's description of who attended the launch of a Reproductive Health Clinic was made at the July 15, 1986 CCCA regular meeting.

[9] Bowen, Beverly. "Teachers coached in fighting abortion." *Globe and Mail*. Friday, July 11, 1986. A11.

[10] Savein, Nelson. "A Doctor's Perspective on Abortion Clinics." CCCA *Newsletter*. (prepared for August, issued in October, 1986)

[11] Editorial. "Grass Fire on Whistler." *Vancouver Sun*. July 31, 1986. B4.

[12] Mason, Gary and Keith Baldery. *Fantasyland: Inside the Reign of Bill Vander Zalm*. Toronto. McGraw-Hill Ryerson. 1989. p.16.

[13] Palmer, Vaughn. "A man who came in from the cold." *Vancouver Sun*. Thursday, July 31, 1986. B4. *Also* Bolan, Kim. "Convention payoff tale called false.' *Vancouver Sun*. Friday, August 1, 1986. B1.

[14] Mason, Gary and Keith Baldery. *Fantasyland*. p.25.

[15] Canadian Press. *Toronto Star*. August 1, 1986 A1. *Calgary Herald*. July 31, 1986. A5. *Montréal Gazette*. August 2, 1986. B1.

[16] Editorial. "Grass fire on Whistler." *Vancouver Sun*. Thursday, July 31, 1986. B4.

[17] "Vander Zalm vows abortion rate study." *Toronto Star*. Saturday, August 2, 1986. A12.

[18] "Premier asks for abortion report." *Vancouver Sun*. Tuesday, August 16, 1986. A12.

[19] Delacourt, Susan. 'Curtailing of abortions shows need for clinics, pro-choice groups say." *Globe and Mail*. June 24, 1986. A18.

[20] Montgomery, Sue. "Abortions in hospitals said costing up to $400." *Toronto Star*. Friday, July 25, 1986. A1.

[21] Morton. F.L. *Morgentaler vs. Borowski*. Chapter 18, pp.218-230, and quote from p. 222.

[22] Thomson, Ann. "CCCA working to establish abortion clinic." *Kinesis*. September 1986. p.1

[23] Macdonald, Joanne. "Abortion clinic slated for city in '87." *Vancouver Sun.* September 13, 1986.

[24] Ibid.

[25] 'A-G serves warning against abortion clinic." *Vancouver Sun.* September 17, 1986.

[26] Written statement from the CCCA Steering Committee, presented at the September 16, 1986 CCCA meeting, and item in the Minutes of the same meeting, recording that the motion of censure carried, with one abstention.

[27] Author's notes of a September 24, 1986 phone call from a CCCA activist.

[28] Author's notes of October 18, 1986 CCCA conference to discuss opening a clinic, with Toronto guests Dr. Nikki Colodny, Carolyn Egan, and Norma Scarborough. Participants' comments are as exact as possible, but because they are not corroborated by a written record, they are identified within half quotation marks.

[29] Ibid.

[30] "Access crisis in Powell River." *Pro-Choice News.* Quarterly publication by CARAL Toronto. Summer 1986. p. 9.

[31] Fletcher, Anne. "Abortion splits MDs in Vernon." *Vancouver Sun.* November 10, 1986. *Also* Mullens, Anne and Chris Wong. "Doctors oppose board for position on abortion." *Vancouver Sun.* November 1986. *Also* Hall, Neal. "Hospital faces abortion issue power struggle." *Vancouver Sun.* December 23, 1986.

[32] Mullens, Anne. "St. Paul's Hospital won't rule out all tubal ligations." *Vancouver Sun.* October 17, 1986.

[33] Cox, Sarah. "Abortion clinic due in city within year." *Vancouver Sun.* October 17, 1986.

[34] Mason, Gary and Keith Baldrey. *Fantasyland; Inside the Reign of Bill Vander Zalm.* 1989. p.64.

[35] Mason and Baldrey. p. 59.

[36] Hall, Neal. "Premier draws fire for abortion fee probe." *Vancouver Sun.* December 20, 1986 A1.

[37] Fletcher, Anne. "Doctor counters abortion stand." *Vancouver Sun.* December 22, 1986. A1.

[38] Tose, Chris. "Adoption bid backed to reduce abortions." *Vancouver Sun.* December 24, 1986. A1.

[39] See photo by Greg Finch, *Vancouver Sun,* December 1988, included in Mason and Baldrey. *Fantasyland.*

[40] Mason and Baldrey. p. 60.

Notes for Chapter 13 — 1987 — The BC Coalition for Abortion Clinics

[1] Lee, Jeff. "Abortion clinic vowed despite closure threat." *Vancouver Sun.* January 23, 1987. A3.

[2] Fitterman, Lisa. "Premier's moral stand against abortion seen as election winner." *Vancouver Sun.* January 30, 1987. B2.

[3] Ibid.

[4] Price, Cathie. "End run to outlaw legal abortions." *Vancouver Sun.* January 9, 1987. Letters page.

[5] Stowe, Barbara, Johanne Paradis, Katharine D. Hunt. "The butchers are history." *Vancouver Sun.* January 27, 1987. Letters page.

[6] Nichols, Marjorie. "Vander Zalm's BC: it's anti-abortion...but hates kids." Column in *Vancouver Sun.* January 16, 1987.

[7] Editorial. "Parliament must act on abortions." *The Province*. Sunday, January 18, 1987. *Also*, several articles on abortion by Ann Rees, *The Province*, January 18, 1987. pp.4-5

[8] "Abortions belong in clinics, not hospitals, doctor says." *Vancouver Sun*. January 14, 1987. A1.

[9] Actually, CCCA had received a letter dated January 19, 1987 from the NDP Women's Rights Committee, signed by Sadie Kuehn and Sandra Bruneau, advising us of its plans. It said the WRC was holding meetings to "get clear in our own minds what the differences are between the NDP policy on abortion...and your position to push for free-standing clinics...We felt it was important for you...to know that at the [January 25 clinic coalition founding] meeting, many of us will be supporting a position consistent with NDP policy: full health-care clinics which provide abortion and other health care services for women. The Women' Rights Committee of the Party has taken this position, because (a) we believe it to be the right one for women's total health care, and (b) we believe the position stands a greater chance of acceptability by the people of this province, perhaps even by the government." However, CCCA did not share this letter with conference organizers.

[10] Minutes of Conference to Establish a BC Abortion Clinic Coalition, Sunday, January 25, 1987, p.6.

[11] Goodman, Ellen. "The central character keeps disappearing." *Vancouver Sun*. January 22, 1987.

[12] For example, because more doctors refused to refer women for hospital abortions, the number performed at the Toronto Morgentaler clinic more than doubled in 1986, from 1600 in 1985 to 3,500. Adamick, Paula. "Abortions at Morgentaler clinic doubled because MDs refuse referrals, women told." *Toronto Sunday Star*. January 11, 1987. A12.

[13] Barrett, Tom. "Abortion: More BC Hospitals say no." *Vancouver Sun*. March 4, 1987. B1-B2.

[14] "Teen has abortion after court fight." *Toronto Star*. January 2, 1987. A22.

[15] "Teenager says 'I'm glad' of abortion." *Vancouver Sun*. January 2, 1987. A10.

[16] Harrington, Denise. "Special abortion clinics urged." *Toronto Star*. January 30, 1987. A1.

[17] "Area abortion centres urged for Ontario." *Vancouver Sun*. January 30, 1987. A10.

[18] Scarborough, Norma. "Crombie's wise decision." Pro-Choice News. Winter 1987. p.3

[19] Canadian Press. "Abortion penalties predicted." *Vancouver Sun*. March 23, 1987. The article refers to a study for the federal solicitor-general's department by Simon Fraser University criminologist, Ezzat Fattah, who found in 1976 that "Canadians who favour the death penalty also generally favour use of the strap in schools and harsher sentences for all crimes. He said they also generally oppose abortion and parole or early release of offenders." A University of Western Ontario professor was quoted to the effect that "Fattah's profile of capital punishment advocates has been found 'again and again' in countless other studies."

[20] The story was given continuing coverage in *Pro-Choice News*: Winter, 1987, p.2; Spring, 1987, p. 2; Summer, 1987, pp.8-9.

[21] "Anti-Choice Win Vernon Board Election." CARAL. *Pro-Choice News*. Fall/Winter 1987. p.13.

[22] "Dueck spurns doctors in abortion dispute." *Vancouver Sun*. April 21, 1987. A10/

[23] "Abortion committee called illegal." *Vancouver Sun*. February 12, 1987.

[24] Bolan, Kim and Gary Mason. "Abortion legalities checked." *Vancouver Sun*. April 22, 1987.

[25] Compiled from: Fletcher, Anne. "Kamloops board chief won't act on abortion refusal." *Vancouver Sun*. April 28, 1987. A3. *Also* Teichroeb, Ruth. "Teenage abortion refused." *The Province*. April 28, 1987. p.4 *Also* "Abortion rejection jolted referring MD." *Vancouver Sun*. April 29, 1987. *Also* Teichroeb, Ruth. "Father's Fight." *The Province*. April 29, 1987. p.3.

[26] Fletcher, Anne. "Pro-choicers win Kamloops abortion battle." *Vancouver Sun*. June 19, 1987. A22.

[27] Fletcher, Anne. "Pro-choicers still control Lions Gate." *Vancouver Sun*. June 25, 1987. A16.

[28] Based on notes of the meeting taken by the author.

[29] Based on typed Minutes of the meeting and detailed notes taken by the author.

[30] From author's detailed notes of the March 22, 1987 BCCAC general membership meeting.

[31] Remarks attributed to participants at the March 22, 1987 BCCAC general meeting are based on the typed Minutes and on the author's detailed notes. Because hastily noted quotes may not be exactly right, they are not placed in full quotation marks. The gist of each speaker's intention is given, as faithfully as possible.

[32] "The abortion report...should help put to rest a myth or two — prime among them the perception that many women rely on abortion as a form of family planning. The report found that just isn't the case." Editorial. "Abortion stand off." *Vancouver Sun*. March 31, 1987. B4.

[33] Mullens, Anne. "Report receives mixed reaction." *Vancouver Sun*. March 31, 1987. B3.

[34] Barrett, Tom. "Premier predicts tighter abortion control in BC." *Vancouver Sun*. March 31, 1987. B3.

[35] Knickerbocker, Nancy. "Morgentaler supports policy free of religion." *Vancouver Sun*. April 4, 1987.

[36] Rauhala, Ann. "Religion is key for anti-abortionists, study finds." *Globe and Mail*. April 2, 1987. A1, A5. *Also* "Religion called central to abortion foes' lives." *Vancouver Sun*. April 2, 1987 A6.

[37] Author's notes of meeting held April 5, 1987 at Britannia community centre.

[38] "NDP resolution urges abortion clinic here." *Vancouver Sun*. April 11, 1987. A1. *Also* Baldrey, Keith and Tom Barrett. "NDP backs labour ties, abortion clinic, poverty fight.' *Vancouver Sun*. April 13, 1987. A3.

[39] "Langley teachers opposed to clinic." *Langley Times*. March 8, 1987.

[40] Barrett, Tom and Douglas Todd. "Victoria would fight bid to set up abortion clinics, premier says." *Vancouver Sun*. March 17, 1987. A10.

[41] Minutes of August 10, 1987 meeting of BCCAC clinic sub-committee. It was agreed to take a proposal to find a doctor to the October general membership meeting. Meantime, a letter to doctors went through many drafts by members of the clinic sub-committee, on which the author sat.

[42] Horwood, Holly. "Doctors hold off." *The Province*. October 19, 1987. p.4.

[43] Every news story about the demo quoted the $800,000 figure — the first BCCAC had heard of it. See 'Pro-choice group seeks defence fund." *Vancouver Sun*. October 19, 1987. p.1. *Also* Horwood, Holly. "Doctors hold off." *The Province*. October 19, 1987. p.4. *Also* Howes, Noreen. "BC Coalition for Abortion Clinics: building support." *Kinesis*. November 1987. p.3

[44] Minutes of BCCAC Steering Committee meeting, October 21, 1987.

Notes for Chapter 14 — Morgentaler and Vander Zalm

[1] Makin, Kirk. "Abortion law scrapped; women get free choice." *The Globe and Mail.* Friday, January 29, 1988. A1. *Also,* Dunphy, Catherine. *Morgentaler: A Difficult Hero.* Toronto. Random House of Canada. 1996. pp. 306-307.

[2] Boei, William, Kim Bolan and Gary Mason. "Pro-choice groups vow fight against BC abortion stand." *Vancouver Sun.* Friday, January 29, 1988. A1, A2.

[3] Ibid.

[4] Ibid.

[5] Fraser, Graham. "Ottawa promises to act quickly to establish new abortion policy." *Globe and Mail.* Saturday, January 30, 1988. A1, A2.

[6] Makin, Kirk. "Abortion law scrapped; women get free choice." *Globe and Mail.* January 29, 1988. A1, A2, A7, A9-A10.

[7] Day, Shelagh and Stan Persky, Eds. *The Supreme Court of Canada Decision on Abortion.* Vancouver. New Star Books. 1988.

[8] Wilson, Justice Bertha. "Reasons for Judgment in Morgentaler, Scott, and Smoling. In Day and Persky, eds. p. 127.

[9] Wilson, Justice Bertha. p. 133.

[10] Wilson, Justice Bertha. p. 133.

[11] Wilson, Justice Bertha, as quoted in the Commentary by Shelagh Day, ed., in *The Supreme Court of Canada Decision on Abortion.* Vancouver. New Star Books. 1988. p. 180.

[12] Wilson, Justice Bertha. p. 143.

[13] Wilson, Justice Bertha, and quotations from Joad, C.E.M., "Guide to the Philosophy of Morals and Politics." In Day and Persky, pp. 140-142.

[14] "...Court" *Vancouver Sun.* Thursday, January 28, 1988. A2

[15] Information about the provinces' responses, condensed from "Across Canada: In the Wake of the Supreme Court's Decision," CARAL, *Pro-Choice News,* Spring 1988, pp. 4-6: abortions remained unavailable in PEI and Newfoundland; in Nova Scotia, access dropped because one of the 10 hospitals that had had TACs withdrew all abortion service. Vandals hurled rocks through the windows of the Morgentaler clinic in Montréal, and while the TACs at 30-35 hospitals in Québec were disbanded, pro-choice activists charged that some of these hospitals quit providing the service. The Morgentaler Clinic in Winnipeg eventually re-opened, after a fight for return of the equipment seized by police and a renewal of the doctors' licences by the College of Physicians and Surgeons. In provincial elections, the Manitoba NDP was replaced by the Tories under Gary Filmon, who campaigned on a promise of permitting no abortion clinics, but after months of obduracy, Filmon was forced to back down. The best response was in Ontario, where TACs were scrapped, and the government began paying for doctor's fees (but not for overhead or operating costs) in clinics. The governments of the western provinces — Saskatchewan, Alberta, and BC — dug in their heels, sought to retain TACs, and one way or another prohibited abortions.

[16] "Dueck Fights Clinics: BC refuses to pay for abortions on demand; Morgentaler Wins Historic Case." With two pages of stories by Holly Horwood, Barbara McLintock, and Olivia Scott. *The Province.* Friday, January 29, 1988. pp. 1, 4-5.

[17] Horwood, Holly and Olivia Scott. "First BC clinic may open by June." *The Province.* Friday, January 29, 1988. p. 5.

[18] Scott, Olivia. "Pro-lifers slam stand by BCMA." *The Province.* Wednesday, February 3, 1988. p. 4

[19] "BC doctors to defy Dueck on abortion committees." *Vancouver Sun.* Tuesday, February 2, 1988. A1,A2.

[20] Hendrickson, Bob. "Dueck to stand by his guns." *The Province.* Tuesday, February 2, 1988.

[21] "BC doctors to defy Dueck on abortion committees." *Vancouver Sun.* Tuesday, February 2, 1988. A1,A2.

[22] Bolan, Kim. "Dueck claims he can find MDs for panel." *Vancouver Sun.* Wednesday, February 3, 1988. A3.

[23] Mason, Gary and Keith Baldrey. *Fantasyland: Inside the Reign of Bill Vander Zalm.* Toronto. McGraw-Hill Ryerson. 1989. P. 180. *Also,* Corbella, Licia. "Dueck vs. Docs." *The Province.* Sunday, February 7, 1988. p.3.

[24] Mason, Gary and Keith Baldrey. *Fantasyland.* p.181.

[25] Corbella, Licia. "Dueck vs. Docs." *The Province.* February 7, 1988. p. 3

[26] Horwood, Holly. "'I had to do it'— Premier." *The Province.* Monday, February 8, 1988. p. 4.

[27] Mason and Baldrey. *Fantasyland.* pp. 181-183.

[28] Ibid.

[29] Ibid. pp. 184-185. *Also* Baldrey, Keith. "Abortion option rapped." *Vancouver Sun.* Wednesday, February 10, 1988. B7.

[30] Editorial. "Abortion policy mocks justice." *The Province.* Monday, February 8, 1988. p. 18.

[31] Mason and Baldrey. *Fantasyland.* p. 185.

[32] McLintock, Barbara. "Funding Cut." *The Province.* Tuesday, February 9, 1988. p. 3

[33] Boei, William. 'Hospitals question government abortion policy." *Vancouver Sun.* Tuesday, February 9, 1988. A9.

[34] Boei, William. "Hospitals readied for paid abortions." *Vancouver Sun.* Wednesday, February 10, 1988. A1,A2.

[35] Bolan, Kim and William Boei. "BC doctors referring women to U.S. clinics for abortions." *Vancouver Sun.* Tuesday, February 9, 1988. A1,A2. *Also* Scott, Olivia. 'Some sent to Wash." *The Province.* Tuesday, February 9, 1988. p.3

[36] Boei, William. "Hospitals readied for paid abortions." *Vancouver Sun.* Wednesday, February 10, 1988. A1,A2.

[37] Bolan, Kim. "$205 fee, possible second opinion among new abortion rules at VGH." *Vancouver Sun.* Friday, February 12, 1988. A3.

[38] Boei, William. "Hospitals readied for paid abortions." *Vancouver Sun.* Wednesday, February 10, 1988. A1A2.

[39] Scott, Olivia. "Girl, 12, wants abortion." *The Province.* Wednesday, February 10, 1988. p. 4. *Also* Boei, William. "Hospitals readied for paid abortions." *Vancouver Sun.* Wednesday, February 10, 1988. A1,A2.

[40] Kieran, Brian and Licia Corbella. "'Halt Funding'" *The Province.* Sunday, February 7, 1988. C3

[41] Bolan, Kim. "Pro-choice group vows to fight Vander Zalm on abortion issue." *Vancouver Sun.* Monday, February 8, 1988. B8.

[42] Tytherleigh, Mike. "Premier shows hostility to women." *The Province.* February 10, 1988. p. 6.

[43] Boei, William. "Civil liberties group plots abortion action." *Vancouver Sun.* Wednesday, February 10, 1988. B7.

[44] Parton, Nicole. "A dangerous man surrounded by simpering sycophants."*Vancouver Sun*. February 11, 1988.

[45] Parton, Nicole. "Welcome to the backlash, Mr. Vander Zalm." *Vancouver Sun*. February 12, 1988. B3.

[46] "Socred breaks ranks over abortion policy."*Vancouver Sun*. Friday, February 12, 1988. A1,A2.

[47] Baldrey, Keith. "Three more Socreds query abortion stand." *Vancouver Sun*. Saturday, February 13, 1988. A1,A2.

[48] Editorial. "A citizen's arrest is the only route." *Vancouver Sun*. Saturday, February 13, 1988. B4.

[49] Boei, William. "Second opinions on abortions creates controversy." *Vancouver Sun*. Saturday, February 13, 1988. A3.

[50] Ibid.

[51] "Richmond abortions end: hospital fears legal problems."*Vancouver Sun*. Wednesday, February 17, 1988. A1,A2.

[52] Bolan, Kim. "Abortion fund for rape, incest no answer, pro-choicers say." *Vancouver Sun*. Friday, February 19, 1988. A3.

[53] "VGH wants cash up front for abortions." *Vancouver Sun*. Thursday, February 18, 1988. A1.

[54] "BC premier a 'fanatic' on abortion: Morgentaler." *Montréal Gazette*. Saturday, February 13, 1988. A3.

[55] Bolan, Kim. "Abortion policy skipped BC medical committee." *Vancouver Sun*. Monday, February 15, 1988. A1,A2.

[56] "12-year-old got abortion with gifts." *Vancouver Sun*. Monday, February 15, 1988. A2.

[57] Bolan, Kim. "BC policy on abortion faces challenge." *Vancouver Sun*. Tuesday, February 16, 1988. A1,A2.

[58] Ibid.

[59] Ibid.

[60] "VGH wants cash up front for abortions."*Vancouver Sun*. Thursday, February 18, 1988. A1.

[61] "5th MLA at odds on abortion." *Vancouver Sun*. Tuesday, February 16, 1988. A2.

[62] Volkart, Carol. "McCarthy favours second abortion look."*Vancouver Sun*. February 17, 1988. A3.

[63] Mason, Gary and Kim Bolan. "Abortion pay available: Criminal act fund open to rape, incest victims."*Vancouver Sun*. Thursday, February 18, 1988. A1,A2.

[64] Editorial. "Abortion shift changes little."*Vancouver Sun*. Friday, February 19, 1988. B2.

[65] Parton, Nicole. "Verily, verily, what fresh revelations." *Vancouver Sun*. February 18, 1988. B3.

[66] Mullens, Anne. "Abortion policy hypocritical, BC's female doctors say."*Vancouver Sun*. Friday, February 19, 1988. A1

[67] "Doctors asked for abortion policy." *Vancouver Sun*. Thursday, February 18, 1988. B6.

[68] "Abortion ruling sets off provincial policy scramble." *Vancouver Sun*. Friday, February 19, 1988. F12.

[69] Boei, William. "Cash-first abortions challenged." *Vancouver Sun*. Saturday, February 20, 1988. A1,A2.

[70] Bolan, Kim. "'Back-door' abortions ruled out." *Vancouver Sun*. Monday, February 22, 1988. A1.

[71] "BC Catholics urged to fight eased abortion laws." *Calgary Herald*. Tuesday, February 23, 1988. C2.

[72] Editorial. "Mature consensus needed on abortion." *Vancouver Sun*. Wednesday, March 2, 1988 B2.

[73] Pemberton, Kim. "Secularism felt factor in poll." *Vancouver Sun*. Monday, March 7, 1988. A1.

[74] Bolan, Kim. "Doctors volunteer their time: Pro-choice group drafts plans for abortion clinic." *Vancouver Sun*. Monday, February 22, 1988. A3.

[75] Mason, Gary and Keith Baldrey. "Socred still firm on abortions." *Vancouver Sun*. Tuesday, February 23, 1988. B1,B4.

[76] Baldrey, Keith. "Abortion issue draws protests." *Vancouver Sun*. Thursday, February 25, 1988. B5.

[77] Mason, Gary. "Premier says Poole acted correctly." *Vancouver Sun*. February 24, 1988. A10.

[78] Mason, Gary and Keith Baldrey. "Abortions not only issue, premier says." *Vancouver Sun*. Wednesday, February 24, 1988. A11.

[79] Parton, Nicole. "Resign, gentlemen, resign." *Vancouver Sun*. Wednesday, February 24, 1988. B3.

[80] Palmer, Vaughn. "Socred hand language speaks volumes." *Vancouver Sun*. Thursday, February 25, 1988. B2.

[81] Baldrey, Keith. "Vander Zalm pledges to block abortion clinic." *Vancouver Sun*. Saturday, February 27, 1988. A1,A2.

[82] Bolan, Kim and Gary Mason. "Premier welcomes debate on abortion." *Vancouver Sun*. Monday, February 29, 1988. A3.

[83] Mullens, Anne. "Early fetus said unable to feel pain." *Vancouver Sun*. Wednesday, March 2, 1988. B1,B7.

[84] Vander Zalm, William. Text of ministerial statement to the legislature, printed in full under the head "Abortion: The premier lays down his views" in *Vancouver Sun*. Tuesday, March 1, 1988. F8.

[85] Mason and Baldrey. *Fantasyland*. pp. 189-191.

[86] Baldrey, Keith. "Surrey NDP MLA expelled for calling premier coward." *Vancouver Sun*. Tuesday, March 1, 1988. A2.

[87] "Government pay favoured 2-1, CBC poll says." *Vancouver Sun*. Tuesday, March 1, 1988. A2.

[88] Mason and Baldrey. *Fantasyland*. p.187-188.

[89] Vander Zalm, William. Text: "Abortion: The premier lays down his views." *Vancouver Sun*. March 1, 1988. F8.

[90] Boyd, Denny. "Moderate majority awaits a reasoned debate." *Vancouver Sun*. March 3, 1988. A3. *Also* Parton, Nicole. Column. "Such unforgivable ignorance." *Vancouver Sun*. March 2, 1988. B3.

[91] "Socred raps premier's hard line." *Vancouver Sun*. Thursday, March 3, 1988. A1,A2.

[92] Palmer, Vaughn. "The premier should be a better listener." *Vancouver Sun*. March 3, 1988. B2.

[93] Boei, William. "BC says no to premier." *Vancouver Sun*. Saturday, March 5, 1988, A1,A8. *Also* Baldrey, Keith. "'I have never governed by polls.'" *Vancouver Sun*. Saturday, March 5, 1988. A8. *Also* Editorial. "Premier must heed those he serves." *Vancouver Sun*. Saturday, March 5, 1988. B4.

[94] "PM ponders free vote on abortion." *Vancouver Sun*. Monday, March 7, 1988. A1.

[95] Boei, William. "Abortion policy sunk; B.C. chief justice vetoes Socred regulation." *Vancouver Sun*. Tuesday, March 8, 1988. B7.

[96] Boei, William and Gary Mason. "Premier vows to fight on; Court rules medicare must pay for abortions." *Vancouver Sun*. Tuesday, March 8, 1988. A1,A2.

[97] Parton, Nicole. "Where there's Bill there's a way." *Vancouver Sun*. Wednesday, March 9, 1988. B3.

[98] Mason, Gary and Kim Bolan. "BC doctors must decide when abortion necessary, BCMA says." *Vancouver Sun*. Thursday, March 10, 1988. A3.

[99] Bolan, Kim. "Province to refund all abortion fees." *Vancouver Sun*. Friday, March 11, 1988. A3.

[100] Baldrey, Keith. "Premier vows to court on abortion." *Vancouver Sun*. Saturday, March 12, 1988. A1,A2.

[101] Bolan, Kim. "Anti-abortion policy to stress marriage." *Vancouver Sun*. Monday, March 14, 1988. B5.

[102] The $4.4 million figure was cited in Bolan, Kim. "Women doctors urge birth control measures." *Vancouver Sun*. Saturday, March 12, 1988. A12.

[103] Bolan, Kim. "Anti-abortion policy to stress marriage." *Vancouver Sun*. Monday, March 14, 1988. B5.

[104] Bolan, Kim. "Family aid group shuns abortion issue." *Vancouver Sun*. Tuesday, March 15, 1988. B7.

[105] Southam News. "No agreement on abortion law." *Vancouver Sun*. Saturday, March 19, 1988. A7.

[106] Bryden, Joan. "Ottawa considering abortion limits." *Vancouver Sun*. Thursday, March 10, 1988. A8.

[107] "Turner balks at airing party abortion policy." *Vancouver Sun*. Wednesday, March 30, 1988. A10.

[108] "Clinic backers oppose bid to restrict abortions." *Vancouver Sun*. Thursday, March 17, 1988. B1.

[109] "Coalition argues women better off without any national abortion law.' *Vancouver Sun*. Friday, March 25, 1988.

[110] Baldrey, Keith. "BC awaits federal abortion move." *Vancouver Sun*. Tuesday, March 22, 1988. B4.

[111] "Group challenges BC on abortion." *Calgary Herald*. Wednesday, March 24, 1988. A3.

[112] Volkart, Carol. "Abortion row in Richmond shaping up." *Vancouver Sun*. Friday, March 18, 1988. A3.

[113] "No-abortion hospitals challenged." *Vancouver Sun*. Saturday, September 24, 1988. A1.

[114] Sarti, Robert. "Family campaign panned; NDP critic says women ignored." *Vancouver Sun*. Wednesday, April 6, 1988. B5.

[115] Mason and Baldery. *Fantasyland*. p. 194

[116] Palmer, Vaughn. "Four days that shook Social Credit." *Vancouver Sun*. Friday, April 8, 1988. B2.

Notes for Chapter 15 — A Summer of Excitement

[1] Bettie Scheffer, interview by author, August 20, 1992, Vancouver, BC, tape recording. Further quotes from Scheffer, or other members of the BCCAC Steering Committee, are taken from the interviews listed here.

[2] Anne Hamilton, interview by author, August 23, 1992, Vancouver, BC, tape recording.

[3] Ibid..

[4] Joy Thompson, interview by author, August 20, 21, 25, 1992, Vancouver, BC, tape recording.

[5] Hilda Thomas, interview by author, July 16, 1992, Vancouver, BC, tape recording.

[6] Pat Katagiri, interview by author, August 8, 1992, Langley, BC, tape recording.

[7] Drena McCormack, interview by author, July 27, August 10, 1992, Vancouver, BC, tape recording.

[8] Ruth Houle, interview by author, July 17, 1992, Vancouver, BC, tape recording.

[9] Sharon Hager, interview by author, August 26, 1992, Vancouver, BC, tape recording.

[10] Jean Rands, interview by author, September 3, 1992, Vancouver, BC, tape recording.

[11] Author's notes of April 13, 1988 BCCAC Steering Committee meeting.

[12] Author's notes of May 4, 1988 BCCAC Steering Committee meeting, and interview with Pat Katagiri.

[13] Parton, Nicole. "Former A-G Smith admits pro-choice group spied on: Detectives worked undercover." *Vancouver Sun*. Tuesday, July 26, 1988. A1,A2.

[14] Parton, Nicole. "The infiltration caper: why Brian Smith had to talk." Column in *Vancouver Sun*. Wednesday, July 27, 1988. B3.

[15] Baldrey, Keith. "Knowledge of secret probes part of resignation, Smith says." *Vancouver Sun*. Thursday, August 25, 1988. A1.

[16] Mason, Gary, Keith Baldrey, Kim Bolan. "Changing the Guard: McCarthy exit shakes Socreds." *Vancouver Sun*. Wednesday, July 6, 1988. A1,A2.

[17] Nicole Parton, interview by author, August 18, 1994, North Vancouver, BC, tape recording.

[18] Parton, Nicole. *Vancouver Sun*. Tuesday, July 26, 1988. A1, A2.

[19] Parton, Nicole. *Vancouver Sun*. Wednesday, July 27, 1988. B3.

[20] Crane, Donald, for the BC Law Union. Letter to the *Vancouver Sun*. Saturday, July 30, 1988. B4.

[21] The figure of $145,337 appeared in the *Sun* on Wednesday, July 27, 1988, p. A2. Smith's estimate of $12,000 for the spy caper appeared in Nicole Parton's original scoop on Tuesday, July 26, 1988, p. A2.

[22] Kieran, Brian and Don Hauka. "Spies since '83." *The Province*. Thursday, July 28, 1988. p. 5

[23] Cruikshank, John. "Vander Zalm denies role in spying on group." *Globe and Mail*. Wednesday, July 27, 1988. A1. *Also*, Kavanagh, Jean, Gary Mason and Keith Baldery. "Release of A-G reports, spying probe demanded." *Vancouver Sun*. Wednesday, July 27, 1988. A1,A2.

[24] Editorial. "Abortion caper a very bad joke." *The Province*. Wednesday, July 27, 1988. Cartoon by Murphy. p. 22 cc. *Also* 'Bill's root cause of spying fiasco." Editorial. *The Province*. Thursday, July 28, 1988. p. 26.

[25] Editorial. "Who in Victoria stooped to snoop?" *Vancouver Sun*. July 27, 1988.

[26] Except for the reference to Georgetti in the *Province* (note 30, above), all other quotes are from Kavanagh, Jean, Gary Mason and Keith Baldrey. "Release of A-G reports, spying probe demanded." *Vancouver Sun*. July 27, 1988. A1,A2.

[27] Rose, Chris and Sarah Cox. "Investigation of pro-choice group heavy-handed, police say." *Vancouver Sun*. Thursday, July 28, 1988. A1,A2.

[28] Cox, Sarah. "Morgentaler amused, enraged by spy caper." *Vancouver Sun*. July 29, 1988. A8.

[29] Rose, Chris and Sarah Cox..*Vancouver Sun*. July 28, 1988. A1, A2.

[30] Volkart, Carol. "Ombudsman to investigate pro-choice spying complaints." *Vancouver Sun*. July 29, 1988. A1,A2. *Also* Wilson, Deborah. "BC Ombudsman probes spying case." *Globe and Mail*. July 30, 1988. A5.

[31] Parton, Nicole. "NDP milking spy scandal, detectives say." *Vancouver Sun*. July 28, 1988. A10. Note: Nicole Parton came to have confidence in the professional skills of Larry and Marzena Banks, and at her request, the two gave me an interview on July 13, 1995. They were both very aggrieved by the public lack of appreciation for their work and the doubts cast upon their integrity, which they defended to me for two hours. In the end, they added nothing to what had been reported in the media in 1988.

[32] Baldrey, Keith. "Abortion spying poor judgment, Owen finds." *Vancouver Sun*. August 24, 1988. A1,A2.

[33] "Text of abortion motion" presented by the federal minister of state Douglas Lewis on July 26. *Globe and Mail*. July 27, 1988. A4.

[34] O'Neil, Peter. "BC Tory urges more emphasis on birth control." *Vancouver Sun*. July 27, 1988. *Also* Bryden, Joan. "MPs poles apart in abortion debate." *Vancouver Sun*. July 27, 1988. *Also* Fraser, Graham. "McDougall calls for choice as House debates abortion." *Globe and Mail*. July 28, 1988. A1,A3. *Also* "MPs can't make law." *The Province*. July 29, 1988. p. 6. *Also* O'Neil, Peter. "MPs defeat all motions on abortion." *Vancouver Sun*. July 29, 1988. A1.

[35] Bryden, Joan. "Anti-abortion Tories rebel: MPs want no delay in court case." *Vancouver Sun*. July 15, 1988. A8.

[36] Canadian Press. "Supreme Court rejects request to delay hearing abortion case." *Vancouver Sun*. Tuesday, July 19, 1988. A1

[37] Diamond, Sara. *Spiritual Warfare: The Politics of the Christian Right*. Boston. South End Press. 1989. p. 91.

[38] Brozan, Nadine. "503 Held in Abortion Protest on E. 85th St." *New York Times*. May 3, 1988. *Also* Brozan, Nadine. "Effectiveness of Abortion Protests is Debated." *New York Times*. May 8, 1988. A28.

[39] "Anti-Abortion Demonstrators Face Fines of $25,000 a Day." *New York Times*. May 5, 1988. B3.

[40] Smothers, Ronald. "Atlanta Protests Prove Magnet for Abortion Foes." *New York Times*. August 13, 1988. A6.

[41] Associated Press. "134 Against Abortions Are Arrested in Atlanta." *New York Times*. July 20, 1988. A19. *Also* Associated Press. "Abortion Foes Jailed in Atlanta." *New York Times*. July 30, 1988. *Also* Associated Press. "69 More Opponents of Abortion Jailed in Atlanta Protests." *New York Times*. August 7, 1988. A20. *Also* Smothers, Ronald. "Atlanta Protests Prove Magnet for Abortion Foes." *New York Times*. August 13, 1988. A6. *Also* "31 Abortion Protesters Freed in Atlanta After 40 Days in Jail." *New York Times*. August 29, 1988.

[42] Interview with Anne Hamilton.

[43] Author's notes of BCCAC Steering Committee meeting, August 30, 1988.

[44] Author's notes of BCCAC Steering Committee meeting, September 6, 1988.

Notes for Chapter 16 — Everywoman's Health Centre Opens

[1] Blain, Joanne. "Abortion clinic to bill Victoria." *Vancouver Sun*. September 10, 1988. A22. *Also*, Dawson, Lea. "Everywoman's Health Centre opens soon." *Kinesis*. October 1988. p. 4.

[2] Author's recollections of BCCAC general membership meeting, September 10, 1988, and author's notes of BCCAC Steering Committee meeting, September 13, 1988.

[3] MacDonald, Gary. "Pro-choice groups ponder court fight for clinic funding." *Vancouver Sun*. September 12, 1988. A8.

[4] Ibid.

[5] Editorial. "Clinic plan an answer to abortion." *The Province*. September 9, 1988. p.34

[6] Letter to: "All Affiliates" from the B.C. Federation of Labor Executive Council and president Ken Georgetti, dated September 15, 1988. Copy in author's files.

[7] Parton, Nicole. "A simply outrageous MALE accusation." *Vancouver Sun*. September 14, 1988. B3.

[8] Hunter, Justine. "Three more quit board of anti-abortion organization." *Vancouver Sun*. September 22, 1988. A3. *Also* Hunter, Justine. "Anti-abortion group said to be in turmoil." *Vancouver Sun*. September 15,1988. A15.

[9] Leidl, Pat. "Anti-abortion group leader under fire from ex-members." *Vancouver Sun*. October f3, 1988. B4.

[10] Lorena Kanke, M.D., interview by author, December 23, 1992, Vancouver, BC, tape recording.

[11] Ibid.

[12] Culbert, Lori. "Botched abortion spurred crusade." *Vancouver Sun*. July 12, 2000. p. A3.

[13] Minutes and author's notes of September 20, 1988 BCCAC Steering Committee meeting.

[14] Vienneau, David. "Pro-life activist brings remains of two fetuses to Supreme Court." *Toronto Star*. October 5, 1988. p. 3

[15] McQueen, Ken. "Hearing lacks abortion law." *Vancouver Sun*. October 4, 1988. A6.

[16] Morton, F.L. *Morgentaler v. Borowski: Abortion, The Charter, and the Courts*. Toronto. McClelland and Stewart. 1992. pp. 271-272.

[17] Horwood, Holly. "Abortion clinic sparks fury." With color photo of anti-abortionist on page one. *The Province*. October 7, 1988, pp. 1,3. *Also* Hunter, Justine. "Clinic site picked, anti-abortionists say." *Vancouver Sun*. October 7, 1988. A1, A9.

[18] Los Angeles Times wire service. "Abortion clinics hit by protesters." *Calgary Herald*. October 5, 1988. A15.

[19] Associated Press. "Anti-abortionists regroup." *Calgary Herald*. October 8, 1988. B4.

[20] Associated Press. "Police arrest 2,000 activists." with photo. *Calgary Herald*. October 30, 1988 A3

[21] Joy Thompson, interview by author, August 25, 1992, Vancouver, BC, tape recording.

[22] Reported to BCCAC Steering Committee meeting of October 12, 1988. From author's notes.

[23] Patricia Katagiri, interview by author, August 8, 1992, Langley, BC, tape recording.

[24] Minutes of BCCAC Steering Committee meeting, November 16, 1988.

[25] Telephone code names hark back to the legendary network of lay activists who ran 'Jane,' an underground abortion service in Chicago from the late '60s, until *Roe v. Wade* made abortions legal in 1973. They performed at least 11,000 abortions, and none of their clients died.

[26] Author's notes of October 26, 1988 BCCAC Steering Committee meeting.

[27] Author's notes of November 9, 1988 BCCAC Steering Committee meeting.

[28] Bolan, Kim. "Abortion foes plan to march outside first B.C. clinic." *Vancouver Sun*. Friday, November 4, 1988. A12. *Also* Minutes of November 9, 1988 BCCAC Steering Committee meeting.

[29] Author's notes of Dr. Kanke's report to October 26, 1988 BCCAC Steering Committee meeting.

[30] Ibid.

[31] Minutes of November 9, 1988 BCCAC Steering Committee meeting.

[32] Helene Wisotzki, interview by author, September 2, 1992, Vancouver, BC, tape recording.

[33] "Premier invited to abortion clinic opening." *Vancouver Sun*. October 25, 1988. F8.

[34] Bolan, Kim. "300 protest abortion clinic opening." *Vancouver Sun*. November 5, 1988. A3.

[35] Collins, Anne. *The Big Evasion: Abortion, the Issue That Won't Go Away*. Toronto: Lester & Orpen Dennys. 1985. p. 13.

[36] Speeches by Robin LeDrew, Dr. Lorena Kanke, Margaret Mitchell, Johanna den Hertog, Anne Harvey, Elaine Bernard, and Hilda Thomas, to the Everywoman's Health Centre rally at the Hotel Vancouver, Saturday, November 5, 1988. Tape recording by author.

[37] Author's notes of Monday, December 5, 1988 BCCAC Steering Committee meeting.

[38] Author's notes of December 7, 1988 BCCAC Steering Committee meeting.

Notes for Chapter 17 — Blockades

[1] Minutes of BCCAC Steering Committee Emergency Meeting, Sunday, Dec. 18, 1988.

[2] Ward, Doug. "Abortion protesters carried off by police." *Vancouver Sun*. December 15, 1988. A1.

[3] Joy Thompson, interview by author, August 21, 1992, Vancouver, BC, tape recording. Other quotes from Thompson are from this interview.

[4] Joy Thompson interview. Also information supplied by Bill Coller, one of the volunteer legal team.

[5] Hendrickson, Bob. "69 carted off." *Province*. Friday, December 16, 1988. p. 3.

[6] Bill Coller, written report on his involvement with Everywoman's Health Centre. 1993. Quotes from Coller in this chapter are from this report.

[7] Lautens, Trevor. "Consorting with criminals." Column. *Vancouver Sun*. Saturday, December 17, 1988. B5.

[8] Laura Parkinson, interview by author, November 1, 1994, Vancouver, BC, tape recording.

[9] Minutes of emergency BCCAC Steering Committee meeting, Sunday, December 18, 1988.

[10] Laura Parkinson, interview.

[11] Star Rosenthal, interview by author, November 18, 1992, Vancouver, BC, tape recording.

[12] Bill Coller, written report, p. 6.

[13] "Abortion clinic backers ponder counter-protests." *Vancouver Sun*. Monday, January 23, 1989. A3.

[14] Canadian Press. "Abortion clinic appeal for money falls on deaf ears." *Vancouver Sun*. Wednesday, January 18, 1989.

[15] Boei, William. 'Police baffled in search for unidentified anti-abortionists." *Vancouver Sun*. Wednesday, January 25, 1989. A3.

[16] Pemberton, Kim. "Priest freed despite abortion stand." *Vancouver Sun*. Tuesday, January 24, 1989. A1.

[17] Editorial. "Abortion frustration." *Vancouver Sun*. Tuesday, January 24, 1989. A12.

[18] Skelly, Richard. "Rally marks court ruling on abortion." *Vancouver Sun*. Monday, January 30, 1989. A3.

[19] Bryden, Joan. "Abortion: Obstacles abound year after ruling." *Vancouver Sun*. Saturday, January 28, 1989. B1.

Notes for Chapter 18 — Circuses in Court and IWD

[1] Taylor, Lisa. "Abortion foes picket 2 doctors' homes." *Vancouver Sun*. July 3, 1989. C1.

[2] Moya, Miguel. "Neighbours seek end to abortion protests: Keeping the Crowds Away." *Vancouver Sun*. January 31, 1989. A3.

[3] Ibid.

[4] Anne Harvey, interview by author, June 2, 1993, Richmond, B.C., tape recording.

[5] Slotnick, Lorne. "Appeal court to hear union dues case." *Globe and Mail*. June 16, 1988. A15.

[6] Trickey, Mike. "Union activism facing court test." *Vancouver Sun*. June 18, 1988. B7.

[7] Sarick, Lila. "Give precedence to union's rights, court told." *Globe and Mail*. June 21, 1988. A16.

[8] "An Urgent Message to All Union Members." Half-page advertisement sponsored by the Chilliwack, BC Pro Life Society. *Chilliwack Times*. January 17, 1989.

[9] Todd, Douglas. "Teachers want right to choose: BCTF policies cause concern in Abbotsford." *Vancouver Sun*. March 15, 1989. B1.

[10] This anti-abortion case was heard and appealed several times, until, in 1991, the Industrial Relations Council ruled in these teachers' favour. The North Vancouver Teachers' Association, the Confederation of Canadian Trade Unions, and the BC Federation of Labor presented arguments for union rights, to which the IRC gave partial recognition, but, ultimately, the anti-abortionists won. However, a mere handful of teachers availed themselves of the ruling and refused to join or pay dues to the teachers' union. [See 'Wasilifsky and North Vancouver Teacher's Association' as cited in *Canadian Labour Relations Boards Reports*, 12 CLRBR (2d), pp. 161-212. I am indebted to Laura Parkinson for a copy of the report on this case.] Nonetheless, anxiety over the case spurred the BCTF to divest itself of most of its pro-choice policy before the final IRC decision was handed down. By that time, however, abortion was legal, and there were clinics in BC, so the policy was less needed.

[11] Sun News Service. "Court rules unions free to spend dues." *Vancouver Sun*. January 31, 1989. A7.

[12] Needham, Phil. "Clinic blockade justified, lawyers say." *Vancouver Sun*. February 7, 1989. B8.

[13] "Abortion protesters arrested: Judge calls demonstration at clinic blatant defiance." *Vancouver Sun*. February 7, 1989. A1. The *Sun* carried the story of the February 7 blockade at the top of page one in three of its four editions that day.

[14] Needham, Phil and William Boei. "Abortion protesters head back to court." *Vancouver Sun*. February 8, 1989. A1, A2.

[15] Needham, Phil and William Boei. "12 jailed anti-abortionists offered review." *Vancouver Sun*. February 10, 1989. A1, A9.

[16] Boei, William and Phil Needham. "Abortion foes choose jail." *Vancouver Sun*. February 9, 1989, A1, A9.

[17] Ibid.

[18] Sun Victoria Bureau. "Ree says protests could lead to anarchy." *Vancouver Sun*. January 24, 1989. A1.

[19] Boei and Needham. "Abortion foes choose jail."

[20] Editorial. "A-G should police abortion contempt." *Vancouver Sun*. February 10, 1989. A14.

[21] Skelly, Richard. "New abortion legislation felt answer to protests." *Vancouver Sun*. February 13, 1989. A12.

[22] Parton, Nicole. "Inmates slam abortion foes." *Vancouver Sun*. February 14, 1989. A3.

[23] Boei, William. "Abortion foes to admit obstruction, court told." *Vancouver Sun*. February 24, 1989. A1, A2.

[24] Ibid.

[25] Boei, William and Ben Parfitt. "City police still want court order in any future abortion clinic action." *Vancouver Sun*. February 24, 1989.

[26] Fayerman, Pamela. "Clinic wars expected to subside." *Vancouver Sun*. February 27, 1989. A3.

[27] Ibid.

[28] NY Times News Service. "Abortion foes caught by law." *Vancouver Sun*. March 4, 1989.

[29] Bellett, Gerry and Phil Needham. "Defence of necessity pushed; Ruling due on bid in abortion cases." *Vancouver Sun*. February 28, 1989. A3.

[30] Bellett, Gerry. "Fetus remark draws gasps in courtroom." *Vancouver Sun*. March 1, 1989. A3.

[31] Still, Larry. "Abortion foes hear conduct unjustified." *Vancouver Sun*. March 2, 1989. C1.

[32] Still, Larry. "Lawyer says abortion foes won't apologize to court.' *Vancouver Sun*. March 2, 1989.

[33] Still, Larry. "Anti-abortionists get their say in court." *Vancouver Sun*. March 3, 1989. A1.

[34] Still, Larry. "Probation indicated for protesters." *Vancouver Sun*. March 4, 1989. A1, A2.

[35] Boei, William. "Enemy runs court, tapes teach." *Vancouver Sun*. March 3, 1989. D5.

[36] Needham, Phil. "Protesters get terms suspended; Obey the law or face prison, judge warns anti-abortionists." *Vancouver Sun*. March 6, 1989. A1.

[37] "Pro-choice rally told equality means freedom." *Vancouver Sun*. March 6, 1989. A3. Caption on photo reads: "Scuffle: pro-choice demonstrators try to stop CBC cameraman Robb Douglas from filming protest."

[38] "Break the law, Borowski says at abortion rally." *Vancouver Sun*. April 8, 1989. A1, A2.

[39] Copy of leaflet "Satanism and Bolshevism" in author's files.

[40] Boei, William. "Abortion clinic fears protesters calling in extreme right wing." *Vancouver Sun*. May 6, 1989. A5.

[41] Author's copy of notes taken by disguised pro-choicers at the April 28, 1989 conference on "Satanism and Bolshevism" at the Croatian Cultural Centre. These were the notes that also went to the media and formed the basis for William Boei's article on May 6, 1989.

[42] Gould, Terry L. "Men Who Love to Hate." *V Magazine* [a short-lived monthly supplement to the *Vancouver Sun* that was distributed only in affluent neighbourhoods) May 1989. pp. 22-52.

[43] Boei, Wiliam. "Abortion clinic fears protesters calling in extreme right wing."

[44] Chapman, Paul. "Videotape stirs up demand for probe." *Province*. March 12, 1995.

[45] Tam, Chui-Ling. 'Pro-life group denies connection to KKK." *Calgary Herald*. May 13, 1988. B2.

[46] Canadian Press. "Anti-abortion KKK welcome." *Calgary Herald*. May 12, 1988. A14.

[47] Kuehn, Donovan. "The Nazis are coming." *New Directions Magazine*. May-June 1989. p. 18.

[48] Will Offley, interview by author, Vancouver, B.C. August 12, 1992. tape recording.

Notes for Chapter 19 — The Struggle Continues...

[1] Calami, Peter. "States can bar some abortions, top US court rules." *Vancouver Sun*. July 3, 1989. A1. *See also,* Morton, Brian. "US ruling fuels Vancouver debate.," and "U.S. ruling follows Canada." *Vancouver Sun*. July 4, 1989. A11. *Also* Marcus, Ruth. "US justices hesitate to overrule abortions," and Kamen, Al. "Reagan legacy controls top court," and Will, George, 'Rolling back the Roe rule," all in *Vancouver Sun*. July 5, 1989. A3. A9. *Also* Kines, Lindsay. "Pro-choicer warns BC" and "Abortion issue holds risk for US parties." *Vancouver Sun*. July 6, 1989. C8.

[2] "Abortion halt called no victory." *Vancouver Sun*. July 5, 1989. A6.

[3] Bolan, Kim. "Society running clinic finally gets tax-number." *Vancouver Sun*. November 29, 1991. B6.

[4] "Fetus-saving judge wrote anti-abortion article for book." *Vancouver Sun*. July 7, 1989. A9.

[5] "Dodd regrets abortion." *Vancouver Sun*. July 19, 1989. A1.

[6] "Man fails to halt abortion." *Vancouver Sun*. July 8, 1989. A16.

[7] "Abortion necessary, single mother claims." *Vancouver Sun*. July 11, 1989. A5.

[8] "$25,000 won't stop planned abortion." *Vancouver Sun*. July 13, 1989. A10.

[9] "Decision fuels debate: Québec court backs injunction, citing rights of 20-week fetus." *Vancouver Sun*. July 18, 1989. A1,A2.

[10] Ibid.

[11] "Abortion ruling challenged." *Vancouver Sun*. August 4, 1989.

[12] Nelson, Lou. "'Tremendous anger at judges' blatant contempt.'" *Kinesis*. September 1989. p. 3.

[13] "Choice under Attack." Executive Board Statement to the Labour Council of Metro Toronto & York Region. August 3, 1989. copy in author's files.

[14] Morton, F.L. p. 278.

[15] "Abortion to protect fetus, Daigle says." *Vancouver Sun*. August 14, 1989.

[16] Bindman, Stephen. "Ruling not expected to aid Ottawa." *Vancouver Sun*. August 10, 1989.

[17] Boei, William."Police reject criticism after opening clinic." *Vancouver Sun*. April 14, 1989. A3. *Also* Boei, William. "Clinic lauds word of jail terms for abortion protesters." *Vancouver Sun*. May 2, 1989. A15.

[18] Trask, Peter. "Protesters cut away from clinic." *Vancouver Sun*. July 4, 1989. A1

[19] Kavanagh, Jean."Anti-abortionists' explosive threat roundly criticized." *Vancouver Sun*. July 10, 1989. A5.

[20] McIntyre, Greg. "2000 join pro-choice action rally." *Province*. October 15, 1989.p.8.

[21] Boyle, Theresa. "Proposed abortion law stirs protests." *The Globe and Mail*. October 16, 1989. A9.

[22] Horwood, Holly. "Sole voice of approval from minister handling bill." *Province*. November 3, 1989. p. 5

[23] Delacourt, Susan. "Abortion bill draws hail of criticism." *Also* Makin, Kirk. "New law likely to face challenges, experts say."both in *The Globe and Mail*. November 4, 1989. A1.

[24] Editorial. "Commons or court will kill the bill.' *Vancouver Sun*. November 4, 1989.

[25] "New abortion law sparks rally." *Vancouver Sun*. November 6, 1989. *Also* What they"re saying", story with photo of rally. *Province*. November 5, 1989. *Also* "Pro-choice group rallies to show opposition to bill." Story with large colour photo. *Vancouver Sun*. November 7, 1989. B1

[26] Environics Research Group. "Canadian Attitudes Toward Abortion."Poll prepared for Canadian Abortion Rights Action League, between November 15 — 29, 1989.

[27] Bindman, Stephen. "Fetus is not a human being, top court rules in Daigle case." *Vancouver Sun*. November 16, 1989. A1. *Also* Makin, Kirk. "Men can't stop abortion choice, top court rules." *Globe and Mail*. November 17, 1989. A1. *Also* Editorial. "Now it's clear: fetus has no rights." *Vancouver Sun*. November 18, 1989.

[28] "Abortion bill passes; Now the battle moves to review panel." *Province*. November 28, 1989. p. 5.

[29] Dawn Black, interview by author, October 23, 1994, New Westminster, BC, tape recording. Further quotes from Black are taken from this interview..

[30] Mullens, Anne. "Document discussions, doctors told." *Vancouver Sun*. October 5, 1990.

[31] Parton, Nicole. "Proposed abortion statute would be retrogressive." *Vancouver Sun*. May 9, 1990.

[32] Applebe, Alison."Campbell Defends Abortion Bill." *Vancouver Courier*. June 3, 1990. p. 1

[33] Young, Huguette. "Abortion bill survives last-minute NDP kill tactic." *Vancouver Sun*. May 25, 1990. A8.

[34] Canadian Press. "NDP abortion ploy irks Tories, Liberals." *The Globe and Mail*. May 26, 1990. A5.

[35] PC MP Bill Attewell (Markham-Whitchurch-Stouffville), quoted in Mackie, Richard. "PM leads troops in defeating amendments to abortion bill." *The Globe and Mail*. May 24, 1990. A10.

[36] O'Neil, Peter. "Turner's vote helped pass bill in narrow win." *Vancouver Sun*. May 30, 1990. A7.

[37] Ibid.

[38] Baldrey, Keith."Vander Zalm tells caucus to toe line: 'you're in or you're out'." *Vancouver Sun*. January 18, 1990. A1.

[39] "Vancouver abortion clinic gets accreditation for three years." *Vancouver Sun*. February 7, 1990. A10.

[40] Joy Thompson, interview.

[41] Platiel, Rudy. "Coalition says abortion bill must go in wake of death." *The Globe and Mail*. June 14, 1990. A12.

[42] Pulling, Nicola. "Doctors' commitment shaken by abortion law." *The Globe and Mail*. July 2, 1990. A5.

[43] Canadian Press. "Withdraw abortion bill, MDs urge Campbell; CMA fears harassment of physicians." *The Globe and Mail.* Tuesday, August 21, 1990. A3.

[44] Simpson, Scott. "Socreds won't block new clinic; Abortion clinic has legal right, Vander Zalm says." *Vancouver Sun.* September 17, 1990. B1

[45] Needham, Phil. "Abortion protests blocked." *Vancouver Sun.* October 27, 1990. A8.

[46] Needham, Phil. "Abortion protests blocked; court upholds injunction preventing blockade outside Vancouver clinic. *Vancouver Sun.* October 27, 1990 A8.

[47] Jessica Gossen, interview.

[48] Todd, Douglas. "Abortion-fighters will pay $45,000 legal bill." *Vancouver Sun.* January 27, 1994.

[49] Between 1993 and 1999, Delta Police Constable Steven Parker, treasurer for BC Campaign Life Coalition, was found to have illegally run at least eleven licence-plate numbers of Everywoman's Health Centre staff and patients through a police computer, in order to identify the cars' owners. Parker was disciplined, but not dismissed from his job.

[50] Young, Mary Lynn. "Abortion foes seek election issue." *Vancouver Sun.* February 1, 1991. A1,A2.

[51] Carney, Pat. *Trade Secrets, a Memoir.* Toronto. Key Porter Books. 2000.p.333.

[52] Carney, Pat. p. 334.

[53] Patricia Katagiri, interview.

[54] Jessica Gossen, interview.

REFERENCES

Anderson, Doris. *Rebel Daughter: An Autobiography.* Toronto. Key Porter Books. 1996.

Antonyshyn, Patricia, B. Lee and Alex Merrill. "Marching for Women's Lives: The Campaign for Free-Standing Abortion Clinics in Ontario." In Cunningham, *et al.* Eds. *Social Movements/Social Change.* Toronto. Between the Lines Press. 1988. pp.129-156.

Bank Book Collective. *An Account to Settle: The Story of the United Bank Workers (SORWUC).* Vancouver. Press Gang Publishers. 1979.

Brodie, Janine, Shelley A.M. Gavigan and Jane Jenson. *The Politics of Abortion.* Toronto. Oxford University Press. 1992.

Canadian Supreme Court. *Decision on Abortion.* Edited by Shelagh Day and Stan Persky. Vancouver. New Star Books. 1988.

Canadian Women's Educational Press. *Women Unite!* Toronto. 1972. [anthology]
Includes:
Bernstein, Judy, Peggy Morton, Linda Seese, Myrna Wood. "Sisters, Brothers, Lovers... Listen... pp.31-39
Kreps, Bonnie. "Radical Feminism I." p. 74.
Power, Doris. "Statement to Abortion Caravan, May 1970." pp.121-124.

Carney, Pat. *Trade Secrets: A Memoir.* Toronto. Key Porter Books. 2000.

Collins, Anne. *The Big Evasion: Abortion, the Issue that Won't Go Away.* Toronto. Lester & Orpen Dennys, Ltd. 1985.

Creighton, Phyllis, ed. *Abortion: An Issue for Conscience.* Task Force on Human Life. Toronto. Anglican Church of Canada. 1974

Cuneo, Michael W. *Catholics Against the Church: Anti-Abortion Protest in Toronto,* 1969-1985. Toronto. University of Toronto Press. 1989.

Diamond, Sara. *Spiritual Warfare: The Politics of the Christian Right.* Boston. South End Press. 1989.

Dunphy, Catherine. *Morgentaler: A Difficult Hero.* Toronto. Random House of Canada. 1996.

Evans, Sara. *Personal Politics: The Roots of Women's Liberation in the Civil Rights Movement & the New Left.* New York. Vintage Books. 1980. Includes the SNCC (Student Non-Violent Co-ordinating Committee) *Position Paper (Women In the Movement.)* November, 1974. This inspired the paper written by Canadian women titled *Sisters, Brothers, Lovers, Listen...)*

Faux, Marian. *Roe v. Wade.* New York. Macmillan Publishing Co. 1988. (paper edition: Penguin Books. 1989.)

Faux, Marian. *Crusaders: Voices from the Abortion Front.* New York. Birch Lane Press and Toronto. General Publishing. 1990.

Ferraro, Patricia and Patricia Hussey, with Jane O'Reilly. *No turning Back: Two Nuns' Battle with the Vatican over Women's Right to Choose.* New York. Poseidon Press. 1990.

Fitzgerald, Maureen, Connie Gruberman and Margie Wolfe, eds. *Still Ain't Satisfied: Canadian Feminism Today.* Toronto. Women's Press. 1982.

Francke, Linda Bird. *The Ambivalence of Abortion.* New York. Dell Publishing. 1978

Gifford-Jones, W., M.D. *On Being a Woman: The Modern Woman's Guide to Gynecology.* Toronto. McClelland & Stewart. 1969. *Paperback*

Government of Canada, Ministry of Supply and Services. *Report on the Operation of the Abortion Law.* Robin F. Badgley, Chairman. 1977.

Government of Canada. *Report of the Royal Commission on the Status of Women In Canada.* Florence Bird, Chairman. 1970.

Lader, Lawrence. *Abortion II: Making the Revolution.* Boston. Beacon Hill Press. 1973.

McGill Students Society. *Birth Control Handbook.* Montréal. 1969.

McDonnell, Kathleen. *Not an Easy Choice: A Feminist Re-examines Abortion.* Toronto. The Women's Press. 1984.

McLaren, Angus and Arlene Tigar McLaren. *The Bedroom and the State.* 2nd edition. Ontario. Oxford University Press. 1997.

McLaren, Angus. *Our Own Master Race: Eugenics in Canada, 1885-1945.* Toronto. McClelland & Stewart. 1990.

Maginnis, Patricia, and Lana Clarke Phelan. *The Abortion Handbook for Responsible Women.* North Hollywood, California. Contact Books. 1969.This is probably the earliest publication on abortion by feminist activists in North America.

Mason, Gary and Keith Baldrey. *Fantasyland: Inside the Reign of Bill Vander Zalm.* Toronto. McGraw-hill Ryerson. 1989.

Merton, Andrew H. *Enemies of Choice: The Right-to-Life Movement and Its Threats To Abortion.* Boston. Beacon Press. 1981.

Mohr, James C. *Abortion in America: The Origins and Evolution of National Policy.* New York. Oxford University Press. 1978. (paper edition, 1979.)

Morgentaler, Henry, M.D. *Abortion & Contraception.* Toronto. General Publishing. 1982.

Morton, F.L. *Morgentaler v. Borowski: Abortion, the Charter, and the Courts.* Toronto: McClelland & Stewart. 1992.

Muldoon, Maureen. *The Abortion Debate in the United States and Canada: a Source Book.* New York. Garland Publishing. 1991.

Pelrine, Eleanor Wright. *Abortion in Canada: The Reform That Hardly Was.* Toronto. new press. 1972.

Pelrine, Eleanor Wright. *Morgentaler.* Toronto. Signet Books, an imprint of New American Library of Canada. 1975.

Reagan, Ronald. *Abortion and the Conscience of the Nation.* New York. Nelson. Copyright by the Human Life Foundation. 1984.

Staggenborg, Suzanne. *The Pro-Choice Movement: Organizaton and Activism in the Abortion Conflict.* New York. Oxford University Press. 1991. (describes the evolution of the movement in Chicago and the US midwest)

Tribe, Laurence H. *Abortion: The Clash of Absolutes.* New York. W.W. Norton. 1990.

United Church of Canada, Proceedings of the 19th General Council. 1960. *Toward a Christian Understanding of Sex, Love, and Marriage.*

Watters, Wendell W. *Compulsory Parenthood: The Truth About Abortion.* Toronto: McClelland & Stewart. 1976.

Weddington, Sarah. *A Question of Choice.* New York: Grosset/Putnam. 1992. (Sarah Weddington was lead counsel in arguing *Roe v. Wade* in the US)

Journals and Newsletters (in alphabetical order)

American Journal of Theology and Philosophy January 1985 issue (see endnote 22 on page 277).

CCCA Newsletter (December 1981 — October 1987)

The Democrat — monthly publication of the BC New Democratic Party

Kinesis — former monthly publication of the Vancouver Status of Women

New Directions

The Pedestal — former monthly publiction of the Women's Caucus

Priorities — monthly publication of the BC NDP Women's Rights Committee

Pro-Choice News — former publication of Canadian Abortion Rights Action League (CARAL), Toronto

Pro-Choice Press — published by the BC Pro-Choice Action Network

Spokeswoman — published by the Canadian Women's Coalition to Repeal the Abortion Laws. Toronto 1972-1973.

Telus — former journal of the Planned Parenthood Federation of Canada

V Magazine (short-lived, selectively distributed, monthly insert in *Vancouver Sun*)

Women's Liberation News — published by the Women's Liberation Alliance. Vancouver 1970-1971.

INDEX

Listed here are names of pro-choice women whose contributions were no less important, but which are grouped together for ease in finding.

ISBN 1-41204247-X

9 781412 042475